SEXUAL RHETORIC

SEXUAL RHETORIC

Media Perspectives on Sexuality, Gender, and Identity

Edited by
META G. CARSTARPHEN
and **SUSAN C. ZAVOINA**

Contributions to the Study of Mass Media and Communications
Number 57

Greenwood Press
Westport, Connecticut • London

Library of Congress Cataloging-in-Publication Data

Sexual rhetoric : media perspectives on sexuality, gender, and
    identity / edited by Meta G. Carstarphen and Susan C. Zavoina.
        p. cm.—(Contributions to the study of mass media and
    communications, ISSN 0732–4456 ; no. 57)
        Includes bibliographical references and index.
        ISBN 0–313–30788–1 (alk. paper)
        1. Mass media and sex. 2. Sex differences in mass media. 3. Sex
    role in mass media. 4. Mass media and culture. I. Carstarphen,
    Meta G., 1954– . II. Zavoina, Susan C., 1954– . III. Series.
    P96.S45S49   1999
    306.7—dc21   99–21278

British Library Cataloguing in Publication Data is available.

Library of Congress Catalog Card Number: 99–21278
ISBN: 0–313–30788–1
ISSN: 0732–4456

First published in 1999

Greenwood Press, 88 Post Road West, Westport, CT 06881
An imprint of Greenwood Publishing Group, Inc.
www.greenwood.com

Printed in the United States of America

∞™

The paper used in this book complies with the
Permanent Paper Standard issued by the National
Information Standards Organization (Z39.48–1984).

10 9 8 7 6 5 4 3 2 1

Contents

Part VI: Video

Part VII: Film

Part VIII: Cyberspace

Illustrations

TABLES

Preface

The purpose of this book is to present electronic, print, and "new" media depictions through case studies and critical analysis of:

1. the ways in which the media intervene in the understanding of popular culture,
2. stereotypical portrayals of women and men and their contexts, and
3. sociopolitical implications of symbols and images used to portray gender roles in society.

There has been a tremendous upsurge of scholarship and interest concerning gender roles in our society. Such inquiry invites a study of the mass media's role in the creation and depiction of men, women, sexuality, and social roles. A need exists for scholarship that reflects how the print media (newspaper, magazines, books), the electronic media (radio, television, movies, music), and the new media (computer-mediated communication) represent and portray sex-defined images. Such a comprehensive view delves into the evolving ways in which individuals come to know and perceive men and women, and how they negotiate the relationships between mass media and contemporary culture.

Collections of critical analyses and case studies that explain through example, illustration, and rhetorical inquiry are rare in the discussion of mass media representations of men and women. While some collections, largely concerned with women's gender representations, contain some articles that attempt to address the issue of culture and mass media, their primary focus has been on empirical research devoted to gender issues from ideological perspectives. This book broadens that focus by concentrating on concrete illustrations and case studies that encompass issues affecting both men and women and use rhetorical perspectives to instruct readers on ways to "read" these messages.

ACKNOWLEDGMENTS

The co-editors are deeply grateful and indebted to many people for their help and support on this project. We wish to thank Dick Wells, our department chair, for helping to subsidize some of our costs. We also thank Nelia Smith for her able and cheerful administrative assistance whenever it was needed.

Every single contributor to this volume has added something fresh and exciting. We greatly appreciate the professionalism with which these authors approached this effort and are grateful for their sharing. And for highlighting the scholarship and ideas within this book, we want to thank Candy Koharchik for her tireless efforts on the index.

Our pathways were guided by the consummate professionals at Greenwood, specifically Pamela St. Clair, Maureen Melino, Heidi Straight, and Peter Kracht. Thanks much!

Last, but certainly not least, we are grateful for the many ways our families and friends supported us during this process, especially Mark, Aubrey, Shea, Chase and Vito.

Introduction

MEDIA RHETORIC: A WAY OF KNOWING

Meta G. Carstarphen

Now more than ever, our senses are titillated and saturated by myriad media. The speed at which images are colliding with our senses accelerates with each passing innovation and invention. At times, it seems we are lost within the morass of messages, unable to interpret their meaning to our lives.

Richard A. Lanham in *The Electronic Word* (1993) characterizes this state as being on "the edge of chaos," an inevitable consequence resulting from life within the Information Age. Importantly, he notes, this epoch is defined not just by the plethora of media and information sources within it but by the accompanying burgeoning of voices within the discourse. Such expanding knowledge borders bring new participants into the conversation and such variety also brings uncertainty. We cannot assume that what we once knew to be true about our world is still true today.

This combination of both opportunity and angst accompanying today's media messages offers increasingly rich fields of exploration for students of the media, as well as those who study society. The two are inextricably intertwined. But the study of the media cannot be limited to an examination of the technology surrounding it and enabling it, although such a view is tempting. However, to look simply at the technical trappings is to look too simply at the world.

Rhetorical interpretations offer potentially invaluable ways of looking more fully at this media world that surrounds us. Rhetoric, defined here as a way of knowing, is presented as a process. What that process involves can be summarized as a five-step journey of recognition, definition, redefinition, consensus, and reflection.

Recognition is that state where our awareness and attention become attached to a medium, and that invariably happens as a result of some performance emanating from it that somehow has meaning for us. A key part of the definition aspect of this rhetorical process is to decide in what ways the media performance has meaning for us. Then, as we push through an assortment of other possibilities to refine our definition, we are redefining meaning through argumentation—an activity that Greek philosopher Aristotle placed at the heart of the rhetorical process when he defined argument as availing oneself to "all available means of persuasion."

Consensus often reflects the artful soul of the rhetorical process. It is the place of arrival that was not necessarily seen at the outset of the intellectual journey, much like a surprise short-cut beckons us away from well-worn pathways. This center of understanding is necessarily fluid, holding together only until, as poet T. S. Eliot warns us, "things fall apart." That is why the rhetorical process cannot be complete until the final stage of reflection. Here, there lies an opportunity for ideas to turn in upon themselves, to emerge either stronger for the test or to find themselves reinvented into more viable representations.

Nowhere does there seem to be more opportunity to lend rhetorical consideration to media messages than in the representations of sex, gender, and identity. Though we tend to think of sex being determined by biological construct and impulse, we know gender to be broader than that in its consideration of the ways in which society establishes roles for men, women, and children. Undoubtedly, at the core of individual identity is the sense of sex and gender. By extension, social identities become enlarged when sex and gender interact within other contexts: class, caste, race, economics, politics, and history. The greatest amplifiers of these competing and often contrasting notions are the collected representations of the media that surround us daily.

In his book *Media Literacy: Keys to Interpreting Media Messages* (1995), Art Silverblatt lays out a map for becoming informed, or literate, about media through an understanding of four key components: process, context, framework, and production values. Collectively, these ideas cover the range of possibilities in media messages, from knowing the way in which they are crafted and distributed to learning about the social contexts in which they appear. The chapters in this book adeptly consider these questions and more in their studied consideration of what we have called *media moments*.

By *media moments* we mean that important juncture where sense and sensibility connect, engraving in our collective awareness an instance of keen attention. This "moment" can be as exhilarating as it is disturbing, as adorned in naked simplicity as it can be wrapped in undeniable complexities. It is the exploration of these such instances, where our focus is held and our intellect is challenged, that comprise the connecting theme of this volume. Look for the media moments, as we review just a few: Phyllis Pearson Elmore's explication of U.S. representative Barbara Jordan's historic call for Nixon's impeachment, Susan Stearns and Meta G. Carstarphen's discussion of Ellen DeGeneres's groundbreaking "outing," and Joseph W. Slade's exposure of the hidden rhetoric behind the video box covers for today's top pornography stars. Each chapter opens with such a sensibility and welcomes you to participate in an exchange of ideas about these important issues of sexuality, gender, and identity in the media.

MEDIA MESSAGES: VISUAL LITERACY/VISUAL RHETORIC

Susan C. Zavoina

Visual imagery dominates media messages. With constant bombardment of visual media our perception of what we "see" gives the false allusion of immediate understanding. Because we are so accustomed to being addressed by images, their total impact is sometimes not fully understood. From newspapers and magazines to television to the Web, our access to visual media messages can be continuous. Photographs, illustrations, film, and video are all used to communicate messages. Our "reading," or perception, of these images shapes our understanding of the visual message. Selection, organization, and interpretation are the stages of perception. However, since perception and meaning are intertwined, the viewer's frame of reference affects perception. Expectations of results from one viewing medium will be carried over to a similar media.

As John Berger states in *Ways of Seeing* (1972), the sharper and more isolated the stimulus memory receives, the more it remembers; the more comprehensive the stimulus, the less it remembers. He explains that this is why black and white photography is paradoxically more evocative than color photography. A faster onrush of memories is stimulated because less visual information has been given—more has been left out. Even with radio, people visualize the events that they hear about using their own context and frame of reference while interpreting the verbal messages. Where television brings images, and thus the illusions of visual reality based on an individual's perception, into our homes, the Web allows unlimited access to a variety of images of our own choosing. Thus, levels of visual literacy or how we "read" these images vary from person to person, culture to culture. For instance, the contrast between a visual interpretation of the world and the actual condition is significant, and this is sometimes consciously recognized. What really matters is whether the perception of visual images can be regarded as critical understanding rather than programmed response—and whether the viewer has a literate, as opposed to reactive, role.

The concept of visual literacy developed from foundational roots, including philosophy, art, linguistics, perceptual psychology, and communication research. The term was coined by John L. Debes, who, along with Clarence Williams, founded the International Visual Literacy Association. As this concept evolves, different interpretations of the meaning of *visual literacy* exist. In *A Visual Literacy Primer* (1974), Donis A. Dondis states that to be considered verbally literate, one must learn the basic components of written language. Therefore, visual literacy must operate somewhat within the same boundaries. As Dondis outlines, the purposes are the same as those that motivated the development of written language: to construct a basic system for learning, recognizing, making, and understanding visual messages that are negotiable by all people.

Visual information may include symbol (text), representational (visual material from the environment replicated in drawing, painting, sculpture, and film), and abstract (understructure of the whole message) components. These components work together to establish a visual syntax. From this viewpoint, text and image are connected and approached as individual elements within the composition. Connecting the verbal and the visual involves combining two distinctive forms of visual data: symbol (text) and representational (replicated visual material). Therefore, the sender crafts the message in anticipation of the audience's probable response, incorporating a "sense" of visual literacy.

Incorporated within the theory of visual literacy lies an underlying theory of visual rhetoric. Rhetoric is an interpretive theory that frames a message as an interested party's attempt to influence an audience. The sender's intention is understood to be manifested in the argument, the evidence, the order of argumentation, and the style of delivery. Formal elements are selected according to the sender's expectations in accordance with how the audience will approach the genre, the speaker, and the topic.

Influences of Powerful Visuals on Gender, Identity, and Sexuality

Research shows that there is considerable continuity between picture perception and everyday, real-life vision. Paul Messaris (1994) and others have stated that realism is a social practice of representation. Messaris states that as identified as the dominant mode of signification in society the constant repetition and cross-echoing of references create a generally perceived picture of what may be regarded as "real" or "realistic," which is not recognized as such—as a picture—but presents itself as precisely the Reality. Visual messages are necessary so the viewer can bridge the gap between concrete experiences and symbolic representations.

Images in mass media affect the way individuals define who they are and who they strive to be through the portrayal of men, women, sexuality, and social roles. This is part of our culture—part of our socialization. Media images intervene in the understanding of news events and popular culture. From the recent public interest in photographs showing Paula Jones's new nose to the much "played" image of Monica Lewinsky hugging President Bill Clinton at a political rally to images of JonBenet Ramsey and Princess Di that still appear in newspapers, magazines, television, and the Web, these images structure meaning and a sense of reality to our world. These images, in turn, reflect and influence our perception of self.

Consequently, several authors in this book emphasize the effect that visual rhetoric may have on the viewer and the influence of news, editorial, and advertising photography. Images may appear to tell us one thing on the surface but be read as much more when contextualized by the viewer. In Chapter 4, "Necrophilia, Pedophilia, or Both?: The Sexualized Rhetoric of the JonBenet Ramsey Murder Case," Diana York Blaine explains that viewer fascination with images of a violent, beautiful death reveals a strong cultural need to view these images to assuage anxiety about human mortality. In other words, the image of a beautiful death is more comforting than the alternative. Blaine argues that the combination of visual beauty and horror explains the longevity of these images in the media.

In Chapter 10, " 'That Undefinable Whatever': Selling Virginity," Elizabeth Dietz examines the visual rhetoric in photographic images of virgins to show not a viewer's desire for the virgin but yet a desire produced by the cultural myth of virginity. It is argued that this powerful cultural fantasy links the virginal (that which cannot be sold or even fully represented in a salable object) with consumer society. The photographic myth is a rhetorical image of commerce.

Voyeurism has long been an outgrowth of the practice of photography and filmmaking as well as currently in media coverage. The curiosity to view what is taboo. The cultural need for fantasy, escapism, and fairy-tale images is in contrast to the reality effect discussed earlier. However, both exist as a part of visual rhetoric. Both types of messages exist within all forms of media. Because of constant bombardment there is little time to filter quantity versus quality and objective attempts for the truthful representation as opposed to conscience falsification of imagery. With digital technology, seeing should not always mean believing. Sadly, this has been the case both in news/editorial photographs as well as in advertising. Our culture strives for the ideal in visual communication.

An interpretation of the attempt for the visual ideal is discussed in Chapter 5, "Media Mirage: The Thin Ideal as Digital Manipulation." Jacqueline C. Hitchon and Shiela Reaves argue that in our culture the media mirage is not viewed in a singular moment but is presented in a barrage of images. It is stated that in recent years the thin ideal has become progressively more digital, beauty manufactured rather than beauty discovered, and that this media mirage is thus disassociating young women from the realities of leading a productive, healthy life. The "untruths" that are part of the visual rhetoric of digitally manipulated images will continue to be part of our visual language in advertising and perhaps in news editorial because of the ever shifting ethical boundaries in image handling.

Visual rhetoric plays an important role in the communication of sexuality. From androgynous model to sex kitten—all is not always as it seems. Subtleties in framing, choice of body type for subject, lighting, use of color, dress, accessories, and language inherent in the pose can all make important visual statements to the viewer. In Chapter 9, "Designed for (Male) Pleasure: The Myth of Lesbian Chic in Mainstream Advertising," Tom Reichert, Kevin R. Maly, and Susan C. Zavoina argue that the coupling of women together in ads such as those by Versace and Guess more closely mirrors images of women engaged in homosexual sexual acts in mainstream pornography than representations of lesbian reality. And, in this case, heterosexuals are viewing lesbians as an extension of heterosexuality.

Rhetoric within visual messages is more prevalent today simply because of the increase in readily available advanced publishing technology and the ease that is inherent in creating sophisticated media images. One goal of this book is to give an overview of media images/media messages in a variety of formats while discussing and analyzing the impact that these images have on the viewer. Historically, media consumers (viewers and readers) have realized the power of the word. It is now imperative that they realize and understand the power of the *image*.

REFERENCES

Berger, J. (1972). *Ways of Seeing*. London: British Broadcast Corporation, Penguin Books, Ltd.

Dondis, D. A. (1974). *A Primer of Visual Literacy*. Boston: MIT Press.

Lanham, R. (1993). *The Electronic Word: Democracy, Technology and the Arts*. Chicago: University of Chicago Press.

Messaris, P. (1994). *Visual Literacy, Image, Mind & Reality*. Boulder, CO: Westview Press.

Silverblatt, A. (1995). *Media Literacy: Keys to Interpreting Media Messages*. Westport, CT: Praeger.

PART I

HISTORIC PERSPECTIVES

Jacqueline Bacon

The *Liberator*'s "Ladies' Department," 1832–37: Freedom or Fetters?

INTRODUCTION

From 1832 to 1837, William Lloyd Garrison's weekly abolitionist newspaper the *Liberator* featured a column devoted to the particular concerns of women. In the inaugural column, Garrison (1832) explained the purpose of the "Ladies' Department":

The fact that one million of the female sex are reduced, by the slave system, to the most deplorable condition—compelled to perform the most laborious and unseemly tasks—liable to be whipped to an unmerciful degree—exposed to all the violence of lust and passion—and treated with more indelicacy and cruelty than cattle, ought to excite the sympathy and indignation of American women. We have therefore concluded, that a Ladies' Department in the Liberator would add greatly to its interest, and give a new impetus to the cause of emancipation. The ladies of Great Britain are moving the sympathies of the whole nation, in behalf of the perishing slaves in the British Colonies. We cannot believe that our own ladies are less philanthropic or less influential. In their hands is the destiny of the slaves. (p. 2)

The "Ladies' Department" was one of many columns featured in the newspaper in the 1830s, including a "Juvenile Department" for children, a column of correspondence entitled "Communications" and the "Slavery Record," which offered exposés about slavery. At the head of most of the "Ladies' Department" columns of 1832 appeared the image of a kneeling slave and the inscription—"Am I not a Woman and a Sister?"—commonly found in women's antislavery publications and artwork (see Figure 1.1). The column usually appeared on the

Figure 1.1
"Ladies' Department" from the *Liberator*

LADIES' DEPARTMENT.

'Am I not a Woman and a Sister?'

For the Liberator.

Image courtesy of UMI from American Periodicals Series.

second or third page of the four-page newspaper and varied in length, sometimes featuring merely one item, other times as many as five. Included in the "Ladies' Department" were essays, poems, letters, fictional dialogues, speeches by women, and constitutions and reports of women's antislavery societies.

Not all of the articles in the "Ladies' Department" were identified as women's writing. Some were anonymous or signed with pseudonyms or initials; others were implicitly or explicitly attributed to male authors. Yet all followed Garrison's assumption that the column should be aimed at a female audience. Although the "Ladies' Department" appeared most weeks in 1832, its frequency varied from 1833 to 1837. In 1836, for example, the column did not appear; other years featured as few as two (1834, 1835) or as many as sixteen (1837). The last column was published in the issue of November 3, 1837.

Garrison's comments about the column—and indeed the very existence of a separate column directed at women—revealed several significant tensions inherent in the views of male abolitionists about women's activism and women's rhetoric. Although Garrison posited a role for women in the abolition movement, he portrayed both antislavery women and female slaves in terms that connoted traditional antebellum notions of femininity—ideals often in conflict with women's public abolitionist activity. While seemingly opening his periodical to include articles by and about women, he neither explicitly invited female abolitionists to argue against slavery in the "Ladies' Department" nor described the column as a repository of antislavery rhetoric. And Garrison's demarcation of the "Ladies' Department" as a discrete section of the periodical was based on various assumptions that threatened to limit women's rhetoric. Women's writing and writing about women, his inaugural column implied, should be separate and different from men's concerns, should address "feminine" subjects such as motherhood and domestic matters, and should appeal to a primarily female audience.

It is not surprising, then, that some abolitionist women found the rhetorical boundaries of the "Ladies' Department" too confining. Speaking at an 1848 Woman's Rights Convention in Rochester, abolitionist Lucretia Mott criticized the "Ladies' Department" as "sickly sentimentality" and applauded the shift to "more substantial food" for women's minds ("Proceedings," 1848, p. 148). Yet the rhetoric of the "Ladies' Department" should not be dismissed as entirely conventional and unassertive. Within the confines of the "Ladies' Department," abolitionists redefined accepted ideals of femininity, expanded the roles available to antebellum women reformers, questioned cultural assumptions that threatened to silence women, and suggested that women could engage political questions usually considered the purview of men. Because the *Liberator* had many African American readers and featured writing by African American as well as white abolitionists, the "Ladies' Department" also articulated the views of women whose experiences challenged traditional gendered rhetoric based on the narrow experiences of upper-class white women.

This chapter explores the simultaneously confining and liberating features of the gendered rhetoric created by abolitionists in the "Ladies' Department." The following section discusses the context within which the column was created, particularly antebellum assumptions about femininity and women's rhetoric, the real-life experiences of antebellum women, and women's roles in the abolition movement during the 1830s. Subsequent sections examine the rhetoric of the "Ladies' Department," focusing on three aspects of contributions that concern women's roles: (1) the rhetorical strategies that enabled abolitionists to negotiate potentially limiting cultural expectations of women and to suggest that women could assume the authority to persuade, even on overtly political topics usually considered "unfeminine"; (2) the appropriation of traditional ideals of womanhood by contributors to the "Ladies' Department" in order to create a public and rhetorical role for women abolitionists; and (3) the challenge to conventional premises about femininity posed by the articulation of women's experiences, particularly those of African American women. As this examination demonstrates, these elements of the rhetoric in the "Ladies' Department" range from relatively indirect and cautious to more radical and direct. The chapter concludes with a consideration of the impact of the "Ladies' Department" on the rhetoric of women abolitionists of the late 1830s and after and a more general reflection on what the column suggests about the potential of gendered rhetoric for women's activism.

THE RHETORIC OF TRUE WOMANHOOD AND THE TRUE LIVES OF WOMEN

During the run of the column, rhetorical formulations of women's proper role in society fit a model often described by historians and scholars of gender as the "Cult of True Womanhood" (Cott, 1977; Epstein, 1981; Smith-Rosenberg, 1985; Welter, 1976). This paradigm proposed that the "woman's sphere"—the domestic realm of the home, family, and motherhood—was sharply divided from the male world of public affairs. The ideal woman was the embodiment of piety, submission, selflessness, and charity. Although women were subordinate to men, they were praised as "morally superior" because the domestic realm for which they were responsible "redeemed" men from the ostensible heartlessness of the public world. Thus women's moral authority was an influence that men presumably could not resist. A wife, John Bolles (1831) commented in the *Ladies' Magazine and Literary Gazette*, should "exert a purifying influence over the heart" by helping her husband to heed "the voice of conscience" (pp. 268–69).

Yet women's influence was not to extend to the public sphere—and, in particular, public argument was inappropriate for women. Catharine Beecher (1837), the influential author of domestic and educational manuals, maintained in her book *An Essay on Slavery and Abolitionism, with Reference to the Duty of American Females* that women must avoid public debate because "whatever, in any measure, throws a woman into the attitude of a combatant, either for herself or others . . . whatever obliges her in any way to exert coercive influences, throws her out of her appropriate sphere" (p. 102). Indeed, as Karlyn Kohrs Campbell (1989) has noted, the qualities of the ideal antebellum woman, who was noncompetitive, modest, and unassuming, contrasted sharply with those of traditionally successful rhetors (p. 10).

Although this rhetoric of femininity was influential in antebellum America, scholars have discovered that, for a variety of reasons, many women's lives did not fit this model (Ginzburg, 1990; Matthews, 1992). African Americans found that they were not considered "true women" because of racist stereotypes, even though they were expected to conform to conventional ideals of womanhood (Richardson, 1987; Yee, 1992). Furthermore, many African Americans and other marginalized women did not fit traditional definitions of the domestic wife and mother because they were compelled by economic necessity to work outside the home. Many women, too, took an interest in public affairs, often seeking newspapers and other reading material that would inform them about political events (Zboray and Zboray, 1996). And the many women in antebellum America of all races and classes who became involved in reform work ventured beyond the domestic sphere and resisted restrictions against public activity. Abolitionist women and other reformers organized to promote causes, worked with men to raise funds, and spoke at meetings. Writing for the "Ladies' Department" was itself a public act. Yet, as Garrison's comments in the first "Ladies' Department" suggested, the power of the rhetoric of domesticity and traditional femininity influenced male abolitionist leaders (see also Friedman, 1982). Thus contributors to the "Ladies' Department" had to negotiate conventional expectations through a variety of rhetorical strategies even as they argued for women's role in abolition.

FEMINIZING "UNFEMININE" TOPICS

Contributors to the "Ladies' Department" often engaged controversial public issues. Yet because convention dictated that the antebellum woman should refrain from any direct discussion of political concerns (see Beecher, 1837, pp. 102–3), contributors often marshaled indirect strategies to frame their arguments in terms that conformed to commonplaces of femininity. Such indirection is characteristic of members of marginalized groups in society, particularly when discussing issues considered the domain of dominant members of society (Kramarae, 1981, pp. 143–44). Writers for the "Ladies' Department" adopted particular forms that were seemingly appropriate in a column directed to women. The presentation of antislavery arguments through letters between women, for example, effectively marshaled an ostensibly private form to grant a political voice to women. Garrison identified a letter printed in the column from Zillah (1832) (the pen name of African American abolitionist Sarah Douglass) as "written to a friend" (p. 115). This framework allowed Zillah to offer strong arguments on a crucial and controversial topic—the question of colonization—while seeming to uphold traditional notions that women's influence should be exercised privately. (Colonization, a plan that proposed sending free African Americans to a colony in Africa or elsewhere, was generally opposed by African Americans [Quarles, 1969, pp. 7–8].) Zillah attempted to persuade her friend, who apparently supported colonization, with bold and well-reasoned claims:

You say, "if we can better our situation by removing, why oppose it?" Believe me, my friend, there is no spot in the known world where people are happier than in America. . . .
    If we should bend our steps to Hayti, there is no security for life and property. . . . If we go to Mexico, it is the same there. Why throw ourselves upon the protection of Great Britain, when thousands of her own children are starving? . . . [T]hough [America] unkindly strives to throw me from her bosom, I will but embrace her the closer, determining never to part with her whilst I have life. (p. 115)

In 1837, Angelina Grimké's series of thirteen letters to Catharine Beecher in the "Ladies' Department" (published in book form the following year) refuted Beecher's *Essay on Slavery and Abolitionism*, which minimized the need for abolitionist activity and advocated a limited sphere for women. In her response to Beecher's text, Grimké offered strong antislavery arguments and defended women's right to join the abolition movement. Framing her rhetoric as private persuasion between women, Grimké ostensibly avoided the "unfeminine" tactic of arguing before a public audience. This strategy enabled Grimké to present many powerful arguments—including even the militant position that it was right to break the law to fight slavery. Significantly, Grimké (1837) presented the latter stance as a response to Beecher's previously published assertions that slaveholders could not legally emancipate their slaves rather than as an autonomously developed argument, thereby seeming less directly confrontational. Yet she still attacked Beecher's argument and strongly condemned her deference to slaveholders: "[S]o far from thinking that a slaveholder is bound by the *immoral* and *unconstitutional* laws of the Southern States, we hold that he is solemnly bound as a man, as an American, to *break* them, and that *immediately* and openly. . . . *We* promulgate no such man-pleasing doctrine as that set forth by thee" (p. 106).

The presentation of antislavery arguments through dialogues between women similarly allowed a female voice to express political arguments within a traditional framework. "Slavery" (1832) presented a conversation between female friends Helen and Ruth in which the latter strongly countered the arguments of the former, who criticized the efforts of abolitionists. In response to Helen's suggestion that Northern abolitionists should not interfere with laws of other states, Ruth declared, "We know well that such laws exist, and we know as well that they are unjust. The public mind may, however, become so enlightened as finally to repeal those laws" (p. 75). Ruth exposed the contradiction between Helen's arguments that slaves, if set free, would be "incapable of civil improvement and self government" and her contention that those sent to a colony in Liberia would be "*well taught*" (p. 75). "[Y]our argument is crushed by its own weight," Ruth revealed, "for it seems that you admit they may become refined; and that they are capable of good government, they have amply proved by nearly forty years of civil administration at Hayti" (p. 75). Paradoxically, it was because a woman's strong persuasion was apparently limited to her private acquaintance that it could become public in the pages of the "Ladies' Department."

The dialogic form allowed contributors to the column to engage even the highly charged question of women's abolitionist activity itself. In a dialogue between female participants A. and B., A. championed women's antislavery activity in response to B.'s comments that women "ought not to interfere in this business, on account of its being a political question" that is "not consistent with propriety, and hardly with feminine modesty" ("Dialogue," 1832, p. 86). A. answered,

I own I have never been able to affix any clear meaning to the expression . . . that this is a political question. It appears to me to be peculiarly a religious and moral question; but I suppose the objection must mean . . . that as women are not legislators, they should not interfere in a question which is to come before a legislative body. I cannot see the slightest force in the argument, that because women can have no part in the final decision, they ought not to take any in helping on the subject towards that decision: as well might it be said that it is improper for women to put their poor neighbors in the way of receiving medical aid—wrong to provide them with sittings in a church or decent clothes to appear in there—wrong to help them to pay law expences when they are injured—for women are not physicians, clergymen, or lawyers, and therefore ought not to put themselves forward on medical, clerical, or legal subjects. (p. 86)

Reframing the question in terms of religion and morality, A. demonstrated that B.'s argument against women's involvement in the abolitionist cause was invalid. Because A. was represented as addressing another woman and answering a challenge put to her directly, her response could be stronger than would perhaps otherwise be acceptable. Within the dialogic form, a female voice could explicitly defend women's right to work and to argue against slavery.

In 1835, the "Ladies' Department" featured a letter from "A Member of the Boston Female Anti-Slavery Society" (1835) to the *Boston Courier*. Intended for the public, this letter contained strong rhetoric defending women's right to organize, agitate, and speak against slavery. Yet the writer deflected attention from her own authority by couching her remarks in terms that suggested that she did not wish to argue publicly, that she was, in fact, "forced before the public" (p. 169). Particular instances, she noted, compelled her "[r]eluctantly and painfully, but as a matter of duty" to defend the Boston Female Anti-Slavery Society against recent allegations (p. 169). The society had invited George Thompson, a British abolitionist, to speak at their annual meeting. Boston reacted angrily; newspaper editorials denounced Thompson, and handbills called for him to be attacked physically. The women of the Boston Female Anti-Slavery Society postponed the meeting and invited Garrison instead—who was, incidentally, threatened by a mob when he tried to attend the later gathering. Yet they did not remain silent about the interference with their original plans. The letter from the member declared:

[I]t is our right, and we will maintain it in Christian meekness, but with Christian constancy, to hold meetings and to employ such lecturers . . . best calculated to advance the holy cause of human rights. . . .
. . . We cannot descend to bandy words with those who have no just sense of their own duty or ours. . . . This is a crisis which demands of us not only mint, and annise, and cummin, but also mercy, justice and judgment. (p. 169)

These strong words—including the assertion that abolitionist women need not choose between domestic and public duties—were, the writer suggested, a reaction to public events rather than a direct argument. Yet within the frame of the defense of the Boston Female Anti-Slavery Society, she offered public and strong arguments for women's activism.

APPROPRIATING ANTEBELLUM FEMININITY

Another strategy marshaled by writers for the "Ladies' Department" involved the appropriation of the ideals of conventional femininity—the so-called Cult of True Womanhood. Catherine Clinton (1984) has argued that female reformers of the early nineteenth century "perceived that they might extend female juris-diction into the public and hitherto exclusively male realm by using their 'do-mestic role' as a lever—wedging themselves into positions of power, however limited, through exploitation of their domesticity" (pp. 41–42). Relying on tra-ditional formulations of women's essential nature and social role, contributors to the "Ladies' Department" sought to extend the purview of "women's sphere" to include abolitionist activity beyond the home. Because women were naturally compassionate, unselfish, charitable, and Christian, these writers argued, they were compelled to have antislavery sentiments. The anonymous author of "Our Own Sex" (1832), while lamenting the apathy of many American women on the subject of slavery, asserted that women's true natures would eventually pre-vail: "We cannot believe this general supineness will be of very long continu-ance, for it is not in the nature of the female heart to look unmoved upon scenes of misery. . . . [T]here has gone forth a spirit of compassion that we doubt not will enter widely into the bosoms of our own sex" (p. 2).

Indeed, the author of this piece represented women who are indifferent to the subject of slavery as unfeminine—a strategy associated with the later abolitionist tactic, identified by Kristin Hoganson (1993), of contrasting female slaveholders with "true women." That many American women had no indignation about slavery, the author of "Our Own Sex" (1832) remarked, was "a circumstance scarcely more to be regretted, than it [was] surprising" (p. 2). Implicit in the writer's expressions of shock was the notion that this apathy called into question other charitable activities of American women:

That American ladies, benevolent and enlightened females . . . who will abridge their own comforts, and penetrate fearlessly into the gloomy and hidden retreats of poverty . . . should calmly suffer hundreds of thousand [sic] of their own sex to drink of all the degradation and bitterness of slavery, without one effort to rescue them from their depth of wretchedness, is, indeed, scarcely to be credited. (p. 2)

Similarly, a letter from the antislavery Agnes (1832c) to the apathetic Isabel—originally published in the antislavery periodical the *Genius of Universal Eman-cipation* and reprinted in the "Ladies' Department" of the *Liberator*—repre-sented the indifferent female as selfish and lazy. Responding to Isabel's desire to remain silent on the subject of slavery and her protestations against boycotting products made with slave sugar, Agnes did not hide her contempt:

No, my dear Isabel, it is not sufficient, that you silently disapprove of iniquity—you should openly *avow* your disapprobation. . . . You speak very *pathetically*, to be sure, of the haunting recollections of *pound-cakes* and *ice-creams* doomed so often to be passed by untasted! . . . But what kind of devotion to the cause of justice and mercy can that be, which would shrink from offering a few sacrifices of inclination and luxury upon their altar? (p. 18)

Agnes's references to selflessness and sacrifice were connected to an additional commonplace of antebellum femininity that she marshaled in another letter to persuade the recalcitrant Isabel. The ideal antebellum woman was a devoted Christian, and abolitionists frequently assailed their female opponents with the accusation that they were not Christian—and therefore, by implication, not "true women"—because they supported slavery. Her concern for Isabel's piety allowed Agnes (1832a) to criticize her harshly and to offer strong, even fiery antislavery rhetoric. It was "[s]trange," she lamented, that the usually "pious," "gentle and merciful" Isabel was "so culpably indifferent" on this subject. Framing her remarks in terms of her concern for her friend, she vigorously condemned those who did not openly renounce slavery:

[D]ear Isabel: even you acknowledge that the system of which I speak is a great evil— you admit that it is sinful to press the iron yoke of oppression upon the neck of any of God's creatures . . . and how can you escape the infection of that guilt, unless you openly lift up your hand in remonstrance against it? It is not sufficient that you are not an immediate participant in this iniquity. . . . [W]hen the voice of that blood, crying out from the ground, riseth up into the high courts of Heaven, think you, Isabel, that those will be held guiltless, who have stood by and beheld the iron of his fetters wearing away into his very soul, and yet have lifted no hand to shield, no voice beseeching mercy for the sufferer? Oh, believe it not! (p. 10)

Agnes (1832b) implied, too, that it was her own Christian principles that authorized her harsh words. She defended herself against Isabel's characterization of her "language" as "too strong" by appealing to her Christianity: "Slavery, my friend, must be either positively right, or positively wrong. There is no *middle* point on which it may rest. It is not a thing to be merely *disapproved* of   coldly warred with as a venial offense. It violates *all* the most essential principles of the Christian religion" (p. 14). Her piety—a traditionally feminine virtue—impelled her to persuade strongly, even at the risk of violating another tenet of "true womanhood"—the bonds between women. "You know that I love you, dearest Isabel," she declared, "but even at the risk of alienating your affection, must I speak thus plainly!" (p. 14).

Those who called for women's persuasion did not always advocate public rhetoric. Many "Ladies' Department" contributors described a limited domestic sphere for women's antislavery influence. Contributor L. H. (1832) qualified the claim that women "lift up their voices against" slavery with the proviso that "the voice of woman should not be heard in public debates" (p. 70). Woman's influence, instead, should be in the home: "Let slavery be spoken of as a withering blight . . . at every fireside in the land, and many would rise in their strength to wipe off the foul reproach on our nation" (p. 70).

Some contributors to the "Ladies' Department," though, did not confine women's "naturally benevolent" influence to the domestic sphere. T. H. (1832)—a male abolitionist, it appears, from appeals to "your sex"—extended the power of women's moral influence to embrace public activism. T. H. provided a recitation of "ancient and modern historical facts" to demonstrate that "the concentrated energies of [women] have never been in vain," from women's influence in preventing war in ancient Rome to the endeavors of British women abolitionists (p. 6). T. H.'s examples did not explicitly present women as public rhetors, describing instead their general moral influence on male leaders. Yet he implicitly supported a broad public role for women in fighting slavery: "Can you doubt for a moment, the natural and absolute right you have to exercise any faculty of your natures for the attainment of such an important object?" (p. 6).

Women did indeed involve themselves directly in a debate over public policy—and defend controversial public action for women—in the "Ladies' Department" in 1833. Educator Prudence Crandall, who had lost most white pupils in her girls' boarding school in Canterbury, Connecticut, when she admitted an African American student, proposed to open a school for young African American women. She was harassed by the community and jailed, and her school was destroyed. Articles in the "Ladies' Department" supported Crandall and condemned the outrages against her. Boldly defending Crandall's controversial public efforts, contributors to the column justified her actions by presenting her as an ideal antebellum woman. "[S]he has been persecuted, abused and imprisoned, for her benevolent and self-denying labors," contributor Eliza (1833) asserted. "But she has borne it all with the patience and fortitude of a martyr. She needs our sympathy, and our prayers; need I say that she is entitled to them?" (p. 122). The "Appeal to the Females of the United States: In Behalf of Miss Prudence Crandall" (1833) claimed that Crandall was a "pious and exemplary member of the Baptist Church" and "a lady . . . elevated, and comprehensive in her views" (p. 130). Significantly, Crandall's "true womanhood" empowered women to assert themselves boldly as they vindicated her. "The elements of moral evil are powerfully at work in the midst of us," declared the author of "Appeal to the Females of the United States." "If any thing can save our country from the most dismal scenes, to what earthly influence can we look, but to the gentle yet firm remonstrances of WOMAN? Why should not *her* voice be heard?" (p. 130).

Abolitionists did not only defend white women in the "Ladies' Department." Slave women should be a particular concern of free women, the author of "Our Own Sex" (1832) asserted: "The situation of the slaves of our own sex, certainly claims in a pre-eminent degree the attention of American females" (p. 2). The aforementioned image featured at the head of the column in 1832 (Figure 1.1) graphically illustrated the assumption that bonds of womanhood overrode all other concerns, making "sisters" of slave women and free women. Because the traditional ideology of femininity was essentialist, presumably transcending divisions of class and race (Ginzburg, 1990), contributors to the "Ladies' Department" appropriated conventional gendered rhetoric to assert women's right to agitate on behalf of female slaves. The article "Yes!" (1832)—whose title responded directly to the question posed by the inscription above the kneeling slave image—demonstrated this strategy of empowerment. "We acknowledge that thou art a woman and a sister," the author asserted, "and our sympathies have been awakened in thy behalf. . . . [S]omething must be done: an effort must be made . . . and it is in the power of American women to do much" (p. 42).

But to awaken audience members' sympathy, as Hoganson (1993) has noted, abolitionists needed to present slave women as "true women" worthy of the support of their countrywomen. Thus slave women were presented in traditional maternal and domestic terms that, somewhat paradoxically, authorized free women to challenge the conventional boundaries of "woman's sphere" in order to argue publicly on their behalf. A writer assuming the pseudonym "Protestant" (1832) relied on conventional definitions of femininity to appeal to female readers on behalf of slave women:

Ladies! you that are tender mothers, permit one of your own sex to attempt to vindicate the cause of the poor degraded, enslaved daughters of Africa. . . .
    Mothers—Women—Sisters—Awake! Who of you are prepared to take the place of the African mothers? See her tender suckling torn from her maternal bosom, carried away by ruffian hands! (p. 106)

Equally salient as the image of the slave as mother was the invocation of female chastity. Contributors to the "Ladies' Department" often represented female slaves as modest women whose sexual purity was constantly subject to violation. In a letter to Garrison, Elizabeth Pond (1837)—the corresponding secretary of the Franklin Female Anti-Slavery Society—relied on this commonplace of antebellum femininity to defend free women's right both to organize and to speak against slavery:

We are aware that persons may be found who will think us to have exceeded our proper limits. . . . But is it so? *Ought* females to withhold the tender sympathies of their natures, while the female heart continues to throb, and her person in the absolute power of an irresponsible master? *Ought* we, I ask, *can* we remain silent, while a sister in the human family is constantly liable to be deprived not only of life, but of all that woman holds dear? (p. 127)

The fundamental bonds of their common femininity, Pond implied, not only empowered but compelled free women to advocate for their enslaved sisters.

CHALLENGING "TRUE WOMANHOOD"

Although contributors to the "Ladies' Department" often relied on conventional antebellum assumptions about womanhood, they also frequently challenged them by articulating women's actual experiences that conflicted with the traditional rhetoric of gender. In particular, articles written by African American women—identified by Garrison with the headnote "By a young lady of color"—often undermined conventional gendered rhetoric that excluded many women. As mentioned above, African American female rhetors were generally held to traditional standards of antebellum femininity in order to be considered credible before biracial audiences of men and women. Yet even as they adopted some conventions associated with "true womanhood"—professing, for example, their piety, selflessness, and compassion—they did not hesitate to confront audiences with the hypocrisy of American perceptions of gender and to challenge, redefine, and expand conceptions of womanhood and women's roles.

This process of redefining the ideology of a dominant society is an important feature of the rhetoric of marginalized groups. Anthropologist Edwin Ardener (1972) has asserted that the control of language by dominant members of a society leaves other individuals in a "muted" position because the linguistic models of those in power claim to define them without acknowledging their perceptions, leaving them "voiceless" in terms of the dominant group's discourse. Discussing the rhetorical strategies muted rhetors adopt to negotiate the obstacles that threaten them, Shirley Ardener (1975) has maintained that they may seem to adopt the values and standards of the dominant group. However, muted rhetors often inscribe these values within "a muted counterpart system," an alternative model that more fully represents their needs and perspectives (p. xvii).

In the "Ladies' Department," African American female abolitionists reshaped "true womanhood" in two ways. As they upheld some traditional notions of gender, they argued from personal experience against the narrow formulation of womanhood that privileged the experiences of upper-class white women. In so doing, they articulated a broader conception of women's roles that allowed women more authority beyond the home. In addition, they confronted audiences with their firsthand knowledge of prejudice and oppression, creating a strong mandate for African American antebellum women to argue on public questions that threatened their security and civil rights.

In a lecture at Franklin Hall in Boston in September 1832, subsequently printed in the "Ladies' Department," Maria Stewart (1832b) maintained that many African American women embodied qualities of the ideal antebellum woman, yet they were not considered "true women" because of prejudice and narrow formulations of femininity. "Let our girls possess what amiable qualities of soul they may," Stewart lamented, "let their characters be fair and spotless as innocence itself. . . . It is impossible for scarce an individual of them to rise above the condition of servants. Ah! why is this cruel and unfeeling distinction?

Is it merely because God has made our complexion to vary?" (p. 183). Although Stewart upheld traditional notions of female virtue, she expanded the narrow definition of femininity that ignored the real-life experiences of African American women. Significantly, she confronted her audience with the hypocrisy of judging women who work outside the home to be unfeminine:

O, ye fairer sisters, whose hands are never soiled, whose nerves and muscles are never strained, go learn by experience! Had we had the opportunity that you have had . . . what would have hindered our intellects from being as bright, and our manners from being as dignified as yours? Had it been our lot to have been nursed in the lap of affluence and ease . . . should we not have naturally supposed that we were never made to toil? And why are not our forms as delicate, and our constitutions as slender, as yours? Is not the workmanship as curious and complete? (p. 183)

Stewart called for an ideal that would include the true experiences of African American women—experiences that challenged a rigid distinction between the domestic sphere and the public realm

Stewart's assumption that women need not choose between domestic and public work allowed her to call explicitly for women's public action. Her appeals demonstrate that, as Paula Giddings (1985) has shown, antebellum African American women rejected a sharp division "between domesticity and political activism" (p. 52). In an excerpt from her tract *Religion and the Pure Principles of Morality, the Sure Foundation on Which We Must Build*, featured in the first "Ladies' Department" column, Stewart (1832a) exhorted African American women to "excel in good housewifery," to "[u]nite, and build a store of [their] own," and to "[s]ue for [their] rights and privileges" (pp. 2–3). Using the example of women in Wetherford, Connecticut, who cultivated and sold onions to raise funds for a church, Stewart demonstrated that female virtue was not in conflict with public and even economic activity.

Sarah Douglass's contributions to the "Ladies' Department" also proposed that African American women not only could, but were obligated to, assume public roles. Articulating the effects of prejudice in African American women's lives, Douglass demonstrated that they could not ignore the social and political forces that constituted a constant danger. In particular, all free African Americans in the North were threatened by the Fugitive Slave Act of 1793, which allowed masters to recapture fugitive slaves in the North—and often led to kidnapping both of fugitives and of those who had never been slaves (Quarles, 1969, p. 144; Wilson, 1994). In her address to the Female Literary Society of Philadelphia, reprinted in the "Ladies' Department," Douglass (1832) featured her own realization of this threat:

One short year ago, how different were my feelings on the subject of slavery! It is true, the wail of the captive sometimes came to my ear in the midst of my happiness, and caused my heart to bleed for his wrongs; but . . . I had formed a little world of my own, and cared not to move beyond its precincts. But how was the scene changed when I beheld the oppressor lurking on the border of my own peaceful home! I saw his iron hand stretched forth to seize me as his prey, and the cause of the slave became my own. I started up, and with one mighty effort threw from me the lethargy which had covered me as a mantle for years; and determined, by the help of the Almighty, to use every exertion in my power to elevate the character of my wronged and neglected race. (p. 114)

Douglass demonstrated that she could not remain secluded in the domestic sphere—legal realities and the force of prejudice brought the public world into her home. In the face of this threat, it was impossible for African American women to deny their mandate for public activism.

Although Douglass did not outline explicitly the public actions that could be taken against prejudice, Zelmire (1832) offered a concrete proposal to fight the racism in churches that relegated African Americans to segregated pews. Zelmire eschewed the feminine commonplaces of submission and deference in addressing this subject, stating boldly, "I have often thought of the distinction made in places of *Public Worship* between white and colored persons, and have wondered that the latter should humble themselves so much as to occupy one of those seats provided for them" (p. 118). Zelmire exhorted her audience to take action, to leave these white-dominated churches in protest: "[T]here are places of worship where we can go and hear ministers of our own color; and is it not better to encourage them by attending upon their ministrations . . . than to go where our feelings are injured by this 'most foul, strange, and unnatural' prejudice, which exists among many white christians towards us?" (p. 118). Significantly, Zelmire's boldness included not only advice to African Americans but a strong condemnation of the unchristian principles of white American churchgoers.

CONCLUSION

What was the impact of the "Ladies' Department" on the rhetoric of women abolitionists of the late 1830s and after? This question necessarily involves another: Why did the column end in 1837? Although it is impossible to determine precisely why Garrison discontinued this section of his paper, it appears that, as time went by, the column became less relevant. From 1833 to 1837, items that would seem to fall within the scope of the "Ladies' Department"—such as letters from women, accounts of female antislavery organizations, and women's speeches—began to appear with increasing frequency in other columns. Ironically, it seems that the column itself, by providing a forum in which writers could challenge the boundaries of women's roles, hastened its own demise.

Scholars of antebellum rhetoric have often assumed that stereotypical conventions of gender fettered the sort of rhetoric featured in the "Ladies' Department." They have distinguished between this rhetoric and later discourse that more directly engaged women's right to speak on controversial issues, and they have implied that the former was compromised by its acceptance of premises based on stereotypical notions of gender (Hoganson, 1993; Zaeske, 1995). This chapter demonstrates, however, that these assumptions do not account for the liberties that writers took within the gendered boundaries of the "Ladies' Department" to explore, challenge, and redefine womanhood and women's potential to expand their roles. The column helped bring about a transformation in public discourse that afforded women increasing rhetorical freedom.

The "Ladies' Department" also demonstrates that gendered rhetoric need not require women to unquestioningly accept the premises on which it is based, nor does it prevent them from offering strong, even radical arguments. This finding has implications not only for abolitionist rhetoric but for women's rhetoric in general. Women activists frequently use gendered rhetoric to promote public agendas. Their rhetorical strategies may involve invoking their roles as mothers to advocate for better societal conditions, identifying with women across boundaries of race and class, and expanding traditional domestic identities to include public activism. These strategies can be found in the arguments of women advocates for peace during World War I (Zeiger, 1996); Mexican American community activists in East Los Angeles from the 1950s to the present who have fought to improve schools and fight drugs in their neighborhoods (Pardo, 1991); women of the United Farm Workers who led the grape boycott in the 1960s and 1970s (Rose, 1995); and contemporary ecofeminists who call upon women's biological role as nurturer as the basis for environmentalism (Diamond, 1994; Keller, 1990; Merchant, 1990; Taylor, 1997). Although this discourse, like the rhetoric of the "Ladies' Department," is highly gendered and based on conceptions of womanhood that seem conventional or even essentialist, it calls for radical social change. From the "Ladies' Department" to contemporary discourse, gendered rhetoric need not confine women. Paradoxically, even apparently fettering ideology can be used to remove limitations, to fight restrictions, to gain freedom.

REFERENCES

Agnes. (1832a, January 21). Letters on slavery.—No. I. *Liberator*, p. 10.

Agnes. (1832b, January 28). Letters on slavery.—No. II. *Liberator*, p. 14.

Agnes. (1832c, February 4). Letters on slavery.—No. III. *Liberator*, p. 18.

Appeal to the females of the United States: In behalf of Miss Prudence Crandall. (1833, August 17). *Liberator*, p. 130.

Ardener, E. (1972). Belief and the problem of women. In J. S. La Fontaine (Ed.), *The interpretation of ritual: Essays in honour of A. I. Richards* (pp. 135–58). London: Tavistock.

Ardener, S. (1975). Introduction. In S. Ardener (Ed.), *Perceiving women* (pp. vii–xxiii). New York: Wiley.

Beecher, C. E. (1837). *An essay on slavery and abolitionism, with reference to the duty of American Females*. Philadelphia: H. Perkins.

Bolles, J. A. (1831, May). The influence of women on society. *Ladies' Magazine and Literary Gazette, 4*, 256–69.

Campbell, K. K. (1989). *Man cannot speak for her* (Vol. 1). Westport, CT: Greenwood.

Clinton, C. (1984). *The other civil war: American women in the nineteenth century.* New York: Hill and Wang.

Cott, N. F. (1977). *The bonds of womanhood: "Woman's sphere" in New England, 1780–1835.* New Haven, CT: Yale University Press.

Diamond, I. (1994). *Fertile ground: Women, earth, and the limits of control.* Boston: Beacon.

Douglass, S. (1832, July 21). Address. *Liberator*, pp. 114–15.

Eliza. (1833, August 3). To Christian ladies. *Liberator*, p. 122.

Epstein, B. L. (1981). *The politics of domesticity: Women, evangelism, and temperance in nineteenth-century America.* Middletown, CT: Wesleyan University Press.

Friedman, L. J. (1982). *Gregarious saints: Self and community in American abolitionism 1830–1870.* Cambridge: Cambridge University Press.

Garrison, W. L. (1832, January 7). Editorial commentary in "Ladies' Department." *Liberator*, p. 2.

Giddings, Paula. (1985). *When and where I enter: The impact of black women on race and sex in America.* New York: Bantam.

Ginzburg, L. D. (1990). *Women and the work of benevolence: Morality, politics, and class in the nineteenth-century United States.* New Haven, CT: Yale University Press.

Grimké, A. E. (1837, June 30). Letters to Catherine [*sic*] E. Beecher. No. II. *Liberator*, p. 106.

Hoganson, K. (1993). Garrisonian abolitionists and the rhetoric of gender, 1850–1860. *American Quarterly, 45*, 558–95.

Keller, C. (1990). Women against wasting the world: Notes on eschatology and ecology. In I. Diamond and G. F. Orenstein (Eds.), *Reweaving the world: The emergence of ecofeminism* (pp. 249–63). San Francisco: Sierra Club.

Kramarae, C. (1981). *Women and men speaking: Frameworks for analysis.* Rowley, MA: Newbury House.

L. H. (1832, May 5). Duty of females. *Liberator*, p. 70.

Matthews, G. (1992). *The rise of public woman: Woman's power and woman's place in the United States, 1630–1970.* New York: Oxford University Press.

A member of the Boston Female Anti-Slavery Society. (1835, October 24). Letter to the editor of the [*Boston*] *Courier. Liberator*, p. 169.

Merchant, C. (1990). Ecofeminism and feminist theory. In I. Diamond and G. F. Orenstein (Eds.), *Reweaving the world: The emergence of ecofeminism* (pp. 100–105). San Francisco: Sierra Club.

Our own sex. (1832, January 7). *Liberator*, p. 2.

Pardo, M. (1991). Creating community: Mexican American women in Eastside Los Angeles. *Aztlan: A Journal of Chicano Studies, 20*, 39–71.

Pond, Elizabeth. (1837, August 4). Another female society. *Liberator*, p. 127.

Proceedings of the Woman's Rights Convention, held at the Unitarian Church, in the city of Rochester, August 2, 1848, to consider the rights of woman: Politically, religiously, and industriously. (1848, September 15). *Liberator*, p. 148.

Protestant. (1832, July 7). Men, women, and babes sold! *Liberator*, p. 106.

Quarles, B. (1969). *Black abolitionists.* New York: Oxford University Press.

Richardson, M. (1987). Introduction. In M. Richardson (Ed.), *Maria W. Stewart, America's first black woman political writer: Essays and speeches* (pp. 3–27). Bloomington: Indiana University Press.

Rose, M. (1995). "Woman power will stop those grapes": Chicana organizers and middle-class female supporters in the farm workers' grape boycott in Philadelphia, 1969–1970. *Journal of Women's History, 7*(4), 6–36.

Slavery. (1832, May 12). *Liberator*, p. 75.

Smith-Rosenberg, C. (1985). *Disorderly conduct: Visions of gender in Victorian America.* New York: Alfred A. Knopf.

Stewart, M. (1832a, January 7). Mrs. Steward's [*sic*] essays. *Liberator*, pp. 2–3.

Stewart, M. (1832b, November 17). Lecture delivered at the Franklin Hall, Boston, September 21st, 1832. *Liberator*, p. 183.

Taylor, D. E. (1997). Women of color, environmental justice, and ecofeminism. In K. J. Warren (Ed.), *Ecofeminism: Women, culture, nature* (pp. 38–81). Bloomington: Indiana University Press.

T. H. (1832, January 14). Address to the ladies. *Liberator*, p. 6.

Welter, B. (1976). *Dimity convictions: The American woman in the nineteenth century.* Athens: Ohio University Press.

Wilson, C. (1994). *Freedom at risk: The kidnapping of free blacks in America, 1780–1865.* Lexington: University Press of Kentucky.

Yee, S. J. (1992). *Black women abolitionists: A study in activism, 1828–1860.* Knoxville: University of Tennessee Press.

Yes! (1832, March 17). *Liberator*, p. 42.

Zaeske, Susan. (1995). The "promiscuous audience" controversy and the emergence of the early woman's rights movement. *Quarterly Journal of Speech, 81*, 191–207.

Zboray, R. J., and Zboray, M. C. (1996). Political news and female readership in antebellum Boston and its region. *Journalism History, 22*, 2–14.

Zeiger, S. (1996). She didn't raise her boy to be a slacker: Motherhood, conscription, and the culture of the First World War. *Feminist Studies, 22*, 7–39.

Zelmire. (1832, July 28). Unnatural distinction. *Liberator*, p. 118.

Zillah. (1832, July 21). Extract from a letter written to a friend, Feb. 23rd, 1832. *Liberator*, p. 115.

2

Allessandria Polizzi

To Strengthen the Wings of a Caged Bird: Constructing Woman in Margaret Fuller's *Woman in the Nineteenth Century* and *The Una*

INTRODUCTION

Margaret Fuller's *Woman in the Nineteenth Century* (1845) set a precedent for first-wave American feminist print culture by asking women to develop their own spheres rather than rely on the duties prescribed to them by men. Fuller expounded upon the status of woman in order to convince her readers (who were, in most cases, already convinced or too hostile ever to be convinced) that woman's status should be elevated. "As she stated repeatedly in *Woman in the Nineteenth Century*," remarks Annette Kolodny (1994), "the time had come for women to give over merely following male models and, instead, find 'out what is fit for themselves' " (p. 360). Politically aligned with Fuller's cultural feminism was one of the first American feminist journals, *The Una* (1853–1855). Susan Conrad (1976) notes the connection between Fuller and *The Una*, stating that "Margaret Fuller's spirit seems to preside over each issue" (p. 58).

As participants in the philosophies of cultural feminism, these writers, along with Fuller, argued for women's equality to men and pushed for their education and their freedom to develop naturally in the print culture they were participating in. As feminist writers, Fuller and the writers of *The Una* were defining "a Vision of New Womanhood" (Coultrap-McQuin, 1990, p. 12). Within Fuller's work and the essays of *The Una*, we can see how this new woman was being defined, how they chose to (re)construct the gender of woman through the written word. By examining the essays of *The Una* and Margaret Fuller's *Woman in the Nineteenth Century*, we can see how first-wave feminists chose to construct (and reconstruct) woman's sphere. Ultimately, what these works reveal is a feminocentric realm characterized by feminine intelligence and power.

TEXT

The Una began its monthly publication a few years after the feminist landmark of the Seneca Falls Convention. Deriving its title from an emblem of truth, *The Una* set forth to elevate woman's status (as its subtitle, "A Paper Devoted to the Elevation of Woman," suggests), to promote the politics of its feminist contemporaries, and to spread the ideologies of feminism to women around the country, as well as in the Western world. *The Una*'s editor, Paulina Wright Davis, "envisioned the paper's target audience as all women, who, although diverse in terms of individual circumstances, shared much by virtue of being female" (Tonn, 1991, p. 50). Paulina Wright Davis (1853) made this intention clear in her first edition, in which she set forth that *The Una* was formed "to discuss the rights, sphere, duty, and destiny of woman, fully and fearlessly; and our aim will be to secure the highest good of all. We shall not confine ourselves to any locality, set, sect, class or caste, for we hold the solidarity of the race and believe that if one member suffers, all suffer, and that the highest is made to atone for the lowest" (p. 1).

Essays such as "Reasons Why a Woman Should Define Her Own Sphere" (1853), "The Moral Character of Woman" (1853b), and "The Legal Rights of Women" (1854) illuminate just how the writers in *The Una* were able to accomplish this goal of elevating women through discussing their place in American culture. "Alas, for woman!" wrote Davis, "we ask for her inherent rights, the right of franchise, the rights of conscience, and the liberty to pursue happiness in her own way, defining for herself her own sphere" ("Legal," 1854a, pp. 244–46). It is toward woman "defining for herself her own sphere" that many of *The Una*'s essays dwell.

"Nineteenth Century women, for the first time in history, recognized a collective experience for members of their sex and defined that as a position of subjugation" (Gordon, Buhle, and Schrom, 1992, p. 17). Their recognition of gender as a domain was a strong element in their sense of self. As Jean Matthews remarks, "[N]ineteenth-century Western culture increasingly encouraged individuals to think of themselves in essentially gendered terms" (1993, p. 61). With the introduction of the division between the domestic and the public, these new gendered spheres were becoming an economic cage built around women in order to keep them closely tied to the home. Gendering this economic division made the classification less fluid. Fuller and the writers of *The Una* hoped that a feminist discussion of "the rights, sphere, duty, and destiny of women," which Davis described, in the printed culture would allow women to construct their own definitions of womanhood in their everyday lives.

But reading this construction fruitfully is problematic on many levels. Now influenced by Freudian analysis, Lacanian psycholinguistics, and sociological theories of gender unknown to these writers, we must step back in time to determine the nature of these (re)definitions. Unfortunately, were one of these time machines to exist, we could never remove the fine dust of the latter twentieth century from our eyes. For my purposes here, a few things must be understood, even if these writers lacked the terminology to name them. As historian Joan Scott (1992) points out, "[F]eminists have in a more literal and serious vein begun to use 'gender' as a way of referring to the social organization of the relationship between the sexes" (pp. 445–46). As a feminist, I, too, see the term *gender* in this light.

As Fuller and the writers in *The Una* argue and as researchers have attempted to prove throughout the last century, gender is a cultural construction, "the entirely social creation of ideas about appropriate values for men and women. It is a way of referring to the exclusively social origins of the subjective identities of men and women. Gender is, in this definition, a social category imposed on a sexed body" (Scott, 1992, p. 443). As Paulina Wright Davis describes it in "The Moral Character of Woman," "[I]t is not a question of sex, but a question of conditions, not a question of difference between man and woman, but a difference between freedom and slavery" (1853b, p. 104). The writers I am discussing here, as I will reveal, saw gender in just this way. In (re)defining gender, they were establishing a feminine sphere, a sphere that differs significantly from that imposed upon them. Their hopes were that the sphere they created in their writings would extend itself to the culture in which they lived.

Second, Anglo American culture emphasizes difference. While these writers saw "gender" as a social construction placed upon them, they still valued and celebrated what they saw as inherent differences between the socially constructed masculine and feminine. "One of the central elements in gender systems is the taboo against the sameness of male and female," say sociologists Myra Marx Ferree and Beth B. Hess (1987, p. 16). Although in some instances questioning it, Fuller and the writers of *The Una* worked within this paradigm. Their understanding of the new sphere of womanhood therefore participated in this cultural system. However, these writers argued for a feminocentric sphere developed by women and nature rather than one formed like a cage around them. They wrote toward a freedom of self-definition.

Our current understanding of nineteenth-century womanhood is quite limited. Most visions of the past are, like Nancy Woloch's in *Women and the American Experience* (1984), Nancy Cott and Elizabeth Pleck's in *A Heritage of Her Own* (1979), and Sarah M. Evans's in *Born for Liberty: A History of Women in America* (1989), based on the gender constructions found in popular women's periodicals, such as *Ladies' Magazine* and *Godey's Lady's Book*. Woloch (1984) describes this view as follows:

The middle-class wife, like the *Ladies' Magazine* reader of 1828, remained at home while her income-earning husband went to work outside it, in office or in store, business or profession. . . . The doctrine of sphere, as expounded in the *Ladies' Magazine, Godey's*

Lady's Book, and countless other publications, celebrated the new status of the middle-class woman, along with her distinctive vocation, values, and character. It also described an unspoken bargain between middle-class women and men. While men were still heads of families, their real domain was now in the world of business, professions, politics, and money making. (p. 114)

As shown above, "a heightened awareness of the distinctiveness of women, even a celebration of that distinctiveness, does not necessarily lead to a principled challenge to that doctrine of separate spheres nor a demand for equality with men in the state" (Matthews, 1993, p. 62). Rather, women, such as the ones described by Woloch, embraced their sphere and their special place as ruler of the heart and home.

Restricted and restrained, this sphere was one of the main social concerns Fuller and the writers in *The Una* argued against. "I repeat, therefore, the question is not now what is woman's sphere?" writes the Reverend A. D. Mayo in "The Real Controversy Between Man and Woman." "She has answered that in her own soul; and there possesses every inch of ground worth having occupied by man" (1853, p. 3). By maintaining the same sphere in our own historical vision, we participate in its maintenance. While this gives us historical "accuracy," it dismisses other attempts by first-wave feminists to deconstruct and rebuild woman's sphere.

A DOCTRINE OF DIFFERENCE

To Fuller and the writers in *The Una*, women were hindered from developing equally to men, from developing naturally and fully. The assigned domestic sphere imposed upon them by the patriarchal system restrained them from growing naturally. "Men and women are in fact and effect, just what their accidental developments make of them," wrote Paulina Wright Davis ("Inequality," 1854b, p. 214). The minister T. W. Higginson, author of "Woman and Her Wishes," agreed: "Nature has everything to dread from constraint, nothing from liberty" (1853, p. 61). "What woman needs," added Fuller (1845), "is not as a woman to act or rule, but as nature to grow as an intellect to discern, as a soul to live freely and unimpeded, to unfold such powers as were given her when we left our common home" (p. 261). We are also introduced to Fuller's Miranda, an autobiographical figure. She is a woman who was able to develop naturally and is the ideal woman in Fuller's eyes. "Of Miranda I had always thought as an example, that the restraints upon the sex were insuperable only to those who think them so, or who noisily strive to break them. She had taken a course of her own, and no man stood in her way" (1845, p. 262). According to this (re)vision of gender, were women able to develop naturally, they would become self-reliant and powerful in their own feminine way.

What these writers saw as the natural development of women emphasized equality but difference. They saw men and women as made from the same elements but perceived that essential differences lie within the gendered spheres. "For Margaret Fuller, every self combined masculine and feminine natures, continually passing and repassing into one another as the self strives towards greater development" (Matthews, 1993, p. 64). "Male and female represent the two sides of the great radical dualism . . . and of this world of causes, this approximation to the region of primitive motives, women I hold to be especially capable. . . . Should these faculties have free play, I believe they will open new, deeper purer sources of joyous inspiration," said Fuller (1845, pp. 310–11). Alike in essence but different in manifestation. This was the new understanding of woman.

Examining this critically, Nancy Theriot (1996) comments that "proponents of separate spheres, from outright misogynists to domestic feminists, agreed that differing sexual roles were the result of differing sexual 'natures' " (p. 66). Categorizing these two groups together based on their slightly essentialist notions is problematic, however. These "domestic feminists" differ from the "misogynists" Theriot describes in that they did not see women as less than men, as misogynists or traditionally male-identified women would. Rather, they argued for their own equality. As Matthews (1993) points out, this position was a common one among early feminists: "[W]ithin the feminist movement, there has been . . . [a] long-standing, though not always overt, tension between equality and 'difference,' between those who seek to expand the area of genderless space available for individual growth and those who affirm a distinct female identity" (p. 61). It was in enabling women to participate in the gendered construction of their sphere that writers like Fuller and those in *The Una* differ from other constructions of gender.

Unlike "the doctrine of sphere," Fuller and the writers in *The Una* consistently argued for the equal valuing of the gendered construction of men and women. These feminist thinkers saw women as "human beings like men with aspirations for achievement and only incidentally wives and mothers" (Coultrap-McQuin, 1990, p. 12). "While they had an acute awareness of being socially classified as 'women,' they precisely did not 'define themselves first as women' " (Matthews, 1993, p. 63). The cultural acceptance of this revisioning of woman's sphere as equal to men's was their most sought-after goal. As Fuller described in her introduction to *Woman in the Nineteenth Century*: "I believe that the development of the one cannot be effected without that of the other. My highest wish is that this truth should be distinctly and rationally apprehended, and the conditions of life and freedom recognized as the same for the daughters and the sons of time; twin exponents of a divine thought" (1845, p. 261). In *The Una*'s "The Intellect of Woman," we see a similar assertion: "The sexes are thus alike in essence, and thus varied in manifestation and acclaim, and in their natural reciprocities is to be found the perfected humanity out of the great strife with the material elements which surround us" (Davis, 1853c, p. 40). This vision of woman sees her as essentially human first, a socially constructed woman second. According to this understanding of woman's sphere, it is most important to see it as dwelling within that of humanity rather than as hovering outside of it.

PROMOTING SIMILARITIES

While maintaining the taboos of sameness by still placing women away from men, these writers saw women and men as made of the same essence and thus capable of similar accomplishments. The most widely discussed similarity between this feminocentric (re)construction and the masculine standard is woman's intellectual capabilities. Fuller again used the example of Miranda to show how well able women are to learn. Raised, as Fuller was, with access to education, Miranda "took her place easily, not only in the world of organized being, but in the world of the mind" (1845, p. 261). That women were able to learn and develop intellectually as much as men is a great part of this new vision of womanhood. *The Una* devoted many essays to this topic. "I do not fear contradiction when I make the assertion that the inner life of woman now covers the whole ground of the life of man. She hopes, thinks, feels, and wills with man," writes the Reverend A. D. Mayo (1853, p. 3). In "The Intellect of the Sexes," we also see the same assertion: "[T]he intellect of woman, which is so remarkable for striking out the highest and best results of reasoning, without traveling to them by the route of demonstrative ratiocination, is imminently fitted to take up the complete issues of the masculine reason, and to hold and employ them in their highest forms effectively" (Davis, 1853c, p. 120).

This position was, according to Frances Cogan (1989), a popular one at the time. In discussing advice books, domestic novels, and periodicals like *The Una*, she writes: "[N]ot only do the writers of these works seem to feel that women are as intellectually capable as men, but they insist that it is woman's God-given duty to develop her mind and her social and patriotic duty to use it" (p. 65). While this construction portrays women as able to learn and reason as well as men, the writers still argued that women did not have access to as high an education as men. "How can we expect any better things of those females brought up, trained from the cradle to be ball-room belles? The thing they receive, mis-named education, what is it? Examine it; analyze its various parts, and see if it does not necessarily make women just the inutile things they are" (L.A.M., 1854, p. 324). This explanation for difference in womanhood from manhood also reveals the push for essential equality these writers were striving for. As intellectually capable as men, women were only limited by the social norms built around them. But T. W. Higginson (1853) writes, "[T]o give 'education' without giving an object, was but to strengthen the wings of a caged bird" (p. 57). With this image, we see the equality within difference so prevalent in their (re)constructions of woman's sphere. Unlike the eagles around them, these birds seem only ornamental. But able to fly, this bird need only be given its chance to do so.

In establishing women's essential equality to men, the writers in *The Una* discussed the assumed moral superiority of women over men with great fervency. "In morals," wrote Paulina Wright Davis in "The Moral Character of Woman" (1853b), we are constrained to say she has been as much misunderstood [as in her intellect], though in a very different way, but strangely enough, with equal injury to her just rights, among her brethren. . . . We are unwilling to be worshiped, for well we know that in the world's religion it means turning us out of the earth, under pretense of sending us to heaven. . . . The difference, in the morals of the sexes is just the difference of their culture and conditions; both alike, can exhibit the virtues of slavery and its vices, the faculties of freedom and its glories. . . . We claim equality here too, as elsewhere, and cannot accept a gratuitous exemption, at the cost of so much restraint and wrong as men would impose upon us. (pp. 72–73)

In order to demonstrate that women and men possess equal morals, both Fuller and the writers in *The Una* did a very interesting thing: They discussed the immorality and flaws found in women. "We answer that women are vicious in proportion as they are degraded; that they are weak, silly, mean, and false to the degree that they are enslaved" (Davis, 1853c, p. 73). This image of womanhood, strikingly different from the morally pure image of woman seen in *Godey's*, is consistent with that described by feminist activists of the day. Lucretia Mott, for example, "voiced the sentiments of her Congregational sisters when she objected to the very 'language of flattering compliment' that portrayed women as more devoted, spiritual, and altruistic as men" (Hewitt, 1986, p. 32). This position appeared in Fuller's work, as well. These are the women "whose whole character is tainted with vanity, inherited or taught, who have early learnt the love of coquettish excitement, and whose eyes restlessly search of a 'conquest' or a 'beau.' " These are the women to whom Fuller called out, "Clear your souls from the taint of vanity" (pp. 321–25).

Rather than relying on the power found in their male-oriented conquests, Fuller called out for women to develop their own self-reliance. To submit that women are able to possess such independence was a radical notion for the nineteenth century. Women were supposed to be devoted mothers and wives, dependent upon the needs of others for their identity. "The necessity of female self-sacrifice, womanly submission, and the equation of self with gender role was part of the gender script middle-class daughters of the mid-century period inherited from their mothers" (Theriot, 1996, p. 66). But a self-defined woman finds strength within herself. As Davis described this powerful womanhood, self-designed women should "woman-like, make our fabric strong and whole" (1853c, p. 41). Fuller's vision of womanhood contradicted this dependence on others, demanding that women look internally for their strength and power and that women possess a power within themselves.

It is not the transient breath of poetic incense that women want; each can receive that from a lover. It is not lifelong sway; it needs but to become a coquette, a shrew, or a good cook, to be sure of that. It is not money or notoriety, nor the badges of authority that men have appropriated to themselves. If demands, made in their behalf, lay stress on any of these particulars, those who make them have not searched deeply into the need. It is for that which once includes these and precludes them; which would not be forbidden power, lest there be temptation to steal and misuse it; which would not have the mind perverted by flattery from a worthiness of esteem. It is for that which is the birthright of every being capable to receive it, "freedom, the religious, the intellectual freedom of the universe, to use its means; to learn the secret as far as nature has enabled them, with God alone for their guide and judge." (1845, p. 276)

Woman's accountability to God rather than to men was an important element in this (re)construction of gender. "This is not whether man or woman shall rule; whether women shall take this or that position; but it is the principle of human accountability, that male and female are accountable alike to God" (Price, 1853, p. 10). Again, allowed to develop naturally according to God's design, women could construct their own definition of self.

Self-reliance also moves the sphere of woman into the sphere of the public. These writers saw participation in public matters, in many cases as a result of winning the vote, as part of their self-definition. Once a part of the public realm, women would bring their valuable qualities to that world. "The policy of government, now so intricate, so dark a contexture of fraud and force that the worst men are its best ministers, will also be redeemed and reformed, so that the acknowledged excellencies of feminine morality and woman's directness and clearness of intellect, will be the highest qualification for national government," writes Paulina Wright Davis in "The Intellect of Woman" (1853c, p. 41). In "Woman and Her Wishes," T. W. Higginson (1853) also comments upon this expansion of woman's sphere: "[O]nce we recognize the political equality of the sexes, all questions of legal, social, educational, and professional equality will soon settle itself." He adds later, "[W]e repress a woman's tongue in public and then complain if she uses it disproportionally in private. But if she has anything worth saying in the one case, why not in the other?" (pp. 59–60).

WOMAN'S NATURE

While promoting self-reliance, Fuller and the writers of *The Una* also privileged what they saw as woman's inherent intuitiveness. Fuller called this an "electrical element" (1845, p. 302), which was "commonly expressed by saying that her intuitions are more rapid and more correct" (p. 309). Woman's intuition makes her more aware of what goes on around her, more sensitive to the needs and actions of others, but it also better enables her to perceive the truth more clearly. "The special genius of woman I believe to be electrical in movement, intuitive in function, spiritual in tendency. She excels not so easily in classification, or re-action, as in an instinctive seizure of causes" (Davis, 1853c, pp. 41–42). Intuition enables women to see what is. At a time when the pursuit of "truth" was so heavily emphasized, especially among the members of Fuller's intellectual circle, this inherent ability helped to raise the status of woman's sphere.

The writers of *The Una* also saw this side to woman's sphere. "Woman is not the strong struggler in the regions of materialism, mechanics, bloody warfare, and political gymnastics; but the science of all these cleared of falsehood; the natural honest truth comes to her clearly, and is adapted to her management" (Davis, 1853c, p. 42). For these writers, woman's sphere included a sense of truth unavailable to men, an insight into reality unavailable to men who were more concerned with the unnatural urge to rule and dominate. Womanhood's value thus increases because it is accompanied by this clearer sense of truth. Their intuition raised them to equal status with men because it was to them more valuable than the male inclinations. "But the question between men and women is, the intrinsic worth of all this paraded superiority. We answer, it is a superiority in inferior things" (ibid.).

The writers of *The Una* also privileged what they saw as the empathetic nature of woman. While we don't see this as clearly in Fuller's work as we do in *The Una*, we can surmise that a finely tuned empathy may be closely related to the intuition Fuller celebrated. This may be the lamb Fuller saw as taking the place of the lion as the emblem of nations. Once accomplished, "both men and women will be as children of one spirit, perpetual learner of the word and doers thereof, not hearers only" (Fuller, 1845, p. 309). Woman's "natural" empathy gives women a more peaceful rule, much like the lamb Fuller describes. The writers of *The Una*, therefore, often tied women's empathetic nature to what they saw as her natural political tendencies. "The fugitive slave law could not have been passed in a congress of women, even if in a fish market; and Nebraska could never be made a territory for the extension of slavery, nor the Missouri compromise repealed if women were co-equal in the government" (Davis, 1854c, pp. 252–53). Woman's political equality would, in this vision of womanhood, lead them to more empathetic actions. "Her heart dictates right action in all questions where the heart should direct" (p. 252). In constructing their own sense of a gendered self, then, women were asked to develop, in a manner seen as natural, their empathetic individuality.

These writers were introducing a new vision of independence foreign to the domestic female paradigm. In order to argue successfully for woman's construction of her own sphere, Fuller and the writers of *The Una* needed to construct solid arguments ripe with plentiful examples. These examples helped them to more clearly construct the sphere of woman for their readers by using a few individuals to represent the status of the natural sphere of woman. According to Gregory Clark and S. Michael Halloran (1993), this was a fundamental trait in Fuller's rhetorical style. "It was Fuller's position as a woman in a culture dominated by men that led her to transform the politics of self-culture from one that designates the individual a majority of one into one that makes the individual an activist working to establish a new majority coalition" (p. 13). The examples Fuller and the writers of *The Una* used to express their visions of woman's sphere are therefore that much more enlightening to the culture of womanhood they were creating. The most prevalent method was the use of historical figures as examples of a natural sphere of woman. As Susan Conrad (1976) tells us, Caroline Dall looked upon her work for *The Una* as that of a "house historian" (p. 167). We see this use of history in Dall's serial essay "The Duties and Influences of Woman" (1853). In it, she used such figures as Donna Olympia Maldachini and Madame Pompadour to show woman's ability to misuse her power. Her argument fit with the stance discussed earlier of women and men as equally moral. These historical figures helped to clarify the moral equality of men and women, which these writers saw as a basic reflection of woman's inherent humanity.

In asserting a similar argument, Davis also used women from the past as support: "[I]n the most advanced societies [women] are as criminal, as cruel and tyrannical as their conditions happen to induce. Mary and Elizabeth of England, were in their way, quite as wicked as their infamous father. . . . Catherine the second of Russia was as licentious as Charles the second. The Jews had a Jezebel as well as a Deborah" (1853b, p. 72). These women are woven through the fabric of our Western history. In using them, Davis and Dall succeed in bringing their vision of womanhood into the reality of their readers. As recognizable figures, they presented a historical basis for, and thus further legitimacy to, their constructions of woman's sphere.

This is only one of the many ways in which these writers used women who influenced history to show their vision of new womanhood. "There never was a time when there were not highly educated women, according to the standard of their age," wrote T. W. Higginson. "Isis and Minerva show the value set upon feminine intellect by the ancients. . . . We forget the long line of learned and accomplished English women from Lady Grey to Elizabeth Barrett. We forget that wonderful people, the Spanish Arabs, among whom women were public lecturers and secretaries of kings, while Christian Europe was sunk in darkness" (1853, p. 56). Rather than choosing examples of less admirable women, Higginson argues here that women are equal to men intellectually. Like the previous use of historical figures, however, these also established the equality of the sexes. These individuals, therefore, not only represented what is inherently female but what is inherently human. Fuller used women from history in order to demonstrate their worth, as well. Admirable women, such as Joan of Arc, graced her pages as women of great strength and nobility. These women from history proved how capable women are to achieve greatness; they demonstrated women's equality to men. They helped to fully construct a vision of woman as self-reliant and able to develop her own sphere.

Within their examinations of historical representations of their argument and within their own searches for the "natural" state of womanhood, these writers also turned to primitivistic readings of other cultures in order to discover and to demonstrate the natural sphere of woman. The primitivism of the day privileged the "uncivilized" cultures as more natural, as closer to what was essentially human. Through their primitivistic interpretations of other cultures, these writers found examples of what they perceived to be "pure" womanhood. In attempting to prove woman's moral equality to man, for example, Davis (1853b) stated that "in semi-civilized nations, women are found as blood-thirsty, as cruel, as eager for war, and as wildly ambitious as men. We have looked in heathen mythology for a Goddess, having in her nature what we conceive to be the true feminine element" (p. 88). Fuller (1845), however, used her primitivistic impulse to demonstrate woman's plight: "You know how it is with the natives of this continent. A chief had many wives whom he maintained and who did his household work; those women were but servants, still they enjoyed the respect of others and their own" (p. 321). While her fundamental argument was different from Davis's, her example remained the same. To Fuller, this example demonstrated the natural tendency for women to accept subjugated positions. Just as women of her own day gladly accepted their assigned domestic spheres, these women were happy in their roles as servants to men.

Fuller and the writers of *The Una* used more chronologically familiar examples for their readers, as well, by using examples of women from their own day. Fuller's Miranda is a fictional woman made to seem a contemporary model of pure womanhood allowed to develop naturally. Fuller also used Miss (Catharine Maria) Sedgewick, a woman who Fuller saw as "a fine example of the independent and beneficent existence that intellect and character can give a woman, no less than a man, if she knows how to seek and prize it" (1845, p. 339). Fuller found in Miss Sedgewick all of the qualities she thought inherent in natural womanhood, and she used her to show how well able women are to develop these admirable qualities.

DEVELOPING HER OWN SPHERE

How woman will develop her sphere now that gendered lines have been drawn economically, socially, and philosophically was a common concern for these writers. What we see them develop in their writings closely reflects their own (mis)understandings of woman's nature. "Mothers will delight to make the nest soft and warm. Nature would take care of that; no need to clip the wings of any bird that wants to soar and sing, or finds itself the strength of pinion for migratory flight unusual to its kind" (Fuller, 1845, p. 346). While nature may make women from the same elements as men, it also emphasizes certain qualities in the male and female. To be a woman, then, for the writers in *The Una* and for Fuller, was to be free to develop the special qualities, qualities of equal worth to those of men, that nature has given them. As Paulina Wright Davis writes in "The Moral Character of Woman":

Differences of sex are marked throughout their respective constitutions in every quality; attribute and action, physical, intellectual, and moral; but education, habit, conditions, opportunity and artificial influences, so greatly influence manifestation, that an almost miraculous penetration is required to trace appearances to their causes, and discover the essential character of the springs in the primitive constitution from which they flow. (1853b, p. 104)

While equal to men in worth, women possess a special aptitude for empathy. The differences inherent to women, according to this reading, are not as sharply divided from maleness as were the more popular constructions of womanhood. "What set most leaders of the antebellum woman's movement apart from other activist women and women in general," argues Matthews (1993), "was a much more fluid sense of self" (p. 63). Their fluidity of selfhood allowed them to embrace what they saw as strongly feminine qualities, qualities that they admired not because they were forced to but because, at least in their minds, they represented the power of the feminine.

While we may now recognize that their own understanding of "natural femininity," a deep empathy for others that is often demonstrated by motherly nurturing or concerns for the oppressed, is closely tied to the gendered system imposed upon them, the difference lies in how they see its construction. Womanhood, for these writers, is what develops naturally in women. And, as Davis commented above, the subjugation of women keeps us from fully discovering this "essential character." Thus, for the writers of *The Una* and for Fuller, to fully realize what this essence of woman is, women must first be free to soar or to nestle.

REFERENCES

Clark, G., and Halloran, S. M. (1993). Introduction. *Oratorical culture in nineteenth-century America*. Carbondale: Southern Illinois University Press.

Cogan, F. B. (1989). *All-American girl: The ideal of real womanhood in mid-nineteenth-century America*. Athens: University of Georgia Press.

Conrad, S. P. (1976). *Perish the thought: The intellectual women in Romantic America, 1830–1860*. New York: Oxford University Press.

Coultrap-McQuin, S. (1990). *Doing literary business: American women writers in the nineteenth century*. Chapel Hill: University of North Carolina Press.

Dall, C. (1853). The duties and influences of woman. *The Una*, 1 (9), 167.

Davis, P. W. (1853a). Prospectus. *The Una*, 1 (1), 1.

Davis, P. W. (1853b). The moral character of woman. *The Una*, 1 (5), 104–5.

Davis, P. W. (1853c). The intellect of woman. *The Una*, 1 (3), 40.

Davis, P. W. (1854a). The legal rights of women. *The Una*, 2 (4), 244–46.

Davis, P. W. (1854b). Inequality of women in marriage. *The Una*, 2 (2), 214.

Davis, P. W. (1854c). Discussion in the Franklin Lyceum on woman's right to vote. *The Una*, 2 (3), 252–53.

Fuller, M. (1845). Woman in the nineteenth century. In Jeffrey Steele (Ed.), *The essential Margaret Fuller* (1995) (pp. 243–378). New Brunswick: Rutgers University Press.

Gordon, A., Buhle, M. J., and Schrom, N. E. (1992). Women in American society: An historical contribution. In Nancy Cott (Ed.), *Theory and method in women's history* (p. 17). Munich: K. G. Saur.

Hess, B. B., and Ferree, M. M. (1987). Introduction. *Analyzing gender: A handbook of social science research*. London: Sage.

Hewitt, N. A. (1986). Feminist friends: Agrarian quakers and the emergence of woman's rights in America. *Feminist Studies*, 12 (1), 32.

Higginson, T. W. (1853). Woman and her wishes. *The Una*, 1 (4), 61.

Kolodny, A. (1994). Inventing a feminist discourse: Rhetoric and resistance in Margaret Fuller's *Woman in the nineteenth century*. *New Literary History*, 25, 360.

L.A.M. (1854). Duty versus fame. *The Una*, 2 (9), 324.

Matthews, J. V. (1993). Consciousness of self and consciousness of sex in antebellum feminism. *Journal of Woman's History*, 5 (1), 61.

Mayo, A. D. (1853). The real controversy between man and woman. *The Una*, 1 (1), 3.

Price, A. H. (1853). Reasons why a woman should define her own sphere. *The Una*, 1 (1), 10.

Scott, J. (1992). Gender: A useful category of historical analysis. In Nancy Cott (Ed.), *Theory and method in women's history* (pp. 443–46). Munich: K. G. Saur.

Theriot, N. M. (1996). Mothers and daughters in nineteenth-century America: The biosocial construction of femininity. Lexington: University of Kentucky Press.

Tonn, M. B. (1991). *The Una*, 1853–1855: The premiere of the woman's rights press. In Martha Solomon (Ed.), *A voice of their own: The woman suffrage press, 1840–1910* (p. 50). Tuscaloosa: University of Alabama Press.

Woloch, N. (1984). *Women and the American experience*. New York: McGraw-Hill.

PART II

NEWSPAPER

3

Gene Murray

War in the Ranks: Newspaper Coverage of Sexual Harassment in the Military

INTRODUCTION

Some of the biggest battles fought by the U.S. military forces during 1996–97 involved the war against sexual harassment. Reports of the war appeared frequently in the headlines. In July 1996, the news was upbeat, as results of a Department of Defense 1995 worldwide survey were announced, headlined "Harassment Statistics Looking Better, But Are Far From Perfect," according to the *Army Times* (Compart, 1996a, p. 10).

However, within the next few months, cases such as those involving drill instructors and trainees at Fort Leonard Wood, Missouri, and Aberdeen Proving Ground, Maryland, became hot news topics. In early 1997, Sergeant Major of the Army (SMA) Gene McKinney was accused of sexual harassment and suspended from his duties as the top enlisted adviser to the Army Chief of Staff.

The purpose of this examination of newspaper coverage of sexual harassment in the military services during 1996–97 is to see to what extent newspapers covered the topic, what editorial comments they made, and what issues were raised. After opening with an overview of the sexual harassment situation in the military, this chapter examines coverage of key sexual harassment incidents by seven daily newspapers and three military-oriented weekly newspapers. Also summarized are findings from a pilot survey of equal opportunity advisers' perceptions of how such coverage could affect the military services and their perceptions of some issues raised in the newspapers.

HISTORICAL BACKGROUND

For several years, sexual harassment has been recognized as a serious problem in both civilian and military organizations. As more women joined the workforce, sexual harassment became more evident. One measure giving some protection was the Civil Rights Act of 1964 outlawing discrimination in employment on the basis of an individual's race, color, religion, sex, or national origin (Goldman, 1995, p. 2). Title VII of the act defined sexual harassment as a legal concept (Harris and Firestone, 1994, p. 51). The first sexual harassment court case, *Corne v. Bausch & Lomb*, raised the question of the legality of a supervisor's unwanted sexual advances toward his subordinates. The plaintiffs, who claimed they quit their jobs because of their supervisor's repeated verbal and physical advances, lost (Goldman, 1995, p. 2).

In November 1980, the Equal Employment Opportunity Commission (EEOC) issued *Guidelines on Discrimination Because of Sex*, outlining the two types of prohibited sexual harassment: (1) *quid pro quo*, or "this for that" harassment, when unwelcome sexual advances are made and an employee is required to submit either to get or keep employment or because employment decisions or benefits for the individual could be affected, and (2) *hostile environment*, where unwelcome sexual conduct or comments have the purpose or effect of interfering with an employee's work effort by creating an intimidating, abusive, or insulting work environment (Harris and Firestone, 1994, p. 51)

The EEOC guidelines defining sexual harassment in 1980 read:

Unwelcome sexual advances, requests for sexual favors, and other verbal or physical conduct of a sexual nature constitute sexual harassment when submission to such conduct is made either explicitly or implicitly as a term or condition of an individual's employment, submission to or rejection of such conduct by an individual is used as the basis for employment decisions affecting such individual, or such conduct has the purpose or effect of unreasonably interfering with an individual's work performance or creating an intimidating, hostile, or offensive working environment. (Harris and Firestone, 1994, p. 51)

Department of Defense (DoD) Directive 1350.2 defining sexual harassment closely parallels the EEOC guidelines. The directive and guidelines are included in instruction at the Defense Equal Opportunity Management Institute (DEOMI).

In 1986, the U.S. Supreme Court heard its first sexual harassment case, *Merritor Savings Bank v. Vinson*. The Court ruled that a sexually hostile work environment is illegal even if it does not cause economic harm to the victim. Besides guaranteeing everyone a right to a harassment-free environment, the decision recognized that hostile environments are unlawful under Title VII. "Unwelcome" actions by the harasser became a key part of the offense. The Court rejected the idea that companies are to be held strictly liable for acts of "hostile environment" harassment. An act of harassment that occurs completely outside of work is unlikely to result in liability for the employer, according to the decision.

After examining 163 sexual harassment complaints filed in the Air Force during fiscal year 1987, Popovich found most victims were white, female, enlisted personnel, and most cases consisted of multiple incidents of sexual harassment in which the offender acted alone. She called for establishment of effective training programs to deal with the problem (Popovich, 1988, pp. 30, 31).

Calling sexual harassment "a complex problem in the military and any other setting," Pryor in 1988 wrote that "a first step in reducing sexual harassment in the military is to identify some of the organizational and personal factors that are related to its occurrence." He recommended a DoD survey with its findings used to develop organizational policies and training programs aimed at reducing sexual harassment (Pryor, 1988, p. 13).

The DoD worldwide survey was conducted in 1988 with results announced in 1990. The 1988 DoD Survey of Sex Roles in the Active Duty Military showed that 64 percent of women and 17 percent of men reported they had been sexually harassed at least once during the year prior to the survey (Bastain, Lancaster, and Reyst, 1996). In most cases, victims are female, single, and new to the unit. Their harassers outrank them. Twelve percent of those harassed reported the harassment-related use of annual leave or sick leave. Firestone and Harris have produced at least three analyses of the 1988 survey results (Firestone and Harris, 1994a, 1994b; Harris and Firestone, 1994).

In 1991, sexual harassment drew national attention during the Senate confirmation hearings for now–Supreme Court Justice Clarence Thomas. Although Thomas was confirmed, Anita Hill raised many questions in the minds of the American public. The television spectacle served at least one important purpose: It focused the nation's attention on the issue of sexual harassment in the workplace, wrote Susan Crawford (1994). She added that relationships between employers and employees, and between men and women, will never be quite the same (p. 48).

The Navy's infamous Tailhook incident occurred in late 1991 during a convention of Navy and Marine Corps pilots in Las Vegas. At least twenty-six women, half of them officers, were forced to run a gauntlet of rowdy conferees and were mauled and pawed. One of the women, Navy Lt. Paula Coughlin, testified that men grabbed her breasts and buttocks and pulled at her pants until she thought she was going to be raped. She filed a complaint and finally went public with her story. Six months later, more than 1,000 officer promotions were delayed, and Navy Secretary H. Lawrence Garret and some high-ranking officers were forced to resign. His replacement, J. Daniel Howard, ordered the entire Navy to "stand down" one day for sexual harassment training. In light of the Tailhook incident, the Navy proposed that the Uniform Code of Military Justice (UCMJ) be amended to deal specifically with sexual harassment. DoD has not yet made such an amendment (Niebuhr, 1997, p. 260).

Although publicity surrounding the convention made it appear sexual harassment is a problem unique to the Navy, a growing number of studies confirm that sexual harassment exists in most organizations, both military and civilian (Culbertson and Rosenfeld, 1994). Coughlin forever altered the relationship between men and women, wrote Rowan Scarborough in the *Washington Times*. "Miss Coughlin's complaints about the 1991 Tailhook Association convention helped usher in complaint hotlines, zero tolerance for sexual harassment and women in combat aviation" (Scarborough, 1997, p. 3).

A 1994 memorandum from Secretary of Defense William Perry further clarified the military's sexual harassment policy to indicate that hostile environment harassment "need not result in concrete psychological harm to the victim, but rather need only be so severe or pervasive that a reasonable person would perceive, and the victim does perceive, the work environment as hostile or abusive." The memorandum indicated that the definition applied both on or off duty for military members and that anyone in DoD "who makes deliberate or repeated unwelcome verbal comments, gestures, or physical contact of a sexual nature in the workplace is also engaging in sexual harassment" (Dansby, 1997, p. 20).

A 1995 DoD-wide sexual harassment survey was sent to 90,000 active-duty service members—65,000 women and 25,000 men. When results were made public in July 1996, they showed that 55 percent of the women and 14 percent of the men said they had experienced unwanted or uninvited sexual behavior within the past year. These figures represent a drop from the 1988 DoD survey, when 64 percent of the women and 17 percent of men said they had experienced harassment. The 1995 survey shows sexual harassment declining, but it remains a major concern within DoD, said Edwin Dorn, Undersecretary of Defense for Personnel and Readiness. "One person who experiences sexual harassment is too many. Sexual harassment affects people's performance, good order and discipline," Dorn added (Kozaryn, 1996, p. 1).

Not long after favorable news about the decline in sexual harassment was disseminated to the public, other incidents or "scandals" surfaced. The accusations and the aftermath of these cases received widespread publicity—two cases at Army training posts because of the volume of complaints and the other because of the status of the person accused, Sergeant Major of the Army Gene McKinney. Results of his court-martial were announced in March 1998. He was reprimanded and demoted one rank by a jury that convicted him of obstruction of justice in a sexual misconduct case. The jury sentenced him on one conviction, and he was found innocent of eighteen counts involving sexual harassment.

NEWSPAPER SEARCH

The news media report, reflect, and influence public opinion. In the United States, most reputable news media advocate the social responsibility theory of the press in which the media seek to uphold their obligation to inform and educate the public—the audience members. News media also serve a "watchdog" function to inform the public of wrongdoings in government agencies, such as the military services. Most journalists intend to be fair and accurate, but sometimes they let the drive to beat deadlines or to top the competition take control. Some members of the general public might perceive reporting as negative because it points out flaws in a system. However, it may be a matter of perspective. Some persons may view the rash of reported sexual incidents as bad publicity for the military, whereas others might view the same situations as the military taking action to try remedy the matter.

Journalists consider news judgment elements when reporting the news. These factors include audience appeal, affect and effect, proximity, conflict, curiosity, celebrities and public people, and timeliness (Vivian and Murray, in press). Since most Americans have served in the military or know someone who has served, many of the factors apply to the sexual harassment stories. Newspaper readers pay attention to such articles. News media influence and reflect public opinion, including that of members of the armed services.

Examined for this study were articles, editorials, and columns from the Associated Press (AP) and seven daily newspapers: *Baltimore Sun, Los Angeles Times, New York Times, St. Louis Post-Dispatch, USA Today, Washington Post*, and *Wall Street Journal*. The study also included the *Air Force, Army*, and *Navy Times*, widely circulated unofficial weekly newspapers. The Baltimore and St. Louis papers were selected because they were the area metropolitan newspapers covering two of the biggest sexual harassment cases—at Ft. Leonard Wood, Missouri, and Aberdeen Proving Ground, Maryland. The other newspapers were selected because they represent opinion leaders. A one-year period from July 1996 to June 1997 was chosen.

The newspaper search began with a chronology of events as reported in the newspapers. The AP, which provides news services to all the newspapers in the study, offered forty-three stories for the newspapers' use during that period. Articles were counted to determine how many stories and of what type were printed by each newspaper. Items were classified into two broad categories: news coverage and opinion/commentary consisting of columns, editorials, analyses, and letters to the editor. Stories that reported factual information with attributed opinions were classified as news stories.

Most of the opinion/commentary materials were labeled as such or appeared on editorial pages or "op-ed" pages facing editorial pages. Opinion materials were analyzed to determine their overall tone or theme. Table 3.1 shows the circulation of each newspaper, along with the number of stories and opinion pieces in each publication.

Headlines such as "Sexual Harassment Declining, Women in the Military Report" (Weiner, 1996, p. 18) and "Sexual Harassment Slows" (Compart 1996b, p. 10) greeted the July 2, 1996, announcement of the results of the 1995 survey. On the other hand, the *Los Angeles Times* took this approach: "Pentagon survey finds much sex harassment," indicating a "pervasive problem despite Defense Department efforts to stamp it out" (Kempster, 1996, p. 1). Syndicated columnist

Table 3.1
Newspaper Search Results

Newspaper		Circulation*	News Stories	Opinion/Editorials
Baltimore Sun		320,986	22	4
Los Angeles Times		1,021,121	25	4
New York Times		1,107,168	36	17
St. Louis Post-Dispatch		326,330	18	3
USA Today		2,040,000	24	14
Wall Street Journal		1,841,188	5	5
Washington Post		854,000	44	25
Air Force Times	(w)	79,063	18	4
Army Times	(w)	104,759	37	3
Navy Times	(w)	81,245	22	4
Totals		**7,775,860**	**251**	**83**

*Figures provided by newspaper staffs in June 1997.

Harry Summers, a retired Army colonel, noted that women comprised 18 percent of the military's new recruits in the six-month period ending March 31, 1996. He advocated focusing efforts on getting rid of the "real harassment" such as unwanted touching, coercive proposals for sex and sexual assault (p. 62).

In November 1996, "sex scandals" erupted at two Army posts—Fort Leonard Wood, Missouri, and Aberdeen Proving Ground, Maryland. At Fort Leonard Wood, three drill sergeants were scheduled for court-martial on charges of sexual misconduct with trainees, including "offensively touching" them. Seven other drill sergeants were suspended.

Meanwhile at Aberdeen, the number of claims involving drill sergeants' mishandling of trainees expanded. On the day the first drill sergeant pleaded guilty at Fort Leonard Wood, Army officials announced that investigations of sexual harassment were being expanded to all seventeen of its training centers. The *New York Times, Washington Post, Baltimore Sun, Los Angeles Times* and *St. Louis Post-Dispatch* were among newspapers publishing feature accounts of the witnesses and reactions from soldiers.

Gen. Dennis Reimer, Army Chief of Staff, promised "zero tolerance." After more incidents were revealed at Aberdeen, the Army opened a hotline for complaints. *USA Today* published the Army hot line number. A total of 3,102 calls were logged during the first week of the hotline, and 341 were referred to the Army Criminal Investigation Command for scrutiny. During November 1996, at least sixty-three news stories appeared in the ten papers. Some papers that had not run the survey results earlier referred to the statistics to illustrate at least half of military women had been sexually harassed in some manner.

Some columns and editorials dealt with power and responsibility, accountability, trust, reemphasis on leadership, fraternization, and discipline. One columnist wrote that in the military consensual relationships and harassment are swept under the rug together (Estrich, 1996, p. 23). The *Wall Street Journal* compared the Aberdeen scandal with Tailhook, concluding that although the offenses at Aberdeen were worse, the Army had the capacity to correct the situation (Moskos, 1996, p. 22).

Linda Chavez (1996) wrote in *USA Today* that "maybe it's time to move more cautiously in this whole experiment with a unisex military." She listed lessons the Army could learn from Tailhook:

• Don't turn this investigation into a politicized witch hunt.

• Don't violate due process.

• Avoid applying double standards. (p. A15)

Among news stories appearing in December 1996 was one about McKinney speaking to soldiers at Aberdeen. The *Army Times* quoted him as saying, "[T]here are few manuals out there that tell you how to deal with people. We've got to teach our leaders how to show compassion," especially in the case of sexual harassment (McHugh, 1996, p. 1). The same issue of *Army Times* announced Secretary of the Army West's Senior Review Sexual Harassment Panel, which included McKinney. Meanwhile, a Fort Leonard Wood drill sergeant was sentenced to eighteen months in prison with a bad conduct discharge, while another was cleared of all charges. Lawyers for the accused soldiers at Aberdeen asked for a gag order, claiming "adverse publicity generated by officials' comments will make it difficult for their clients to get fair courts-martial" (Valentine, 1996, p. B1). The judge refused.

An article in the *Baltimore Sun* showed that most sex misconduct cases at Fort Jackson, South Carolina, involved drill sergeants. The *Los Angeles Times* reported that as of December 26, 1996, the Army hotline had fielded nearly 6,600 calls, with 977 of the calls deemed worthy of investigation.

One January 1997 story was about a private who hanged himself rather than face rape charges at Aberdeen. Sara Lister, Assistant Secretary of the Army for manpower and reserves, told *Army Times* the future is still bright for women in the Army (Patterson, 1997, p. 8). The Navy was investigating allegations of racial and sexual harassment charges at a brig in Charleston, South Carolina, and a former airman had filed a sexual harassment suit. Departing Secretary of Defense Perry stated he favors increasing roles of women in the military. In a *USA Today* commentary, Jill Nelson (1997) wrote that the Army has an opportunity to learn from its sex scandals (p. 14).

In February 1997, new Secretary of Defense William S. Cohen at his first Pentagon press conference declared a zero-tolerance policy on sexual harassment. More actions continued in the Aberdeen case, and the Navy announced no harassment was found at its training bases. Meanwhile, at least ten women alleged they were sexually assaulted by their male instructors at a Darmstadt, Germany, training center.

However, the "shocker," as the *Army Times* called it, came when retired Army Sgt. Maj. Brenda Hoster accused McKinney of sexual harassment (Patterson, 1997, p. 8). The top-ranking enlisted adviser to the Army Chief of Staff was removed from the sexual harassment panel and eventually suspended from his duties. Later other women filed claims against McKinney. He denied all charges.

The NAACP (National Association for the Advancement of Colored People) in March 1997 raised the question of racism in the Aberdeen Proving Ground case, noting all thirteen men facing charges are black, whereas the majority of their accusers are white women. The NAACP contended black men also have been disproportionately accused in Army cases pending elsewhere. McKinney's accusers are white women.

"The allegations of racism are likely to further complicate the Army's efforts to resolve the sexual harassment investigations in a way that is politically, as well as legally, satisfactory," wrote Paul Richter in the *Los Angeles Times* (1997, p. A17). Meanwhile, some women in the Aberdeen case recanted or changed their statements concerning their sex encounters. Five women at a press conference said their charges were coerced by investigators.

On March 20, Capt. Derrick Robertson, a company commander, pleaded guilty to adultery and sodomy. He was ordered to serve four months in prison and was dismissed from the Army. In a March 18 editorial titled "Ghosts of Sexism and Racism," the *St. Louis Post-Dispatch* stated: The "latest development in the Army sexual harassment cases at the Aberdeen proving Grounds seems to have set racism and sexism, two virulent, volatile strands of bigotry, on a collision course. In the process, the controversy threatens to undermine the progress made toward the racial and sexual integration of the armed forces." The editorial concluded that the Army's option was to proceed carefully and fairly. National Association for the Advancement of Colored People (NAACP) President Kweisi Mfume "raises issues that must be examined, but they shouldn't derail the process of justice now under way" ("Ghosts of Sexism and Racism," 1997, p. B6).

As April 1997 closed, *USA Today* ran a story entitled "For Army, the Focus Now Turns to Remaining Cases." The article was accompanied by a drawing of Staff Sgt. Delmar Simpson, the drill sergeant found guilty on eighteen of nineteen cases of rape and several other charges. Twelve soldiers, their charges, and status were listed. All were drill sergeants or instructors except Robertson (Curley and Komarow, 1997, p. A6). The *Baltimore Sun* stated that drill sergeants called sleeping with trainees "the game," and willing female soldiers were "locked in real tight" (Wilson and Bowman, 1997, p. 1).

The *Washington Post* on April 25 ran "capsule sketches" of six of Simpson's alleged rape victims. Meanwhile, twenty women who claimed they were raped or sexually harassed while serving in the military joined two congresswomen to call for a civilian commission to investigate sexual misconduct in the nation's armed forces (Knight, 1997, p. 4). At Fort Leonard Wood, a drill sergeant admitted he posed nude for two young women who had just graduated from his platoon (Levins, 1997, p. B1). "Gene McKinney is not a quitter" was the lead paragraph in an *Army Times* story headlined "McKinney: Resignation Not an Option" (McHugh, 1997, p. 4).

On May 6, 1997, Simpson was sentenced to twenty-five years in prison. "Simpson's lawyers said he was unfairly singled out because he is black. . . . Chris Lombardi, spokeswoman for a group of former servicewomen who say they were sexually harassed or otherwise abused, said a tough sentence in one splashy case will not solve the problem," according to *USA Today* (Komarow, 1997, p. A4).

The next day McKinney was charged with assault, adultery, solicitation, making threats, and trying to obstruct an investigation. He was charged with mistreating three women subordinates and a female sailor. On May 29, a *Los Angeles Time* article quoted the Army's top training official as saying possible remedies for the military's sex scandal would include better screening and perhaps psychological testing to ensure the service does not give its powerful drill instructor jobs to the wrong people (Richter, 1997, p. A15).

Editorials for May included one in the *Baltimore Sun* concluding: "Superiors and soldiers need a resource, perhaps outside normal channels, where they can get counsel and report improper advances and worse before circumstances devolve to the point they did in the landmark case of Delmar Simpson" ("Verdict," 1997, p. 20). The *Washington Post* editorialized on May 1: "In the end, what happened at Aberdeen strikes us less as a case of hormones inevitably running rampant than as a blatant failure of command. Where were the higher-ranking officers while the accused drill sergeants organized their sex ring? They obviously were not communicating the Army's admirable policies on sexual harassment" ("Women," 1997, p. 22). A *New York Times* columnist referred to Simpson's court-martial as "an intriguing, even disturbing, look at the messy, unresolved issues of sex and power within the ranks" (Sciolino, 1997, sec. IV, p. 4).

During June 1997, sexual harassment incidents shared the spotlight with adultery charges against and admissions by military officers. One casualty was Army Maj. Gen. John Longhouser, whose career ended after someone called a hotline set up to cope with the scandal at Aberdeen, where he was commander. There were claims that his adulterous behavior five years earlier could have compromised his handling of sexual misconduct cases brought against soldiers at Aberdeen. Meanwhile, after requesting retirement, McKinney remained suspended in limbo, while one of two sergeants major named to handle his duties was his twin brother. In late June, a hearing began to determine if McKinney's case would go to court-martial. Lawyers for McKinney, his accusers, and the news media petitioned for and got an open hearing.

Also, convictions for sex-related offenses spread overseas as a military jury in Darmstadt, Germany, found an Army sergeant guilty of eleven counts of sexual misconduct and another guilty of rape and sodomy. The Army closed its sexual harassment hotline June 15, saying the volume of calls had waned, and the operation had been misused at times for acts of vengeance. In seven months, the operation fielded 8,305 calls and passed 1,354 tips to investigators, with 350 still under investigation as of June 16, 1997 (Graham, 1997, p. 11). The Navy's Adviceline, set up after Tailhook, registered 1,521 calls from men and 1,422 from women during 1993–96. The Adviceline remains open (Ginsburg, 1997, p. 17).

Seeking remedies to prevent abuses during training, some Congress members led by Sen. Robert Byrd advocated separate basic training for males and females. Gen. William Hartzog, commander of the Army's Training and Doctrine Command, defended gender-integrated training.

Published opinions were numerous during June 1997. Several editorials and columns called for strong leadership and adherence to strict, clear standards to rectify the sexual misconduct situation. Columnist Bill Press in the *Los Angeles Times* wrote: "I was one of millions of young Americans who marched in protest against the Vietnam War, carrying banners that urged the military to 'Make Love, Not War.' Now I understand why the generals ignored us. It wasn't because they preferred to make war, after all. The generals just knew more than we did. They knew, way back then, that making love instead of war could get them into a whole lot more trouble" (Press, 1997, p. B7).

A *Washington Post* columnist summed up the situation: "The military, for some good reasons, has taken a lot of grief over the past few weeks. But the truth is that the armed services are working out in public what the rest of society has been trying, with only limited success, to work out for the past 30 years" (Dionne, 1997, p. 29).

ISSUES RAISED

The press presented both news and views with newspaper columnists and editorials while raising some pertinent questions, such as:

1. Were accusations against the drill sergeants and SMA McKinney racially motivated?
2. Will the negative publicity affect recruiting, especially females?
3. Should there be more sexual harassment training for military members?
4. Should the services look more closely at potential drill instructors?
5. Should basic training be gender-integrated or separate?
6. Are hotlines useful tools against sexual harassment, even though revenge and crank calls may be received along with legitimate complaints?
7. When will leaders take responsibility for what happens within their commands?

In response to these and other questions raised in the newspapers, a pilot perception survey was administered to 166 persons studying to be military equal opportunity specialists. Respondents were asked to answer eleven opinion questions. Responses ranged from "1 totally agree" to "5 totally disagree." T-tests were used to compare means of various groups' responses: active with reserve, women with men, enlisted personnel with officers, and African Americans with whites. The most meaningful differences were found between enlisted members and officers and between African Americans and whites.

When replying to the statements that racism is involved in sexual harassment cases at Aberdeen and with McKinney, African Americans were in the "moderately agree" range, whereas whites were in the "moderately disagree" area. A meaningful difference between male and female responses concerned separate training where women had a mean of 4.28 (strongly disagree it should be separate) compared to the men's 3.85. Overall, the respondents strongly favor keeping gender-integrated training, which supports the stands of the commander of the Army's Training and Doctrine Command.

CONCLUSION

In summary, both the daily newspapers and the service-related commercial weeklies thoroughly covered sexual harassment in the military from July 1996 through June 1997 and raised several issues. Obviously, the military is trying to cope with its sexual harassment problem and is cooperating with the press in reporting the facts. Presented here was an examination of selected newspapers' coverage of sexual harassment in the military and a survey to obtain perceptions about effects of issues raised by the press coverage.

Apparently, as more sexual harassment surfaced, the news media provided more thorough coverage and commented on it. Some readers might see SMA McKinney as representing the roles of sexism and racism in the military, but any man in his high position possibly would have attracted attention. Since McKinney is an African American who rose through the ranks to the highest enlisted position, he was more closely watched than some lower-ranking person might have been.

On March 16, 1998, McKinney said he planned to retire and move on after he was reprimanded and demoted one rank by a jury that convicted him of obstruction of justice in his sexual misconduct case.

"We did OK," McKinney said, standing by his wife, Wilhemina, after the jury sentenced him on one conviction. He was found innocent of eighteen counts involving sexual harassment. McKinney had faced a possible five years in prison and a reduction of rank to private on the obstruction of justice conviction for coaching one of his six accusers about what to tell Army investigators: "Just tell them that we talked . . . no inappropriateness at all, just that we talked," he said in a taped telephone conversation played during the six-week court-martial.

The twenty-nine–year veteran was the first black man to become sergeant major of the Army and was forced out of the position after being charged. If convicted on all counts, he could have faced up to 55.5 years in prison and a dishonorable discharge. Now, with a lower rank of master sergeant and reprimand, McKinney lost some retirement pay and his reputation as a good soldier, said Lt. Col. V. Montgomery Forrester, one of his attorneys (Myers, Associated Press, March 17, 1998).

The press can be an effective tool to inform and educate the American public, and through the press the audience can better understand the issue of sexual harassment.

The military's war against sexual harassment rages on, and the press continues to publicize it. Perhaps the press can be an effective tool to expose it and eradicate it. Leaders throughout the Department of Defense can utilize newspapers, both within their commands and in the civilian realm, as effective weapons to spread information about sexual harassment and how to combat it.

REFERENCES

Bastain, L. D., Lancaster, A. R., and Reyst, H. E. (1996). *Department of Defense 1995 sexual harassment survey.* Arlington, VA: Defense Manpower Data Center.

Chavez, L. (1996, November 13). Tailhook lessons for the Army. *USA Today*, p. A15.

Compart, A. (1996a, July 15). Harassment statistics looking better, but are far from perfect. *Army Times*, p. 10.

Compart, A. (1996b, July 15). Sexual harassment slows. *Air Force Times*, p. 10.

Crawford, S. (1994, August). A brief history of sexual-harassment law. *Training, 3* (8), 46–49.

Culbertson, A. L., and Rosenfeld, P. (1994). Assessment of sexual harassment in the active-duty Navy. *Military Psychology, 6* (2), 69–93.

Dansby, M. R. (1997). Cultural diversity and gender issues. In C. Cronin (Ed.), *Military Psychology.* Boston: Simon & Schuster.

Dionne, E. J., Jr. (1997, June 13). The sex war. *Washington Post*, p. 29.

Estrich, S. (1996, November 13). Reality in the ranks. *Washington Post*, p. 23.

Firestone, J. M., and Harris, R. J. (1994a). Perceptions of effectiveness of responses to sexual harassment in the active duty military. In *Proceedings: Defense Equal Opportunity Management Institute Equal Opportunity Research Symposium* (pp. 51–59). Patrick Air Force Base, FL: Defense Equal Opportunity Management Institute.

Firestone, J. M., and Harris, R. J. (1994b). Sexual harassment in the U.S. military: Individualized and environmental contexts. *Armed Forces & Society, 21*, 25–43.

Ghosts of sexism and racism. (1997, March 18). *St. Louis Post-Dispatch*, p. B6.

Ginsburg, Y. (1997, June 2). Harassment hotline draws more men than women. *Navy Times*, p. 17.

Goldman, J. L. (1995). *The issue is . . . sexual harassment!* (DEOMI Special Topics Series Pam 95–1). Patrick Air Force Base, FL: Defense Equal Opportunity Management Institute.

Graham, B. (1997, June 16). Army shuts sexual harassment hot line. *Washington Post*, p. 11.

Harris, R. J., and Firestone, J. M. (1994). Individual responses to sexual harassment in the U.S. military. In *Proceedings: Defense Equal Opportunity Management Institute Equal Opportunity Research Symposium* (pp. 51–59). Patrick Air Force Base, FL: Defense Equal Opportunity Management Institute.

Kempster, N. (1996, July 3). Survey finds much sex harassment. *Los Angeles Times*, p. 1.

Knight, H. (1997, April 30). Civilian panel sought to probe sex abuse in military. *Los Angeles Times*, p. 4.

Komarow, S. (1997, April 30). For Army focus now turns to remaining cases. *USA Today*, p. B6.

Komarow, S. (1997, May 3). Army sergeant sentenced to 25 years for raping trainees. *USA Today*, p. A4.

Kozaryn, L. D. (1996, July). Sexual harassment declining, remains major concern. Press Release. Washington, DC: Armed Forces Press Service.

Leavins, H. (1997, April 22). Drill sergeant admits posing nude. *St. Louis Post-Dispatch*, p. B1.

McHugh, J. (1996, December 2). SMA speaks to soldiers at Aberdeen. *Army Times*, pp. 1, 22.

McHugh, J. (1997, April 28). McKinney. Resignation not an option. *Army Times*, p. 4.

Moskos, C. (1996, November 14). The Army's Aberdeen is not the Navy's Tailhook. *Wall Street Journal*, p. 22.

Myers, L. (1988, March 17). Army sex. Associated Press wire story.

Nelson, J. (1997, January 31). Opportunity exists for Army in sex scandals. *USA Today*, p. 14.

Niebuhr, R. E. (1997). Sexual harassment in the military. In W. O'Donohue (Ed.), *Sexual harassment: Theory, research, and treatment*. Boston: Allyn & Bacon.

Patterson, K. (1997, January 20). Lister: Future still bright for women in the Army. *Army Times*, p. 8.

Popovich, P. M. (1988). *An examination of sexual harassment complaints in the Air Force for FY 1988* (DEOMI Report No. 88–5). Patrick Air Force Base, FL: Defense Equal Opportunity Management Institute.

Press, B. (1997, June 4). Free the military of '50s prudery sex: Let officers make love if they can't make war. *Los Angeles Times*, p. B7.

Pryor, J. B. (1988). *Sexual harassment in the United States military: The development of the DoD survey* (DEOMI Report No. 88–6). Patrick Air Force Base, FL: Defense Equal Opportunity Management Institute.

Richter, P. (1997, May 29). Higher drill instructor standards urged. *Los Angeles Times*, p. A17.

Scarborough, R. (1997, June 12). Promotion rules expected to change after adultery cases. *Washington Times*, p. 3.

Sciolino, E. (1997, May 4). The Army's problems with sex and power. *New York Times*, sec. IV, p. 4.

Summers, H. (1996, July 15). Go after the real harassment. *Air Force Times*, p. 62.

Valentine, P. (1996, December 9). Lawyers seek gag order on Pentagon. *Washington Post*, p. B1.

Vivian, J., and Murray, G. (In press). News judgment. In *Editing the news*. Boston: Allyn & Bacon.

Weiner, T. (1996, July 3). Sexual harassment declining, women in the military report. *New York Times*, p. 18.

Wilson, S., and Bowman, T. (1997, April 17). At base, sex was "the game." *Baltimore Sun*, p. 1.

Women in the military. (1997, May 1). *Washington Post*, p. 22.

4

Diana York Blaine

Necrophilia, Pedophilia, or Both?: The Sexualized Rhetoric of the JonBenet Ramsey Murder Case

INTRODUCTION

This chapter begins with a shocking proposition: Our cultural obsession with the eroticization of children's bodies and our overwhelming fear of natural death leave us fascinated with the case of JonBenet Ramsey. Since the night of the crime in December of 1996, the six-year-old Colorado girl's murder, unsolved at the time of this writing, has been featured in every major news outlet across the United States. *Vanity Fair, The New Yorker, People, Time*, and *Newsweek* have joined the *Globe,* the *Star,* and the *National Enquirer* in carrying stories about the case, as have all three national network newscasts and the increasingly popular newsmagazines *Prime Time Live, 48 Hours,* and *20/20.* Simply put, JonBenet Ramsey has become the most popular dead girl in America, a country that loses up to six of its children to violence every day. The major difference between this murdered child and the others is painfully clear: Because of her participation in beauty pageants we have access to hundreds of images of JonBenet, all conforming exactly to our idea of perfect female beauty. The availability of these images, coupled with the loud reverberations of incest surrounding the murder, make this lascivious tale extremely attractive. Her face sells airtime, sells magazines, sells soap, because looking at JonBenet Ramsey satisfies two central cultural desires at once: to fantasize about the sexuality of children and believe in our own immortality.

NATIONAL OBSESSION WITH CHILD SEXUALITY

Because of the potential for offense caused by the assertion that we want to fantasize about children's sexuality, this issue will be addressed first. The idea

that there could be some national interest in the sexuality of children diametri-
cally opposes another fundamental cultural myth, that children are asexual beings, empty innocent vessels waiting to be filled slowly with adult
characteristics. According to social theorists Phillipe Ariès and Lawrence Stone,
this historicized construction of childhood as a separate innocent time began
somewhere around the eighteenth century and gained full speed with the Romantic movement (Cox, 1996, p. 2). Formerly seen as small adults, they were
now presumed to come trailing clouds of glory, becoming by the Victorian era
prominent cultural symbols of purity and grace. James R. Kinkaid argues that
it is this very concept of purity that left the idea of childhood ripe for eroticization. "By insisting so loudly on the innocence, purity and asexuality of the
child," he says, "we have created a subversive echo: experience, corruption,
eroticism" (Kinkaid, 1992, p. 5). The assertion that childhood and sexuality are
mutually opposed has in effect guaranteed their linkage. Couple this with Catharine MacKinnon's theory that we eroticize hierarchy, actually constructing
sexual desire out of unequal power dynamics, and we can begin to understand
why Lolita, and JonBenet Ramsey have become omnipresent mythic figures of
desire in twentieth-century America (MacKinnon, 1997, p. 170).

In accounting for the overwhelming popularity of the JonBenet Ramsey tale,
it must be noted that we all participate in the creation of it. Whether active
purchasers of the magazines and viewers of the television programs or not,
nearly every single one of us has consumed and propagated the JonBenet Ramsey narrative in one way or another. Looking at her image at the checkout stand,
murmuring shocked disapproval to each other ("How could her mother have
dressed her up like that?"), speculating about who the murderer is—all of these
behaviors help to construct the JonBenet story, to keep the conversation going.
Even more important, every one of us participates in the institutionalized sexism,
racism, and classism that make this narrative resonate so seductively. JonBenet's
parents are wealthy, she is white, her tiny image conforms perfectly to our
notions of ideal femininity. Far from being on society's margins, as much of
our desperate distancing of ourselves from this story and its tragic conclusions
seeks to place them (*Newsweek* referred to "the strange world of JonBenet"),
the Ramseys are possessors of the all-American Dream par excellence: rich
white daddy, doting wife, and incredibly beautiful blond daughter. Kinkaid
(1992) notes that "we keep the story [of pedophilia] alive and before us, being
told over and over. At the same time, we find ways to deny emphatically that
we are authoring this story, much less serving as its leading players" (p. 341).
The harder we point at the Ramseys, the more cultural currency we give this
story and the more we fashion ourselves as its authors.

And, indeed, as stories go, it is a lurid one. The day after Christmas in 1996,
the breathtaking beauty JonBenet Ramsey, 1995 Little Miss Colorado, 1996
America's Royale Miss, and certain contender for a future Miss America title,
was found dead in the basement of her parents' lavishly decorated mansion
(" 'Everything in that house was way beyond what you usually see, even in

Figure 4.1
JonBenet Ramsey

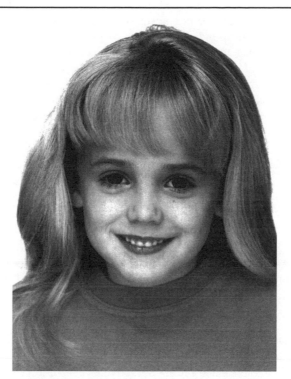

Courtesy of City of Boulder, Colorado.

Boulder,' " one woman reported to *People* magazine in the January 20, 1997 issue [Hewitt, 1997]). Her skull had been crushed, a cord was wrapped about her neck, and duct tape sealed her mouth. Since the six-year-old's corpse was found in the basement, the presence of a ransom note (from a self-described "small foreign faction") only added more confusion to the scene. Allegations that she had been sexually abused surfaced regularly, with no confirmation coming from official sources. Twenty-nine months after the father discovered her body, no one had been arrested for the crime and a cloud of suspicion hung over her parents, in spite of their insistence that a mysterious stranger had invaded the home.

To tell the story of JonBenet Ramsey requires mention of her contest titles, her beauty, for without these there would be no story to tell, and she would presumably have disappeared into the anonymous swamp to which we relegate almost every other victim of violent crime in the United States, adult or child. The exceptions, the celebrities, are often notable for their beauty, at least in the case of women, and so JonBenet inherited from Nicole Brown Simpson (and competes with Princess Diana for) the dubious honor of being the beautiful dead blond white female being featured on the most magazine covers. In this way members of the media construct and then reify normative gender expectations. The dead women who matter the most, we learn, are those who clearly reflect and perpetuate central, foundational myths of blond, white, youthful, innocent beauty. That JonBenet was a princess makes her all the more perfect, all the more precious, for her part as Sleeping Beauty. Like Princess Diana, JonBenet and her wrinkle-free image of physical perfection will forever be with us. She has achieved the "happily ever after" that we acculturate our little girls to long for, becoming a permanent princess with no unbecoming desire for independence or unappealing signs of age.

For cultural expressions of outrage aside, JonBenet's age does not prevent her from fulfilling our desire for blond dream-girls; indeed, it facilitates it. This clean-cut cutie, heir to Shirley Temple's nubile erotic crown, can represent female perfection largely because female perfection is modeled on the features of the girl, not the woman. Susan Sontag (1972) points out that we may have two standards of beauty for the male, boy and man, but for women only the characteristics of the girl child suit our definition of attractiveness (p. 35). So JonBenet's tight skin, lack of body fat, and youthful glow are exactly what make her beautiful to us. She is no pedophile's fantasy—she is ours.

SUSPICIONS ABOUT MOTHER

As we rush to indict Mrs. Ramsey for accentuating her daughter's blond good looks, we are more able to trip lightly over our own complicity in the saga. We continue to place great value on the attractiveness of little girls, and in taking them to see films such as Disney's *Beauty and the Beast, The Little Mermaid*, and *Pocahontas* (which we of course also watch and enjoy ourselves), we make sure that they understand their power will come from being able to attract, from being sexual. Before the murder JonBenet's mother took her daughter to beauty pageants, and no one cared or blamed her; participation in these rituals did not make national news; no charges of child abuse were bandied about. At this point in history few can pretend not to know that Miss America rarely steps on stage for the first time during that televised contest. Years of youthful pageants precede this moment. Kinkaid reports in *Child-Loving* that many national pageant winners are minors, thus "proclaiming to one and all that the most sexually prized among us are not sexual beings at all, cannot be by law" (Kinkaid, 1992, p. 376). Such astonishing contradictions and hypocrisy seem difficult to comprehend. As we rush to sexualize our own little girls we strain just as earnestly to insist that they are asexual and that being attracted to them connotes monstrous perversion. The fact that as I write this chapter I sit surrounded by hundreds of magazines featuring pretty JonBenet, pouting, posing, smoldering, magazines purchased not from some seedy purveyor of smut but at your local grocers, reveals a culture in massive denial. Valerie Walkerdine (1997) notes in

Daddy's Girl that the "complexity of this phenomenon, in terms of both the cultural production of little girls as these ambivalent objects and the way in which little girls themselves as well as adults live this complexity, how it produces their subjectivity, has not begun to be explored" (p. 171). We cannot acknowledge what is right in front of us lest the implication destroy our notion of the deviant pedophile versus the normal citizen.

Much has been made of Mrs. Ramsey's own pageant history, her failure to capture the coveted crown of Miss America in spite of having been Miss West Virginia (as had her sister). One two-page spread in the January 1997 *People* featured not only three cheesecake photos of JonBenet, two in stages of undress, but several of her mother as well. In these photos Patsy is young and beautiful herself, striding down the runway in a bathing suit, her pageant sash marking her as competitor for most sexually desirable young woman in the country. In spite of the breathless and shocked tone of *People*'s coverage of the case (a tone shared by every other media report), it managed to devote over half of this page to photos of nearly naked girls. Much of the vituperation leveled at Patsy was for having her six-year-old involved in exactly the type of beauty contests for which her mother had received such lavish approval (and eventually a billionaire husband). But, goes the story, Patsy had a "choice" to compete as a teenaged girl, unlike JonBenet, who presumably was only following her mother's wishes.

Such arguments avoid consideration of what might make Patsy, and tens of thousands of other women, "choose" their own objectification—or to put it more generously, "choose" to try and be made the most popular and celebrated women in their country (and thus satisfy tens of thousands of mothers' wishes as well). "All women live in sexual objectification the way fish live in water," says Catherine MacKinnon. "With no alternatives, the strategy to acquire self-respect and pride is: I chose it" (1997, p. 171). And why assume that JonBenet was not capable of making the same "choice"? As Valerie Walkerdine shows in her study, little girls understand clearly the benefits of participating in their own objectification and can find it quite thrilling. The feeling of being free, of having choices, stems from making choices that result in enormous outpourings of cultural approval. Of course, as Susan Bordo (1993) points out, the desire to conform to coercive standards of beauty is based on the misapprehension that what feels like power in any given situation will translate into real cultural power in the long run (p. 262).

But none of the popular coverage of this tragedy has explored any of these complicated issues. Instead, we are told, and believe, that Patsy maliciously and mindlessly forced JonBenet to follow in her footsteps down that runway. Why? Keeping it in the family, perhaps, but more insidiously because she was presumably living through her daughter, no longer sexually interesting or viable herself and so all too willing to engineer her little girl into the new erotic female Ramsey. The popularity of this narrative, one that again ignores the stunningly banal commonality of capitalizing on girls' bodies in the United States, permits the circulation of other popular cultural fantasies, those of the evil mother, the sexually frustrated older woman, and the incestuous competition between mother and daughter. Without needing to believe these characters and dramas actually exist, we would not be able to partake in the JonBenet saga. "Evil Mom Exposed!" screams the headline of *Globe* magazine. This cover features a large photo of dark-haired Patsy wearing a white show-girl costume, all legs and bare shoulders. Underneath, in an insert, we see little JonBenet wearing a similar outfit. The accompanying article suggests that in dressing JonBenet as a tiny version of her earlier youthful self, Patsy is actually competing with her daughter. "Renowned psychiatrist" Carole Lieberman explains that Patsy "is like the evil queen who bitterly resented her stepdaughter Snow White's beauty" ("JonBenet," 1997, p. 4). Other unnamed "experts" inform us that "the photograph suggests that Patsy may have been molested in her youth and set up tragic JonBenet to be a victim of sexual abuse too."

These ludicrous conclusions permit us to heap blame on the woman who is violated, thereby ignoring the agency of men, an omission that is necessary for our sexually stratified culture to retain its structure. Perhaps JonBenet was attacked because her mother dressed her like a woman, suggests one version of the story that plays on our cultural belief that rape victims ask for it and simultaneously ignores the role of a violent male perpetrator. The coroner of Allegheny County, Pennsylvania, says JonBenet "was 6 going on 23. I don't think the person who did this ever had any intention of killing her. It was a game" (Harrell, 1997, p. 25). Or perhaps Mrs. Ramsey was jealous of her daughter's beauty and killed her, hints another narrative. Like Charlotte and Dolores Haze in Nabokov's *Lolita*, Patty and JonBenet must have been locked in competition for the attention of the father/husband, "daddy," and this competition must have been fatal.

POWER OF THE FATHER'S GAZE

Of course, without the concept of the "daddy," none of these narratives would be possible. And the magazine headlines make sure we know that "daddy" is involved. "How Daddy's Little Girl Really Died" leered the *National Enquirer* (1997, January 21). The adjacent photo showed a wan JonBenet, eyes cast upward toward an implied father figure, an image clearly meant to eroticize the helplessness of girl children. Thus the element of incest infuses the story, adding explicit sexual overtones to those already created by JonBenet's erotic image. The " 'ideal' spectator is always assumed to be a male," writes John Berger (1985), "and the image of the woman is designed to flatter him" (p. 64). Laura Mulvey (1993) says as much and more in "Visual Pleasure and Narrative Cinema": "The determining male gaze projects its fantasy onto the female figure, which is styled accordingly. In their traditional exhibitionist role women are simultaneously looked at and displayed, with their appearance coded for strong visual and erotic impact so that they can be said to connote *to-be-looked-at-*

ness. Woman displayed as sexual object is the *leitmotif* of erotic spectacle" (p. 436). In this sexual saga, this erotic spectacle, we can have no doubt who is doing the looking: It is JonBenet's so-called daddy. Much can be said about the appeal of implied incest, how its very forbidden nature sets up the conditions for desire. MacKinnon notes that often "taboos are treated as real restrictions— as things that really are not allowed—instead of as guises under which hierarchy is eroticized" (1997, p. 164).

Clearly in the JonBenet case we are dealing with eroticized hierarchy, the implied sexual relations between father and daughter fueling our interest and perpetuating a notion that the violent possession of those less powerful is sexy. Bram Dijkstra (1986) argues that the increasing pressures of capitalism caused men to begin to fantasize about girl children, rather than their adult mothers, in order to avoid having to expend any undesired energy on an overly eager spouse. "To escape the frighteningly physical and emotional demands grown women tended to place on them," says Dijkstra, "many men . . . began to yearn for the purity of the child they could not find in women. These men seem to have come to the conclusion that if woman's grown body soiled the passive purity of her childlike mind, it was better to seek all the positive qualities, all the passive, compliant qualities of woman, in the child itself" (p. 185). This late nineteenth-century phenomenon remains with us today in the construction of the JonBenet saga. Daddy could not resist the charms of his little beauty, goes the story, because he was fatally attracted to the very purity that makes its violation so heinous. Dr. Michael Weiner, faculty member at New York University, says that "this was an accidental murder, the result of a perverse sex game gone too far" (Allison, 1997, p. 4). And of course, by implication, it is the very "perverse" nature of the "game" that makes it attractive. "Taboos founded on terror are not only there to be obeyed," says Bataille. "There is always another side to the matter. It is always a temptation to knock down a barrier; the forbidden action takes on a significance it lacks before fear widens the gap between us and it and invests it with an aura of excitement" (Bataille, 1986, p. 48). And so the *National Enquirer* promises us the "Beauty Queen's Nightmare Life of Sex Abuse" (Harrell, 1997), knowing we are as helplessly interested in reading about it as her father was in allegedly perpetrating it. Hot stuff.

THE ROLE OF CRIME REPORTING

We would not be reading about it, whether "it" actually occurred or not, were the little girl in question not dead. JonBenet's death opens up a number of important possibilities, for while Neil Postman (1982) points out in *The Disappearance of Childhood* that we dedicate enormous amounts of effort to putting our children on display in various pageants, recitals, organized sporting events, school plays, and so on, "not for the sake of doing it but for some external purpose, such as renown, money, physical conditioning, upward mobility, national pride" (p. 131), we cannot often justify exposing young nearly nude girls in provocative and overtly erotic poses to the nation at large via the media. The exception, of course, is advertising, which uses extremely young models. News outlets, however, need to have some reason for regularly broadcasting reports of various violated children, as did a recent *48 Hours* that offered nothing but lascivious minutiae about three lurid sexual scandals involving minors and adults, all the while pretending that the national interest was being served by offering us every nasty detail. As Kinkaid (1992) says: "The religious Right and the radical Left join happily to repeat the same erotic chant; we are all, as it were, compelled to speak it, have it with our corn flakes every morning, start the day off not with a song but a little child sex talk. It's part of our pledge of allegiance to power" (p. 378).

In this milieu, the JonBenet case comes as a clear bonanza, offering not only hundreds of images of provocative child sexuality but a built-in excuse to discuss them endlessly. She has been killed, so of course it becomes our business to know every single tiny detail of her life beforehand, concern with veracity notwithstanding. "One can make any claim, as long as it is shocking," says Kinkaid of our desire to perpetuate and revel in child sex narratives (p. 377). "We do not want it to be all over with" (p. 341). And the JonBenet saga is not over with, perhaps never will be, since officials in such a public case are loath to bring charges that they cannot make stick. Her death, in effect, delivers her to us directly in our homes, safely, without any taint of immorality shading our own enjoyment of the erotic images. We are even invited to become armchair detectives, perusing JonBenet's body with quasi-gynecological specificity. One popular image featured the highlighting of a tiny bruise on her arm. Ogle this little purple spot, we are invited, and imagine the perverse spectacle that caused it. No part of her body remains private, presumably because the public has a right to know. In 1854, Fitzjames Stephen criticized Dickens's description of Nell's death in *The Old Curiosity Shop* with language that recalls our own fixation with JonBenet Ramsey's: "He gloats over the little girl's death as if it delighted him; he looks at it . . . touches, tastes, smells and handles it as if it was some savory dainty which could not be fully appreciated" (Lerner, 1997, p. 204).

THE EROTICISM OF FEMALE DEATH

Not only does JonBenet's death make her image available to us upon demand, but it also plays into a long history of the appeal of the highly eroticized dead girl. Poe tells us in "The Philosophy of Composition" that "the death . . . of a beautiful young woman is, unquestionably, the most poetical topic in the world," a statement left long unchallenged and played out in his own "Annabel Lee" as well as *Lolita*, Nabokov's hommage to Poe's poem and to the erotic charge left by the notion of a dead girl (Poe, 1998, p. 1533). Indeed insofar as aesthetic sensibilities are culturally constructed, it is "true" that this is our most poetical topic, for that object of the male gaze that Mulvey invokes is invariably female and passive. A dead female, then, reflects our desire to look at objectified women taken to its furthest logical extent. In addition to this aesthetic argument for the appeal of dead women, Bram Dijkstra (1986) offers a Christian and economic one by maintaining that as the increasingly immoral capitalist marketplace demanded ever-greater uncharitable behavior from its men, the need for ownership of a spiritual spouse became paramount. Getting into heaven necessitated having a moral wife at home, and her inner morality was frequently imaged as outward physical debilitation. The more frail, the sicker, the thinner the woman, the closer she was presumed to be to heaven. And of course dead women are as unearthly and ethereal as possible. So dead women become the ideal, one with us today. (This adoration of the beautiful young dead woman explains the beatification of Princess Diana, who might instead have been remembered as an adulterous bulemic.)

JonBenet's tragic murder continues the link between women and death that began with Eve. Elisabeth Bronfen (1992) and Beth Ann Bassein (1984) both catalog manifestations of the conflation of woman and death and suggest that by feminizing death we in effect create the position of the immortal male who gazes at the materiality and chaos that is mortal femininity but is safely distanced from it. Men, and all of us enjoying the masculine position as active viewers, find solace in seeing death figured as female, poised prettily on the canvas and seemingly contained by the framing structures of art. So we revisit the Victorian obsession with the Beautiful Death through JonBenet's (and Diana's) demise. If the universal subject position in the United States is male, white, adult, and alive, JonBenet can serve as its near opposite, female, young, and dead. Her whiteness, then, serves as the one characteristic shared by those on the privileged half of the binary and so allows enough identification on their part to make projection possible. This explains why our many dead females venerated in mainstream art (Millais's *Ophelia*, for example) are never women of color. While we certainly exploit the image of the black female, we do so only when she is ostensibly "alive," thus permitting enough viewer identification to make the image titillating. In *The Sexual Politics of Meat*, Carol Adams (1990) suggests a similar dynamic occurs in our representation of nonhuman animals as female; when this anthropomorphism is done, as in the happy pink pig displayed outside of a restaurant eagerly awaiting your fork, the image is invariably white—even though pigs in reality rarely are. One characteristic needs to serve as an anchor in the privileged side of the binary lest the image become too Other and eliminate the possibility of identification.

So because of her specific historical position and context, JonBenet can represent the Beautiful Death; she is shown to us because of her tragic murder yet radiantly alive. Death is small, death is female, death is alive. These images assuage our secular society's anxieties about dying just as the Victorian depiction of dying children showed them longing to be taken home by a God merely lonely for their presence, neither cavalierly ignoring their pain nor seeking to destroy the lives of the bereaved families left behind. Ernest Becker suggests in

The Denial of Death (1973) that the fear of mortality constructs our very identity as human beings, and we need to pretend our own transcendence in order to function. JonBenet's miraculous presence suggests just this sort of transcendence, for in almost every image we see of her she is alive, even as she represents death. Nor does the lone exception to this, two photographs of her actual corpse published in *Globe* magazine (Harrell, 1997), offer an unmediated view of the dead girl. One depicts her body covered by a sheet, and the other, the only photo of her actual bare corpse published in the popular press, is of her hand. The rest of JonBenet's corpse lies shrouded in mystery, its absence protecting us from the full horror of mortality and helping us uphold our fantasy that death is beautiful.

But if the *Globe* participates in our massive cultural fantasy that death is young, beautiful, and female, why did it publish the photo of her hand? Obviously to show the face of this girl's corpse would be too much—bereft of makeup, airbrushing, styled hair, and costume, JonBenet would not look like a foxy little wench who attracted her own abuser. We might be forced to acknowledge that children are not raped because they ask for it any more than adult women are. In addition, it would be difficult to pretend that death, violent death in this case, is at all pretty. Her corpse would function as a reminder of what Julia Kristeva (1992) terms abjection, that realization of our own all-too-human status as organic and finite, not transcendent and immortal (p. 3).

So again, why publish that photo of her dead hand? Geoffrey Gorer (1984) argues that our fear of natural death, one magnified in the twentieth century by our lack of familiarity with its specifics since most people no longer die at home, plays itself out through an obsession with unnatural death. "While natural death becomes more and more smothered in prudery," he says, "violent death has played an evergrowing part in the fantasies offered to mass audiences" (p. 29). He notes the absence of deathbed scenes in modern literature, perhaps made impossible because they permit the unthinkable reality of natural death to enter our anxious age. Far more comforting now, and titillating as well, violent death pervades our movies, television shows, comic books, magazines, and news stories. Tapes like *Faces of Death* circulate obsessively; indeed, we seem to be all the more eager to watch "real" violent death as we apparently become inured to the fictional variety. And so JonBenet's corpse is exposed to us, as well as numerous magazine covers that have the words "Murder" and "Death" directly juxtaposed with her image. In one *Globe* article (Allison, 1997), a full-page photo of JonBenet in elegant evening dress has the words "BEATEN," "STRANGLED," "BOUND," "ABUSED," and "BRUISED" next to it; these are connected to the supposedly relevant parts of her body by helpful and quasi-scientific red lines. The word "ABUSED" is connected to her vaginal area.

Even as the *Globe* risks upsetting the balance between the desire to see images of violent death and the need to be assured that we will not die, several factors serve to control and contain the abjection of these images. Gorer (1984) notes that "the natural processes of corruption and decay have become disgusting, as

disgusting as the natural processes of birth and copulation were a century ago
. . . the ugly facts are relentlessly hidden; the art of the embalmers is an art of
complete denial" (p. 29). JonBenet's pretty airbrushed image (and Princess Diana's) acts as the embalmer's art in this case, and while the corpse's flesh ought
to cause feelings of fear in the viewer, her hand is shown next to a coroner's
tag, an official-looking black and white laminated document that hangs straight
down by the fingers. Such documentary evidence of the presence of authorities
helps write her hand back into the hegemony—the chaos of the corpse is safely
under rule of law, tagged, marked, and named. No abject horror, this dainty
hand with its golden ring (which as we know men give their best girls) and its
paternal seal in the guise of the coroner's tag reveal the proper place of women
within American culture, their potential sexual and moral chaos controlled by
men or, in this case, *the* man. The murder weapon below, a "grisly garrote" as
the lurid caption reads, also has an accompanying coroner's tag, which has not
only identifying numbers but a tiny ruler as well. "Everything's under control
folks," the image seems to suggest. "You can go back to your homes now."

CONCLUSION

In this chapter no differentiation has been made between the tabloid coverage
of the case and that of the so-called legitimate media. The more extensive space
dedicated to the story in the *National Enquirer*, the *Globe*, and the *Star* does
not translate into qualitative differences between their reporting and other media
outlets. We are not dealing with marginalized perversions or issues pertinent
only to those from whom we would presume to separate ourselves. The dynamics that serve to make JonBenet's life, and death, resonate so horrifically for us
are, sadly, those of everyday American life. This recognition causes our strong
reactions to her story. As when we slow down to watch an accident on the
freeway, we look on at this death with relief, glad to know that we have escaped
harm, yet fully cognizant of the fact that we are traveling down the same road
in a similar make and model car.

REFERENCES

Adams, C. (1990). *The sexual politics of meat: A feminist-vegetarian critical theory.*
    New York: Continuum.
Allison, Lynn. (1997, March 4). JonBenet: It was a family member. *Globe*, pp. 4–5.
Bassein, B. (1984). *Women and death: Linkages in Western thought and literature.* West-
    port, CT: Greenwood Press.
Bataille, G. (1986). *Erotism.* San Francisco: City Lights Press. (Original work published
    1957)
Becker, E. (1973). *The denial of death.* New York: Free Press.
Berger, J. (1985). *Ways of seeing.* London: British Broadcasting Corporation.

Bordo, S. (1993). *Unbearable weight: Feminism, Western culture and the body.* Berkeley and Los Angeles: University of California.

Bronfen, E. (1992). *Over her dead body: Death, femininity, and the aesthetic.* New York: Routledge.

Cox, Roger. (1996). Shaping childhood: Themes of uncertainty in the history of adult-child relationships. New York: Routledge.

Dijkstra, B. (1986). *Idols of perversity.* New York: Oxford University Press.

Gorer, G. (1984). The pornography of death. In E. Shneidman (Ed.), *Death: Current perspectives* (3rd ed., pp. 47–51). Palo Alto, CA: Mayfield.

Harrell, Ken. (1997, January 21). Little beauty tortured to death. *Globe,* pp. 24–36.

Hewitt, Bill. (1997, January 20). Lost innocent. *People,* pp. 38–45.

JonBenet: Eerie photo bares mom's sick obsession. (1997, September 30). *Globe,* pp. 4–5.

Kinkaid, J. (1992). *Child-loving.* New York: Routledge.

Kristeva, J. (1992). *Powers of horror: An essay on abjection* (L. Roudiez, Trans.). New York: Columbia University Press.

Lerner, L. (1997). *Angels and absences.* Nashville, TN: Vanderbilt University Press.

MacKinnon, C. (1997). Sexuality. In L. Nicholson (Ed.), *The second wave: A reader in feminist theory.* New York: Routledge.

Mulvey, L. (1993). Visual pleasure and the narrative cinema. In R. Warhol and D. Herndl (Eds.), *Feminisms: An anthology of literary theory and criticism.* New Brunswick, NJ: Rutgers University Press.

National Enquirer. (1997, January 21). Cover photo.

Poe, E. A. (1998). The philosophy of composition. In P. Lauter (Gen. Ed.), *The Heath anthology of American literature.* Lexington, MA: D. C. Heath and Co. (Vol. 1, pp. 1449–57).

Postman, N. (1982). *The disappearance of childhood.* New York: Delacorte Press.

Sontag, S. (1972, October). On the double standard of aging. *Saturday Review of the Society,* pp. 34–38.

Walkerdine, V. (1997). *Daddy's girl: Young girls and popular culture.* Cambridge: Harvard University Press.

PART III
THE VISUAL IMAGE IN MEDIA

5

Jacqueline C. Hitchon and
Shiela Reaves

Media Mirage: The Thin Ideal as Digital Manipulation

[M]erely being a woman in society means feeling too fat.
—Rodin, Silberstein, and Striegel-Moore, "Women and Weight," 1985

INTRODUCTION

The media moment captured and analyzed in this chapter occurs frequently to most women in the United States. Every time they pick up a fashion magazine and leaf through the pages of female forms, they experience moments of complex, conflicted thoughts and emotions. Their longing to resemble the slender media image combines with miserable dissatisfaction at their actual appearance.

Recent research has shown that exposure to magazines predicts the drive for thinness that fuels dysfunctional eating behaviors (Harrison and Cantor, 1997). Eating disorders have had a persistent and perplexing impact on American youth, with 61 percent of college women reporting some form of eating behavior problem (Mintz and Betz, 1988). Although only a relatively small proportion will develop clinical cases of anorexia nervosa or bulimia, those individuals experience severe physical symptoms that culminate in some cases in death. And generations of women have experienced an impoverishment of their imaginations, as they fret constantly over their inability to achieve the thin ideal rather than expending their valuable mental energy aspiring toward more meaningful goals (Kilbourne, 1995).

For the thin ideal is not merely a flimsy goal: waiflike, focused on the superficialities of appearance, and elusive. Rather, it has become a mirage. To young women hungry for life, the media mirage may seem to offer thirst-quenching substance with no forbidden calories, like life-giving water. But today the picture of the female form reflected at them from glossy magazines is the product of artistic creation and computer technology. Digitally manipulated, she is no longer a real woman.

Previous criticisms of the thin ideal from media scholars and educators have pointed out that very few women can achieve its broad-shouldered, slim-hipped, and elongated shape (e.g., Stice and Shaw, 1994; Stice et al., 1994). The observation that even the few thin, extremely tall models are now fictionalized to create the image is rarely articulated. This chapter reviews research to date on the thin ideal and on digital manipulation in order to explore the implications of the media mirage and to set priorities for future research.

CREATING THE MEDIA MIRAGE OF DIANA ROSS

Digital photography eliminates the need for negatives, the analog version of traditional photography (Mitchell, 1994). Negative-based photography is chemical and imposes limits to alterations while also providing a record of the original scene. In contrast, digital photography can duplicate parts of pictures in microseconds, and it can send images rapidly over telephone and computer networks. The image is scanned into a computer and converted to millions of binary computer data called "bits," which have a numerical value of zero or one (on or off). Since the computer is working with binary data, dramatic changes are merely a result of sophisticated computer algorithms. In this way, an image captured in a photograph can be dramatically transformed—into a mirage.

In our demonstration, Diana Ross has been elongated 10 percent, and her skin has been lightened (see Figure 5.1). Skin tone changes permit advertisers to better reflect racial demographics in readership or to create a more exotic image. Diana appears thinner, younger, and more intense. These changes are more conservative than many magazines now allow on a routine basis (Reaves, 1995a). Yet we suggest that such manipulations alter our perceptions to an important extent. In the moment of comparing Diana's body to her own, the reader is no longer able to identify with the real person but instead with a subtly changed, thinner fiction.

EATING DISORDERS AND THE THIN IDEAL

Positive life experiences such as success and happiness are often associated with people who are thin (Stice and Shaw, 1994). Women are under more pressure than men to be thin because their social opportunities are traditionally affected by their beauty, and a sense of beauty becomes an important aspect of a young woman's self-concept (Mazur, 1986). Indeed, being sexually attractive is viewed as a form of empowerment by young women (Baldwin, 1999). Even in such a traditionally male domain as politics, a female candidate's appearance

Figure 5.1
Diana Ross Photographs: Unretouched and Digitally Manipulated

Unretouched.   Digitally manipulated—elongated 10
Courtesy of Shiela Reaves.   percent, waist thinned, skin lightened.

is more salient than a man's, producing higher levels of recall (Hitchon and Chang, 1995). Society thus lays greater stress on appearance, and on achieving a thin appearance, for women than men.

Media messages reflect this gender difference. Silverstein et al.'s (1986) content analysis found the total number of ads for diet foods in forty-eight women's magazines to be sixty-eight, whereas a total of forty-eight men's magazines yielded just a single ad for diet food. More recently, Andersen and DiDomenico (1992) found that the most popular women's magazines contained 10.5 times as many ads and articles promoting weight loss as the most popular men's magazines. The fact that 95 percent of victims of eating disorders are female suggested to Andersen and DiDomenico that a dose-response relationship may exist between "injections" of thinness-promoting media messages and the response of dysfunctional eating patterns.

Research on dysfunctional eating behaviors indicates that several factors contribute to their development, including biological, psychological, familial, and sociocultural factors (Harrison and Cantor, 1997). For example, obesity and depression among parents and close relatives is associated with bulimia. Most pertinent for our research is the contribution of the media to the sociocultural category of risk factors. Indeed, media depictions of the thin ideal are cited most frequently by women as the primary cause of their dysfunctional eating behaviors. Peer and family pressure, respectively, are considered the next two important sources of influence (Irving, 1990).

Both bulimic and anorexic individuals are overly concerned with body weight and have a morbid fear of becoming fat (White, 1992). Anorexia nervosa is a potentially life-threatening disorder characterized by an intense fear of gaining weight even though underweight, maintenance of body weight 15 percent below the minimum considered normal for her age and height, misperceptions about her shape and size, and amenorrhea (cessation of menstruation). Bulimia nervosa is a related disorder characterized by a pattern of binging and purging—eating large quantities of food followed by attempts to compensate by vomiting, using laxatives, overexercising, or fasting (American Psychiatric Association, 1994). Age of onset of both disorders usually occurs in adolescence.

Exactly how do media depictions play into the loss of self-esteem among girls and young women? While Andersen and DiDomenico's (1992) dose-response reasoning served to focus attention on the role of media in promoting the thin ideal, it fails to reflect the psychological impact of years of media moments on young women. And ultimately, if we are to combat the impact of the media mirage, we need insight into the psychological process that takes place between message exposures and the behavioral response of dieting attempts, semistarvation, or binging and purging.

PSYCHOLOGICAL PROCESS BETWEEN MEDIA EXPOSURE AND EATING BEHAVIOR

Some psychological insight into the impact of the media mirage is available from research on the effects of advertising images of women in general. The effects of two broad stereotypes have been explored in early research: domestic and sex object. Although neither early stereotype provides an exact match to the thin ideal, both can serve to illuminate the effects on viewers of images of women achieving goals that real women fail to achieve. The domestic woman kept a perfect house; the sex object poured all her energy into looking provocative and thereby pleasing her man; the thin ideal possesses invulnerable self-control, which can be misconstrued as a form of empowerment. In each case, the goals are flawed but gain stature over repetitions.

In an early study based on cultivation theory, Tan (1977) found that exposure to television commercials that emphasized the desirability of being beautiful cultivated perceptions about the social and personal value of being physically attractive. Subjects exposed to beauty commercials rated being beautiful as significantly more important for being popular with men than subjects exposed to neutral commercials; moreover, subjects exposed to beauty commercials rated beauty as significantly more important to them personally than subjects exposed to neutral commercials. In this way, advertising appears to present women with a standard, or ideal, with which they compare themselves; this standard then influences women's perceptions about how they would like to be.

In an experiment designed to compare the effects of stereotypical and reversed-role ads, Jennings, Geis, and Brown (1980) found that women exposed to stereotypical ads displayed less self-confidence when speaking in public and greater desire to conform with average views than women exposed to reversed-role ads. Confronted with stereotypical depictions of themselves, then, women lost confidence in their own independent judgment and performance abilities. Comparing oneself unfavorably with the thin ideal and a consequent loss of self-esteem are two stages in the psychological process that scholars posit occurs between message exposure and dysfunctional eating behavior. In research that specifically addresses media's impact on eating disorders, McCarthy (1992) suggests that comparing oneself with the thin ideal renders appearance of greater import and creates dissatisfaction with one's body. Stice and Shaw (1994) subsequently found that exposure to the thin ideal produced feelings of depression, reduced self-confidence, and increased body dissatisfaction. Indeed, those with low self-esteem become more vulnerable to negative media effects than those with high self-esteem (David and Johnson, 1998). A strong and alarming link has thus been established in our culture between ratings of perceived appearance and levels of self-esteem (Harter, 1993).

A degree of consensus has thus emerged among researchers regarding negative perceptions and feelings elicited in female viewers by the thin ideal: a comparison unfavorable to the viewer, perception that appearance is very important, loss of self-esteem, dissatisfaction with her body. Although women in Myers and Biocca's (1992) experimental study reported decreased depression levels after watching programming and ads with a thin ideal emphasis, the authors suggest that subjects' upbeat moods were likely to have been short-lived, wearing off once they realized that the aesthetically pleasing ideal is not easily attained.

Not all women who are dissatisfied with their bodies, and preoccupied with vain attempts at dieting, develop anorexia or bulimia. Only a proportion of women who experience the negative perceptions and feelings outlined above progress to a motivational state, termed "drive for thinness." Motivational (conative) states reflect an intention to behave, and drive for thinness is linked to anorexic and bulimic behavior.

Harrison and Cantor (1997) made a significant contribution to the research exploring the connection between media consumption and eating disorders. Their survey revealed that consumption of magazines predicted drive for thinness and consequently eating-disordered behavior. They suggest that the reason exposure to magazines but not television may be a crucial variable is that magazine content explicitly stresses measures to lose weight, whereas television's depictions of thin women relatively rarely show them in explicit relation to dieting or food.

In sum, previous research has developed a model of the psychological process that evolves from those media moments when women visually confront a thin image. By virtue of its selection by the media, the thin image has acquired the stature of an ideal. The fundamental problem with the thin ideal, however, is that it is not simply unworthy; whereas the domestic stereotype, for example, is unworthy in suggesting that a woman is fulfilled by a life of cleaning and decisions about brands of cleaners. The thin ideal is impossible, to the extent that even supermodels are digitally enhanced on a routine basis.

Important questions arise then concerning how our perceptions are affected by a manipulated thin image as opposed to an unaltered image. We need to establish whether a healthy psychological process may be strengthened through education to disrupt the path from media exposure to eating disorder symptomology. Once women are more aware of the routine use of digital manipulation to alter the appearance of models, are they better able to combat the effects of exposure to goals they can never reach? We also need to consider whether digital editing of images should be so widespread. How might the same ethical constraints and dialogues that operate in the news industry be absorbed into the fashion and magazine culture?

MANIPULATING THE MIRAGE

The drive for thinness is now compounded by women trying to emulate not only the thin ideal but also fake bodies falsely created on a computer screen. Since the mid-1980s, our cultural norms of beauty and glamour are based not on thin models but more and more on computer confections. The damage is that we soak up the false image of thinness (Wolszon, 1998)—but not the understanding of the technology that produced the mirage.

The digital revolution that spawned personal computers, digital cameras, and the World Wide Web also transformed media photography. The drive for thinness is now supported by digital manipulation of photographs. These changes allow creative directors to imagine women who are thinner, more beautiful, and more perfect. Digital manipulation can stretch bones, digitally liposuction skin bulges, and clone muscles on a body that is then perceived as belonging to a living model.

Our society tolerates and even winks at the airbrushing of wrinkles and blemishes of models and celebrities in photographs. Magazine covers are routinely airbrushed for blemishes. However, new technology has introduced "morphing," the digital cutting and pasting of elements with extreme ease, speed, and sophistication (Reaves, 1991). Digital photography is so accessible that novice photographers are encouraged to pick up the camera and correct flaws on the computer. "Anyone can take the photo, and we can improve it in Photoshop," advise professional users of a standard photo editing software (Toner, 1997, p. 40).

Mia Consalvo (1997) observes the irony of a new technology that fabricates beautiful images and then labels the false image as "natural":

Many fashion and beauty editorials in *Glamour* also suggest that the "natural" look is now in. The best way for women to achieve this natural look, however, is by using products/technologies. Further, the natural look promoted is itself a fake, the result of air-brushing and digital enhancements. In this system, women are persuaded to want more naturally healthy skin, but must turn to science and technology to achieve this; and what they are trying to achieve (the picture in the magazine) is itself a fabrication of science and technology. (p. 109)

Consalvo (pp. 110–11) also argues that women in magazines, so often blond, can "never be too rich, too thin, or too white."

Cover photography suggests that magazines have embraced this new technology (Blonsky, 1991). In 1993 *Time* magazine morphed a face for their special issue on diversity. Apparently a real person of color was not as appropriate as digitally morphing a composite "face." A 1994 *Mirabella* magazine cover morphed together five different faces to create one composite face that it ironically called "The Face of America." It is not only the photograph that is intoxicating to its audience; the technology itself captivates its practitioners because of its creativity and sophistication. The photographer, Hiro, noted, "Manufacturing a new beauty was more challenging, more intellectual" (Wilson, 1994, p. 36).

The magazine industry embraced digital technology with more creative enthusiasm than the newspaper industry because digital manipulation creates dramatic illustrations with greater ease, amazing speed, and less expense. Magazines depend on dramatic covers in order to compete on the newsstand. Digital manipulation can splice together separate photos that appear lifelike and documentary, such as stunt planes writing the words "New York" near the Chrysler building from three separate images. Magazines argue that covers are illustrations and also that their readers understand their motives (Reaves, 1995a).

By contrast, news organizations protested when *National Geographic* moved the pyramids of Giza closer together in order to fit a cover. Despite a more conservative approach to digital editing in the news profession, many have argued that news photos have never been objective or neutral (e.g., Schwartz, 1992). Cultural analysts have rightly argued that photojournalism's "slice of reality" construct promoted since the nineteenth century is actually misleading (Sekula, 1975; Snyder and Allen, 1975; Walton, 1984). However, before the computer revolution, there were limits to traditional manipulation because of technical constraints in film and slow darkroom processes. With the computer revolution, photojournalism loses its credibility as a witness to history with every digital mishap in newspapers or magazines.

The newspaper industry has issued digital protocols out of a sense of survival (Alabiso, 1990; Reaves, 1993). Newspaper editors have set limits and, as a rule, only allow enough digital alterations that mimic the traditional tools used in the darkroom, such as cropping and darkening or lightening parts of the photo to improve reproduction. The creative use of digital manipulation is allowed by newspapers only when the news illustration is so obvious in its exaggeration or artifice that the reader is not fooled by the technology. Wheeler and Gleason (1995) coined the term, "The Pregnant Bruce Willis Test," when they applauded a digitally outrageous *Spy* magazine that spoofed the *Vanity Fair* cover of a pregnant Demi Moore. *Spy* spliced the head of Bruce Willis onto the pregnant body, and this incident has since become a metaphor for using digital technology for creative illustrations that cannot fool readers.

It appears that magazines are not as concerned with visual ethical boundaries. Visual ethics are not a recognized part of a corporate culture that values creativity and dramatic visual impact (Reaves, 1991). In a recent survey, magazine editors consistently embraced digital changes, whereas newspaper editors did not (Reaves, 1995a). Another industry survey of 1,164 publishing executives concluded that "self-interest rules the day." Magazine editors were not as concerned over journalistic ethics and noted "a big silence out there" on the topic (Silber, 1994). Instead, the main concern of magazine executives is a potential copyright problem (Angelo, 1994). Magazines do not want to be sued for violating copyright when using part of a photo owned by another photographer for a photo montage.

In fact, ethical guidelines for art directors are seen as a chilling effect on artistic vision and creativity. These illustration values give media editors the license to morph and change at will on the basis of creative self-expression. Artistic directors and editors have always made a big assumption: "The reader understands we are creating illusions." This unexamined assumption—"our readers understand"—has nevertheless backfired (Reaves, 1995b). *Texas Monthly* was surprised when readers questioned how they convinced then-Governor Ann Richards to dress as a motorcycle rider in tight leathers and chains (she didn't). *Time* magazine was surprised when readers were outraged that they darkened O. J. Simpson's face with sinister lighting (manipulating a police mug shot). *Vogue* magazine was embarrassed when Madonna protested a cover in which editors digitally filled in the gap in her teeth. *Newsweek* was criticized for digitally straightening the teeth of Iowa's septuplets mother Bobbi McCaughey.

It is apparent to communication educators teaching female students about media issues that they remain largely unaware of the pervasive presence of altered images; and, when apprised, they do not understand it as benign. They seem particularly sensitive to its use in enhancing thinness. We suggest that the psychological path from media exposure to dysfunctional eating behaviors may be disrupted by informing women at a young age of the technological developments and the ethical problems that have fostered the creation of the media mirage.

CONCLUSION

Scholars in the area of eating disorders suggest that increasing preferences for thin body shapes in women may be related to increases in the prevalence of eating-related problem behaviors (Irving, 1990). Indeed, content analyses of *Playboy* magazine and scrutiny of Miss America Pageant contestants show that even women recognized for curvier figures than catwalk models have become progressively thinner (Garner and Garfinkel, 1980; Wiseman et al., 1990). Meanwhile, the average weight of women in the general population has risen. Women appear to be combatting these contradictory trends by striving to become thinner.

In our culture, physical appearance and image factors are important cultural elements, particularly for women. Many of us dismiss advertising as a nuisance factor in our lives, yet most advertising consistently and pervasively extols beauty, thinness, and sexuality (Rockett and McMinn, 1990). Such ads may reinforce a culture that values and rewards appearance over skills, providing incentives for young women to cultivate a particular look rather than developing and expanding their talents and abilities.

Research linking media consumption to eating disorder symptomatology points to magazine images, which are largely advertisements, as the key component. Indeed, scholarship specifically addressing the effects of media on the thin ideal has built on early insights from advertising research regarding the negative impact of stereotypical portrayals on self-esteem. Comparisons between themselves and media images tend to elicit in women perceptions that appearance is very important, dissatisfaction with their own bodies, loss of self-confidence, dieting attempts, and in some, a drive for thinness that is associated with eating disorders.

If we cannot persuade the fashion, advertising, and magazine industry to favor truth in images, then the only logical step is to educate the audience on technological deception. Technological literacy may turn out to be an alternative to medical doctors advising at-risk women to "limit your exposure to the mass media and find new role models" ("Body Image," 1997).

One task of researchers is to incorporate "before and after manipulation" images into experiments. So much of previous research has been correlational that causal designs need to be afforded a priority. Furthermore, future research should include process-oriented measures that allow women to express how a mirage makes them feel and think. It is important to test whether conscious awareness of the impossibility of achieving the thin ideal disrupts the process from unfavorable comparison with self to loss of self-esteem and beyond.

In our culture, the media mirage is not viewed in a singular moment but is presented in a barrage of images. It possesses a cumulative impact. In recent years, the thin ideal has become progressively more digital; beauty manufactured rather than beauty discovered. The media mirage thus threatens to disassociate young women from the realities of leading productive, healthy lives.

With better education about industry norms, the public may not only condemn the creation of the media mirage but be able to resist its effects to the extent that its fabrication no longer benefits advertisers and the media they support. The fullness of Diana Ross in Figure 5.1 (left) elicits warm recognition of her authenticity in us. Why be misled by the false svelteness and elongated shape of Diana Ross in Figure 5.1 (right) that can so easily fill young women with a sense of alienation?

REFERENCES

Adverting Age. (1996, September).

Alabiso, V. (1990, November 26). The ethics of electronic imaging and photo content. *AP Log*, p. 1.

American Psychiatric Association. (1994). *Diagnostic and statistical manual of mental disorders* (3rd ed.). Washington, DC: Author.

Andersen, A. E., and DiDomenico, L. (1992). Diet vs. shape content of popular male and female magazines: A dose-response relationship to the incidence of eating disorders. *International Journal of Eating Disorders, 11* (3), 283–87.

Angelo, J. M. (1994, May). Altered states. *Folio*, pp. 60–62.

Baldwin, C. (1999). Sexualized imagery as power in advertising: The development of self-efficacy in young women. *Visual Communication Quarterly, 6* (1), 4–7.

Blonsky, M. (1991, September). The retouching epidemic. *Allure*, pp. 28–31.

Body image: The last frontier of women's rights? (1997, December): *Women's Health Advocate Newsletter*, pp. 4–6.

Consalvo, M. (1997). Cash cows hit the Web: Gender and communications technology. *Journal of Communication Inquiry, 21*, 98–115.

David, P., and Johnson, M. A. (1998). The role of self: Third-person effects about body image. *Journal of Communication, 48* (3), 37–58.

Garner, D. M., and Garfinkel, P. E. (1980). Socio-cultural factors in the development of anorexia nervosa. *Psychological Medicine, 10*, 647–56.

Harrison, K., and Cantor, J. (1997). The relationship between media consumption and eating disorders. *Journal of Communication, 47*, 40–63.

Harter, S. (1993). Causes and consequences of low self-esteem in children and adolescents. In R. F. Baumeister (Ed.), *Self-esteem: The puzzle of low self-regard*. New York: Plenum Press.

Hitchon, J. C., and Chang, C. (1995). Effects of gender schematic processing on the reception of political commercials for male and female candidates. *Communication Research, 22* (4), 430–58.

Irving, L. M. (1990). Mirror images: Effects of the standard of beauty on the self- and body-esteem of women exhibiting varying levels of bulimic symptoms. *Journal of Social and Clinical Psychology, 9*, 230–42.

Jennings, J., Geis, F. L., and Brown, V. (1980). Influence of television commercials on women's self-confidence and independent judgment. *Journal of Personality and Social Psychology, 38* (2), 203–10.

Kilbourne, J. (1995). *Slim hopes: Advertising and the obsession with thinness*. North-ampton, MA: Media Education Foundation.

Mazur, A. (1986). US trends in feminine beauty and overadaptation. *Journal of Sex Research, 22* (3), 281–301.

McCarthy, M. (1992). The thin ideal, depression and eating disorders in women. *Behavioral Research Therapy, 28*, 205–15.

Mintz, L., and Betz, N. (1988). Prevalence and correlates of eating disordered behaviors among undergraduate women. *Journal of Counseling Psychology, 35*, 463–71.

Mitchell, W. J. (1994, February). When is seeing believing? *Scientific American*, pp. 68–73.

Myers, P., and Biocca, F. A. (1992). The elastic body image: The effect of television advertising and programming on body image distortions in young women. *Journal of Communication, 42* (3), 109–30.

Reaves, S. (1991). Digital alteration of photographs in consumer magazines. *Journal of Mass Media Ethics, 6*, 175–81.

Reaves, S. (1993). What's wrong with this picture?: Daily newspaper photo editors' attitudes and their tolerance toward digital manipulation. *Newspaper Research Journal, 13–14*, 131–55.

Reaves, S. (1995a). Magazines vs. newspapers: Editors have different ethical standards on the digital manipulation of photographs. *Visual Communication Quarterly, 2*, 5–9.

Reaves, S. (1995b). The unintended effects of new technology (and why we can expect more). *Visual Communication Quarterly, 2*, 11–15.

Rockett, G., and McMinn, K. (1990). You can never be too rich or too thin: How advertising influences body image. *Journal of College Student Development, 31*, 278.

Rodin, J., Silberstein, L., and Striegel-Moore, R. (1985). Women and weight: A normative discontent. In T. Sonderegger (Ed.), *Psychology and gender. Nebraska Symposium on Motivation, 1984* (pp. 267–307). Lincoln: University of Nebraska Press.

Schwartz, D. (1992). To tell the truth: Codes of objectivity in photojournalism. *Communication, 13*, 95–109.

Sekula, A. (1975). On the invention of photographic meaning. *Art Forunr, 13*, 36–45.

Silber, T. (1994, February 15). A big silence out there. *Folio*, pp. 48–101.

Silverstein, B., Perdue, L., Peterson, B., and Kelly, E. (1986). The role of the mass media in promoting a thin standard of attractiveness for women. *Sex Roles, 14* (9–10), 519–32.

Snyder, J., and Allen, N. W. (1975). Photography, vision and representation. *Critical Inquiry, 2*, 143–69.

Stice, E. M., Schupak-Neuberg, E., Shaw, H. E., and Stein, R. I. (1994). The relation of media exposure to eating disorder symptomatology: An examination of mediating mechanisms. *Journal of Abnormal Psychology, 103* (4), 836–40.

Stice, E. M., and Shaw, H. E. (1994). Adverse effects of the media portrayed thin-ideal on women and linkages to bulimic symptomatology. *Journal of Social and Clinical Psychology, 13* (3), 288–308.

Tan, A. S. (1977). TV beauty ads and role expectations of adolescent female viewers. *Journalism Quarterly, 56*, 283–88.

Toner, M. (1997, October). Photo realism: A special report. *Presstime*, pp. 38–43.

Walton, K. L. (1984). Transparent pictures: On the nature of photographic realism. *Critical Inquiry, 11,* 246–77.

Wheeler, T., and Gleason, T. (1995). Photography or photofiction: An ethical protocol for the digital age. *Visual Communication Quarterly, 2,* 8–12.

White, J. (1992). Women and eating disorders, part I: Significance and sociocultural risk factors. *Health Care for Women International, 13,* 351–61.

Wilson, S. (1994, September 15). *Mirabella* discovers a new face. *Folio,* p. 36.

Wiseman, C. V., Gray, J. J., Mosimann, J. E., and Ahrens, A. H. (1990). Cultural expectations of thinness in women: An update. *International Journal of Eating Disorders, 11* (1), 85–89.

Wolszon, L. R. (1998). Women's body image theory and research: A hermeneutic critique. *American Behavioral Scientist, 41,* 542–57.

6

Cecelia Baldwin

The Historical Development of Women's Posing from the Post–Gold Rush Era to the Present Print Media

INTRODUCTION

In order to grasp the depth of passive learning that has taken place in the continued objectification of women, it becomes important to explore the historical development of female posing and the use of sexualized imagery in the print media. The post–gold rush era (1860s–1880s) presents a unique set of historical circumstances that led to the promotion of visually sexualized rhetoric in the media with the convergence of sexualized language rhetoric. Four areas that led to this convergence were examined:

- first, the semiotic comparison of images of saloon girls, actresses, and prostitutes of the post–gold rush era with current images in women's magazines;

- second, the exploration of the historicity of the era by examining the lives of the women of the post–gold rush era who were the subjects for the mass media images of the time;

- third, a discussion of how these women's lives were influential to the development of the current media; and

- fourth, the critical examination of how these women may have demonstrated a resistance to eastern Victorian society, and its correlation to our postmodern era.

There is substantial research that has demonstrated that the use of women as decorative objects and the use of sexually explicit posing of women continue to increase (Courtney and Lockeretz, 1971; Courtney and Whipple, 1983; Craig, 1992; Ferguson, Kreshel, and Tinkham, 1990; Rudman and Hegira, 1992; Sullivan et al., 1988). Women's attitudes about self can be shaped by the media; Kellner (1995) posits that girls negotiate and construct their own gendered identities through different definitions of what it means to be a woman from their families, their peers, the school, and the media. Most studies view the posing of women as decorative objects and sexualized imagery as commencing in the 1960s, but this study reveals the extended historical development of the posing of women in the print media and the extent of the objectification that has taken place and its potential to shape attitudes and self-identities. This research found that the post–gold rush era appears to be the origin of many of the specific poses of women we see in today's print media images. It reviews the progression of what was found to be a single era, beginning with the post–gold rush era and continuing through the present, and discusses the influence early sexualized imagery had on mass communication. When viewing decorative objectification as an extended historical period, its implications become more significant.

THE POST–GOLD RUSH ERA

Female Scarcity

The post–gold rush era became known for its saloon girls and brothels, but in actuality it may have been the lack of women that led to this renown. Men far outnumbered women in the Old West; as Hittell (1878) states, "[O]nly the padres found this advantageous. Young women were locked up at night by old women. As they were fewer in number than the men, the friars were careful to give the desirable girls as wives to the most industrious of the young men, who thus had strong motives to be faithful to the church" (p. 5).

In 1847, one year after the United States had won the war with Mexico, and the year before gold was discovered, Yerba Buena (now San Francisco) had a total population of 459 persons, of whom 138, or nearly a third, were females. Breaking these figures down, there were 128 white females to 247 males. There were 8 female Indians to 26 males. There was 1 African American female to 9 males, and 1 Hawaiian female to 39 males. After the gold rush these ratios rapidly changed. It is estimated that, during the first half of 1849, 10,000 people landed at San Francisco; only about 200 were women. Over the next six months some 24,000 gold seekers arrived by sea, with only about 500 females among them. In 1850, 34,000 people landed in San Francisco, but less than 700 were female (Soule and Gihon, 1854). As late as 1880 the men still outnumbered the women 2 to 1. And still the ratio of women to men was much higher in San Francisco than in the mining areas (Gentry, 1964).

It would seem quite certain that the low percentage of the female population gave new power and value to women and sexuality because of female scarcity. But did this major demographic upheaval contribute to a new social order? The possibility that this new order also may have ushered in the current era of mass media is explored, because female scarcity may have been one reason why the scandalous style of William Randolph Hearst was initiated. In examining images of the post–gold rush era, and additionally examining the women themselves whose images were portrayed, the women who were the subjects of the gossip columns are examined. Furthermore, these women also became the subjects of the front pages as a Hearst style of journalism emerged.

SEMIOTIC COMPARISONS

Method

To compare the posed imagery of the women of the post–gold rush era to the posed images of women today, a semiotic comparison was used because, as Pease (1985) discusses, semiotics is the social communication of images as they communicate messages that symbolically link people as representatives of social structures and processes. Social scientists have employed semiotic theory to discern the values and beliefs that are widely shared among the public. Additionally, both Cox (1993) and Kuypers and Bengtson (1993) have pointed out how semiotic theory is utilized to explain how individual roles and identities are partially determined through the transference of meaning through images.

Comparative images in women's magazines today and media images of the 1860s and 1870s were selected and analyzed. Fifteen images from the post–gold rush era were preselected from posters, playbills, stereoscopic cards, and promotion photos. Each was coded as to the specific position of the pose (arms, legs, and body configuration of the image) and were also coded as to additional semiotic content (other images in photo, general type of dress, amounts of body exposed). Nine issues from 1995–1996 fashion magazines (*Mademoiselle, Harper's Bazaar*, and *Vogue*) were randomly selected. The preselected fifteen post–gold rush images were compared, by a second researcher, to the images in current women's fashion magazines in order to find similar correlating imagery, to determine how many of the original poses could be found reproduced, and generally to compare imagery.

FINDINGS

To the surprise of both researchers, all fifteen original posed configurations were reproduced, and many poses were reproduced over and over, in the current women's fashion magazines. They were reproduced in posed configurations (position of body, arms, legs, etc.), and they were often reproduced in accompanying imagery. Even one specific post–gold rush era image of a woman having lunch with a dog at a table, depicting the dog as a human companion, was reproduced in a current magazine.

For example, see Figure 6.1 for a specific comparison of imagery from the post–gold rush era to current imagery. Note the extent of the similarity of the configuration of the pose, with one leg resting on a stool. It is important to note

Figure 6.1
Gold Rush Girl versus Contemporary Ad Image

Contemporary image.   Gold rush image.
Courtesy of Peter Lindbergh, *Harper's Bazaar*, November 1995, p. 179.

that the extension of the leg in both cases is much too large to be in a comfortable resting or leaning position: Both images have the high-heeled right foot significantly above the left knee, whereas a typical resting position might have the foot resting at a midcalf area. Both the left arms are angled, and the left hands are touching the left hips at the waist. The bodies are both slightly leaning to the right, and the right elbows are both placed at the right knees. Additionally, the right hands are at the right cheeks with the index fingers towards the eye. Both smiles are also similar, and the general dress, given the difference in history, is very similar in amount of skin covered, with the earlier image in tights, the predecessor of the later image's panty hose. In all fifteen images, both myself and the second researcher found the similarity of corresponding images much greater than was ever anticipated.

Interestingly, one specific pose that was introduced in the late 1860s was called the Grecian bend. This pose "combined a tightly laced corset, which forced the body into an exaggerated s-shaped configuration (bust thrust outward in front, buttocks behind), and high heel shoes, which projected forward the upper part of the body even more. To further emphasize the hips, the uppermost part of a double skirt was pulled up at the sides and gathered at the back" and designated as "the most erotic style of the century" (Allen, 1991, p. 141). Although the corsets and gathered skirts no longer embellish the pose, the Grecian bend–posed configuration was also found in current imagery.

After finding the striking similarity of images, a search was conducted for earlier images that depicted the posing configurations that were found in the post–gold rush era and then currently. This included viewing pre–gold rush images, drawings, artifacts, and fine art of earlier eras. The only posing configuration used previously to the post–gold rush era was the "odalisque," which is a partially dressed or nude laying on her side. Generally in fine art the painter Ingres is credited with creating the odalisque pose in 1814 (Janson, 1986). Ingres's odalisque is truly a nude reclining rather than the contrived posing of hands, shoulders, and heads that we began to see in the post–gold rush era and continue to see today. In 1864 Ingres did begin to create poses for women that were more similar to the post–gold rush images, although his images were more fluid and "natural" rather than the stiffer contrived poses of the post–gold rush era. And, of course, 1864 is now within the post–gold rush time period. Generally speaking, Toulouse Lautrec is often thought to be the originator of female posing from the brothels and dance halls of France, but in fact, Lautrec was born in 1864, and most of his paintings were done in the 1890s. With the possible exception of the odalisque, the posing configurations were not produced earlier; therefore, the conclusion was reached that the post–gold rush era was indeed a defining era. This was of particular interest because this study had not set out to define a single era but in its revelation allows for a historical pattern of female depiction in which we are still engaged. Therefore, the posed images of the women not only have significance as present images, but have been embedded in our culture for over a hundred years.

CONTEXTUALIZING THE IMAGES OF THE POST–GOLD RUSH ERA

In order to understand current female posing and the initiation of sexualized imagery into the media, a historical context becomes important. Aronowitz and Giroux (1985) contend the issue of historical understanding is dependent upon deconstructing events, texts, and images of the past. Thus, in exploring the deconstruction of the posed imagery of the post–gold rush era, the lives of some of the women who became the subjects of this imagery—who came to the West in the mid- to late 1800s to work as actresses, saloon girls, and prostitutes— were viewed. Furthermore, the interchangeability of the three professions was also observed. It was these young women who became the images of mass entertainment. In exploring resistance to middle-class definitions of women's roles, we find some of the reasons that brought the women of the post–gold rush era to seek out a different life in the West. Additionally, portions of resistance theory are utilized to explore the high percentage of violence that was inflicted upon these women.

The same year gold was discovered in California, the feminist movement in the United States was commencing, for in July 1848 the first women's rights convention was held in Seneca Falls, New York. Johnston (1992) noted that the response to the Seneca Falls Convention was swift and negative. The *Philadelphia Public Ledger and Daily Transcript* wrote from a Victorian perspective as it denounced the convention and its "unfeminine" behavior. The newspaper stated, "A woman is nobody. A wife is everything. A pretty girl is equal to ten thousand men, and a mother is, next to God, all powerful. . . . The ladies of Philadelphia, therefore, under the influence of the most serious, sober second thoughts, are resolved to maintain their rights as Wives, Belles, Virgins and Mothers, and not as Women" (Ryan, 1975, pp. 22–23). The initiation of the women's rights movement was indeed a healthy resistance to these attitudes personified by an eastern Victorian society, but the movement was often relegated to a relatively few educated women.

In critically examining the era and the contradictions and conflicts contained within the context of the Philadelphia newspaper account, it becomes likely not only that would resistance take many forms at this juncture but that traveling west was one way to resist an eastern Victorian society. But it cannot be overlooked that in the lives of these young women who worked as saloon girls, actresses, and prostitutes in the Old West there was a high percentage of violence. Saloon girls were often beaten and sometimes "would take the morphine route out" and "suicide was in fact a common end for these poor girls"; furthermore, "most newspapers had daily court columns, and they all carried examples of assaults against prostitutes" (Barnhart, 1986, p. 112). Moreover, Goldman (1981) states, "Visions of dance hall girls with their customers seem benign compared with [real] images of addict-prostitutes writhing in agony. Alcohol abuse, however, was at least as problematic as opiate abuse . . . but alcoholism caused as much physical suffering and contributed to public violence in ways that opiates did not. While drug abuse did not drive women to prostitution, drugs sustained them in dangerous, degrading daily routines" (p. 132). In the Comstock Lode area the "suicide rates were high, and they were almost unbelievable for prostitutes" (p. 134). Prostitutes' suicides were so common that the *Enterprise* referred to one victim as merely "one more unfortunate" (p. 134, quoting *Territorial Enterprise*, 1886).

Therefore, it becomes important to review one of the most powerful aspects of oppression, which is a culture's ability to continue to reproduce oppression in the face of resistance. Marcuse (1955) examines this phenomenon as he states that "the struggles against freedom reproduce . . . in the psyche of man [and woman] as the self-repression of the repressed individual, and his self-repression in turn sustains his masters and their institutions" (p. 16). Therefore, one embraces a resistance that is endemic within the oppression. We can readily see that in the equation of one pretty woman to 10,000 men there is indeed a relationship of power to be embraced by young women, but it is a power given by a distorted Victorian ideology that ultimately would act as a self-repression when used as a resistance to the powerlessness and even, as the quote suggested, the actual nonexistence of a woman as an individual. It is this phenomenon of resistance as a function of self-repression that was employed as women traveled west in the post–gold rush era to become the actresses, saloon girls, and prostitutes of the time.

LIVES OF WOMEN IN THE POST–GOLD RUSH ERA

Gentry (1964) tells of several women who became madams in the post–gold rush era. One was Belle Cora who kept a brothel on Waverly Place. In the varying accounts of her life, we see the contradictions and conflicts of a Victorian order. Later in this chapter, it will be shown how Belle's life in San Francisco became an ongoing topic for newspaper reporters and gossip columnists: "Like Cleopatra, she was very beautiful, and, beside the power that comes of beauty, rich; but oh so foul! Flaunting her beauty and wealth on the gayest thoroughfares, and on every gay occasion, with senator, judge, and citizen at her beck and call" (p. 76).

Gentry continues to tell two different stories of her life. One was as a daughter of a Baltimore minister who had been abandoned by her family because of a pregnancy and was subsequently rescued by a madam in New Orleans. This story fits the ideological dependency and shame of a scorned woman and helpless prostitute. It also fits the Victorian view of female helplessness and the sentimentality of shame. But there is another version of Belle's early years, which is believed to be the true version of Belle's life. It is not a life of helplessness and shame but a life of adventure and resistance to her "expected" role as a woman in eastern Victorian society. It is based on an account given by San Francisco Police Detective Ben Bohen. Bohen knew Belle, and his recollections, given in a newspaper interview some years after Belle's death "are in their particulars explicit enough to have been drawn from the official police records" (p. 78). According to Bohen, her parents were respectable, though nonministerial, Irish Catholics. Belle had a sister, Anna, two years her senior, and in their early teens, both girls quit school to work in Betsy Osbourn's dressmaking establishment on North Street in Baltimore. Among Betsy's customers were young women who frequented the Lutz, a place visited by English sea captains. In time it occurred to the sisters that it would be easier and more profitable to wear the dresses than to make them. They, too, then frequented the Lutz. Belle left Baltimore to eventually live in Charleston, leaving Anna behind. There she became the mistress of a man who was later killed. She never had a child. In 1848, either in Charleston or in New Orleans, she met Charles Cora, a famed gambler.

Information is then pieced together about Belle's life. They left for San Francisco on the ship *The California* on December 5, 1849, Belle and Charles Cora sailed from New Orleans to Colón. The group crossed the Isthmus, as was usual, on horseback to Panama City. It is assumed they reached their destination because in the early 1850s Belle opened a brothel in Sonora and soon moved her business to San Francisco, where Miller (1964) discusses how she became a highly successful madam, and her life became the subject of many gossip columns throughout the San Francisco area.

Gentry (1964) also discusses another famous madam and gambler, Mme. Eleanore Dumont, as she was registered by the Wells Fargo Stage that brought her to Nevada City, California. "She was young, apparently about twenty." According to a spectator she was "pretty, dark-eyed, fresh-faced. And she was attired as any women cared to be when riding a dusty . . . coach. By all precedent, she should have done one of two things: been met by husband, relative, friend; or inquired the way to . . . the town's red-light district. She did neither" (p. 177).

Barnhart (1986) and Drago (1969) tell how Dumont opened a brothel and became a legend as the most famous gambling woman in the history of the American West. She opened brothels in Idaho and Montana, where one of her prostitutes was sixteen-year-old Martha Jane Canary, alias "Calamity Jane." After Montana there are conflicting reports. One report is that she bought a ranch in Nevada, married, and was swindled out of her money by a "worthless husband." Another report is that she went to Wyoming and followed the construction of the Union Pacific Railroad. Records then show her as a brothel owner in San Francisco, then in Wild Bill Hickok's Cheyenne in the 1870s, in Eureka in 1877, in Deadwood in 1878, and in Nevada County in Bodie where in 1879 she apparently committed suicide.

DEVIANT OR RESISTANT

Saloon girls and prostitutes were often seen as deviant in their behavior. But were their actions deviant or resistance to the Victorian view of women? In analysis of the literature of the Old West, Armitage (1984) describes women's economic interaction with dependency and violence as it occurred in that era. Some women in the post–gold rush era believed that they could evade violence by remaining single. Yet these women recognized the economic pressures on women to marry. Additionally it is pointed out that some women compared marriage to prostitution and recognized the causes of violence in the unequal distribution of economic power (Armitage, 1984). Middle-class Victorian society declared any woman who was outside of the sexual norm as deviant. "Throughout the latter half of the nineteenth century, doctors, reformers and the legal system devised ways to control women who 'transgressed' bourgeois sexual norms—from female castration and clitoridectomy (the latter first performed in the United States in the late 1860's) if she were middle-class, to declaring a woman feeble minded or criminal if she were working-class" (Allen, 1991, p. 144). Therefore, in resisting the expected sexual roles of the time, women were labeled as deviant.

BURLESQUE'S INTERACTION

In the mid-1860s Dolly Adams entered the world of madam by way of the theater. She was billed as the Water Queen in the brothels she owned (Gentry, 1964). A play opened in New York in 1866 known as *The Black Crook*, which was produced the following year in San Francisco. Gentry quotes Sol Bloom (1948) who described it as "an uncommonly silly allegory in which virtue triumphed over the Forces of Darkness." Bloom continues:

The real attraction was the golden-haired Stalacta, Queen of the Fairies who appeared, as did all the ladies of the ensemble, in low-cut bodice and wearing tights. It was America's first leg show.... Legs, of course, had been revealed before.... But "The Black Crook" was the first large-scale entertainment, in a respectable theater, which had been devised almost exclusively to "glorify" the female body.... Burlesque ... had been born. So, for that matter, had the musical comedy and the revue. Flo Ziegfeld's Follies, George White's Scandals, and the sophisticated inventions of Richard Rogers and Oscar Hammerstein are all lineal descendants (p. 165).

Thus the mass entertainment media was born and with it "[b]urlesque became emblematic of the way that popular entertainment developed a pattern of displaying the complexities and ambiguities of cultural contradictions" (Allen, 1991, p. 27).

The Black Crook was soon followed by imitators. One of the most famous was Lydia Thompson's Company, "The British Blonds." "[Lydia] discussed tights as Einstein might have philosophized about the theory of relativity" (Sobel, 1956, p. 20). Allen (1991) designated Lydia Thompson as "the figurative mother of Sophie Tucker and Mae West and the grandmother of Bette Midler" as he discusses burlesque as "a model for the sexual objectification of women in popular entertainment" (p. 27). Zeidman (1967) additionally points out how this genre of entertainment was also performed at brothels and led to an exchange of the two professions of performer and prostitute. "Burlesque owed much, at its beginnings, to the minstrel show, the beer and dance hall.... A popular [burlesque] stunt ... was swinging out over the heads of the audience in trapezes ... furnishing a closer erotic view of fleshy thighs. This device was appropriated from the beer gardens and brothels" (p. 20).

Dolly Adams was one of the most famous of those combining professions from actress to prostitute to madam. "There have been many who, like Dolly Adams, entered the world of the demimonde by the way of the theater, but not with quite the same splash" (Gentry, 1964, p. 166). Dolly Adams first appeared on the stage of the Bella Union Theater about 1873, billed as The Water Queen. "Of her parentage and background little is known; her age at the time was eleven" (p. 166). She was said to have been "taken under the wing" by one of San Francisco's madams who was "taken with the vivacious brunette teenager"

(p. 166). In the late 1870s Dolly became a madam herself and opened a brothel on Ellis Street. "The address, 225 Ellis, was to become one of the best known in the annals of San Francisco prostitution" (166). Her association with the mass media was long and clear as she and her activities became a continual source of "news." But at her death Hearst's the *Examiner* quoted a ship's doctor who stated that she was so "horribly ravaged by disease she appeared to be a woman well in her seventies. She was twenty-six years old" (p. 168).

The financial panic of 1873 lent further impetus to developing burlesque shows. "Burlesque thrives on depression" (Zeidman, 1967, p. 29). In this statement we can see the interaction of sexuality not only as needed escape by men but also as needed economic escape by women.

A NEW JOURNALISM

At this time W. R. Hearst walked through the door opened by "new" theater and brought sexual scandal into everyone's living room. Gentry (1964) points out that the son of Senator George Hearst, William Randolph Hearst, upon assuming ownership of the *San Francisco Examiner*, in 1887, "promptly set about printing all manner of scandal concerning even close friends and political allies of the family" (p. 160). At this time there was a popular rhyme describing the native Californian: "The miners came in forty-nine. The whores in fifty-one; and when they got together—They produced the native son" (p. 161). Hearst made a journalism empire on his style of new journalism, and the term *yellow journalism* was coined.

This project revealed that during this time period the development of visual sexual rhetoric as exemplified in posed configurations of the female body was converging with the commencing of language developed sexual rhetoric in journalism. This was observed not only as sexual imagery became content for news stories but in the development of the traditional format of newspaper design, since it was also revealed that, in what appears to be the reporting of a scandalous marriage, a new template for newspaper design was initiated.

William Chambliss came to San Francisco and allied himself with the *Examiner*. He wrote a periodic column as well as publishing a book of scandal listing the publisher as himself but with Hearst's New York Office as the address. Sexual gossip and scandal became a part of newspaper journalism, and the saloon girls and women of the brothels became its subjects not only for visual rhetoric but also for language rhetoric of the media. The following excerpt from the *Examiner* is one example of this interaction. It is Dolly Adams (The Water Queen madam referred to earlier) to whom he refers as he states: "Perhaps the mention of her name will remind certain prominent members of the Bohemian, the Olympic, and the Pacific Union Clubs [all meeting places of San Francisco's powerful and elite] of many a pleasant midnight party from a certain Ellis Street establishment . . . for among her effects were photographs of several prominent members of the above mentioned clubs. How she got these photographs I will ask the reader to decide" (Gentry, 1964, p. 160).

Swanburg (1961) notes that Hearst was not a newsman in the conventional sense. He invented, produced, and arranged the news. Cited by Swanburg as an example was the marriage of Maud Nelson to the son of James Fair. The senior Fair was one of the four "Silver Kings" of the Comstock Lode, whereas Nelson was the proprietress of a brothel. The *Examiner*'s first account of the marriage was a complete four columns. It included a drawing of the bride and a facsimile of the wedding license. The story continued to be followed for several weeks. Invention was indeed part of the equation as the *Examiner*, in describing the groom stated, "His bloodshot eyes, his swollen face and generally fatigued appearance yesterday when he started on his wedding trip indicated that his stay indoors for the last few days at the Post Street house was in the nature of one of his regular carousals" (Gentry, 1964, p. 176), since this passage, in addition to detailed descriptions of their dress, was merely invented as the reporter writing the story had missed the train that they were supposed to have left on (Gentry, 1964).

But equally as significant to the development of the mass media is that in addition to the convergence of posed imagery and the scandalous content of the reporting of the news, the design of this unique presentation of the news was to become part of the emergence of the "traditional format in newspaper design that dominated newspaper design in the United States for a century" (Conover, 1990, p. 333). Before this point, printers felt that to break the column rule— that is, "to spread a layout over two or more columns—disfigured a page. The *New York Herald* ran two column headlines in 1887, but it left the rule between the columns in place and divided the headline on either side of the rule" (p. 335). A few years later Hearst not only broke the column rule line but expanded a layout over four columns with accompanying imagery. This four-column design was continued in the weeks to come as the scandalous story of James Fair's son unfolded. Furthermore, "W. R. Hearst . . . would utilize many of the same [journalistic] campaign tactics in successfully launching the Spanish American War" by incorporating the layout design generated for the marriage of Maud Nelson and Charles Fair (Gentry, 1964, p. 170), thus establishing a format whose influence has remained for over a century in the way we view the news.

CONCLUSION

The significance of this project is in the revealing of the long history of the convergence of visual and language sexual rhetoric that has been employed by the media. It has been demonstrated that for over 100 years visual and language sexual content have been incorporated into the public sphere through the media. In defining this era, it allows for the continued study and evaluation of this convergence and its historical context.

Further, in viewing the historical development of the specificity of posed configurations of women and the continued repetition of those poses that have been reproduced for more than a century leads us into issues of social control and the importance of passive learning, as "seemingly harmless fun products like the movies, popular music, advertising and TV serve to transmit dominant myths, ideologies and values of the U.S. society, and thus serve to influence how we see, experience, understand and act in our social lives" (Kellner and Exoo, 1987, p. 108). Additionally, Kellner (1995) has shown that attitudes about one's self are learned by the media and has emphasized that girls negotiate and construct their own gendered identities through different definitions of what it means to be a woman through the media, thus adding to the importance not only of the critical examination of the current media but of its history to fully evaluate the possible social construction that has taken place. In defining the development of posed configuration of females and sexual content in a historical context, and subsequently seeing ourselves as part of an era that has continued for over a hundred years, it is easier to grasp the depth of the passive learning in which we have engaged.

Moreover, a contextual analysis of the incorporation of female sexuality into the media may be seen as both an oppressive inequality and a creative struggle of attempted resistance. It therefore becomes important to recognize that context in order to dismantle the spheres of power that have arisen in the continued objectification of women and thereby maximize the ability to enact an effective resistance to objectification that will allow both men and women to engage in an authentic sexuality. It is with the articulation of a historical context that productive resistance can more readily take place because "that space within oneself where resistance is possible remains: It is different then to talk about becoming subjects. That process emerges as one comes to understand how structures of domination work in one's own life, as one develops critical thinking and critical consciousness, as one invents new alternative habits of being" (hooks, 1990, p. 15).

REFERENCES

Allen, R. (1991). *Horrible prettiness*. Winston-Salem: University of North Carolina Press.

Armitage, S. (1984). *The women West*. Norman: University of Oklahoma Press.

Aronowitz, S., and Giroux, H. (1985). *Education under siege*. New York: Bergin & Garvey.

Bancroft, H. H. (1888). *History of California, popular tribunals* (Vols. 1–2). San Francisco: History Company.

Barnhart, J. (1986). *The fair but frail prostitution in San Francisco 1849–1900*. Reno: University of Nevada Press.

Bloom, S. (1948). *The autobiography of Sol Bloom*. New York: Putnam.

Conover, T. (1990). *Graphic communications today*. St. Paul, MN: West.

Courtney, A., and Lockeretz, S. (1971). A woman's place: An analysis of the roles portrayed by women in magazine advertisements. *Journal of Marketing Research, 8* (1), 92–105.

Courtney, A., and Whipple, T. (1983). *Sex stereotyping in advertising.* Lexington, MA: Lexington Books.

Cox, H. G. (1993). *Later life: The realities of aging.* Englewood Cliffs, NJ: Prentice-Hall.

Craig, S. (1992). The effect of television day part on gender portrayals in television commercials: A content analysis. *Sex Roles, 26* (5–6), 197–211.

Drago, H. (1969). *Notorious ladies of the frontier.* New York: Dodd, Mead.

Ferguson, J., Kreshel, P., and Tinkham, S. (1990). In the pages of *Ms.*: Sex role portrayals of women in advertising. *Journal of Advertising, 19* (1), 40–51.

Fine, M. (1991). *Framing dropouts.* New York: State University of New York Press.

Gentry, C. (1964). *The madams of San Francisco.* New York: Doubleday.

Goldman, M. (1981). *Gold diggers and silver miners: Prostitution and social life on the Comstock Lode.* Ann Arbor: University of Michigan Press.

Hittell, J. (1878). *The history of San Francisco and incidentally the state of California.* San Francisco: A. L. Bancroft and Company.

hooks, b. (1990). *Yearning: Race, gender, and cultural politics.* Boston: South End Press.

Janson, H. W. (1986). *History of art.* New York: H. N. Abrams; Englewood Cliffs, NJ: Prentice-Hall.

Johnston, C. (1992). *Sexual power.* Tuscaloosa: University of Alabama Press.

Kellner, D. (1995). Cultural studies and multiculturalism and media culture. In G. Dines and J. Humez (Eds.), *Gender, race and class in media* (pp. 5–17). Thousand Oaks, CA: Sage.

Kellner, D., and Exoo, C. P. (1987). *Democracy upside down: Public opinion and cultural hegemony in the United States.* New York: Praeger.

Kuypers, J. A., and Bengtson, V. L. (1993). Competence and social breakdown: A social-psychological view of aging. *Human Development, 16* (3), 181–201.

Leiss, W., Kline, S., and Jhally, S. (1986). *Social communication in advertising: Persons, products and images of well being.* New York: Methuen.

Marcuse, H. (1955). *Eros and civilization.* Boston: Beacon Press.

Martin, C. (1974). *Whiskey and wild women.* New York: Hart Publishing.

McRobbie, A., and Garber, J. (1975). Girls and subcultures. In S. Hall and T. Jefferson (Eds.), *Resistance through rituals* (pp. 37–51). London: Hutchinson.

Miller, R. (1964). *Shady ladies of the West.* Los Angeles: Western Lore Press/Dodd, Mead.

Pease, O. (1985). *The responsibility of American advertising.* New Haven, CT: Yale University Press.

Rudman, W., and Hegira, A. (1992). Sexual exploitation in advertising health and well-ness products. *Women and Health, 18* (4), 77–90.

Ryan, M. (1975). *Womanland in America from colonial times to the present.* New York: New Viewpoints.

Sobel, B. (1956). *A pictorial history of burlesque.* New York: Putnam's Sons.

Soule, F., and Gihon, J. H. (1854). *The annals of San Francisco.* New York: D. Appleton.

Sullivan, G., O'Connor, T. V., Belknap, P., and Leonard, W. M. (1988). A conceptual replication and extension of Erving Goffman's study of gender advertisements. *Sex Roles, 25* (3–4), 103–118.

Swanburg, W. (1961). *Citizen Hearst.* New York: Charles Scribner's Sons.

Thomas, C., and McRobbie, A. (1980). *Girls and counter-school culture* (Melbourne Working Papers). As cited in K. Weiler (1988), *Women teaching for change: Gender, class & power*. South Hadley, MA: Bergin & Garvey Publishers.
Zeidman, I. (1967). *The American burlesque show*. New York: Hawthorn.

PART IV

MAGAZINE

7

Debra Merskin

That Time of the Month: Adolescence, Advertising, and Menstruation

INTRODUCTION

"Special fashion marathon!" "Cool hair—How to get it!" and "Your period—The real deal" scream the article teasers on the cover of a recent issue of *Seventeen* magazine. Advice giving is a primary function of teen girl magazines—how to dress, look, diet, behave, and think about boys are typical topics. Given that magazines play a significant role in adolescent socialization, and that issues associated with the female body are frequently discussed in their pages, analyzing messages associated with menstruation is important in gaining an understanding of how this medium might contribute to a girl's self-image.

Several scholars have suggested that women are judged not on what they do but rather on what they look like (Bordo, 1993; Jacobs-Brumberg, 1997; Kilbourne, 1987; Wolf, 1991). Body self-consciousness often begins during adolescence when a girl feels conflicted about her developing body. Magazine advertising typically portrays the ideal as boyish—flat-chested, slim-hipped. The maturing adolescent girl often feels betrayed by her naturally developing breasts and hips. Given that menstruation is one of the key indicators of the transition from girlhood to womanhood, portrayals of activities associated with this event are intimately connected to understanding how magazines contribute to a girl's developing sense of self. Often thought of as a "guide to life," magazines play an important role in the lives of teenage girls (Rowland, 1995).

Frye's (1990, p. 179) conceptualization of feminist epistemology serves as a strategy for this research: "Our process has been one of discovering, recognizing, and creating patterns. ... [P]attern recognition/construction opens fields of

meaning and generates new interpretative possibilities. Instead of drawing conclusions from observations, it generates observations. . . . What we do is sketch
a schema within which certain meanings are sustained." A combination of techniques is used in this chapter to uncover the portrayals of adolescent girls'
sexuality (as portrayed in feminine hygiene advertisements) in *Seventeen* and
Teen magazines. The nature of adolescent experience for girls, the importance
of menstruation in that process, and how magazine advertising conveys important information about participating in girl culture will be examined.

This analysis is important for three primary reasons: (1) The teen market
represents an increasingly important target market, thereby receiving more attention from advertisers, (2) magazines are important sources of adolescent socialization information, and (3) the research will contribute to the relatively lean
literature on teen magazines and adolescent girls.

ADOLESCENCE: THE AGONY AND THE ECSTASY

A time of awkwardness and opportunity, adolescence represents a critical time
of identity formation for both boys and girls. It is a "biopsychological" process
that involves psychological and emotional changes with "a large variation of
what's 'normal' " ("Helping Teens," 1994). Adolescence is a time of "searching
and introspection in which the individual is constantly faced with the perplexing
question, 'Who am I?' " (Avery, 1979, p. 53).

Typically, the age range for adolescence is twelve to eighteen years of age
when puberty (the biological process) and adolescence (the social and personal
process) meet. Scholars such as Erikson (1968), Piaget (1972), and Kohlberg
(1976) have all described the unique characteristics of this time, one of the most
notable being the concern with the evaluative judgments of one's peers. During
adolescence, the peer group is the major source of socialization for adolescents
because "adolescents are looking to each other rather than to the adult community for their social rewards" (Coleman, 1961, p. 138). Once the adolescent
has moved through this time, he or she is equipped with an understanding of
what will be expected in adulthood. The importance of laws, rules, mores, and
sex roles have been internalized so that he or she is equipped with a mental
guidebook for navigating the social and cultural sea he or she will inhabit as an
adult.

Generally, adolescents look to a "collective cultural consciousness" (often
found in music, movies, and magazines) rather than to their parents or local
community norms for guidance and support (Ianni, 1989, p. 674). According to
Elkind (1967), the changes in body shape that accompany puberty generate a
belief that other people are also preoccupied with one's appearance. Research
by Cavior and Dokecki (1973) suggests that early adolescents view physical
attractiveness as being more important than compatibility of personal beliefs
when it comes to choosing friends. Today's emphasis on physical appearance

encourages a thin physique, yet the physical changes that accompany puberty can conflict with that ideal.

GENDER AND ADOLESCENCE

Certainly much of the confusion that accompanies adolescence is experienced by both girls and boys. Adolescents are faced with a bewildering array of tasks. These include gaining independence (from parents), developing interpersonal skills, and forging a new identity. This third component includes accepting a new body image, evaluating peer codes, learning to feel comfortable with sexual feelings, planning a career path, and formulating his or her own opinions ("Helping Teens," 1994; Strasburger, 1995, p. 12).

In terms of identity and self-esteem formation, however, something very different happens with girls than with boys. Whereas boys are encouraged to experience life widely, enjoy changes in voice and physicality such as growth of the penis and an increase in body hair, girls become less confident in both their bodies and their abilities. Lerner (1976) suggests that girls are culturally denied knowledge about their bodies, particularly their genitals. Parents often find cute names for a boy's body parts (for example, "wee-wee"), yet girls' genitals are most often referred to as "down there" or "private parts" (Martin, 1996, p. 23). This lack of identification contributes to a girl's sense that her body is something to be kept hidden, particularly functions associated with sexuality. This missing knowledge about one's body can thereby contribute to a sense of having little control over it. Given this lack of general knowledge, when a girl's body develops on course, she can easily perceive it as out of control.

This loss of identity and self-knowledge associated with adolescent girls has been widely discussed in the literature (Brown and Hendee, 1989; Gilligan, 1977, 1984; Horney, 1926; Orenstein, 1994; Pipher, 1994). Most widely associated with the work of Carol Gilligan (1977, 1984), disavowal of self is a key characteristic of adolescent girls. Horney (1926) linked the development of this characteristic to comparisons teen girls made between their own behavior and expectations and that of boys. Finding they were unable to measure up, girls were left with feelings of inadequacy. Girls who enter adolescence with a firm sense of who they are often "renounce and devalue their perceptions, beliefs, thoughts, and feelings" (Stern, 1991, p. 105). According to Orenstein (1994, p. xvi), although all young people experience a kind of confusion during adolescence, "girls' self-regard drops further than boys' and never catches up."

These changes and feelings of self-worth are intimately connected to menstruation. As Lott (1981, p. 115) points out, "[T]o damn one's body monthly is not conducive to feelings of self worth." Both symbolically and in actuality, menses is the indicator of the transition from girlhood to womanhood, a biological validation of femaleness when girls are keenly aware of role prescriptions. This framing carries with it the weight of dominant culture beliefs that

can be traced to the distant past yet manifest themselves in modern communications.

THE IDEOLOGY OF MENSTRUATION

Symbolically marked in some cultures while hidden in others, a common
theme surrounding menstruation is the transition to adulthood—the girl becomes
a woman (and can become a mother). Known by a variety of names (the month-
lies, a visit from Aunt Flo, being "on the rag"), the onset of menses is anticipated
as a sign of womanhood yet feared as a target of ostracism. In dated parlance,
these beliefs or myths have been called "old wives' tales." Those associated
with menstruation are among the most prevalent and persistent. For example:

• Menstruation is a sign of being unclean and in less-than-perfect health.
• Exercise, particularly swimming, should be avoided.
• Cold foods should be avoided.
• Given that women are physically vulnerable during their periods, regular exercise
  should be avoided.
• Don't water plants.
• Neither dental fillings or permanents will take. (Allen and Fortino, 1983, p. 18)

Inspired by fear and often confused with defilement, taboos help order a
society. A taboo "expresses itself essentially in prohibitions and restrictions"
(Voigt, 1984, p. 97). To remain stable a society needs order, and dirt "offends
against order" (Douglas, 1966, p. 92). Therefore, the "curse" is a taboo dating
to the time of Eve that presents menstruating women as "filthy, sick, unbalanced,
and ritually impure" (Daly, 1978/1990, p. 248).

As a society we have beliefs that separate, classify, and organize to create
social structures designed to withstand natural disasters, punish transgressions,
and demarcate. In many cases it is necessary to exaggerate differences in order
to create a semblance of order. For example, distinctions between men and
women are made visible and exaggerated through differences. Given that only
women menstruate, the biological fact of blood determines their cultural and
social distinction during adolescence. Menstruation then becomes a hygienic
rather than a maturational issue. Lien (1979, p. 120) points out that women are
subjected to a kind of "menstrual discrimination" marked by "contempt and
isolation."

SANITIZING PUBERTY

Girls are entering menses earlier than ever before. Changes in nutrition
(better-nourished girls are able to maintain body fat), growth hormones added
to chicken and beef, and electricity (when exposed to sufficient light, bodies

will enter puberty earlier) all contribute to this process (Pipher, 1994, p. 53). Many American girls now begin menstruating as early as nine (Steinberg, 1985, p. 44).

Much of the fear associated with menses comes from the lack of input from parents (Gainotti, 1986; Konopka, 1986; Thornburg, 1975). When there is parental involvement, the information typically comes from the mother (Fox, 1980; Gainotti, 1986). Several scholars have suggested that mothers often react after the fact, rather than preparing their daughters for the event, resulting in uncertainty and even trauma—an experience that reinforces the fundamental nature of taboo—bleeding, pain, fear, and the unknown (Gainotti, 1986; Jacobs-Brumberg, 1997; Konopka, 1986). One of the reasons taboos die so hard is that they are "rigorously taught to youngsters who dare not question them" (Delaney, Lupton, and Toth, 1988, p. 22). Rodin (1992) relates Phillipa's story about her first period:

In my family everybody was really private about their bodies. I was the only girl and when I had my first period my mother hurriedly handed me some sanitary napkins and mumbled some instructions. My brothers started laughing and making fun of me because they saw the box of sanitary napkins. I went to bed that night thinking my body was a curse. (p. 55)

In twentieth-century America, preadolescent and adolescent girls learn to menstruate in a way that differs from their counterparts of earlier times. No longer confined to couches, clutching hot water bottles, girls today are generally active during their periods. Although there has been a shift from inactive to active and from homemade to commercial products, Brumberg (1997) suggests that there has been an "unintended consequence" to this newfound freedom. When they do begin to menstruate, girls and their mothers "typically think first about the external body—what shows and what doesn't rather than the emotional and social meaning of the maturational process" (p. 29). This suggests that, along with other behaviors such as dieting, physical appearance is a primary developmental concern. According to Brumberg, "[M]odern mothers typically stress the importance of outside appearances for their daughters: keeping clean, avoiding soiled clothes, and purchasing the 'right equipment.' Hygiene, not sexuality, is the focus of maternal discussions with girls" (p. 30). Coupled with messages that reinforce the beauty ideal of thinness, the psychological changes associated with menstruation also influence a girl's developing body. Hayne (1987) describes the story of a girl who expressed dislike for her developing body:

Sometimes my body looks so bloated, I don't even want to get dressed. I like the way I look for exactly two days each month. . . . [E]very other day my breasts, my stomach, they're just awful lumps, bumps, bulges. My body can turn on me at any movement; it is an out-of-control mass of flesh. (p. 213)

Given the importance of peer groups, normal bodily changes that accompany adolescence conflict with expectations of looking good and right and fitting in. Body image is of particular concern to teen girls. A Canadian study found that while 60 percent of girls aged eight to nine reported being "happy with the way they are," by the time these girls were sixteen, only 29 percent felt content with their bodies (compared with 48 percent of similarly aged boys) ("Helping Teens," 1994).

Certainly confusion about bodily changes is typical of adolescence. However, control of the activities associated with this process is central to the socialization of adolescent girls. Menstruation clearly offers the opportunity for dominant culture to direct the attitudes, beliefs, and behaviors of girls. A century ago, mothers lengthened their daughters' skirts or allowed them to put their hair up as a sign of maturing. Today American girls and their mothers typically head for the mall where growing up is acted out through purchases—bras, lipsticks, high heels, or ear piercing.

Given the many changes in contemporary society, such as social and geographic mobility, and changing family structure, information transferral from parent to teen becomes increasingly strained and perhaps unavailable. Although the media would ordinarily play only a supplemental role in providing important information on how to participate in society, today this role may become nearly exclusive.

ADOLESCENCE GIRLS AND MEDIA USE

Reach a girl in her *Seventeen* years and she may be yours for life.
                    —*Advertising Age* (cited in advertisement, September 1996)

Except for increases in use when a new magazine is introduced, there is little evidence of any substantial change in print media use from childhood through adolescence (Avery, 1979). Magazine reading, however, appears to be greater among adolescents than it is among younger children. Content preferences also become clear during this time.

Long-term exposure to stereotypical role portrayals of women in advertising may encourage women to internalize values and ideals (Jennings-Walstedt, Geis, and Brown, 1980). In Tan's (1979) study of beauty ads, cultivation effects were found even after short-term exposure, and it was posited that longer-term exposure would likely lead to more intense effects. In addition, there is a substantial body of research that suggests that mass media messages have the power to influence behaviors, worldviews, and self-image of readers and viewers. Today, young women not only tend to look to the mass media for guidebooks for daily living but also tend to compare themselves to the models and actresses in the articles and advertisements. Richins's (1991) study of female images and advertising found that seventy-one of her respondents stated, "[W]hen I see models in clothing ads, I think about how well or how badly I looked compared to the models" (76). Dissatisfaction with physical appearance (perceived as imperfections) has been found to negatively impact educational priorities. In her study of female students, Foster (1994) found that most of the female students would rather lose five pounds off their thighs than to get an A in their classes. Imperfections in their bodies were considered to be personal rejections and much more serious than poor grades.

Magazines in particular are important tools of socialization for preadolescent and adolescent girls. In her analysis of ads and editorial content in *Seventeen* magazine, Peirce (1990) found that few of the stories offered anything but traditional socialization messages for teenage girls. In their analysis of content of *Sassy, Seventeen*, and *YM*, Evans et al. (1991) found that success for girls (and hence, women) is measured through personal attractiveness; there was little emphasis on identity themes (career, education); and the content, both advertising and editorial, focused on white, slim, blond hairdo, blue-eyed girls.

Duffy and Gotcher (1996) examined dramatized images that appeared in *YM*, analyzing how reality is shaped through rhetorical strategies used in editorial and advertising content. They found that *YM* presents a "dramatized curriculum for ideal female behavior" (p. 45).

Magazine advertising can be a particularly powerful tool of socialization, as it suggests to adolescents what is new and popular and, therefore, desirable. In her 1990 study, Yanni argued that women's representation in advertising is part of a negative system of representation that reinforces patriarchal meaning. Several scholars have suggested that the media serve an important role in naturalizing and reinforcing the roles of women as dominated by men and that their bodies are appropriate objects of desire (Dolan, 1988; Duffy and Gotcher, 1996; Wolf, 1991). The following section describes research that has focused specifically on the communication of feminine hygiene information.

THE GIRL BODY AND HYGIENE ADVERTISING

Most investigations of American girls' menstrual experiences have relied upon personal interviews (Koff and Rierdan, 1995; Predergast, 1989; Whisnant and Zegans, 1995). Other researchers have conducted interviews internationally, in countries such as Bangladesh (Nazmuh, 1984), the United Kingdom (Konopka, 1986), Italy (Gainotti, 1986), and Spain (Thuren, 1994). The findings of these studies are consistent with those in the United States—girls aren't receiving advice from their mothers and continue to view menstruation as a shameful, dirty process.

The use of educational materials in socializing girls in the preparation for, and process of, menstruation has been evaluated (Havens and Swenson, 1988; Whisnant, Brett, and Zegans, 1975). Typically these studies have found that the majority of film and slide presentations depict female anatomy, but do so through animation. Fear and embarrassment were acknowledged and openness with peers and female adults encouraged.

Additional work has come from the cultural studies tradition. Kaite (1984) presents a history of the feminine hygiene market and relates the development of products to women's involvement in World War I and the marketplace. Treneman (1989) investigated the mythical imagery and text in feminine hygiene advertisements. Kane (1996) looked at the ideology of freshness in television commercials. Kissling (1996) interviewed adolescent girls, focusing on the communication strategies they use to violate taboos against menstrual communication. She found that the use of various linguistic devices "satisfied girls' need to talk about menstruation with friends while maintaining social decorum on the issue" (p. 305).

Studies of the content of print advertisements for feminine hygiene products is extremely limited. Havens and Swenson (1988) content analyzed advertisements for these products over a ten-year period in *Seventeen* magazine. The researchers found that the ads present menstruation as a "hygienic crisis," encourage guilt, diminish self-esteem, and focus on the importance of peer support over that of adults. This chapter not only adds to this limited literature but also analyzes advertisements more extensively while providing a theoretical context for considering this information.

METHOD AND MEASURES

Feminine hygiene and related medicine advertisements were content analyzed in two of the top-selling magazines targeting preadolescent and adolescent girls (*Standard Rate & Data Service*, 1997). A 25 percent sample was taken over a ten-year period in *Seventeen* and *Teen* (1987–1997), yielding thirty-three issues each and 168 ads for tampons, panti-liners, pads, and related medicines (such as Midol). After duplicates were removed, 128 advertisements were analyzed. All ads were coded by the researcher and a graduate student. An average intercoder reliability rate of 96 percent was achieved (Holsti, 1969). To study the content of these advertisements, Havens and Swenson's (1988) framework (described later) was used.

CODING

Two central approaches were key to coding the ads in the Havens and Swenson (1988) study: (1) scientific and (2) athletic. Scientific themes included depictions of special designs (wings), schematics of a pad or tampon, special coverings (shields), or special sizes (slims). Athletic ads featured young women engaged in activities such as attending ballet class, swimming, bicycling, and gymnastics. A preliminary review of the ads for the current study revealed a new approach—stationary figure. In this case, the figure is simply standing or sitting, or otherwise posed, but not engaged in any activity. This approach was added to this coding category.

Each ad was analyzed for recurrent themes (text, context, tone). The text was analyzed for the dominant theme of the ad (fear, freedom, peace of mind, secrecy). Examples of context include making practical arrangements, being worried or embarrassed, feeling ill, or being in class. The tone of the ad identified whether it was written in a conversational style, used a role model, was humorous, or exuded self-confidence. In addition, method of presentation (cartoon, photograph), product features (comfort, ease of use, no bulk), and number and race of models were coded.

In terms of products advertised, 44 percent were for tampons, approximately one-third for pads (32 percent), 16 percent for medicines, and 8 percent for panti-liners. The leading advertisers were Tampax Tampons (28 percent), Always (25 percent), and Playtex (13 percent). The remaining third were distributed among nine other advertisers.

FINDINGS

A stationary figure was found in nearly half (46 percent) of the ads. Examples include a girl sitting on a front porch, looking out a window, or sitting in a park. This approach was followed by the "other" category (44 percent). Ads were placed in this category that did not fit the others, such as product schemata or cartoons. Often these were entirely text. For example, Always offered a question and answer section called "Always Answers." Others used cartoon figures in mock discussions.

Nine percent of the ads employed an athletic approach. In these, girls typically wore either leotards or tight, and usually white, clothing. In some cases the ads focused on the buttocks and/or perineal area. For example, an ad for Always Ultra Plus had the headline "Introducing the No-Worry, No-Show Maxi" and featured the bottom half of four girls in skirts, leotards, and shorts. Another Always ad featured the bottom half of four girls wearing leotards and asked, "Pop Quiz: Who's Wearing the Tampon?" Scientific ads accounted for only 2 percent of the ads.

TEXT, CONTEXT, AND TONE

Text was the dominant "voice" of the ad—what the headline or key topic of the advertisement emphasized as the theme.

As Table 7.1 shows, "peace of mind/trust" was the theme most often used in copy (40 percent). In fact, "Trust is Tampax" was the slogan used by this major advertiser. In one of their ads, trust is emphasized as two young girls are shown bicycling wearing tight, white jeans. In another ad, three young women and two young men were shown in a swimming pool. Freedom is emphasized in ads

Table 7.1
Theme (Text) of Ads

Theme	Frequency	Percent*
Peace of mind/trust	84	40
Comfort	61	29
Freedom	32	15
Secrecy	14	6
Fear	13	6
Other	9	6

*Numbers do not total 100 percent as ads mentioned several themes.

such as one for O.B. tampons that features a young woman in a swimsuit and copy describing how O.B. is designed to free a girl from applicators and bulk.

Secrecy was mentioned in the ads as well (6 percent), as shown in an ad for Stayfree Ultra Thin Tampons that promises buyers that no one need ever "know" when they are menstruating. In a Tampax ad, a young woman was shown from behind in ballet class. Speaking to her friend, she worries that "everyone will know" she's wearing a pad until tampons come to the rescue.

The themes of fear and uncertainty were also used (6 percent). The fear appeal typically focused on virginity and the desire to retain it. Such uncertainty focused on fear of discomfort and product risks. A Tampax ad, for example, shows girls talking at the beach and one asking if "they" are hard to insert. In another scene in a girls' rest room, one girl asks another for reassurance that the tampon "won't hurt."

The context of the ads focused on fears of "showing" or being found out, about locating supplies "just in case," and having to leave class to check. Most ads focused on practical concerns. For example, an ad for Playtex Portables (shown fitting into the front pocket of a tight pair of jeans) touted its product for its newness, its neatness, and its discreetness. Always Slenders for Teens recognized first-day-of-high-school jitters by calling this product a "smooth move" designed to beat the back-to-school blues. The product Tampax Tampons assures girls that while they may do a lot of things to get noticed, "wearing a pad" doesn't have to be one of them. The copy elaborated on this by pointing out that if a girl wears a pad, she "may just be announcing to everyone" that she has her period.

Worries about the signs of one's period showing were also contextual themes. For example, a Tampax ad warns that even pads that boast about being "thin" and "discreet" may still be visible in a "pair of leggings."

Another important part of the ad is the tone. For example, does the copy lecture, instruct, or use humor or a role model to communicate? Who addresses the reader? In nearly all of the ads (88 percent) the tone was conversational, such as the ad where two young women are discussing virginity. In this print ad, a young girl is discussing what she perceives to be the complexity of tampons. She wonders, for example, if a girl needs to be "experienced" sexually to use them. However, by talking with her friend Lisa (whose mother is a nurse), she learns that Petal Soft Plastic Applicator Tampax Tampons pose no threat to virginity. Table 7.2 describes product features.

Protection was mentioned most often (69 percent). An example is a New Freedom pad ad that describes the "unique Center Protection System that helps direct fluid to the center." Product comfort followed (46 percent). An example is a Tampax Tampon ad where Jade M.—sixteen (years)—compares a girl's first bra experience to that of the first tampon, noting how after a while, it was easy to "forget" you're even wearing it.

Ease of use (43 percent) was found in a Playtex ad that countered by having its female model admit she was mistaken to think tampons would be "hard to use." No bulk (20 percent) was another consideration. In one ad a young woman admits to another that she hates wearing pads and compares them to wearing "diapers." Charcy E., age eighteen from Merrimack College, addressed fears of losing a tampon internally when she testified that the only thing a young woman really can lose "are those diapers."

Nearly half of the ads (42 percent) featured one young woman, followed by no models used (27 percent), and two models (18 percent). Five percent of the ads used five or more models. In terms of race, more than half of the models (52 percent) were white, followed by "other" (24 percent), which accounts for cartoon characters and text-only ads. This was followed by 11 percent of the ads that featured both a black and a white model. It was impossible to determine race in 10 percent of the ads.

CONCLUSION

Although few of us like to admit it, as consumers we increasingly rely on advertising for information. This is particularly true of adolescent girls who have fewer resources for gaining private information or may in fact reject the advice of mothers and older women. In this way, advertising has become a forum for discussing personal matters—a kind of social guide.

Despite an increase of feminine hygiene advertising in broadcast media, and liberalization of body-related thinking, "menstruation has not be redefined as something positive" (Havens and Swenson, 1988). Certainly it is inconvenient and often uncomfortable, but it need not result in social ostracism or negative feelings about the bodies of adolescent girls as they enter a critical time of identity formation. It is important also to recognize that, through ads for tampons, napkins, panti-liners, and related medicines, adolescent girls learn not only about the functioning of their bodies but also about how particular products are meant to help them control their developing bodies. The findings of this study suggest that ads for these products are dominated by white girls who deliver

Table 7.2
Product Features

Feature	Frequency	Percent*
Protection	89	69
Comfort	59	46
Ease of use	44	43
Other	27	21
Lack of bulk	26	20
Biodegradable	13	12
Convenience	12	9

*Numbers do not total 100 percent as ads mentioned several themes.

information about products while simultaneously discussing fears of bodily betrayal. Given that the mythology surrounding menstruation is laden with messages about being unclean, unsafe, and unwanted, the use of white models is hardly surprising.

If what Hall (1989) and Williamson (1978) suggest is true, that the media present a vision of the world constructed to support the dominant social system, then the current array of feminine hygiene advertising targeting adolescent girls serves to reinforce an ideology that helps define their social roles and suppress self-esteem. In many ways, the bodies of girls (and hence women) are given meaning that suggests there are times when they are unattractive (if they are not thin or young) or are unclean (if they are menstruating).

Despite increased knowledge about how the female body functions, feminine hygiene advertising continues to present a world akin to the past. It may be a world where girls are permitted to ride bicycles when they menstruate and where skirts can be of any length, yet the ads serve as reminders that an active life is only possible through careful preparation and purchase of a specific brand. Otherwise, these young women face humiliation if any sign of their femaleness should seep through their clothing.

Perhaps due to the availability of birth control the significance of a girl's period has changed, but the weight of the culture remains behind how this event is perceived and how a sense of self develops. Self-esteem becomes intimately connected with body image, one increasingly prescribed by the media.

REFERENCES

Allen, P., and Fortino, D. (1983). *Cycles: Every woman's guide to menstruation.* New York: Pinnacle.

Avery, R. K. (1979). Adolescents' use of the media. *American Behavioral Scientist, 23* (1), 53–70.

Bordo, S. (1993). *Unbearable weight: Feminism, Western culture and the body.* Berkeley: University of California Press.

Brown, E. F., and Hendee, W. R. (1989). Adolescents and their music: Insights into the health of adolescents. *Journal of the American Medical Association, 262,* 1659–63.

Cavior, N., and Dokecki, P. R. (1973). Physical attractiveness, perceived attitude similarity, and academic achievement as contributors to interpersonal attraction among adolescents. *Development Psychology, 9,* 44–54.

Chess, S., Alexander, T., and Cameron, M. (1976). Sexual attitudes and behavior patterns in a middle-class adolescent population. *American Journal of Orthopsychiatry, 46,* 690–701.

Coleman, J. (1961). *The adolescent society.* Glencoe, IL: Free Press.

Daly, M. (1978/1990). *Gynecology: The metaethics of radical feminism.* Boston: Beacon Press.

Delaney, J., Lupton, M. J., and Toth, E. (1988). *The curse: A cultural history of menstruation.* Urbana: University of Illinois Press.

Dolan, J. (1988). *The feminist spectator as critic.* Ann Arbor, MI: UMI Research Press.

Douglas, M. (1966). *Purity and danger.* New York: Praeger.

Duffy, M., and Gotcher, J. M. (1996). Crucial advice on how to get the guy: The rhetorical vision of power and seduction in the teen magazine *YM. Journal of Communication Inquiry, 20,* 32–48.

Elkind, D. (1967). Egocentricism in adolescence. *Child Development, 38,* 1025–34.

Erickson, E. H. (1968). *Identity: Youth and crisis.* New York: W. W. Norton.

Evans, D., Rutberg, J., Sather, C., and Turner, C. (1991). Content analysis of contemporary teen magazines for adolescent females. *Youth & Society, 23,* 99–120.

Foster, P. (1994). *Minding the body: Women writers on body and soul.* New York: Doubleday.

Fox, G. L. (1980). The mother-adolescent daughter relationship as sexual socialization structure: A researcher's view. *Family Studies, 29,* 21–28.

Frith, K. T. (1995). Advertising and mother nature. In A. N. Valdavia (Ed.), *Feminism, multiculturalism, and the media: Global diversities.* Thousand Oaks, CA: Sage.

Frye, M. (1990). The possibility of feminist theory. In D. L. Rhode (Ed.), *Theoretical perspectives on sexual difference* (pp. 173–184). New Haven, CT: Yale University Press.

Gainotti, M. A. (1986). Sexual socialization during early adolescence: The menarche. *Adolescence, 11,* 703–10.

Gilligan, C. (1977). In a different voice: Women's conception of self and morality. *Harvard Education Review, 47,* 481–517.

Gilligan, C. (1984). *In a different voice: Psychological theory and women's development.* Cambridge, MA: Harvard University Press.

Hall, S. (1989). Ideology. In E. Barnouw (Ed.), *International encyclopedia of communications* (Vol. 2). New York: Oxford University Press.

Havens, B., and Swenson, I. (1988). Imagery associated with menstruation advertising targeted toward adolescent women. *Adolescence, 23,* 89–97.

Havens, B., and Swenson, I. (1989). A content analysis of educational media about menstruation. *Adolescence, 24,* 901–7.

Hayne, D. (1987, April). Bodyvision? *Mademoiselle,* p. 213.

Helping teens through adolescence. (1994, June). *Health News* [Online], *12*. Available: Lexis/Nexis.

Holsti, O. R. (1969). *Content analysis for the social sciences and humanities*. Reading, MA: Addison-Wesley.

Horney, K. (1926). The flight from womanhood. *International Journal of Psychoanalysis, 7*.

Ianni, F. A. (1989, May). Providing a structure for adolescent development. *Phi Delta Kappan*, pp. 673–82.

Jacobs-Brumberg, J. (1997). *The body project*. New York: Random House.

Jennings-Walstedt, J., Geis, F., and Brown, V. (1980). Influence of television commercials on women's self-confidence and independent judgment. *Journal of Personality and Social Psychology, 38*, 203–10.

Kaite, B. (1984). *The body and femininity in feminine hygiene advertising*. Unpublished master's thesis, University of Ottawa.

Kane, K. (1996). The ideology of freshness in feminine hygiene commercials. *Journal of Communication Inquiry, 14*, 83–92.

Kilbourne, J. (1987). *Still killing us softly* [Video recording]. Cambridge, MA: Cambridge Documentary Films.

Kissling, E. A. (1996). That's just a basic teenage rule: Girls' linguistic strategies for managing the menstrual communication taboo. *Journal of Applied Communication Research, 24*, 292–309.

Koff, E., and Rierdan, J. (1995). Early adolescent girls' understanding of menstruation. *Women & Health, 22*, 1–18.

Kohlberg, L. (1976). Stages and moralization: The cognitive-developmental approach in theory, research, and social issues. In T. Lickona (Ed.), *Moral development and behavior*. New York: Holt, Rinehart & Winston.

Konopka, G. (1986). *Young girls: A portrait of adolescence*. New York: Harrington Press.

Lerner, H. E. (1976). Parental mislabeling of female genitals as a determinant of penis envy and learning inhibitions in women. *Journal of the American Psychoanalytic Association, 24*, 269–84.

Lien, A. (1979). *The cycling female: Her menstrual rhythm*. San Francisco: W. H. Freeman.

Lott, B. (1981). *Becoming a woman: The socialization of gender*. Springfield, IL: Charles C. Thomas.

Martin, K. A. (1996). *Puberty, sexuality, and the self: Boys and girls at adolescence*. New York: Routledge.

Nazmuh, M. (1984). Age at menarche and the related issue: A pilot study on urban school girls. *Journal of Youth and Adolescence, 13*, 559–67.

Orenstein, P. (1994). *Schoolgirls: Young women, self-esteem, and the confidence gap*. New York: Anchor.

Peirce, K. (1990). A feminist theoretical perspective on the socialization of teenage girls through *Seventeen* magazine. *Sex Roles, 23*, 491–500.

Piaget, J. (1972). Intellectual evolution from adolescence to adulthood. *Human Development, 15*, 1–12.

Pipher, M. (1994). *Reviving Opehlia: Saving the selves of adolescent girls*. New York: Ballantine Books.

Predergast, S. (1989). Girls' experience of menstruation in school. In L. Holly (Ed.), *Girls and sexuality: Teaching and learning*. Philadelphia: Open University Press.

Richins, M. (1991). Social comparison and the idealized image in advertising. *Journal of Consumer Research, 18*, 71–83.

Rodin, J. (1992). *Body traps*. New York: Quill/William Morrow.

Rowland, R. (1995). *It's like a guide to your life: Cultural narratives in teen magazines*. Unpublished master's thesis. University of Oregon.

Standard Rate & Data Service Consumer Media (1997, May).

Steinberg, L. (1985). *Adolescence*. New York: Alfred A. Knopf.

Stern, L. (1991). Disavowing the self in female adolescence. In A. G. Rogers and D. L. Tollman (Eds.), *Women, girls, and psychotherapy*. New York: Harrington Park Press.

Strasburger, V. C. (1995). *Adolescents and the media: Medical and psychological impact*. Thousand Oaks, CA: Sage.

Tan, A. (1979). TV beauty ads and role expectations of adolescent female viewers. *Journalism Quarterly, 56*, 283–88.

Thornburg, H. D. (1975). Adolescent sources of initial sex information. In R. E. Grinder (Ed.), *Studies in adolescence*. London: Collier-Macmillan.

Thuren, B. M. (1994). Opening doors and getting rid of shame: Experiences of first menstruation in Valencia, Spain. *Women's Studies International, 17*, 217–28.

Treneman, A. (1989). Cashing in on the curse: Advertising and the menstrual taboo. In L. Gamman and M. Marshment (Eds.), *The female gaze*. London: Real Comet Press.

Voigt, D. Q. (1984). A tankard of sporting taboos. In R. B. Brown (Ed.), *Forbidden fruits: Taboos and tabooism in culture*. Bowling Green, OH: Bowling Green University Press.

Whisnant, L., Brett, E., and Zegans, L. (1975). Implicit messages concerning menstruation in commercial educational materials prepared for adolescent girls. *American Journal of Psychiatry, 132*, 815–20.

Whisnant, L., and Zegans, L. (1995). A study of attitudes toward menarche in white middle-class adolescent girls. *American Journal of Psychiatry, 132*, 809–14.

Williamson, J. (1978). *Decoding advertisements: Ideology and meaning in advertising*. London: Marion Boyars.

Wolf, N. (1991). *The beauty myth: How images of beauty are used against women*. New York: William Morrow.

Yanni, D. (1990). The social construction of women as mediated by advertising. *Journal of Communication Inquiry, 14*, 71–80.

8

*Kathy Brittain McKee and
Carol J. Pardun*

Face-ism Reconsidered: Facial Prominence and Body Emphasis of Males and Females in Magazine Advertising

The term *face-ism* was first devised in 1983 by Archer et al. for their analysis of gender illustrations in a variety of visual media. Archer et al. defined *face-ism* as "the relative prominence of the face in a photograph, drawing, or other depiction of a person" (p. 726). The researchers argued that men and women were given significantly different ratios when pictured in drawings or photographs. Men were shown with an emphasis on their faces, which the researchers interpreted to mean that men were regarded as more intelligent and rational. Women were depicted with an emphasis on their bodies, which the researchers interpreted to mean that women were depicted in a more physical, less intellectual manner. In essence, the illustrations were read to say that women had bodies; men had brains. However, the research described in this chapter sought to determine if a change in such depiction had occurred in the ten-year period following the original study. This analysis employed systematic content analysis of gender depictions in advertisements in sampled issues of *Good Housekeeping, Time*, and *Sports Illustrated* from 1983 to 1993. Statistical analysis of the contents revealed that there were significant differences in the depictions of male and female images, but analysis showed a different direction in the difference in advertisements in *Time* and *Good Housekeeping* than had previous studies. Overall, in these two magazines, women models were depicted with a greater "face-ism" index than were men models. The advertisements within these two periodicals were then reexamined to discover what patterns existed between gender representation and the products that were advertised and what patterns were apparent when analyzing genders and numbers of models within the ads, such as females together, females alone, males and females together, and so on. Such an analysis revealed that the measurement of face-ism alone was insufficient to explain the dominant or subordinate role of models within the ad. Apparently within these magazines, a large "face" image was not a visual indicator of mental acuity or social role, as Archer et al. had concluded. Instead, a large face was more likely used as a palette for demonstration of cosmetic enhancement or hair coloring. The use of a single quantitative index as a standard of social role measurement was therefore questioned.

GENDER PORTRAYALS IN MEDIA

The portrayal of men and women in various media has been analyzed by a number of researchers, many of whom have concluded that media portrayals of both men and women tend to fall into the stereotyped "traditional" roles. (For an excellent review of early research, see Courtney and Whipple, 1983; for more recent research, see Klassen, Jasper, and Schwartz, 1993; Robinson, 1994.) Courtney and Lockeretz (1971) examined eight magazines published during the week of April 18, 1970, and coded 729 advertisements. They found that only 12 percent of the ads showed women in working roles. When men appeared with women, the men tended to be in nonworking roles, and women were rarely shown interacting with other women. Klassen, Jasper, and Schwartz summarized the magazine studies: "Like the general-readership magazine studies, examinations of advertisements in magazines targeted specifically at female and male audiences, such as *Good Housekeeping* and *Sports Illustrated*, concluded that women frequently appeared in traditional stereotypical roles" (1993, p. 31). In what has come to be regarded as a seminal study of the visual stereotypes often afforded such photographic portrayals, sociologist Erving Goffman (1976) offered a frame analysis of advertising portrayals of men and women in his monograph *Gender Advertisements*. Goffman used a randomly selected collection of magazine advertisements to analyze position and expression used within the illustrations. Goffman argued that such display informed viewers about acceptable gender behavior, role positions, and stereotypes.

Dodd et al.'s (1989) study supported Goffman's idea of the subordination of women in media portrayals with their study that argued that the photographs of women in magazines show them with their mouths open more than men, "presumably portraying less serious expressions" (p. 325), concluding that the portrayal of women's facial expressions in the media is "consistent with sex role stereotypes" (p. 331). One of Whipple's (1992) more recent studies reviewed the content analysis research that has examined gender in advertising. He concluded that investigating "the increasing numbers of cases of women portrayed as sex objects and in fashion roles in products targeted specifically to women is a trend worth following. Currently, it appears that these role portrayals are gaining acceptability for advertising products which are designed to enhance appearance, physical attractiveness and sex appeal" (p. 139). Bernt (1995) conducted a content analysis of 164 trade periodicals to determine if the racial and gender diversity reflected in photographs, bylines, and staffs were correlated with the racial and gender diversity of the 1990 labor force. Males were over-represented in mastheads and bylines, and whites and males were over-represented in photography. Advertising photos, however, were less biased against females and people of color than were editorial photographs. A comparison of the portrayal of men and women on television commercials broadcast in the 1950s and those broadcast in the 1980s conducted by Allan and Coltrane (1996) found a change in the depiction of women, moving toward a diversity of occupations and lessened depictions of women as parents, but found little change in the depiction of men, either occupationally or as parents.

Several recent studies have linked exposure to images within advertising with subsequent attitudes of gender role stereotyping. Lafky et al. (1996) found some differences in gender role expectations between high school students exposed to stereotypical images of women in advertising and those who viewed nonstereo-typic images. They concluded that "even brief exposure to advertisements that rely upon gender stereotypes reinforces stereotypes about gender roles" (p. 385). MacKay and Covell (1997) studied the impact of advertising portrayals on perceived attitudes toward appropriate roles for women. Using a sample of ninety-two undergraduate white middle-class students, the researchers found strong evidence linking viewing sex-image advertisements and attitudes supportive of sexual aggression and a lower acceptance of feminism. Interestingly, however, only a few researchers have investigated the specific products that such magazine advertisements convey. Ferguson, Kreshel, and Tinkham (1990) examined 628 ads from *Ms.*, showing that almost one-third of the advertisements "promote products generally perceived to be 'harmful' " (p. 48). The researchers organized the products from the study into ten categories: alcohol, cigarettes, entertainment, autos, feminine hygiene, nonprofit groups, cosmetics, institutional ads, clothing, and medicine. They also examined the relationship between product category and the female models' "interpersonal sex roles" (p. 44) and found "substantial levels of sexism are, nevertheless, evident in *Ms.* magazine's advertising content" (p. 48). Reid, King, and Kreshel (1995) examined 418 cigarette and alcohol ads published in eleven magazines and found significant differences in the depiction of blacks' and whites' social interactions and roles in such ads. They wrote: "Taken together, the differences here suggest a world where blacks place importance on leisure while whites place importance on work, where black males and females are most often together while white males manage independently of women" (p. 885).

FACE-ISM INVESTIGATED

The issue of face-ism is one method that a variety of researchers have used to examine gender depiction in various media settings. In the initial study, Archer et al. (1983) advocated the face-ism index because it was easy to measure, it had a high level of reliability, and it could be used no matter how large the model appeared relative to the picture as a whole (p. 726). The larger the face-ism index was (with a maximum of 1.00), the more the photograph emphasized the head; conversely, the smaller the index number (with a minimum of 0.00), the more the photo emphasized the body. Archer et al. reported index results from five studies. In the first, analysis of 1,750 photos in magazines and news-papers resulted in a mean index for men of 0.65 and a mean index for women of only 0.45. Study 2 looked at cross-national photos and found a face-ism effect in every culture examined. Study 3 examined photos throughout history and again found a face-ism effect, although it was not as distinct as found in the first study. Finally, studies 4 and 5 used experimental measures to test for the face-ism effect, and again, a different face-ism index for males and females was found. Archer et al. conclude their research by stating that the findings of the face-ism phenomenon "suggest that perceived intellectual (and other) qualities may be significantly and favorably affected by something as simple as the rel-ative prominence of the person's face" (p. 732).

During the past decade, several researchers have attempted to clarify and further investigate the findings of the Archer et al. study. Sparks and Fehlner (1986) examined news photographs published in *Time* and *Newsweek* magazines during a twenty-two-week period preceding the November 1984 presidential elections. They found a statistically significant difference in the face-ism index of men (mean = 0.64) and women (mean = 0.58) across all occupations but found that within occupational categories depicted, there was no difference in the index of men and women. Additionally, they found that pictorial represen-tation of female vice-presidential candidate Geraldine Ferraro actually had a larger face-ism index (mean = 0.63) than vice-presidential candidate George Bush (mean = 0.52). Dodd et al. (1989) also investigated gender depiction in *Time* and *Newsweek* by analyzing the cover photos used by the newsmagazines. They found there was no significant difference in the face-ism index of men and women pictures on the covers, with a male mean = 0.58 and a female mean = 0.53. Again, however, they found a significant difference between different portrayals of social roles pictured, with those in a public official social role having the largest face-ism index than other roles. However, they concluded that "gender was dramatically related to social role" (p. 328), with males pictured in the public official social role more than 97 percent of the time.

Copeland (1989) looked to prime-time television to determine if there were differences in the face-ism index of males and females within entertainment programming. He studied ten-minute segments of fourteen prime-time programs from CBS, NBC, ABC, and Fox selected from a two-week period to select single shots of only one person. Those images were then coded for age and gender, and the actual mean face-to-body ratio at the end of each camera shot was measured. The mean for women (mean = 0.41) was significantly different from that of men (mean = 0.47), indicating that men are shot from a closer perspec-tive. However, the difference shifted directions when different cameras were used. "Contrary to expectation, women appear in tighter framing in single camera than in multiple camera programs and for men the reverse is true" (p. 213). He concluded that "face-ism in prime-time entertainment programming appears to be as prevalent as it is in other media" (p. 213). While not specifically a face-ism index analysis, Kolbe and Albanese (1996) investigated the body characteristics of the sole males depicted in the ads of at least one-quarter page size or larger in male-oriented magazines. Their analysis of ads appearing in *Business Week, Esquire, GQ, Playboy, Rolling Stone*, and *Sports Illustrated*, during 1993, revealed that in all but *Business Week* the majority of advertisements of men contained "full body" or "knees up" depictions. The *Business Week* models with men as "head and full shoulders" "clearly exemplify depictions intended to suggest competency," the researchers asserted (p. 8).

RESEARCH QUESTIONS

The initial purpose of this analysis was to examine photographs and drawings found in full- or two-page advertisements in three contemporary magazines to determine if there were significant differences in the face-ism index between gender and between the magazines. Based on the findings of the previous face-ism studies, this chapter addressed the following research hypotheses:

H1: There will be a significant difference in the face-ism index for males, females, and unknown-gender models in the sampled advertisements in all three magazines during the time frame sampled.

H2: There will be a significant difference in the face-ism index for males and females in the sampled advertisements for each magazine sampled.

METHODOLOGY

This chapter employed systematic content analysis of full- and two-page and cover advertisements in sampled 1983–1993 issues of three magazines: *Time*, the circulation-leading newsmagazine; *Good Housekeeping*, the magazine that leads women's magazines in advertising revenue; and *Sports Illustrated*, the leading sports magazine in both circulation and revenue (Agee, Ault, and Emery, 1994, p. 154). The January and July issues of *Good Housekeeping* were analyzed, yielding 881 advertisements with 1,048 models. The first-weekly issues of the months of January, April, July, and October were randomly sampled for *Time* and *Sports Illustrated*; more months were selected for these magazines than for *Good Housekeeping* to compensate for the comparatively smaller number of advertisements present in these two publications. These three magazines were selected to allow for analysis of advertising geared to a predominantly female, male, and mainstream audience. The ten-year time period reflected the ten-year period of publication following the initial Archer et al. study.

For this analysis, figures within the advertisements were coded for apparent

Figure 8.1
Face-ism Index—Illustration 1

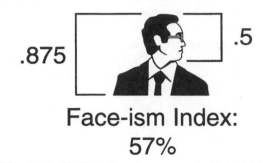

.875   .5

Face-ism Index:
57%

The head size of 0.5 inches in this illustration when compared with the total figure size of 0.875 inches yields a face-ism index of 0.57, indicating there is greater concentration on the head in the image than on the model's body.

gender, with figures categorized as male, female, or unknown; and amount of body shown as categorized into one of five categories: head only; head and partial body; partial body with no head; full body; hands only. Additionally, figures were measured using a standard inch ruler to measure the face-ism index. The index measures the ratio between the distance from the top of the head to the lowest part of the chin of the figure with the distance from the top of the head to the lowest part of the figure's body (Figures 8.1 and 8.2 explain the index procedure). All models appearing in the advertisements were coded, regardless of apparent age.

For the secondary analysis of *Time* and *Good Housekeeping* advertisements, the gender and numerical characteristics of models were addressed, and the product categories of the ads were coded. Initially, coding of models allowed for various racial/ethnic groups, but analysis showed so few people of color that such coding was not used in analysis. Models were coded as follows: man or woman alone; men and women; two or more women; or two or more men.

Categories for the product analysis were: services (which included nonprofit groups such as the Red Cross as well as Visa credit); food; autos; electronics; medicine; health and beauty aids (including cosmetics, shampoo, and deodorant); entertainment (including movies and television programs); household products (which included such items as furniture polish and detergent); cigarettes; clothing; household furnishing such as furniture; and alcohol.

ANALYSIS OF FACE-ISM IN SELECTED
ADVERTISEMENTS

A total of 2,546 figures found in the advertisements were analyzed. Across the three magazines, depictions of males exceeded that of females, with a total

Figure 8.2
Face-ism Index—Illustration 2

.5

3.5

Face-ism Index:
14%

The head size of 0.5 inches in this illustration when compared with the total figure size of 3.5 inches yields a face-ism index of 0.14, indicating there is greater concentration on the model's body in this image than on her head.

of 1,334 males, 1,129 females and 83 unknown-gender depicted in the advertisements. Table 8.1 shows the distribution of men, women, and unknowns for the individual magazines. Overwhelmingly, the most common depiction showed the model's head with partial body, such as a head-and-shoulders photo (N = 1,368). The second most common image was a full-body photograph. This was true for both genders. This supports the conclusions of the statistical analysis of the face-ism indexes.

Investigation of the first hypothesis indicated there was a significant difference in the gender face-ism index means, but the direction of face-ism found in this analysis was different from previous studies. (Table 8.2 contains the face-ism means by gender in each magazine.) Here, females were shown with more face and head than were males. The first ANOVA (Analysis of Variance) investigating the significance of magazine, gender, and the interaction of magazine and gender revealed two significant effects, gender ($f = 3.44$, $p < 0.032$) and the

Table 8.1
**Number of Models Portrayed in *Time*, *Good Housekeeping*, and *Sports Illustrated*
Full-Page Advertisements**

	Men	Women	Unknown
Good Housekeeping	303	711	33
Time	690	318	32
Sports Illustrated	341	100	18
TOTAL	1,334	1,129	83

interaction of magazine and gender ($f = 3.07$, $p < 0.016$) but found magazine
as a variable not significant ($f = 2.76$, $p < 0.064$). However, after analyzing
the means for the three indexes, it was thought that the "unknown" gender means
could be triggering the main significance in the ANOVA, so a second ANOVA
was conducted, using just the means for the male and female models. This
ANOVA investigated the significance of the male and female gender without
other interactions and found it to be highly significant ($f = 18.37$, $p < 0.00$),
with a male mean of 0.379 and female mean of 0.425.

The second series of ANOVAs demonstrated the differences in gender depictions between magazines. The first, which had tested for differences in overall
indexes between the magazines with no interactions and without testing for
gender differences ($f = 15.27$, $p < 0.00$), revealed that the greatest face-ism
for all models was apparent in *Good Housekeeping*, the magazine that used the
most female models (mean $= 0.435$). A second ANOVA added the factors of
male and female gender and the interaction of magazine and gender to the
individual magazines. It showed a significant difference between magazines
($f = 8.63$, $p < 0.00$) but not between genders ($f = 1.31$, $p < 0.253$) or the
interaction of gender and magazines ($f = 1.98$, $p < 0.139$). Both *Good Housekeeping* and *Time* showed females with more "face" than did *Sports Illustrated*,
which followed the more expected face-ism depictions.

But do the depictions of men and women in *Good Housekeeping* and *Time*
really differ from the traditional stereotypical gender roles? To further investigate their advertising depictions, the ads in *Time* and *Good Housekeeping* were
analyzed for products, gender, and ethnicity of models. Some ads were dropped
from this analysis for several reasons, including large crowd scenes for models,
which made identifying gender and ethnicity impossible. Products that were not
clearly defined in any of the twelve categories were dropped as well. For example, the one dog-food advertisement was dropped from the analysis. A total
of 1,047 were then analyzed.

In all the ads in these two magazines, 1,065 ads featured only white models.
Conversely, only 13 ads in the two magazines featured only black models. Fifty
ads showed black and white models together. The largest category for product

Table 8.2
Face-ism Index Means by Magazine

	Men	Women	Unknown
Good Housekeeping	0.407	0.447	0.472
Time	0.362	0.396	0.595
Sports Illustrated	0.388	0.359	0.370

representation was health and beauty products, which had 268 ads for this category. Of those, 199 had a single female as a model (74.3 percent). Interestingly, there were no ads for health and beauty that featured any black models alone.

Products Advertised

Of the 1,047 ads coded for products, the largest categories were for health and beauty (268, 25.6 percent), food (126, 12 percent), and cigarettes (111, 10.6 percent). The rest of the categories were split more evenly. The least number of ads coded were for household goods, with only 24 ads over the ten-year period (2.3 percent). Table 8.3 shows a complete breakdown of the coded product categories.

Gender Representation

The gender representation was more evenly split than past research has indicated, with about equal numbers of men and women represented. Given *Good Housekeeping*'s mission, that should be no surprise. All-women ads were seen 490 times, all-men ads were shown 335 times, and men and women together in the same ad were seen 212 times.

The Relationship Between Gender and Products

In an advertising context, looking at models alone may have offered an incomplete understanding of what is intended or actually communicated. The products, goods, or services being advertised must also have been considered, and the interplay between model and products in this analysis offered insights into the limitations of the face-ism index as a single measure of gender stereotyping. For example, in these two magazines, even though women models were represented in the ads 68.4 percent of the time, the vast majority of those ads are for health and beauty products. Of the 268 ads for health and beauty, only 7 featured only male models. But in cigarette ads, 67 featured male-only models, whereas only 17 had female-only models. Besides cigarettes, male models were

Table 8.3
Product Representations in Sampled *Good Housekeeping* and *Time* Full-Page Advertisements

	Total	Male Only	Female Only	Male & Female	Male & Male	Female & Female
Services	83	34	10	29	9	1
Food	126	32	42	32	5	15
Autos	84	35	6	33	7	3
Electronics	88	44	16	13	13	2
Medicine	72	18	23	20	3	8
Healthy & Beauty	268	6	199	24	1	38
Entertainment	93	26	22	28	9	8
House Products	52	8	26	10	1	7
Cigarettes	111	48	13	27	19	4
Clothing	46	4	22	10	7	3
Household Goods	24	4	8	6	2	4

shown mostly in auto and electronic ads, whereas women were more likely than men to be seen in food ads and clothing ads.

CONCLUSION

According to the sampled advertisements, face-ism was still an indicator of the different ways men and women are presented through illustrations—even ten years after the initial Archer et al. (1983) findings. However, face-ism, at least within two of these magazine's advertisements, had shifted its presence. No longer did the mainstream magazine *Time* just offer "women as bodies, men as brains" images as indicated by the face-ism index, and neither did the traditional women's magazine *Good Housekeeping*. The index means for their portrayal in the original Archer study of *Time* advertisements were male = 0.51 and female = 0.39 (p. 728); in this study, the means for both genders in *Time* were smaller than the original female mean index, and females were rendered with more face-ism than were males. However, it also should be noted that the index means for this magazine were markedly smaller than the means reported in the Archer et al. or Dodd et al. studies. They were more similar to those reported by Copeland, which may suggest a trend toward more equal representation of genders in recent years. Table 8.4 offers a comparison of means found in earlier studies with this present research.

However, this research also suggested that the face-ism index alone may be an incomplete measure of role status when used to measure advertising depictions. Other factors, such as the number of images within the total, the product represented by the ad, and the social role depicted by the model must also be

Table 8.4
Comparison of Magazine Face-ism Index to Indexes from Earlier Analyses

Study	Male Index Mean	Female Index Mean
Archer et al. (1983)	0.65	0.45
Sparks and Fehlner (1986)	0.64	0.58
Dodd et al. (1989)	0.58	0.53
Copeland (1989)	0.47	0.41
McKee and Pardun (1994)	0.38	0.43

considered. For example, the growing number of advertisements featuring women models did not necessarily mean that women are finding different roles in advertising or society. Still 33.8 percent of the total number of coded ads that featured women models were for health and beauty products. Although the readership of *Good Housekeeping* was heavily skewed toward women, nearly half of the ads coded were from *Time*, and many other products were represented in both *Time* and *Good Housekeeping*. If the 268 health and beauty ads were removed from the sample, then males dominate the visuals, with 334 (32 percent) ads having only male models in them and only 243 (23 percent) ads having women in them. This was a reversal of the percentages of women in ads when looking at the total number of ads in the original sample. While a majority of ads in *Good Housekeeping* featured a lone woman, even in this women's magazine, about a third of the ads showcased male models only. With readership for *Good Housekeeping* measured at only 11 percent male ("Consumer Magazine," 1991), it seemed incongruous to have nearly three times as many ads with males in them than the readership of the magazine.

The frequent use of women in health and beauty and household product categories may have indicated that the traditional social paradigm for women was perpetuated in advertisements. Was it more cerebral for a woman to be shown full-face in an ad for cosmetics than to be shown full-figured standing in an office setting? Probably not. Whether women or men were shown with their full bodies or just by heads or faces should not be considered out of the context of the product if one sought fully to understand the societal role signified by the ad. For example, according to the paradigm presented by most of these sampled advertising images, women still spent most of their disposable income on clothing and makeup; men still bought the cars and the stereos; women and men interacted for fun, cigarettes, and alcohol; and people of color were still outside the economic mainstream. Within these magazine ads, women used cosmetics; men used machines. Women cooked; men drove. Women cleaned; men smoked.

It was the sports magazine that characterized males and females in the most familiar face-ism manner. Yet while the mean index for males was slightly larger in *Sports Illustrated* than the mean for females, again, the means were smaller than those found in the earlier studies. Whether this treatment of females and males within the advertisements was deliberate or unintentional, the sports magazine's ads showed more of women's bodies than did the newsmagazine or the women's magazine.

This analysis of face-ism within three leading magazines offered evidence that a visual change in depiction of genders within magazine advertising was occurring. The findings of this analysis were in sharp contrast to the means found by earlier analyses; at least in two of these three magazines, the depictions of males and females had changed in visual presentation. Whether this indicated a shift in perception of gender roles or merely changes in advertising fads will require broader research.

REFERENCES

Agee, W. K., Ault, P. H., and Emery, E. (1994). *Introduction to mass communications* (11th ed). New York: HarperCollins.

Allan, J., and Coltrane, S. (1996). Gender displaying television commercials: A comparative study of television commercials in the 1950s and 1980s. *Sex Roles, 35* (3–4), 185–203.

Archer, D., Iritani, B., Kimes, D. D., and Barrios, M. (1983). Face-ism: Five studies of sex differences in facial prominence. *Journal of Personality and Social Psychology, 45*, 725–35.

Bernt, J. P. (1995, August). *Race and gender diversity in trade and business periodicals as reflected in editorial and advertising images, mastheads, and bylines.* Paper presented to the Magazine Division of the Association for Education in Journalism and Mass Communication, Washington, DC.

Consumer magazine and agri-media rates and data. (1991). *Standard Rate and Data Service*, p. 691.

Copeland, G. A. (1989). Face-ism and primetime television. *Journal of Broadcasting and Electronic Media, 33*, 209–14.

Courtney, A. E., and Lockeretz, S. W. (1971). A woman's place: An analysis of the roles portrayed by women in magazine advertisements. *Journal of Marketing Research, 8*, 2–5.

Courtney, A. E., and Whipple, T. W. (1983). *Sex stereotyping in advertising*. Lexington, MA: Lexington Books.

Dood, D. K., Harcar, V., Foerch, B. J., and Anderson, H. T. (1989). Face-ism and facial expressions of women in magazine photos. *Psychological Record, 39*, 325–31.

Ferguson, J. H., Kreshel, P. J., and Tinkham, S. F. (1990). In the pages of *Ms.*: Sex role portrayals of women in advertising. *Journal of Advertising, 19* (1), 40–51.

Goffman, E. (1976). *Gender advertisements*. Cambridge, MA: Harvard University Press.

Klassen, M. L., Jasper, C. R., and Schwartz, A. M. (1993). Men and women: Images of their relationships in magazine advertisements. *Journal of Advertising Research, 33*, 30–39.

Kolbe, R. H., and Albanese, P. J. (1996, Winter). Man to man: A content analysis of sole-male images in male-audience magazines. *Journal of Advertising, 25* (4), 1–20.

Lafky, S., Duffy, M., Steinmaus, M., and Berkowitz, D. (1996). Looking through gendered lenses: Female stereotyping in advertisements and gender role expectations. *Journal and Mass Communication Quarterly, 73* (2), 379–388.

MacKay, N. J., and Covell, K. (1997). The impact of women in advertisements on attitudes toward women. *Sex Roles, 36* (9–10), 573–82.

Reid, L. N., King, K. W., and Kreshel, P. J. (1995). Black and white models and their activities in modern cigarette and alcohol ads. *Journalism Quarterly, 71*, 873–86.

Robinson, G. J. (1994). The study of women and journalism: From positivist to feminist approaches. In C. J. Hamelink and O. Linné (Eds.), *Mass communication research: On problems and policies. The art of asking the right questions in honor of James D. Hamelink* (pp. 191–202). Norwood, NJ: Ablex.

Sparks, G. G., and Fehlner, C. L. (1986). Faces in the news: Gender comparisons of magazine photographs. *Journal of Communication, 36*, 70–79.

Whipple, T. W. (1992). The existence and effectiveness of sexual content in advertising. In S. R. Danna (Ed.), *Advertising and popular culture: Studies in variety and versatility* (pp. 134–40). Bowling Green, OH: Bowling Green State University Popular Press.

9

Tom Reichert, Kevin R. Maly, and
Susan C. Zavoina

Designed for (Male) Pleasure: The Myth of Lesbian Chic in Mainstream Advertising

> Lesbian chic. It's oh so acceptable to be a gay girl nowadays. People think it's cute. Got this full picture of lipstick lesbians in their heads like they all resemble Alyssa, while most of them look just like you.
> —Hooper (Dwight Ewell) to Holden McNeil (Ben Affleck) in *Chasing Amy*
> (Miramax Films, 1996)

INTRODUCTION

Lesbian chic is certainly "in" nowadays. Homoerotic images of women in film, television, and other media are hip, hot, and increasingly prevalent. Lately, these images are popping up in mainstream consumer advertising as well (see Figures 9.1 and 9.2). While advertising is not shy about brandishing sexual sizzle and titillation, using homoerotic imagery to sell might be seen as somewhat stunning, given advertising's tendency to promote the ideal, along with its general reluctance to offend mainstream audiences. In a recent Guess ad, two young, blond, female models are seductively positioned with regard to each other and gaze invitingly at the viewer. Versace, no stranger to using hot beefcake in ads, features two naked women "spooning" amidst his Home Signature pillow collection. In yet another Versace ad, the same two women are engaged in a provocative, semiprivate gymnastics routine, clothed only in designer jeans (and white gloves). And the promotional ad for the film *Romy and Michelle's High School Reunion* features Mira Sorvino and Lisa Kudrow "pressing the flesh." These are only a few instances of steamy "girl/girl" ads appearing in mainstream advertising that display the phenomenon of "lesbian chic."

Figure 9.1
Ad for Guess Belts

Courtesy of Guess. Used by permission.

At first glance, these images are relatively incongruent with the literature related to gay/lesbian representation in the media. Numerous voices have argued that portrayals of homosexuals in mainstream media have been relatively non-existent. What few homosexuals seep through are, more often than not, de-meaningly stereotypical and often pathological beings (Gross, 1991; Inness, 1997; Parish, 1993). Schulman (1998) notes a recent stereotype in which homosexuals are portrayed as "a privileged elite with more money and power than heterosexuals," contrary to data that indicate lesbian women and gay men earn less than their heterosexual counterparts (pp. 18–20).

What, then, of the relatively flirtatious and fresh-faced images in the ads examined in this chapter? These models, clearly portrayed in a homoerotic fashion, are surely benign. Or are they?

The purpose of this chapter is to suggest that the meanings embedded in these advertising images have little to do with "lesbianism" per se. Using methods of semiotic analysis, we will argue that these images mirror those of women engaged in "lesbian" sex in mainstream heterosexual pornography. These images

Figure 9.2
Ad for Guess Footwear

Courtesy of Guess. Used by permission.

are powerful and become part of a system in and through which women, both lesbian and heterosexual, become socially constructed objects. Further, these ads function to tell women what they must do to market themselves as consumer goods designed to satisfy the desires of heterosexual males.

SEMIOTICS AND DECONSTRUCTION

Semiotics (or *semiology* as it was first called) derives from the work of Swiss linguist Ferdinand de Saussure (1907/1966). Saussure's work was extended and modified by French writer Roland Barthes (1957/1972) and Italian linguist Umberto Eco (1976). Semiotics, according to Barthes, is the task of interpreting *signs*. For Barthes, visual signs in particular cry out for interpretation. Because they masquerade as straightforward and natural, beyond social force, visual signs especially are freighted with undetected ideological constructs that perpetuate and extend the status quo. Signs, according to Barthes, carry with them the mythologies of a culture. However, the mythic constructs carried by signs are not readily apparent and are all too easily overlooked. These mythic constructs dwell less with the denotative level and more with the connotative level. Eco states that "semiotics is in principle the discipline studying everything which can be used in order to lie" (1976, p. 7). Denotation, that which is on the surface, is seldom the problem. Connotation, however, works by stealth; the connotative potential of the socially constructed sign is hidden. The task of semiology is to deconstruct the sign so that lies may be brought to light.

Three terms are essential to semiotics: *sign, signifier*, and *signified*. The sign is composed of a signifier and a signified. We'll use the picture of a blond woman on a page. The picture, in itself and prior to socially constructed meaning, is a signifier. On one level this picture could be thought of as "merely" denotative, a photographic representation of a woman. Beyond being a representation of a woman, however, social constructs are signified. In the dominant cultures of at least the United States, the image of a blond carries with it a whole series of connotations. We "know" that blonds are "dumb." We remember that "blonds have more fun." We think of Marilyn Monroe and the on-screen antics of her characters when we see the blond woman. And when our thinking is less than clear, we are said to be having a "blond moment." That which is signified by the image of the blond woman (the signifier) consists of all these constructs and more. The sign, then, is the combination of the visual image of the blond (signifier) and the many connotations (the signified) that attach to the image of the blond woman. Barthes, especially in some of his later work (1974/1974) maintained that an innocent denotation ("It's just a picture of a blond woman!") only appears to be the first, the "natural" meaning. However, says Barthes, "denotation is not the first meaning, but pretends to be so . . . it is ultimately no more than the *last* . . . the one which seems to both establish and to close the reading" (p. 7). The *seems* is important here. The appeal to denotation is used to hide the ideological and hegemonic baggage inhering to connotation. It is to attempt to establish that the picture of the blond is only that and nothing more, and it is to attempt to close off any deconstructive efforts. These appeals are essential in any attempt to forestall the inquiry that would expose how the sign perpetuates and extends the values of the status quo.

Barthes and Eco also show that any examination of signs is, of necessity, an examination of the system or systems to which the signs belong. No one sign can be looked at in isolation. As we look at a print advertisement, for instance, we cannot isolate one sign, such as *blond hair*, from the other signs in the ad, nor the ad from other signs and systems of signs extant in the socially constructed world. The ad is a system of many signs embedded in other systems of signs that together operate with and upon one another "like an algebra"— and a complex algebra at that (Barthes, 1957/1972, p. 17).

THE SIGN SYSTEM OF THE "LESBIAN CHIC" AD

In all of the ads described in this chapter, two female models are tightly joined together. In an ad for Guess belts (see Figure 9.1), the models hold hands, and

Figure 9.3
Ad for Guess Jeans

Courtesy of Guess. Used by permission.

their joined hands rest on the breasts of one of the models. The lips of one model are slightly parted. Bellies and breasts are thrust out toward the viewer. Hair is tousled, with the "just got out of bed" look. The models are locked in a sideways hug, the breasts of one pushed against the breasts of the other.

In another Guess ad for jeans, the most prominent model has large, supple breasts accentuated by tight, minimal clothing. Most of the breasts of the model in the foreground are revealed, and the nipple is emphasized and compositionally placed in the focal point of the image. A cross rests directly above her breasts. The model in the back drapes her arms and legs over the model in front. The fingers of the hand in the foreground are spread open in a *V*-shape. The models lean together, head against head (see Figure 9.3).

A Versace jeans ad features one model standing, raring back, the angle of her arms hiding her breasts. She lifts the legs and buttocks of the other model, who cups her hands firmly over her own full, bare breasts. They gaze not at each other but toward the viewer. Hair is wild. Lips are full and prominent. The posture is provocative (see Figure 9.4).

Perhaps the most tame images of this chapter are in a Versace ad. A female couple nest amidst Home Signature pillows. The model's eyes are closed. One

Figure 9.4
Ad for Versace Jeans

Courtesy of KCD Inc. Used by permission.

model has parted lips, and the lips of the other are full and pouty. The women cuddle like a pair of spoons and are covered with pillows. Only their bare shoulders are revealed. Nudity must surely lurk beneath (see Figure 9.5).

Even a verbal description of these signs should suggest that most common system of signs, the signified of which is *SEX*. Svelte, tall bodies, wild, blond hair, full, parted lips, and thrusting, prominent breasts have long been recognized as signifiers that tell the observer that women are desirable objects, playthings, sex kittens (Lambiase et al., 1999; Solomon, Ashmore, and Longo, 1992). The ads in this chapter do not, however, give the viewer a lone woman as toy; the viewer is offered two women for the price of one. And, as an added bonus, these women are positioned in a manner that Ellensweig (1992) would define as homoerotic. Although Ellensweig discusses the homoerotic image, the signifier, within the context of photography, it is directly applicable to advertising images. Homoerotic signifiers depict desire and affection between members of the same sex with an erotic tension that "lurk[s] like a phantom in the background" (p. 73). He goes on to say that homoerotic images aren't necessarily

Figure 9.5
Ad for Versace Home Signature Pillows

Courtesy of KCD Inc. Used by permission.

overtly sexual, but the erotic potential is present. What, then, is the signified of these homoerotic signifiers?

One is tempted to move quickly to conclude that what we have in these ads is lesbian sex. But a semiotic analysis forces us to look at sign systems. Lesbian sex is a common element in both soft- and hard-core pornography. Women having sex with women is a standard narrative device for heterosexual titillation. Williams (1989) calls it the "girl/girl number." Lesbian sex in mainstream pornography is even listed as an important convention for stimulating male arousal in Ziplow's (1977) manual for would-be pornography producers, *The Film Maker's Guide to Pornography*. In addition, feminists have long held that such pornography is produced by males, distributed by males, and is primarily consumed for male pleasure (for review, see Linz and Malamuth, 1993). As such, women are presented as sexual objects whose primary importance is wish fulfillment for men, and men's ideas and men's perceptions of what sex should be like constitute the status quo. Further, research has shown that men find images of "lesbian erotica" particularly arousing (Adams, Wright, and Lohr, 1996; Gillan and Frith, 1977). These signifiers rarely, if ever, signify the "girl/girl number" as anything more than a prelude to the heterosexual encore—as constructed by the heterosexual male. This construct is documented by Eliason (1997), who found that college-aged males are tolerant and accepting of bisexuality in women. That "bisexuality" means the "girl/girl number" is made manifest by these males reporting a desire to date a woman who would be open to the possibility of a ménage à trois with another woman.

Confirming this equation, Duncker (1995), a lesbian feminist, argues that "lesbianism" in male oriented, mainstream pornography is "a heterosexual spectator sport." She finds the separation between lesbian lives and the representation of lesbian sexuality in pornography to be unequivocal: "Narratives of all these erotic reviews insist that Lesbians are everywhere, that any woman can be a lesbian and that this is a simple sexual desire like any other" (p. 12). Inness (1997) finds that even in the editorial content of mainstream women's magazines, lesbianism is viewed either as accidental or as a simple sexual adventure. In this system, the lesbian is reduced to an object of sexual encounter. This sexual encounter is, again, for the benefit of the heterosexual male and his fantasy life. Inness argues that in the "landscape of women's magazines . . . the lesbian body frequently loses all association with real lesbians" (p. 58). The model/signifiers, she says, "fail to look like any lesbian I have ever encountered, although I recognize that some exist" (p. 65). Viewers are given "models who look stereotypically heterosexual pretending to be lesbians." What is signified by these images is "an implicit understanding that these are not 'real' lesbians." These sanitized lesbians become a domesticated commodity that offers the male viewer "titillation without threat" (pp. 65–66).

The gaze of the "lesbian" signifiers and the environments of the ads reinforce the offering. In most of the ads in this chapter, both models together gaze out at the viewer with an invitation to join in on the fun. The models do not gaze at each other with anything close to understanding or shared intimacy that might be expected in a dyadic lesbian encounter. The gaze is accompanied by full, red lips that make the women seductive and seemingly eager to provide the third-party viewer with steamy sexual adventure. The environments of the ads are sparse and unidentifiable and provide a secluded space that isolates the two women for the pleasure of the viewer. Little text, outside of the designers' names, is visible to complicate the system of signs being presented. The hegemonic discourse, the "simple" offering of the "girl/girl number" for heterosexual male consumption, remains undetected. Ample space is created for the innocent reply that "they're just a couple of pretty girls."

This cry of innocence can be well defended by pointing out that these are ads that promote products for women, and heterosexual women at that. But why the sexual innuendo? Conventional wisdom, of course, tells us "sex sells." Surely the message of the presentation is that if a woman purchases these designer products, some of the models' appeal will accrue to the buyer. But to what end? For the woman's self? Or for the attraction and ultimate pleasure of men? The kinship that the sign systems of these ads share with the "girl/girl numbers" proffered by soft- and hard-core pornography for consumption by heterosexual males makes clear that what we have here is, functionally, an instruction manual for women that advises women how to market themselves as consumer objects. "Here, girls, this is how to make yourselves marketable to (heterosexual) men: Buy these goods and you will be transformed into the ultimate porn fantasy of those hot heterosexual men. You too, girl, can achieve that ultimate success: to become a man's possession. And you will like it."

One could argue at this point that there is little difference between "lesbian chic" ads and those that feature a lone female model or a woman on the arm of a man. Indeed, these as well function as marketing manuals for women. And they are, by and large, placed in women's magazines that are themselves guides that instruct women, albeit indirectly, through connotation, in how to successfully offer themselves up as consumer goods. Yes, women are taught to objectify themselves in these lone-female and male-female sign systems. The difference between these and the "lesbian chic" ads is one of degree and perhaps one of kind. Lesbian chic ads serve to further the objectification process already in place, but they also publicly do what was formerly done in the semiprivacy of pornography—they add lesbians to the public commodity offering. A difference of kind occurs in that, formerly, mainstream ads taught women that a relatively garden variety of thin, girl-next-door sexiness was the packaging necessary for the successful sale of one's self to a male. The lesbian chic phenomenon in mainstream media, however, publicly suggests that one must somehow participate in the packaging portrayed in pornography. Gone now is any suggestion that something like "love" or "romance" might be included in the bargain. The pornographic woman is completely objectified, one in being with the images bought in "adult" bookstores and video arcades. "Take her, fuck her and her girlfriend, smack 'em around some if that's your thing, and then get rid of the both of 'em, 'cause there's always more where they came from. That, my girl, is what a man wants, and that's what you're here to give him."

OTHER READINGS?

Signs, especially visual signs as Barthes pointed out, are subject to multiple readings depending on the systems in which they participate. In a series of focus groups conducted with separate groups of male and female college students, half of the women read the Guess belts ad as a sign of female resistance signifying independence and defiance of male domination. These women saw "lesbian" sex, or bisexual sex between two women, as a sign that women can now "do what they want." The sign systems of the ad offered the message that women are free to make their own decisions and are no longer subjugated to male definitions of female pleasure. Indeed, these young, heterosexual women interpreted these ads as signs of a "hip" resistance movement.

What of lesbians themselves? Duncker (1995) and Inness (1997) are clear that the female images in lesbian chic presentations do not accurately depict lesbians (nor many heterosexual women, for that matter). But as Schulman (1998) points out, "Lesbians . . . have spent lifetimes translating subtext and innuendo in order to have the normative pleasure experience of seeing themselves represented" (p. 18). So while "pseudolesbian images are being used to market to straights," lesbians are adept, from long practice, at personalizing nonlesbian images.

CONCLUSION

Taking our cue from semiotics, we have argued that "lesbian chic" ads present a system of signs that mirrors "lesbian" coupling in soft- and hard-core pornography that is produced for the sexual gratification of heterosexual males. The female signifiers in these ads and in pornography have little to do with the lived lives of real lesbians. The lesbian chic ads share one aspect in common with ads that feature a lone woman or a male/female dyad. Both ad types function as instructional manuals for women, telling them what they must do to market themselves to men. Women are taught to become objects of consumption. Lesbian chic shares in the sign system of heterosexual pornography and thereby functions as hegemonic discourse that tells women that they must become like the pornographic image: a thing to be used, abused, and discarded.

REFERENCES

Adams, H. E., Wright, L. W., and Lohr, B. A. (1996). Is homophobia associated with homosexual arousal? *Journal of Abnormal Psychology, 105* (3), 440–445.

Barthes, R. (1972). *Mythologies* (A. Lavers, Trans.). New York: Hill and Wang. Original work published 1957)

Barthes, R. (1974). *S/Z* (R. Miller, Trans.). New York: Hill and Wang. (Original work published 1974)

Duncker, P. (1995). "Bonne excitation, orgasme assure": The representation of lesbianism in contemporary French pornography. *Journal of Gender Studies, 4* (1), 5–15.

Eco, U. (1976). *A theory of semiotics.* Bloomington: Indiana University Press.

Eliason, M. J. (1997). The prevalence and nature of biphobia in heterosexual undergraduate students. *Archives of Sexual Behavior, 26* (3), 317–26.

Ellenzweig, A. (1992). Gay images in photography: Picturing the homoerotic. In W. R. Dynes and S. Donaldson (Eds.), *Homosexuality and homosexuals in art* (pp. 73–79). New York: Garland.

Gillan, P., and Frith, C. (1977). Male-female differences in responses to erotica. In M. Cook and G. Wilson (Eds.), *Love and attraction* (pp. 461–64). Oxford, England: Pergamon Press.

Gross, L. (1991). Out of the mainstream: Sexual minorities and the mass media. *Journal of Homosexuality, 2* (2), 19–46.

Inness, S. A. (1997). *Lesbian menace: Ideology, identity, and the representation of lesbian life.* Amherst: University of Massachusetts Press.

Lambiase, J. J., Reichert, T., Morgan, S. E., Carstarphen, M. G., Zavoina, S. C., and Callister, M. (1999). Gendered bodies still thrive in (post)modern magazineland. In M. G. Carstarphen and S. Zavoina (Eds.), *Sexual rhetoric: Media perspectives on sexuality, gender, and identity.* Westport, CT: Greenwood.

Linz, D., and Malamuth, N. (1993). *Pornography.* Newbury Park, CA: Sage.

Parish, J. R. (1993). *Gays and lesbians in mainstream cinema: Plots, critiques, casts and credits for 272 theatrical and made-for-television Hollywood releases.* Jefferson, NC: McFarland.

Saussure, F. de (1966). *Course in general linguistics* (W. Baskin, Trans.). New York: McGraw-Hill. (Original work published 1907)

Schulman, S. (1998). The making of a market niche. *Harvard Gay & Lesbian Review, 5* (1), 17–20.

Solomon, M. R., Ashmore, R. D., and Longo, L. C. (1992). The beauty match-up hypothesis: Congruence between types of beauty and product images in advertising. *Journal of Advertising, 21* (4), 23–34.

Williams, L. (1989). *Hard core: Power, pleasure, and the "frenzy of the visible."* Berkeley: University of California Press.

Ziplow, S. (1977). *The film maker's guide to pornography.* New York: Drake.

10

Elizabeth Dietz

"That Undefinable Whatever": Selling Virginity

> Now I wish to introduce the following idea. Between the age limits of nine
> and fourteen there occur maidens who, to certain bewitched travelers, twice
> or many times older than they, reveal their true nature which is not human,
> but nymphic (that is, demoniac); and these chosen creatures I propose to
> designate as "nymphets."
>
> —Nabokov, *The Annotated Lolita*

INTRODUCTION

The narrator of Vladimir Nabokov's *Lolita*, Humbert Humbert, speaks as the
watcher, and more particularly the lover, of young girls. Looking is the mode
through which Humbert customarily enjoys his infatuation with "nymphets."
Despite his abduction and possession of *Lolita*, his narrative returns again and
again to linger on moments of verbal looking—hovering almost orgiastically
over every seen and unseen detail. Yet it is obvious as well that seeing Lolita
through the text, or rather the "nymphet" within the adolescent Dolores whom
he christens Lolita, is far from straightforward. It involves the necessity of ap-
prehending some ineffable, undefinable element ("Certain mysterious characteristics, the fey grace, the elusive, shifty, soul-shattering, insidious charm"
[Nabokov, 1970, p. 19]), a charm that is so elusive that Humbert claims it
functions as a demonic attraction. He cannot identify what he sees—and here,
as in photography, seeing is akin to desiring—although his description promises
to "limit" "reveal" and "designate" precisely those essential qualities by which
the nymphet is known. Here and elsewhere in *Lolita*, the title character is pic-

tured for us repeatedly yet appears only incompletely; Humbert's feverish encounters with nymphets in the park, for instance, yield at different times a foot, slim bare arms, the strap of a roller skate, auburn ringlets, but never the whole girl (p. 22). Humbert's apparently perverse love of young girls employs the mythical connotation of virginity as the limit of what one can see, the place where vision turns back at some "undefinable whatever," to quote Steve Mills from *The Brooke Book* (Shields, 1978), one of the photographers who made Brooke Shields's image as the child-woman a ubiquitous Lolita image for late twentieth-century American culture.

Photographs that situate young girls as objects of desire may be, at times, challenging or downright distasteful. Yet what is manifested in these photos, this chapter argues, is not a desire for a virgin or any other material object but the production of desire by the cultural myth of virginity. And this mythology in turn conceals its own ideological interests—interests that subject the general population of consumers to the complicated pleasures of looking at the virginal, purchasing items that promise to convey some of its mythic qualities. Ultimately it is the elusive cultural connotations behind this mythology, not the intrinsic qualities of the photographic image itself, that powers its consumer appeal. This chapter will attempt to show how and why photographic images of virgins obscure their origins in a powerful cultural fantasy—a fantasy that surprisingly links the virginal (that which cannot be sold or even fully represented in a salable object) with consumer society.

THE VIRGINITY MYTH IN ADVERTISING

Simone de Beauvoir's landmark work on the cultural construction of femininity, *The Second Sex* (1983), curiously echoes Humbert's stance as a fascinated observer of virginity.

Virginity is a myth . . . the virgin would seem to represent the most consummate form of the feminine mystery; she is therefore its most disturbing and at the same time its most fascinating aspect. (p. 154)

In their work on the uses of virginity in perfume advertising, Ventada Boyd and Marilyn Robitaille (1994) explore Simone de Beauvoir's sense that the image of the virgin is at once innocent and mysterious: An ad for Esteé Lauder's Beautiful perfume pictures a bride as "the epitome of the virginal young woman. Her eyes are modestly downcast; makeup is understated; her elegant dress, although lowcut, has puffed sleeves and a ruffled skirt. . . . She is unadorned with jewelry except for classic pearl earrings" (p. 51). The recent television ads for Beautiful repeat that archetype with models who are simply dressed and presented in a natural setting. (Nudity, of course, is a more "natural" sign altogether in Hamilton's collections.) The other elements of the picture continue to code her as an innocent. The more physically adult woman in this case, one who must be dressed in the ads, is often accompanied by young children: The model's overall impression of purity suggesting that, rather than giving birth to them, these (usually girl) children are her natural companions. The virginal woman here is a rare distillation of the repeated signs of innocence that surround her. Her purity belies her adult physique in the advertisement, which carefully erases its ties to manufactured goods.

As de Beauvoir points out, such an image is the creation of the photographer (or the commercial filmmaker) utilizing a cultural myth; the model's simplicity, her surroundings, are carefully staged for the camera to produce an appearance of innocence. An innocence that not only replaces or masks, with its guise of passivity, an artificial product that takes on the attributes of this created archetype, but that represents its value as a salable commodity. That is, the virginal attribute is not valuable only as a set of associations that contribute to the value of the perfume. Rather, the perfume is valuable (and the ad effective) because it can confer an aura of purity—yet that aura of purity is something that the ad itself has created. Here again is the "ineffable" quality of the virginal, a myth that seems to have been generated without a point of origin—which has, seemingly, a virgin birth. While virginity seems here to have no fundamental relation to its commercial, artificial setting, this chapter suggests that it is the operation of the myth itself that acts to disguise its own origins in, and as, commerce. And it does so through the visual rhetoric of virginity, a rhetoric that signifies rarity and above all naturalness by carefully distancing its product from the ordinary means of production.

THE RHETORIC OF THE VIRGINAL IMAGE

Innocence

David Hamilton's *The Age of Innocence* (1995), a photo collection of nude or seminude young girls roughly between the age of nine and fourteen, features softly lit models in anonymous surroundings. The photos are accompanied by a high-toned yet erotic narrative that laments the inevitable progression their subjects will make from innocence to sexual experience. This collection recently made news headlines when its sale at the national chain of Barnes & Noble bookstores caused local protests across the United States. It features the same strategy of looking and not seeing offered by Humbert Humbert's narrative.

While the publication of *The Age of Innocence* appears to be an isolated incident of a work of "soft" pornography passing into the regular market for books, and thus becoming available to consumers at large, a look at the film and advertising career of child-star Brooke Shields (and later echoes like Kate Moss or the recent cinematic remake of *Lolita*, banned in the United States) makes that explanation less plausible. Images of the child-woman often circulate profitably and freely in society, for whom they have a peculiar attraction: Barnes & Noble continues to sell Hamilton's work, despite the protests of many local groups of book buyers. In this collection, as in *Lolita*, there is a kind of suavely wrought erotic frustration that almost passes (as it does for Humbert) for satisfaction. In a specific example from Hamilton's book an anonymous girl looks directly at the camera, frowning slightly. She is seated on a rough rug, arms crossed under her breasts, legs more loosely crossed with one knee raised; her labia are clearly visible in the shadow of her thigh. This particular shot, which also exists in Hamilton's earlier collection, is repeated at least six times in *The Age of Innocence*. Other variations include a nude girl with a garment partially obscuring the genitals, or girls turned slightly away from the camera so that a direct view of their genitals have been obscured. This repeated image comes to represent a motif of virginity, that this chapter will explore.

Like all pictures, this image is and is not "about" its subject, the girl whom Hamilton has chosen to photograph. Its meaning is not predetermined by the particular girl it pictures, an individual who has a proper name, favorite foods, and so on. Instead, the photo's meaning is constructed by the photo's pictorial composition, its place in the collection, the social and visual codes surrounding both the subject of the photo (the virgin) and the photo itself as a particular type of object (a device for seeing, remembering, acquiring).

That the girl is both turned away and open, available, to give one example, sets up a tension between her knowledge and her ignorance—does she know what she is doing?—which we try to read through signs that point either to her apparent age or to her innocence. But because both types of signs are present (the sexually provocative, on the one hand, and the child's seeming disengagement from her own sexuality), it is possible to see in this pose the oxymoron of Hamilton's title: an age of innocence. Where age is intuitively linked to experience, age and innocence cannot be said to coexist. In a preface written by poet Liliane James, this paradoxical quality is celebrated as virginity's identifying mark. "These opposites," writes James, "perfectly reflect the prize that all men long for: an untouched female and an experienced, all-caring figure who yields pleasure and familiarity" (Hamilton, 1995, p. 7).

These paired opposites of age and experience suggest a narrative progression; the girl in the photograph will acquire experience, a particular kind of sexual experience with the reader, which will in turn make her image infinitely more familiar. Yet the photo also stalls the narrative's movement toward experience; it deliberately stages this threshold of intimacy without crossing it. In the photo's visual cues, it is not the resolution of this tension in designating the image either "innocent" or "knowing" that gives the viewer pleasure but rather the continued conflict that delays familiarity. The very problem elucidated by Hamilton's antithetical title and uneasy designation of the term "nymphet" for the virgin is one in which the image of a human being resists gender fixing. Formerly neither child nor woman, she would thus become fully acquirable herself, categorized and objectified: woman. But for now, the virgin-girl, or child, what-have-you, remains maddeningly elusive even to the possessor of the photograph. This pleasure, the pleasure derived from the problem of that unfixable, ungraspable child-woman, is opposed to what we would normally take to be the point of these photos, were they pornographic: the viewer's material (and erotically imagined) possession of their subject. But the real pleasure these photographic images offer proceeds from a delay in knowing, (visually) surveying, or (verbally) naming these figures, with the resulting continuation of a desire that has not been fulfilled. The visual rhetoric thus centers around conflicting terms—innocence, experience, and familiarity—that define the image in such a way as to preserve undetected what they claim to discover.

Experience

The experience these photos generate in place of the satisfaction of ownership is a pleasure directed toward a space that is taken to be innocent of meaning or ideological intent, a yet-unconscious psychical space that (in semiotic terms) lacks the awareness to dissemble but is itself, purely and unconditionally. The viewer is invited to inhabit this threshold between childhood and female sexuality, figured as the ultimate self-fulfillment. Hamilton's captions often raise the notion of experience as a threat to that satisfaction. Note, for example, a verse of Dryden's: "He that has me first is blest,/For I may deceive the rest" (Hamilton, 1995, p. 203). The image of the virginal girl suits this pleasure absolutely, because she is apparently untainted by the smallest conscious motives: Even the girls' names, in Hamilton's collection, are replaced by captions containing scraps of traditional verse celebrating virginity as a preconscious state. It is no accident that Sally Mann's corrective attempt at photographing young girls, *At Twelve: Portraits of Young Women* (1988), will instead insist on framing particulars within the photographs—names, family photos, and personal possessions—as a way of resisting or remarking on the problems of such assumptions.

Spectatorship

The photos and the accompanying narrative text linking the photos in these collections offer the ultimate gendering of the virgin (as woman) only as a future event, something that is bound to happen later. And this gendering occurs in Hamilton's collection (or will have occurred) as the virgin's sexual awakening, her first (future) encounter with a male who will "open" and "know" her, repeating and extending the attempt of the spectator to see and know. To mark this conclusion, the photo narrative concludes with two brief sections entitled "First Love" and "The End of Innocence." Captions in these sections alternate between poetic epithets and a narrative imagined to be the girl's speech. It is as if she is emerging into consciousness for the first time. For example, in "First Love" she wonders, "Who is he?":

In her daydreams she thinks about this man who will one day come to her in answer to her questions. Perhaps he is a prince, a man on a white stallion, a man in a military uniform? Perhaps he is the pop-star in the signed photograph on the bedroom wall? Perhaps the boy she passed in the street, good-looking and carefree? Perhaps a man in a blazer, flannels, and straw hat with a cane under his arm? Perhaps the handsome man in those tiny swimming trunks, swaggering along the beach? Perhaps a man, or a boy, naked, like her, and ready. (Hamilton, 1995, p. 212)

Looking at Hamilton's collection, the spectator finds himself "at home," reflected back at himself from a space that has not yet been claimed as feminine or, alternatively, claimed by the masculine. Gender, then, determines the direction of the narrative, its goal, a final moment in which spectator (as subject, possessor, masculine) acquires a stable identity through the fantasy of possessing the image (as objectified, possessed, feminine). Yet because the book never arrives at this moment, gendering these photos is radically uncertain. Instead of marking an end, gender here is being used to support the fashioning of a narrative event for the viewer who progresses toward discovery and (visual) possession of the object. Gender, in other words, is a mobile symbol, used not to define but to loosen and manipulate the identities of spectator and object. The sexuality of both the anonymous girls and their viewers does not signify as itself but masks the underlying effects of this visual dialogue.

Since the photo is coded as a feminine, objectified, aestheticized subject, we may assume it is constructed in relation to a masculine gaze, a masculine possessor. But it is clear also that gender involves multiple and contradictory signs. For instance, this particular combination of openness and closure works because it is embodied in a child on the verge of becoming woman—becoming aware, in a way that children are not represented as being aware of their bodies. What are we to make of this pose? And the fact that this image is not coded as a woman or as a child but belongs to some strange resistant in between? Analagous to the sense that she is in two places at once, the girl in the photo offers us two distinct foci—one is her own eyes, staring back at us. The other is her genitals. As orifices to the hidden interior of her body, both might be said to give us a guarded, withdrawn look; they focus our gaze on the moment of discovery, of unveiling that is always about to happen in these photos. This ambiguity is repeated in the crossed arms and legs that neither fully invite nor curtail our visual investigation.

As a final touch, each photographic image in Hamilton's collection is accompanied by a few lines of verse or prose at the bottom of the page. The caption for this photograph reads, "I know I am almost a woman,/But at heart I am simply a girl" (p. 72). Despite the conventional dynamics of a masterful viewer and the object (of the gaze), this virginal image can undermine the viewer's controlling position. In a word, if this image has been posed for the viewer's pleasure, she is also posing a question that interrogates the viewer: If I am unlocatable, how or where do you find yourself?

Familiarity

This interrogation from within the image might be said to have replaced "experience" as a narrative goal with "familiarity." The prologue cited above establishes the ideal image as "an innocent, untouched female . . . who yields pleasure and familiarity" (p. 7). Familiarity is a curious substitute for the text's original interest in experience. Familiarity is a kind of experience, but one that here indicates a mutual intimacy at odds with a spectator's power. Strangely enough, it is the girl, in James's sentence, who yields familiarity to another. But in the context of the prologue and the book, it is the virgin who must gain sexual familiarity with men. The rhetoric of this introductory passage blurs the distinction between the spectator's pleasure and the pleasure of virginal girls represented in the collection, effectively eliding the onlooker and the image. The viewer's fantasy that a virgin might experience his possession has turned into a double-edged familiarity: Who is the possessor? Who is possessed?

Viewers finds themselves within the virginal image to the point of identifying with it unawares, wishing to forestall their own "fall" from the illusion of naturalness and purity that these images promise to retrieve. These virginal images may engage viewers through a discourse that identifies onlookers as both the preservers and seducers of their objects. But beneath this discourse, they fulfill an ambivalent desire to find oneself in a seemingly pure form. For example, the passage from "First Love," cited above, offers the viewer a split position, as a continued observer and as a participant. Spoken as if it comes from the young girl, the ambivalence registered in this caption registers as strongly for the viewer. Under the guise of reverie, of nostalgia, the reader is led to confuse his (or her) speculations with those of the imagined girl. Who will he be? The man in tiny swim trunks, the boy next door? That is to say, the photo generates a story in which the girl is overheard speculating on her arrival at a sexual identity (in the future). Yet the caption, read aright, makes it clear that such speculations rightfully belong to the viewer and that, after all, it is our own vulnerable state that has been displaced onto the virginal image: "Perhaps a man, or a boy, naked, *like her*, and ready" (emphasis added).

In *The Acoustic Mirror* (1988), Kaja Silverman remarks that images and objects are a kind of mirror that constantly provide us with an opportunity for self-investment. This account draws on Lacan's well-known theory of the mirror stage (see Lacan, 1977). Beginning with the division of mother and child in early childhood, the child arrives at self-perception as a result of the distance between itself and another object. Self-perception is thus "induced through a culturally mediated image which remains irreducibly external, and which consequently implants in the child a sense of otherness at the very moment that identity is gained." Further, "[t]he object thus acquires from the very beginning the value of that without which the subject can never be whole or complete, and for which it consequently yearns. At the same time, the cultural identity of the subject depends upon this separation. Indeed, it could almost be said that to the degree that the object has been lost, the subject has been found" (Silverman, 1988, p. 7).

This theory helps to explain the ambivalence that the spectator brings to the virginal image, as both the seducer who would eliminate the distance from the object and the protector of virginity who would preserve it. What is at stake in these images, though, is the maintenance of an illusion about virginity that hides consciousness from the speaker in the guise of forestalling the loss of innocence figured in the photo. As Liliane James warns in the preface to *The Age of Innocence*, "Virginity is a trauma. . . . Gone is the carefree unconsciousness of childhood; in its place is an intense consciousness of being that brings with it a minefield of unexploded myths" (Hamilton, 1995, p. 7). Ironically, this trauma that James's preface displaces onto the subject of the photographs is actually the spectator's. The "unexploded myths" lie beneath the surface of these images that the spectator both desires and fears to penetrate. The success of these photos, and others like them, lies in their ability to keep these "demonic" truths at bay.

While the images in these photos seem natural, vulnerable, and transparent, this chapter attempts to show that there is nothing natural about the way they are constructed for viewers. The myth of the virginal instead manufactures transparency as a shielding device for the viewer, rendering innocuous a traumatic vision of their own vulnerability. At the same time, the image retains its attraction through the promise of finding oneself reflected by a completely natural object.

Photography, with its indexical resemblance to its subject, is particularly useful in suggesting this immediately and vulnerability. Thus attempts to preserve this "undefinable whatever" through a visual medium are not accidentally paired with photography itself as the preeminent medium for capturing what is real. By examining the interconnection between the concept of the virgin, the aesthetics of the photograph, and the ways in which marketing photos and virgins are similar, this chapter addresses the roots of public interest in this phenomenon.

THE MYTH OF PURITY

Andre Bazin (1967) finds an almost magical power in the photograph's ability to capture the object, seemingly without human intervention or control:

For the first time an image of the world is formed automatically, without the intervention of man. . . . All the arts are based on the presence of man, only photography derives an advantage from his absence. *Photography affects us like a phenomenon in nature, like a flower or snowflake whose vegetable or earthly origins are an inseparable part of their beauty.* (p. 50)

Bazin is not alone in wishing that the photograph could indeed perform "naturally," representing for the viewer the ultimate truth of objects unclouded by artistic intent. Susan Sontag reflects a general assumption when she notes that "[p]hotographs are experience captured" (Sontag, 1990, p. 3; see also Kaja Silverman's *The Acoustic Mirror* [1988, pp. 8–13], Susan Sontag's, *On Photography* [1990], and John Berger's *About Looking* [1991] for accounts of photographs' almost magical realism). Moreover, it is impossible, as Bazin says, to critique what is represented so truthfully: "[W]e are forced to accept as real the existence of the object produced" (1967, p. 50). Photographer Sally Mann's portrait collection of young girls, *At Twelve*, offers a revealing look at those assumptions. In many ways, the photos are an antidote to the treasured illusions built into the viewing experience in Hamilton's collection. The photos of twelve-year-old girls in *At Twelve* offer a response not only to the naturalized process through which their subjects are objectified but an essay on the way in which the photographic medium conspires with this imagery by naturalizing the marks of its own artistic composition. That is, the photograph is the medium whose function is analogous to the virginal image: Both operate by presenting the viewer with a seemingly pure, unadorned image of the thing itself.

Each of Mann's subjects is drawn from the marginal rural community in Rockbridge County, Virginia, where she grew up. Her subjects, in clothes ranging from everyday wear to their mother's prom dresses, are clearly endangered by the poverty and violence of their surroundings. One child is photographed during the hunting season, standing by a shed from which hang several skinned deer. Another is posed by a tree that mysteriously covers her face. It is their context, rather than their nudity, that makes them vulnerable. The viewer's intimacy with these girls is formed through reference to their real social and economic environment rather than the abstract ideal of nude beauty. Since viewers can only accept a position of mastery along with responsibility for their surroundings, the viewing experience is complicit and uncomfortable—observers become witnesses. The same virginal elusiveness is part of each picture, yet both narrative and image work to dispel any sense that greater familiarity with these children would bring comfort. An early caption reading "[W]hat knowing watchfulness . . . at once guarded, yet guileless" (Mann, 1988, p. 14) might have been lifted from Hamilton's collection. And yet a few pages later: "I grew to love those three children in the mournful, deficient way that one loves those beyond reach. As their lives began to unravel, I found them living in the back of a car parked outside an uncle's cabin. Then they were gone" (p. 20).

Despite its dialectic of innocence and experience, these children's world is radically different from that which appears in *The Age of Innocence*. Experience is a brutal enemy present in each of the photos as a threat that has already occurred. Eventually Mann's narrative reveals that Cindy, the girl in the preceding caption, has had a baby. Mann is shown a photo of "her holding the baby and pregnant again" (Mann, 1988, p. 20). The report of this second photo superimposes itself over the first; it is impossible not to read that absent photo's outcome into its visible predecessor. Here the loss of Cindy's innocence becomes fused with the act of looking at the collection; the viewer's gaze is no longer protective but invasive. At the same time, the viewer may be led to associate their own lost innocence with the "lost" photograph of Cindy, the one object that the narrative keeps out of sight.

Mann offers the reality that the work of the photograph is neither transparent nor innocent. Instead, it is predatory, even treating its subjects like puppets to be manipulated and consumed by the camera's (and the spectator's) eye. Many of these images purposely show evidence of having been staged, remarking the presence of the camera. We are told, for instance, that the child posed near the family slaughterhouse was asked to pull her jacket down off her shoulders and spread her legs in a v-shape, echoing the inverted limbs of the deer carcasses that framed her (p. 38). This positioning does not work to place the subject in the idyllic, timeless environment of Hamilton's photos. The viewer's complicity is indistinguishable from the camera's cool aestheticizing eye.

Rather than the object's innocence, it is the spectators' naïveté that Mann's photos attempt to confront and interrogate. By presenting them in everyday contexts and exposing the camera's manipulations, Mann's collection argues what *The Age of Innocence* took pains to deny: "[T]he act of taking pictures is a semblance of appropriation, a semblance of rape" (Sontag, 1990, p. 24).

The outcome of this penetrating eye is symbolically manifested in Mann's photos as the aftermath of sexual exposure. While Hamilton's narrative avoids consummation, many of Mann's twelve-year-old subjects are posed with their own infants. One poignant image crops the picture frame around a pair of nude adolescent thighs stretched out on a beach chair, the crotch "covered" only by an equally naked female infant. The infant's body, also cropped, is positioned so that the baby's genitals are exposed to view (a double irony) in the place of her mother's. This single image offers a profoundly different visual experience than the earlier "crotch shots" of Hamilton's work, but it does so by echoing that original speculation, the desire to "see" virginity. But here the product of that speculation—and the product of sexuality that Hamilton leaves out of his narrative—is beautifully rendered as a real consequence for the girl.

Mann's camera does not subordinate these subjects to the viewer's desires. Whether the child's body is being offered to view as evidence of virginity or as the product of "commercial" activity, the child is a pointed symbol of the complicated relation between the viewer and the image. Yet if Mann's photos seem to suggest that the spectator takes complete control of the viewing experience, they also mark the reciprocal effects of looking that construct the spectator as one who is "subject-ed" to the control of the image.

However much the viewer's pleasure is generated by the thought that he (or she) remains an unseen voyeur, the tension produced by Hamilton's and Mann's very different collections seems to lie in their development of the spectator's ambivalent status. He (or she) is both unseen agent, privy to secrets, and included as a passive "audience" whom these pictures construct in significant ways. This conflicted viewing position is complicated because these two readings (one that frees the viewer from any relation to the viewing subject other than control and penetration, the other that molds a passive viewer in reaction to the rhetorical circumstances of the picture) place the viewer in seemingly opposite positions. Significantly, the viewer is both constructing the image through the narrative's possibilities and is constructed by it. But the nearer the viewer gets to this image, and the closer he or she comes to entering it (whether that motive is conceived as protective or possessive), the more freedom and agency the viewer loses. In short, the ultimate controlling factor in this experience is neither the viewer nor the photographic subject but the myths that produced the image.

CONCLUSION: VIRGINITY AS COMMODITY

Keith Carradine's role in the Louis Malle film *Pretty Baby* (1978) mimics the viewer as consumer of virginity. Carradine plays Bellocq, a photographer fascinated with a twelve-year-old girl (played by then child-actor Brooke Shields). Shields's character is raised in a turn-of-the-century New Orleans whorehouse, where her virginity makes her the target of both Bellocq's and the film's obsessive gaze. Even after a climactic scene in which her virginity is sold to the highest bidder, Bellocq remains enchanted with the child, abducts her, and repurchases her as his prime photographic subject. Through his twin obsession with picture taking and the child, we see that having her is like having a photograph, that the bewitching promise of possessing a "real" object outlasts the claims to purity that that object (the girl) might retain. Virgins and photos, passed from hand to hand, are similar objects of mass consumption. Neither, in *Pretty Baby*, will appease the viewer's need to possess them. At the end, the child is given a white dress and led away by her mother, a reformed prostitute who has married and plans to raise the little prostitute as an ordinary girl. In her final meeting with Bellocq before this departure, the child refuses to recognize him and appears to have uncannily regained her innocence.

Pretty Baby functions as a parable in which the photographic lens promises the object's complete surrender. Through the character of the child-prostitute that surrender is made to occur again and again in a pointedly mercantile context. Yet this repetition is patently absurd; it is precisely the impossibility of regaining virginity that makes it valuable. While the "business" of sex should be incompatible with the image of virginity, screenwriter Polly Pratt makes a shrewd assessment of the child-prostitute's character. "My theory is that she was innocent and she had no sexuality of any kind,' she explains, 'because she was born into it' " (Abramowitz, 1993, p. 97). The "it" into which the child was born is, of course, the sexual commerce of a brothel.

Brooke Shields, the actor playing this child-prostitute, has been dubbed "America's most celebrated symbolic virgin" (Kaplan, 1994, p. 60), in her professional life providing strong evidence of the continued commercial viability of a virginal image. Shields may herself be the best example of commodified virginity: Nearly all of the hundreds of articles written about her marketability play coyly with the notion that she still "has it" in private life. Even after her much publicized relationship with tennis star Andre Agassi (they have since married and divorced), a Broadway theater advertised its surprise casting of Brooke as Rizzo in *Grease* with the slogan "You Can't Be a Good Girl All Your Life" (Bennetts, 1994, p. 212). Recent articles that repeat this rhetoric include "Our Miss Brooke" (Bennetts, 1994, pp. 212–15) and "Endless Comeback" (Kaplan, 1994, p. 60).

In fact, while virginity is understood in our culture as an elusive state of purity, one destroyed by exposure, Brooke Shields's career as "America's most celebrated symbolic virgin" has been fabricated through an inexhaustible circulation, sale, and display of her image to the public. Shields is an example of a virginal image whose commercialization is undeniably successful. But why? In one of a series of seven Calvin Klein jeans commercials in which she starred at age fifteen, for example, the scene contains the familiar signals of innocence and "market" experience:

Shields is sitting on the floor with her legs in a V-position. She is facing the camera directly. One leg is bent with the foot flat on the floor; the other leg is bent and resting on the floor for support. . . . [At first] only a few inches of jeans against the plain background can be seen and it can be hard to understand the visuals. The camera has placed us about four inches from her leg, by proxemic definition, in an intimate relationship with her. The camera lens, however, is not at eye level, as might be expected. It remains just about level with the genital area. (Simpson, 1983, p. 151)

Simpson goes on to note striking similarities between the camera's position and Hamilton's use of the camera to obtain genital poses in *The Age of Innocence*. Referring to that now classic one-liner that Shields whispered, the actress's reproach that "nothing" came between her and her "Calvins" speaks volumes as the camera pulls back from her seated form (p. 151). This ad sold a lot of jeans. And it did so by marketing virginity as something any consumer could purchase: something, in fact, that invited them to recapture a missing part of themselves. As the camera frames this imagined striptease, it "revives the primordial desire for the object only to disappoint that desire, and to reactivate the original trauma of its disappearance" (Silverman, 1988, p. 9).

In Hamilton's collection, the photo itself is the object that comes to substitute for the state of naturalness the image seems to offer; by owning the photo the viewer might own the image. But in advertising, the commodity itself appears within the space left by the disappearing object. Nearly any commodity, in this context, can present itself as an authentic substitute for the virginal image: so natural, its status as a manufactured object is obscured. Through careful advertising, such a commodity appears mythic in Roland Barthes's sense of objects that "lose the memory that once they were made" (1972, p. 142).

In fact, the myth of virginity could be considered as the perfect evolution of commercial advertisement. It will be reproduced and sold to millions of consumers (what could be commoner than blue jeans?), each of whom responded to the ad's implied rhetorical claim that putting on these jeans means suturing that elusive wholeness back onto one's own body. The jeans in the ad that "come between" the camera and the virgin are constructed not merely to hide but to create the appearance of the space that is both hauntingly familiar and eludes sight. Virginity here is nothing other than the trompe l'oeil effect of its covering: The scandal in Brooke's jeans is "nothing."

This, of course, makes the image all the more self-generating, since an aptly named "consumer" will have been constructed with the imperative to find what is unfindable. The success of the virginal advertising image depends on its ability to access cultural constructions of virginity. Yet the virginal is not simply presented through the visual rhetoric described in the Calvin Klein ads above. It is manufactured in such a way as to sever the product's connections to its means of production. The success of virginal advertising lies as much in what is removed from view as what is there to be seen. Like Hamilton's virginal girls, posed in neutral surroundings nostalgically removed from time and change, this ad insists that the genitalia it covers have never been discovered, were not built from the ground up, as it were, by illusory rhetoric. Their value (a value transferred to the jeans that confer it) lies in the rhetorical statement that there is nothing artificial or extraneous there. This is why Mann's image of a twelve-year-old's pelvis overlaid with an infant is at once shocking and illuminating. Unlike the purveyors of illusion, it insists on the productive continuum in which these girls, and their sexuality, exist: a place that has no room for consumers' fantasies.

REFERENCES

Abramowitz, R. (1993, November). She's done everything. *Premiere*, pp. 91–100.
Barthes, R. (1972). *Mythologies* (A. Lavers, Trans.). New York: Hill and Wang.
Bazin, A. (1967). The virtues and limitations of montage. In H. Gray (Trans.), *What is cinema?* (Vol. 1). Berkeley: University of California Press.
Beauvoir, S. de. (1983). *The second sex* (H. M. Parshley, Ed. and Trans.). New York: Knopf.
Bennetts, L. (1994, December). Our Miss Brooke. *Vanity Fair, 57*, 212–15.
Berger, J. (1991). *About looking*. New York: Vintage.
Boyd, V., and Robitaille, M. (1994). Scent and femininity. In L. Manca and A. Manca (Eds.), *Gender and utopia in advertising* (pp. 47–59). Lisle, IN: Procopian Press.
Hamilton, D. (1978). *The young girl: The theme of a photographer*. New York: William Morrow.
Hamilton, D. (1995). *The age of innocence*. London: Aurum Press Limited.
Kaplan, J. (1994, November 21). Endless comeback. *New York*, pp. 60–62.
Lacan, J. (1977). *Ecrits: A selection*. London: Tavistock.
Malle, L. (Director). (1978). *Pretty Baby* [Film].
Mann, S. (1988). *At twelve: Portraits of young women*. New York: Aperture.
Nabokov, V. (1970). *The annotated Lolita* (A. Appel, Ed.). New York: McGraw-Hill.

Shields, B. (1978). *The Brooke book*. New York: Pocket Books.

Shields, B. (1985). *On your own*. New York: Villard Books.

Silverman, K. (1988). *The acoustic mirror*. Bloomington: Indiana University Press.

Simpson, M. (1983 Fall). Advertising art or obscenity? The Calvin Klein jeans ads. *Journal of Popular Culture, 17* (2), 146–53.

Sontag, S. (1990). *On photography*. New York: Doubleday.

11

Jacqueline J. Lambiase, Tom Reichert,
Susan E. Morgan, Meta G. Carstarphen,
Susan C. Zavoina, and
Mark Callister

Gendered Bodies Still Thrive in (Post)modern Magazineland

INTRODUCTION

If magazine ads are viewed as time machines or—as cultural markers of salient ideas within a given time—then gender representations would be one indicator of where in time each advertisement's micronarrative takes place. Dates on magazine covers may provide one clue for readers, but reviewing cultural data within advertising also becomes important in order to determine where along a time continuum these marketing pitches seem at home. A pitch that ignores its cultural setting would seem as out of place as, say, did H. G. Wells's time traveler or Mark Twain's *Connecticut Yankee in King Arthur's Court.*

In order to examine gender representations in magazine advertising in the 1990s, we've combined the tools of rhetorical analysis with the tools of empiricism. First, we'll look at the visual and textual rhetoric of one particular advertisement and its contextualization within a new men's magazine. Then, a content analysis of gender representations in advertising will complement this analysis by offering data that show changes in male representations but no changes in time-tested depictions of women as objects. Together, these approaches provide rhetorical and empirical texts through which to consider gender and these environments of time.

MAXIM'S RHETORIC TEASES POSTMODERNISM AND MALES

Maxim, a new men's magazine, began publication with a May–June 1997 issue featuring a cover shot of Christa Miller, a list of the 100 greatest sports moments of the century, plus articles on loving stress and on "babe management." Above its masthead on the cover each month is this teaser, or frame: "sex, sports, beer, gadgets, clothes, fitness." If there were no text on its cover, *Maxim* (for men) could be mistaken for a *Cosmopolitan* (for women) clone, since nearly every cover of both magazines features a three-quarter shot of a woman and her skin.

Articles inside *Maxim* focus on many of the same topics as *Cosmopolitan*, only from a strongly heterosexual male perspective: past issues advise readers how to "marry a rich girl" (January–February 1997), "score like a celebrity" (March 1998), "outsmart your boss" (September–October 1997), and negotiate "the ins and outs of office sex" (July–August 1997). Taken at face value, *Maxim* might be classified by some as a postmodern artifact, since it does construct male bodies as objects when it offers exercise advice and advertisements on baldness treatment. (Men's bodies are also objectified when a narrow range of idealized male images are featured with more frequency; more on this later.) The same sales appeals made to women in magazine editorial and advertising content—for example, selling them a body image that requires much conscious consumerism to maintain—are now made to men and in more places than just *Maxim*.

One could argue that gender categories of female and male are being blurred in many mass media texts, that women and men are being treated in the same way in order to sell products. Yet much of the editorial and advertising content places its readers into object positions all too familiar from times past. Women have "gained" equality with men, but not in the active, Cartesian-styled subject positions that first-wave feminists would support. Women are receiving more equal treatment in magazine advertising because men, too, are now objects to be sculpted and cosmetically maintained. We've taken a trip to the present, across a landscape of feminist education and egalitarian-filled cant, to find that we really have not arrived at any new destination. Capitalism guides our media landscape and still genders the bodies in it.

"I THINK I'M GONNA LIKE IT HERE"

An advertisement in the March 1998 issue of *Maxim* actually features a time machine and time traveler, a man dressed in an old-fashioned tweed suit and watch chain, à la H. G. Wells (see *Maxim*, pp. 16–17). The product advertised is Camel cigarettes, and one is dangling from his mouth as he takes a first step out of the time machine. He leers at four women, all dressed in short negligees. Three of them sit at his feet, and the one woman who is standing plays a phallic flute. Text above the time traveler tells the reader that "Travis" has emerged from his time machine, lighting a Camel and thinking that the so-called future is a satisfying place. Travis says he is "gonna like it here."

The future? Well, no wonder heterosexual Travis will like the future, for he has stepped into a late twentieth-century harem. Not much in this landscape has changed since the late nineteenth century, from which his travel originated. The crotch of his tweed pants is aglow with green light pulsating from his time machine—go, man, go—and between his legs is the rectangular box of the surgeon general, which reads: "Smoking by Pregnant Women May Result in Fetal Injury, Premature Birth, and Low Birth Weight." Since he's the only one smoking in the advertisement, and since this ad is made for men, then we must surmise that the only ones in need of a surgeon general's warning are the women in the ad who are in danger of becoming impregnated by Travis.

This R. J. Reynolds Tobacco advertisement, it could be argued, is as anachronistic and out of date (or out of time) as its inspiration, Wells's nineteenth-century novel. But it is exactly otherwise: The ad is in time, in sync, with its environment, that of *Maxim*. In the same issue, acting editor-in-chief Keith Blanchard describes this environment in an opening message to readers: "I've devoted my life to making the world a safer place for guys to be guys, and that's what *Maxim*'s all about" (p. 14).

Also in this message, Blanchard announces that his predecessor, Clare McHugh, "has decided to return to the world of women; fans can find her at the helm of *Now Woman* magazine" (p. 14). While the world of men and the world of women are delineated here as if they were completely separate, the paradox is that these targeted markets are now being treated in many ways as if they were the same. A female helped "get *Maxim* off the ground," Blanchard writes, and now he will step into her role and continue making a male world that is safe for his male readers.

Whether it be the vision of a male or a female editor, this approach will be the same. McHugh undoubtedly had previous experience with women's magazines, and her skills were equally useful for men and for *Maxim*. In his work on the masculine gaze, Clay Steinman (1992) asserts that "[m]edia industries and patriarchal differentiations work hand in hand to keep gender in line" (p. 203).

Part of the cultural work performed by the time machine ad within the pages of *Maxim* is the hardening of categories, the sanctioning of the male/female binary as true and good. Travis, the only man in this time machine landscape, is fully dressed and plays a traditional role, whereas the four women are "merely" decorative, dressed as they all are in sexually explicit bedroom attire. Travis is a traveler; the women are nameless, stationary, and submissive.

These characteristics seem all the more relevant when considered alongside empirical data from content analysis, which suggests that women's bodies are being objectified more than ever, especially in the environments of either male or female magazines.

EXAMINING BEEFCAKE, A SIDE DISH IN THE BANQUET OF CHEESECAKE

The content analysis was conducted to assess beefcake and cheesecake depictions of women and men in magazine ads. In order to measure changes in these depictions over time, all full-page ads in three issues of six magazines in

Table 11.1
Portrayal of Advertising Models in 1983 and 1993

	Female Models		Male Models	
	1983	*1993ª*	*1983*	*1993*
Decorative	45%	53%	28%	35%
Traditional	50%	41%	70%	64%
Progressive	5%	6%	2%	1%
	$n = 522$	$n = 441$	$n = 468$	$n = 258$

Note: $n = 1,689$.
ª$p = 0.01$

1983 were coded and compared to ads in the same magazines in 1993. Overall, 2,545 ads were included in the analysis (1,473 in 1983; 1,072 in 1993).

Female and male models within these ads were coded according to three categories adapted from a sex-role scale developed by Pingree et al. (1976). If the model was present merely to enhance the attractiveness of the product, the model was categorized as being "decorative." These portrayals show women and men as having no true functional relationship to the product and typically as nothing more than a nonthinking, two-dimensional object. Often these models were dressed in provocative clothing that accentuated their well-sculpted physiques. The second category was labeled "traditional" and generally featured women and men in stereotypically masculine or feminine roles (e.g., nurses, mothers, fathers, executives, etc.). Depictions of either gender as equal, as managing role reversals competently, or as "whole persons" rather than caricatures were coded as "progressive." The coding was conducted by two trained coders who worked independently. The agreement coefficient for female depictions was 0.81 and for male depictions was 0.82.

The six magazines (*Time, Newsweek, Cosmopolitan, Redbook, Esquire*, and *Playboy*) were chosen because they represent a spectrum of readership interests (general interest, women's, and men's magazines), have high circulations, and are among those commonly sampled in content analyses of gender portrayal in the literature. Three issues of each magazine (March, July, and November) were coded for both 1983 and 1993.

First, we sought to determine and compare the overall depictions of women and men in ads to gain a relative snapshot of cheesecake and beefcake in American advertising. What we see is that overall, a high percentage of women designed to look good decorate the pages of advertisements in magazines (see Table 11.1). A chi-square test revealed that women's depictions differed significantly between 1983 and 1993, $\chi^2(2) = 9.30$, $p < 0.01$. Decorative portrayals of women were more prevalent in 1993 (53%) than in 1983 (45%). There was also an increase in the percentage of men portrayed decoratively, but this dif-

Table 11.2
Portrayal of Advertising Models by Type of Magazine

	Female Models					
	General Interest		Women's		Men's	
	1983	1993	1983	1993[a]	1983	1993
Decorative	16%	26%	55%	61%	30%	33%
Traditional	69%	59%	42%	34%	66%	61%
Progressive	15%	15%	3%	5%	4%	6%
	n = 62	n = 46	n = 345	n = 331	n = 115	n = 64
	Male Models					
	General Interest		Women's		Men's	
	1983	1993	1983	1993	1983	1993[b]
Decorative	19%	20%	19%	23%	36%	48%
Traditional	81%	77%	79%	75%	61%	51%
Progressive	—	3%	2%	2%	3%	1%
	n = 109	n = 69	n = 105	n = 60	n = 254	n = 129

Note: n = 1,689.
[a]$p < 0.10$
[b]$p < 0.05$

ference was not significantly different—about one in four men in ads in 1983 (28%) were depicted as beefcake images, compared to a little over one-third (35%) in 1993.

Second, we examined how both genders were portrayed by magazine type (general interest, women's, and men's). Some interesting patterns emerged (see Table 11.2). First, the most decorative portrayals of either gender are in their respective periodicals. For instance, in 1993, 61 percent of women in *Cosmopolitan* and *Redbook* were portrayed decoratively, as were 48 percent of men in *Esquire* and *Playboy*. These percentages are more than double those in general interest magazines (*Time* and *Newsweek*) and about twice as many in the other magazines. This provides evidence that women and men are seeing more images of themselves as objects of desire adorning products than those for consumption by the opposite sex.

Third, the only significant shifts from 1983 to 1993 toward more decorative portrayals are in those same magazines for men or for women. For instance, a chi-square test revealed a marginally significant difference in female portrayals in women's magazines, $\chi^2(2) = 4.75$, $p < 0.10$. Decorative portrayals of women increased from 55 percent in 1983 to 61 percent in 1993. There was also a significant shift for men in men's magazines, $\chi^2(2) = 6.37$, $p < 0.05$. Male decorative portrayals increased from 36 percent in 1983 to 48 percent in 1993.

There were no other differences in the other magazine types for either gender. These findings suggest that decorative depictions are increasing only in the magazines read by their respective gender. Women see more cheesecake in *Cosmopolitan* and *Redbook*, and men see more beefcake in *Esquire* and *Playboy*. And readers of all these magazines saw women's bodies used more decoratively in 1993 than they did a decade before.

EQUAL OPPORTUNITY IMAGES OF IDEALIZED BODIES

Let us, for a moment, contemplate this grouping of four magazines—*Maxim, Cosmopolitan, Playboy*, and *Esquire*—across the rhetorical and empirical analyses presented above. To paraphase a *Sesame Street* song, one of these things is different from the others. But which one is not like the others? In the male/female binary worlds consciously created by magazines such as *Maxim*, the answer would be simple: *Cosmopolitan*. It is clearly a magazine targeted at women who, when constructed as readers of this magazine, gaze a lot at themselves in advertising as revealed in our study. *Maxim, Playboy*, and *Esquire* are clearly seen as male domains. And within these environments, the time traveler ad fits well with expectations for all three of these magazines' heterosexual audiences.

In other ways, *Cosmopolitan* may be likened to *Maxim* (and for that matter, similar also to *Playboy* or *Esquire*). Male viewers of the latter three magazines are gazing at themselves more than ever before, matching female viewers of *Cosmopolitan* who have been gazing at women's bodies for decades.

One reason for the increase in decorative portrayals of men, especially in men's magazines, is the emphasis on beautification of the male body. In the pages of comic books since the 1950s, Charles Atlas has espoused the benefits of body building and physique enhancement. His primary appeal, however, hinged on bulking up for protection purposes to deter other males from kicking sand in one's face. A substantial number of advertising appeals today hinge on body enhancement for the purposes of becoming visually pleasing, not brawny for the sake of survival.

The eroticization of men's fashion—most notably of underwear by Calvin Klein and Jockey in the early 1980s—and an increasingly large array of men's beauty products, such as facial creams and moisturizers, have sent a consistent message to men to place an emphasis on looking good. These messages have manifested in an increasing proportion of decorative male images in the pages of men's magazines. Wernick's (1987) analysis of men's magazines lends support to this proposition. He argues that since the 1960s men in ads have transitioned from being positioned as voyeurs to objects of voyeurism. Men's bodies have increasingly become objects of visual inspection. Kervin (1990) reached a similar conclusion in a content analysis of men in ads in *Esquire* magazine from the 1920s to the 1980s. Men were depicted as decorative objects in the 1970s and 1980s, a role for men that was nonexistent in the earlier decades. Clearly,

Figure 11.1
Ad with Thin Female and Muscular Male

Courtesy of KCD Inc. Used by permission.

a parallel exists between male decorative roles in advertising and the relatively recent emphasis on men's fashion and beauty products.

Since these heavily gendered bodies shown in both magazine types uphold an ideal, viewers and readers may desire to become the idealized Other. In this psychological view, media imagery is never a literal depiction of reality but, rather, is part of a complex symbolic system that serves to advance particular ideas among particular people at particular times (Kitch, 1997). One well-established cultural ideal in late twentieth-century media imagery has been the thin female body, which is now joined by an ideal for males, that of a V-shaped body that is low in body fat and muscular (see Figure 11.1). In her study of *GQ, Sports Illustrated*, and *Rolling Stone* magazines, Cheryl Law (1998) found that V-shaped images of men increased from 45 percent in 1967 to 80 percent in 1997. She projects that males may now suffer from muscle dysmorphia, just as women have been suffering from anorexia nervosa, perhaps in part after being exposed to unrealistic body images in mass media. In their promotion of thin female bodies and V-shaped male bodies, then, these four magazines—*Maxim,*

Cosmopolitan, Playboy, and *Esquire*—serve the interests of late capitalism without much difference among them.

THRIVING IDEALIZATIONS FOR ALL TIMES

When both male and female bodies are portrayed as hyperperfected in ads, the gulf between real life and advertising increases, consumerism is reinforced (Foster, 1991), and viewers use their gaze to identify symbolically with these images. Perfect, gendered bodies populate these magazines, with male and female readers gazing and "consuming" their own idealized bodies: "[Y]ou create an image which few can attain and you are ensured of a market forever" (Dickey, 1987, p. 76). Some scholars would argue, however, that women's gazing at female bodies and men's gazing at male bodies are fundamentally different. From John Berger's own maxim: "The surveyor of woman in herself is male: the surveyed female. Thus, she turns herself into an object—and most particularly an object of vision: a sight" (1972, p. 47). Liesbet van Zoonen (1994) agrees and asserts that " '[m]asculine' voyeurism of the male body is prevented by visual and narrative codes that signify activity and control by the male pin-up" (p. 104). Men are seen as muscular, athletic, and active; women's bodies are usually characterized by thinness alone.

In this way of reading these images, the idealization of male and female bodies in gendered magazines—like the active role of Travis and the passive roles of his time machine harem—is grounded in patriarchy. From this modernist patriarchy springs the postmodernist impulse of equal opportunity images. Using a body, whether it be male or female, is becoming a dominant frame for advertising discourse. Objectification is now a commonplace in a new way, and this frame will not easily go away for women, now that it has enveloped men. It is a frame that pushes patriarchy beyond its own traditional borders, since magazine advertising imagery now includes more male bodies.

E. A. Kaplan (1996) describes a postmodern world in which "both men and women are victims; all bodies are 'invaded' and exploited because they are no longer adequate to the advanced technologies" (p. 39). This, however, doesn't alter the sheer numbers of objectified female bodies, which are used more relentlessly than ever before since women must maintain an idealized image that wears less clothing than ever before. Just as narcissism has been distorted to seem liberating for women (see Douglas, 1994), so too does the newly gendered, objectified male body seem to be part of women's so-called liberation. The incidence of the male body's reproduction as decorative, when compared to the saturation of female images, reveals its negligible impact in the marketplace (see Table 11.1).

Through the production of idealized forms, whether they be sculptures or paintings or billboards or magazine ads, women have inhabited corsets and endured other restrictions for centuries while being used decoratively. The tyranny of Renaissance-inspired voluptuous figures of women may be no different than

1980s anorexic thinness or 1990s V-shaped muscle men. Misery may love company; however, women's now-virtual corsets are still damned uncomfortable decorations.

This chiasmic interplay of female and male images offers intriguing possibilities for those wishing for a genderless world. At the present moment, men seem to be falling into an idealized tyranny so familiar to women in their own gendered magazines. In fact, *Maxim*'s Blanchard warns his readers about a hostile cultural climate when he suggests that his magazine is "a safer place for guys to be guys." As this new men's magazine conforms to the strategies used for decades by women's magazines such as *Cosmopolitan*, however, his readers will be unprotected and caught in a double-bind similar to that of women's magazines: "the paradox that 'natural' femininity [insert *masculinity* here] can be achieved only through hard labour" (Ballaster et al., 1996, p. 91).

Newly derived, objectified images of men may seem to be a by-product of postmodernism's promised multiplicity of images contained within a genderless world. But Travis, the leering time traveler, reminds us that we still inhabit a modernist time zone that is just a meal away from the ever-popular cheesecake. There are lessons in these contradictory images. And media critic John Fiske (1996) warns us that "Postmodern culture is often characterized as one of extreme multiplicity—a multiplicity of commodities, of images, of knowledges, and of information technologies. . . . Multiplicity is a prerequisite of diversity, but it does not necessarily entail it—more can all too often be more of the same" (p. 239).

REFERENCES

Ballaster, R., Beetham, M., Frazer, E., and Hebron, S. (1996). A critical analysis of women's magazines. In H. Baehr and A. Gray (Eds.), *Turning it on: A reader in women and media* (pp. 87–96). London: Arnold.

Berger, J. (1972). *Ways of seeing*. London: Penguin Books.

Blanchard, K. (1998, March). Editor's letter. *Maxim*, p. 14.

Dickey, J. (1987). Women for sale: The construction of advertising images. In K. Davies, J. Dickey, and T. Stratford (Eds.), *Out of focus: Writings on women and the media* (pp. 74–77). London: Women's Press.

Douglas, S. J. (1994). *Where the girls are: Growing up female with the mass media*. New York: Times Books.

Fiske, J. (1996). *Media matters: Race and gender in U.S. politics*. Minneapolis: University of Minnesota Press.

Foster, H. (1991). *The anti-aesthetic: Essays on postmodern culture*. Seattle: Bay Press.

Kaplan, E. A. (1996). Feminism/Oedipus/postmodernism: The case of MTV. In H. Baehr and A. Gray (Eds.), *Turning it on: A reader in women and media* (pp. 33–43). London: Arnold.

Kervin, D. (1990). Advertising masculinity: The representation of males in *Esquire* advertisements. *Journal of Communication Inquiry, 14* (2), 51–69.

Kitch, C. (1997). Changing theoretical perspectives on women's media images: The emergence of patterns in a new area of historical scholarship. *Journalism and Mass Communication Quarterly, 74* (3), 477–89.

Law, C. L. (1998, August). *Cultural standards of attractiveness: A 30-year look at changes in male images in magazines.* Presentation at the Association for Education in Journalism and Mass Communication national conference, Baltimore.

Pingree, S., Hawkins, R. P., Butler, M., and Paisley, W. (1976). A scale for sexism. *Journal of Communication,* 193–200.

Steinman, C. (1992). Gaze out of bounds: Men watching men on television. In S. Craig (Ed.), *Men, masculinity, and the media* (pp. 199–214). Newbury Park, CA: Sage Publications.

van Zoonen, L. (1994). *Feminist media studies.* London: Sage Publications.

Wernick, A. (1987). From voyeur to narcissist: Images of men in contemporary advertising. In M. Kaufman (Ed.), *Beyond patriarchy: Essays by men on pleasure, power, and change* (pp. 227–97). Toronto: Oxford University Press.

PART V

TELEVISION

12

Linda K. Fuller

Super Bowl Speak: Subtexts of Sex and Sex Talk in America's Annual Sports Extravaganza

A woman who can't speak (the common language of sport) starts any business interaction with a built-in disadvantage. This is not to say that women executives must be able to spout baseball statistics or compare the defensive capabilities of all NBA teams, but rather that any woman with some knowledge of these things will find it easier to relax with her male colleagues; sport is, as we have seen, the perfect nonthreatening way to make small talk.

—Lance, *A Woman's Guide to Spectator Sports*

As discussions and definitions of sexual harassment circle the workplace and academe, one of the clearest conceptions to emerge is the simple discovery of how men and women differ in, among a number of factors, their language choices. Since sports talk is pervasive in male-speak, the aim here is to examine that phenomenon, zeroing in on the example of the rhetoric embedded in the Super Bowl, the largest television event of the year in the United States—drawing some 140 million viewers, along with advertisers anxious to spend $1.3 million per thirty seconds to infotain them. Linguistic deconstruction is only a part of the issue, however: Accumulating research indicates that the frenzy of football's annual finale also coincides with hideous statistics relative to reported instances of domestic violence.

SPORTS, GENDER, AND RHETORIC

A basic assumption of evolving research is that it behooves feminists to consider sports as an important topic of popular culture. It has been an argument a long time in the offing. In addition to fitness author Kathryn Lance's 1980 advice cited in the opening quotation, consider this declaration from The Learning Annex's—a national adult education program—book entitled *How to Talk Sports to Men* (1984), which emphasizes how sports provide a common reference point: "For a woman in business, this means that her words, if couched in the imagery of sports, can be weighed by her male co-workers on the same pscale they use for each other. She becomes easier for them to understand, even if the ideas she expresses remain the same" (p. 8). Sport, according to this publication, "offers a unique window into the psyche of men, both in business and personal life. Sports talk can be extremely revealing, exposing basic facts about an individual's approach to life" (p. 8). Further, "[o]n the most basic level, a woman's interest in, or knowledge of, a sport that fascinates the men around her gives her a natural point of contact with their lives. Instead of alienation during Monday Night Football, there can be togetherness. In the place of long Sundays at home alone, there can be entertaining afternoons at the ball park with the boys" (p. 9). Nearly two decades later, some women are deciding that their best defense is learning more about football (Hoyle and Lanier, 1997), whereas other women are taking the tack that what they prefer is a critical study of sport in our society.

Beginning in the 1970s, feminist perspectives have been incorporated into mainstream dialogues, (hopefully) sensitizing the public to gender issues. Best exemplified by Theberge's 1981 article in *Social Forces*, critiquing sport as "a fundamentally sexist institution that is male dominated and masculine in orientation" (p. 342), the bulk of the literature tends to have a general focus—for example, Gerber et al.'s *The American Woman in Sport* (1974); Oglesby's *Women and Sport: From Myth to Reality* (1978); Twin's *Out of the Bleachers: Writings on Women and Sport* (1979); Boutilier and San Giovanni's *The Sporting Women* (1983); Remley's *Women in Sport: An Annotated Bibliography and Resource Guide* (1991); and Hargreaves's *Sporting Females* (1994).

Then, as Messner and Sabo (1990) state about this theoretical background, "Feminist analyses uncovered a hidden history of female athleticism, examined sex differences in patterns of athletic socialization, and demonstrated how the dominant institutional forms of sport have naturalized men's power and privilege over women" (p. 2). Much of the literature has centered on issues of patriarchy and, by default, hegemony (e.g., Davis, 1997; Hall, 1978).

While there is a long journalistic tradition of sports reporting, particularly autobiographical tell-all publications, the 1980s saw the beginning of academic interest in televised sporting events—for example, Koppett (1981), Powers (1984), Rader (1984), Chandler (1988), Klatell and Marcus (1988), Spence (1988), Himmelstein (1989), O'Neil (1989), Whannel (1992), Creedon (1994), Fuller (1994), and Real (1989a, 1989b, 1996). Sports spectators are the province of studies by Johnson (1971), Underwood (1984), Guttman (1986), Duncan and Brummett (1987), Brummett and Duncan (1990), and Jenkins (1992). Interestingly, there have also been a number of books dealing with sports quotations:

Harvey Frommer's *Sports Roots* (1979), Tim Considine's *The Language of Sport* (1982), and Lee Green's *Sportswit* (1984).

FOOTBALL AND ITS CHAMPIONSHIP GAME: SUPER BOWL

> Football today is a social obsession. Football is a boy-killing, education-prostituting, gladiatorial sport. It teaches virility and courage, but so does war. I do not know what should take its place, but the new game should not require the services of a physician, the maintenance of a hospital, and the celebration of funerals.
>
> —Shailer Mathews, dean of the Chicago Divinity School, on football of the late nineteenth century[1]

"Professional football on television each year occupies more American man-hours than have been expended to date on the entire space program," according to Phil Patton's introduction to *Razzle Dazzle: The Curious Marriage of Television and Football* (1984). Consider some of these "wise words," culled from Larry Adler's *Football Coach Quotes* (1992):

• Ray Berry (New England Patriots, 1984–1989): "It's almost like a marriage. You have to make allowances and understand each other. You get to know each other so well that you know instinctively what to expect in any situation"—*said about the relationship between a passer and receiver.*

• "Bear" Bryant (U. Alabama, 1958–1982): "It isn't the size of the dog in the fight. It's the size of the fight in the dog."

• "Bud" Grant (Winnepeg Blue Bombers, 1957–1966, Minnesota Vikings, 1967–1985): "A good coach needs a patient wife, loyal dog and a great quarterback—not necessarily in that order."

• Woody Hayes (Ohio State, 1951–1978): "Paralyze their resistance with your persistence."

• "Pudge" Heffelfinger (U. Minnesota, 1895): "A man's body must go where his head goes."

• John Heisman (Oberlin, 1892, Rice, 1927): "Thrust your projections into their cavities."

• Tom Landry (Dallas Cowboys, 1960–1988): "You don't build character without somebody slapping you around" and "Football's still primarily emotion. Hitting comes first. Thinking comes second."

• Vince Lombardi (Green Bay Packers, 1959–1967, Washington Redskins, 1969), famous for his "Winning isn't everything . . . it's the only thing," is also attributed with "Pro football is a violent, dangerous sport. To play it other than violently would be imbecile."

• John Madden (Oakland Raiders, 1969–1978): "Football is serious."

- Chuck Noll (Pittsburgh Steelers, 1969–): "If you are doing it right, you don't get hit in the head. You hit the other guy."

- Bill Parcells (NY Giants, 1983–): "To heck with a first down. Let's go deep. I want it all."

- Joe Paterno (Penn State, 1966–): "Women's sports have arrived. They give women another way of feeling good about themselves."

- "Bum" Phillips (New Orleans Saints, 1981–1985): "I take my wife with me everywhere because she is too ugly to kiss good-bye."

- Knute Rockne (Notre Dame, 1918–1930): "Go out there and crucify them"; "Fit to live! Fight to win! Fight to live! Fight to win-win-win!"; "Play tough, play fair, play to win. Don't beef if you lose, but don't lose." "Boys must have an outlet for animal spirits."

- Don Shula (Miami Dolphins, 1970–): "You kick some in the butt, praise others, continue to harass a third group. They're all different and you've got to realize this."

- Barry Switzer (U. Oklahoma, 1973–1988): "Football is a violent physical sport. It's a demanding sport run by demanding coaches who teach huge kids to collide into one another as fast as they can run."

While professional televised football has been called "The Church of Monday Night Football," there is an oft-quoted statement attributed to the late Reverend Norman Vincent Peale to the effect, "If Jesus were alive today, he would be at the Super Bowl." While most of the literature on the Super Bowl (e.g., Green, 1995; Hanks, 1989; Hyman, 1996; Janz and Abrahamson, 1991; Resciniti et al., 1994; Sampson, 1996; Sporting News Staff, 1992) deals directly with statistics and such, Gunther and Carter's (1988) depictions of it seem most appropriate: "The most valuable television property of all time" (p. 15), or "a television extravaganza, the most-anticipated, most-watched, most analyzed program of the year" (p. 240). McAllister (1996) points out, "The high-profile TV event of the year, the Super Bowl has become as well known for the commercial spectacle as for the football spectacle" (p. 118). Its first million-dollar minute came in 1985, a shock at the time but an almost quaint figure these days for what has since become our preeminent secular holiday.

Ever since the merger of the American Football League (AFL) and the National Football League (NFL), the "ultimate" football contest has been waged. First played on January 15, 1967, then officially referred to as the National Football League championship game but unofficially called the Super Bowl by the media, the fans, and the players, the name just stuck. In the beginning the Super Bowl was simulcast by both CBS and NBC, the former known for allegiances to the NFL and the latter for the AFL; then, since 1993, the Fox Network outbid the rights, covering Super Bowl for $1.6 billion until 1997. It is unquestionably corporate Big Business at its peak. Dona Schwartz (1998), reporting on the time Super Bowl XXVI took place in her hometown of Minneapolis–St. Paul, states:

Perpetuating the commerce it venerates, CEOs use the Super Bowl as a vehicle to cement deals, entertain clients, reward productive employees with a free excursion, and simultaneously create tax deductions. The media take advantage of the event they helped craft, and the Super Bowl is placed among items at the top of the week's news agenda. Sportswriters, newscasters, talk show hosts, protesters, and celebrities of every ilk converge on the host city to produce and exploit the media spectacle that unfolds. (p. 2)

Of all the sports that women may want to spectate—assuming that they want to buy into this supreme patriarchal experience—none better exemplifies the nexus of Big Business, big stakes, and big boys than American football. And of all the football games that women and men alike are expected to watch, none can surpass the Super Bowl. A ratings leader,[2] it has become an advertisers' yardstick, drawing as it does more than 140 million viewers and costing more than $2 million a minute.

Not the least of its attractions is the self-conscious hype that the Super Bowl draws, commanding equally lucrative pre- and postgame hoopla. In truth, though, it is common knowledge that the Super Bowl typically is not a demonstration of the best that football has to offer, and more often than not, it is downright boring. The game itself is oftentimes hardly the point; rather, it is the parties, the people, and most important, the products surrounding it.

Super Bowl begins well in advance of its actual showing. In addition to the general hype of Super Week, there are numerous interviews, photo opportunities, even hints of various "new" products that might be unveiled. Each year there is a unique logo, a special theme song, and accompanying special souvenirs. Television adds its own touch, too, oftentimes introducing new technological devices such as the following:

- The "Louma," a camera at the end of a robot arm that premiered for Super Bowl XV in 1981;
- The reverse-angle replay;
- The Telestrator "Video Chalkboard";
- The Precam—a helicopter-mounted means for cameras to follow running backs and receivers, which was introduced for Super Bowl XVII;
- The Goodyear Blimp, which has become inextricably associated with Super Bowl—appropriately, full of hot air.

One especially interesting case study is that of Super Bowl XXV (the New York Giants versus the Buffalo Bills), which took place on Sunday, January 27, 1991, as reported by Fuller's (1992a) narrative analysis. Recalling that at the time of the first Super Bowl, in 1967, the United States was involved in the Vietnam War, parallels were drawn with the ritual's twenty-fifth celebration, falling as it did on the eleventh day of the Persian Gulf War. Considerable media attention had focused on whether the event would even take place in the first place. There were discussions about the safety of many people together in one place at one time, about respecting our fighting troops and their families, about preempting valuable airtime, even about the appropriateness of staging a sporting event in the middle of such a serious period in our history. The Gyrocam 360, an advanced camera, and a remote pan-and-tilt camera had been designed to give new perspective to field goal attempts, but the Federal Aviation Administration banned the blimp from the immediate area, saying that for security reasons it didn't want aircraft over the stadium. But in the end there really was no discussion at all: There was simply too much at stake, commercially. Fortunately, Super Bowl XXV played without incident or complaint. Besides, President George Bush had already taped his halftime message a dozen days earlier, the same day as the United Nations deadline for withdrawal of Iraqi troops from Kuwait.

ABC, that year's winning network, had predicted that about 118 million Americans would be watching the televised spectacle, as well as another 250 million worldwide. Some of those viewers included about a third of the U.S. troops overseas—who viewers at home got to watch, watching television at various strategic places and at various strategic points of the (in)action. Super Bowl XXV also attracted yet another target miche, this one perhaps containing new recruits: all the news junkies who had been glued to their television sets, if typically on CNN, since the Persian Gulf War began. Maybe it is only appropriate to mention that Ted Turner, the media mogul who transfixed an entire nation during those days, is the person who made the immortal statement "Sports is like a war without the killing" (cited in Martin, 1991, p. H29).

The pregame pageantry and commentary reeked with patriotism. *TV Guide* devoted a half-page close-up about the event, commenting that sportscasters Frank Gifford, Al Michaels, and Dan Dierdorf would be "backed by a small army—some 200 strong—of network personnel" and that their "arsenal" would include twenty-two cameras that could be "deployed" for various purposes. Some 72,000 American flags were handed out to the paying customers in the Tampa (FL) Stadium for the Silver Anniversary contest—after they had cleared metal security detectors. Tickets to the event on the fifty-yard line or behind the end zones cost $150 and had an additional security device during the backdrop of war: holograms, created by the Polaroid Corporation. The hologram, depicting the stadium and the Vince Lombardi Trophy, was said to be a particularly valuable collector's item, valued at about $75 postgame. George Young, general manager of the New York Giants, admitted, "Let's face it. We're in show business. We're selling a product, and it's football" (cited in Berkow, 1991, p. S6).

Pregame, viewers were introduced, soap-opera style, to a story from Saudi Arabia featuring soldiers vowing to watch the game despite its 2:18 A.M. kickoff time; later, cameras returned there during the twenty-six-minute commercial intermission known as halftime, when the New Kids on the Block were joined by more than 2,000 "real" kids in a patriotic Walt Disney extravaganza. But perhaps the highlight of anticipation took place when Whitney Houston gave her stirring rendition of the national anthem. And what an image it reinforced, when people around the world had an opportunity to be led in song by a beautiful, young, talented Black woman in a red, white, and blue outfit. As *Entertainment Weekly* (Cagle, 1991, p. 84) pointed out, "The Gulf war fervor has turned Houston's performance into an unlikely, overnight pop hit," just as Francis Scott Key's 1814 ode to the flag was about to celebrate its sixtieth anniversary as America's national anthem. While there had been comments juxtaposing American priorities on what is really important, once the actual kickoff came, pure escapism took over, "affirming the special place of sports in our culture, whether the Americana-steeped World Series or Madison Avenue–driven Superbowl. Despite everything occurring on the outside, [it] was its own isolated impregnable world, a seamless, Scudless Saddamless chamber where one could focus on the benign violence on the field without dwelling on the bigger violence looming elsewhere" (Rosenberg, 1991).

Football, by default loaded with risk, is a violent game, loaded with military argot. It includes terms like *blitz,* which derives from the German *Blitzkrieg,* a term "coined to describe the swift, unstoppable advance of Hitler's troops into Poland in 1939. Now . . . it refers to a defensive tactic of sending in extra players, other than the down linemen, to rush the quarterback" (Hill, 1991). The sport routinely incorporates words like *bombs, offense* and *defense, flanks, victories* and *defeats, casualties,* and *dominance.* It is also characterized by phrases like "blockading the way," "ground and air attacks," "fighting and dying on the frontlines," and "battling in the trenches." Strategies and tactics are inherent, like preventing defenses or sticking to a game plan, using "two-minute drills" or the "two-platoon system," "weaving through minefields," sometimes being reduced to employing "unnecessary roughness," even having both sportscasters and newscasters use "telestrators" for charting movements. In response to her own question, "Why is football a game that maims?" Schwartz (1998) states:

Since its emergence in the 1800s American football has been noted for its violence, but only recently have studies enumerated the risks. Some suggest that steroid use, officially prohibited by the league in 1989, has produced bigger, faster players whose collisions do more damage. Others cite the adverse affects of playing on artificial turf. Yet others attribute the rise in football injuries to television's need for an exciting, dramatic show, in order to keep viewers riveted and guarantee robust advertising sales. As player activists have begun to expose the hazards and stresses associated with professional football, a useful wedge in salary negotiations, the NFL has commissioned its own studies of player injuries. (p. 100)

In addition, football incorporates a remarkably sexualized vocabulary, using terms like "going all the way," "using deep penetration," "grinding it out," using "bump and run" stratagem, "gang-tackling," "naked reverses," and "butt-blocking" techniques. And of course there is always, should it be needed, the possibility of "fakes"!

During the time of Super Bowl XXV, as the Persian Gulf War was being waged, General ("Stormin") Norman Schwarzkopf was widely quoted about his characterization of a strategic plan that bore an amazing similarity to football's "Hail Mary" play—a low-percentage pass that requires a lot of luck. Jansen and Sabo (1992, p. 5) discuss how "[t]he Pentagon public relations officers consciously cultivated the referential system based upon vocabularies and images of sport." For example, the authors contend that the press briefing room resembled sets used by television sports producers, equipped as it was "with instant video-replays and chalkboards reviewing the 'game plans' of the invasion, the sets as well as the choreography of briefings themselves possess[ing] what media professionals describe as 'high-production values.' " The dramaturgical effect was heightened, they argue, by the personae of Schwarzkopf, "whose on-camera presence bore an uncanny resemblance to some of the mythic tough-talking coaches of football/entertainment legend: Buddy Ryan, Vince Lombardi, even Pat O'Brien playing the lead in the film version of the Knute Rockne story."

Both news organizations and war correspondents played into the sport/war metaphor, with CNN anchor Patrick Emory commenting after the earliest salvo, "Last night was about as close to the Super Bowl as you can get. It was as though we had Montana, Marino, and Hostetler in together." Yet it should be pointed out that for Super Bowl XXV sportscasters had been warned to be sensitive to its audiences' apprehensions and especially to respect those families who might have loved ones out on the real fighting field. The tension was palpable. Still, these were the sportscaster terms that were most frequently coded as the game was played:

Term	Number of times cited
Prevent the defense	3
Hurry-up offense	4
Bomb	1
Dominance	6
Regulation	5
Battling in the trenches	1
Shotgun	4
Exploiting	2
Blockading the way	2
Protection	6
Blitz	2
Zone(s)	7

And there was another word that many of us waited for but, fortunately, never heard—a term natural enough to make the crossover from military to football jargon; still, it wasn't used, appropriately enough: *scud*.

Advertisements, which Klatell and Marcus (1988) call "the business of television sports" (p 22),[3] were also kept to a minimum during Super Bowl XXV. Pepsico, Inc. had planned to launch its own Super Bowl spectacle by flashing a toll-free number for viewers to call, whereby three randomly selected callers would be given $1 million; instead it, like rival Coca-Cola, aired self-serving patriotic messages about supporting our troops. Probably the most noticeable commercial was McDonald's narration by a worker with Down syndrome who was touting the company's hiring practices.

By way of comparison, the rhetoric of Super Bowl XXVI the next year was surprisingly similar to its predecessor in tone. As Mariah Burton Nelson (1994) has pointed out, "The language describing men's sports is routinely violent. Teams are beaten, gunned down, destroyed" (p. 70). Played on January 26, 1992, in twenty-two-degree temperatures with a wind chill of minus six degrees at Hubert H. Humphrey Metrodome in Minneapolis, it nevertheless had the requisite tailgate parties and incorporated interviews around the world, interspersed with retrospectives of Operation Desert Storm. Playing to an audience of 79.6 million viewers, 52.3 million in postgame, the twenty-sixth Super Bowl opened with this comment: "Today is the day when grown men become little boys again, playing out their fantasies before all the world . . . on a day made for dreams." Bugle Boy jeans ran a semipornographic simulation of intercourse between a couple overlaid (if you'll pardon the expression) with his golfing buddies talking about how henpecked he was because his "slave"/wife hadn't let him out with them that day. Fruit of the Loom underwear had Sampson and Delilah act out another mock seduction, and Pepsi told us we "Gotta Have It." Nike, in its award-winning campaign, was urging us to "Just Do It." Outside the actual stadium were some 2,000 demonstrators protesting the use of Native American nicknames and mascots in sports, a rally especially aimed at the Washington Redskins.

At a setting for what columnist Ellen Goodman (1998) has labeled "the largest male-bonding, testosterone-loading sporting even of the year," though, the personal becomes particularly subservient to the political. David Newsom (1991), former undersecretary of state, has properly pointed out, "The war in the Gulf was not a Super Bowl. As with all wars, it was a violent and destructive intrusion into the affairs of others. As with past wars, too, its lessons are not easily transferable to other conflicts" (p. 19).

Super Bowl XXXII of 1998, Broncos versus Packers, had more than 400 possible hyperlinks from its central Internet address of www.superbowl.com— mainly men and merchandise, along with virtual tours of host cities, player/coach interviews, animated playbooks with graphical play-by-plays, online chats, and more. Drawing the requisite worldwide viewers for ads now running $1.3 million for each thirty-second spot, Super Sunday is billed by research firms as a tantalizing "three-hour escape."

REFLECTIONS ON SUPER BOWL SPEAK

> When we think about language and gender, especially in relation to media practice, we are referring less to the grammar and structure of the language; more to the relative entitlement of men and women to speak up and be heard, and to define the world we live in.
>
> —Macdonald, *Representing Women*

As feminism continues its long struggle against sexist oppression, discrimination, and exploitation, it behooves us to recall bell hooks's observations from 1984: "Traditionally the battleground has been the home. In recent years, the battle ensues in any sphere, public or private, inhabited by women and men, girls and boys" (p. 34).

Extending that notion of battleground, it becomes frighteningly apparent that earlier comments about Super Bowl's ingrained references to war and violence are, in fact, played out in a number of American homes. In 1993, Anna Quindlen was one of the first journalists to bring to public attention the correlation between football game viewing and domestic violence: "The football game story is omnipresent: the kids make too much noise during a crucial play, or someone steps in front of the screen, or he loses a bet, or he runs out of beer, and 'Pow!' " (p. E17). She then reported how a coalition of groups, under the umbrella of the watchdog organization Fairness and Accuracy in Reporting (FAIR), was requesting that year's Super Bowl network to air public service spots relative to the phenomenon—based on reports and pleas from shelter workers that Super Bowl Sunday is one of their busiest days of the year. Figuring that some 1 million women are abused each year, Quindlen facetiously suggested how, if PSAs (public service announcements) run about a dollar for each one, it would be worth it. She concludes: "So whether or not there's some sick synergy on Super Sunday between beer, betting and beatings, between violence on the field and violence in the home, there is good reason to bring this issue into the national spotlight" (p. E17). No wonder Nelson Frey (1995) has labeled it "The Violence Bowl."

Dissecting the language surrounding sports in general and the Super Bowl in particular hopefully can lead us to better understand inherent conflicts and repercussions, alerting us to linguistic and active alternatives. An examination of the rhetoric surrounding and embedded in a sample of these athletic contests helps explain how violence on the field can translate to our wider infotainment-oriented and hegemonically masculine-powered society.

NOTES

1. Cited in Green (1984), p. 169.
2. The most-watched Super Bowl was in 1986, the Chicago Bears versus the New

England Patriots, which drew a 48.3 rating and a 70 percent share, but a number of the NFL championships have led the Nielsens.

3. The supreme Super Bowl spot came in 1984, when the Macintosh computer was introduced—setting a new standard for future advertising such as the McDonald's "Showdown" of Michael Jordon and Larry Bird vying for a Big Mac while Charles Barkely was the odd man out, the Bud Bowl, Nike and Reebok competitions, Budweiser's Spuds McKenzie, Fred Astaire dancing with a Dirt Devil, green M&Ms as aphrodisiacs, Federal Express's network test pattern in 1998, and many more.

REFERENCES

Adler, L. (1992). *Football coach quotes: The wit, wisdom and winning words of leaders on the Gridiron*. Jefferson, NC: McFarland & Company.

Berkow, I. (1991, January 27). Once again, it's the star-spangled super bowl. *New York Times*, p. S6.

Boutilier, M., and San Giovanni, L. (1983). *The sporting woman*. Champaign, IL: Human Kinetics.

Brummett, D., and Duncan, M. C. (1990). Theorizing without totalizing: Specularity and televised sports. *Quarterly Journal of Speech, 76*, 227–46.

Cagle, J. (1991, February 15). Oh say, can you sing? *Entertainment Weekly*, p. 84.

Chandler, J. M. (1988). *Television and national sport: The United States and Britain*. Urbana: University of Illinois Press.

Considine, T. (1982). *The language of sport*. New York: World Almanac Publications.

Creedon, P. J. (Ed.). (1994). *Women, media, and sport: Challenging gender values*. Thousand Oaks, CA: Sage.

Daddario, G. (1998). *Women's sport and spectacle: Gendered television coverage and the Olympic Games*. Westport, CT: Praeger.

Davis, L. R. (1997). *The swimsuit issue and sport: Hegemonic masculinity in Sports Illustrated*. Albany, NY: State University of New York Press.

Duncan, M. C., and Brummett, B. (1987). The mediation of spectator sport. *Research Quarterly for Exercise and Sport, 58*, 168–77.

Frey, J. (1995, January 29). The violence bowl: One woman's view. *New York Times*, p. 43.

Frommer, H. (1979). *Sports roots: How nicknames, namesakes, trophies, competitions, and expression in the world of sports came to be*. New York: Athenaeum.

Fuller, L. K. (1992a). *Sportstalk/wartalk/patriotismtalk/mentalk: Super Bowl XXV*. Paper presented to the International Association for Media and Communication Research, Sao Paulo, Brazil.

Fuller, L. K. (1992b). Reporters' rights to the locker room. *Feminist Issues, 12* (1) (Spring); 39–45.

Fuller, L. K. (1994). The business of sportscasting. In P. J. Graham (Ed.), *Sport business: Operational and theoretical aspects* (pp. 251–61). Madison, WI: Brown & Benchmark.

Gerber, E. R., Felshin, J., Berlin, P., and Wyrick, W. (1974). *The American woman in sport*. Reading, MA: Addison-Wesley.

Goodman, Ellen. (1998, January 29). Super Bowl sends testosterone raging. *(Springfield, Mass.) Union News*, p. A11.

Green, J. (1995). *Super Bowl chronicles: A sportswriter reflects on the first 30 years of America's game*. Indianapolis, IN: Masters Press.

Green, L. (1984). *Sportswit*. New York: HarperCollins.

Gunther, M., and Carter, R. (1988). *Monday night mayhem: The inside inside story of ABC's Monday Night Football*. New York: Beach Tree Books/William Morrow.

Guttman, A. (1986). *Sports spectators*. New York: Columbia University Press.

Hall, M. A. (1978). *Sport and gender: A feminist perspective on the sociology of sport*. Ottawa: Canadian Association of Health, Physical Education, and Recreation Sociology of Sport Monograph Series.

Hanks, S. (1989). *The game that changed pro football*. Secaucus, NJ: Carol Publishing Group.

Hargreaves, J. (1994). *Sporting females: Critical issues in the history and sociology of women's sports*. New York: Routledge.

Hill, M. (1991, January 26). Football commentary requires tact in wartime. *Baltimore Evening Sun*.

Himmelstein, H. (1989). *Television myth and the American mind*. New York: Praeger.

hooks, b. (1984). *Feminist theory: From margin to center*. Boston: South End Press.

Hoyle, J. C., and Lanier, K. (1997, December 2). Women huddle for lessons in football 101. *Christian Science Monitor*, p. 15.

Hyman, L. J. (1996). *Official book of Super Bowl XXX: Showdown in the desert*. Woodford Press.

Jansen, S. C., and Sabo, D. (1992). *Sport war: The gender order, the Persian Gulf War and the new world order*. Paper presented at the 42nd annual conference of the International Communications Association, Miami, FL.

Janz, W., and Abrahamson, V. (1991). *War of the words: Twenty-five years of Super Bowl head-butts & high-fives*. Minneapolis: Bobble-heads Press.

Jenkins, H. (1992). *Textual poachers: Television fans and participatory culture*. New York: Routledge.

Johnson, W. O., Jr. (1971). *Super spectator and the electric Lilliputians*. Boston: Little, Brown and Co.

Klatell, D. A., and Marcus, N. (1988). *Sports for sale: Television, money, and the fans*. New York: Oxford University Press.

Koppett, L. (1981). *Sports illusion, sports reality: A reporter's view of sports, journalism and society*. Boston: Houghton Mifflin.

Lance, K. (1980). *A woman's guide to spectator sports*. New York: A & W Visual Library.

The Learning Annex. (1984). *How to talk sports to men*. New York: Berkeley Books.

Macdonald, M. (1995). *Representing women: Myths of femininity in the popular media*. London: Edward Arnold.

Martin, D. (1991, January 27). TV view: No football? No problem. *New York Times*, p. H29.

McAllister, M. P. (1996). *The commercialization of American culture: New advertising, control and democracy*. Thousand Oaks, CA: Sage.

Messner, M. A., and Sabo, D. F. (Eds.). (1990). *Sport, men, and the gender order: Critical feminist perspectives*. Champaign, IL: Human Kinetics.

Nelson, M. B. (1994). *The stronger women get, the more men love football: Sexism and the American culture of sports*. Orlando, FL: Harcourt Brace.

Newsom, D. D. (1991, April 10). The Gulf War wasn't a sports match that ended in victory. *Christian Science Monitor,* p. 19.

O'Neil, T. (1989). *The Game Behind the Game: High Stakes, High Pressure in Television Sports.* New York: Macmillan.

Oglesby, C. (Ed.). (1978). *Women and sport: From myth to reality.* Philadelphia: Lea and Febiger.

Patton, P. (1984). *Razzle dazzle: The curious marriage of television and football.* Garden City, NY: The Dial Press.

Powers, R. (1984). *Supertube: The rise of television sports.* New York: Coward-McCann.

Quindlen, A. (1993, January 17). Time to tackle this. *New York Times, 17,* p. E17.

Rader, B. G. (1984). *In its own image: How television has transformed sports.* New York: Macmillan.

Real, M. R. (1989a). *Super media: A cultural studies approach.* Newbury, CA: Sage.

Real, M. R. (1989b). Super Bowl football versus World Cup soccer: A cultural-structural comparison. In Lawrence A. Wenner (Ed.), *Media, sports, & society* (pp. 180–201). Newbury Park, CA: Sage.

Real, M. R. (1996). *Exploring media culture: A guide.* Thousand Oaks, CA: Sage.

Remley, M. L. (1991). *Women in sport: An annotated bibliography and resource guide, 1900–1990.* Boston: G. K. Hall.

Resciniti, A. et al. (1994). *Super Bowl excitement.* Minocqua, WI: Willowwisp.

Rosenberg, H. (1991, January 28). Hussein—a football fan? *Los Angeles Times.*

Sampson, M. (1996). *The football that won.* New York: Henry Holt & Co.

Schwartz, Dona. (1998). *Contesting the Super Bowl.* New York: Routledge.

Spence, J. (1988). *Up close and personal: The inside story of network television sports.* New York: Athenaeum.

Spencer, D. (1998, January 29). Top ten Superbowl commercials of 1998, and other goodies. *The Student Voice,* p. 10.

Sporting News Staff. (1992). *The complete Super Bowl book.* Sporting News.

Theberge, N. (1981). A critique of critiques: Radical and feminist writings on sport. *Social Forces, 60* (2), 341–53.

Twin, S. (1979). *Out of the bleachers: Writings on women and sport.* New York: Feminist Press.

Underwood, J. (1984). *Spoiled sport: A fan's notes on the troubles of spectator sports.* Boston: Little, Brown and Co.

Wenner, L. A. (1989). The Super Bowl pregame show: Cultural fantasies and political subtext (pp. 151–79). In Lawrence A. Wenner (Ed.), *Media, sports, & society.* Newbury Park, CA: Sage.

Whannel, G. (1992). *Fields in vision: Television sport and cultural transformation.* New York: Routledge.

13

Phyllis Pearson Elmore

Agitational Versatility: When Truth Met Jordan

INTRODUCTION

On July 25, 1974, Barbara Charline Jordan came before the television camera to present her position on the impeachment of the president of the United States. Solemn, tired, she hunched over four annotated, amended pages of her own notes and four pages of historical impeachment criteria set against Nixon's actions. Her black-rimmed glasses reflected the glare of the lights as she studied her notes. Then, improvising, she spoke to an unseen and unknown audience in living rooms across the country.

One hundred twenty-three years earlier, another six-footer, a female ex-slave, entered a church at Akron, Ohio, where the Women's Rights Convention was being held. Clad in an oversized smock, comfortable walking shoes, and a shabby head rag situated over her bonnet, she listened as a coterie of white males proselytyzed, via a tortured logic, against granting women—white women—equality before the law. Never one to suffer fools kindly, Sojourner Truth, originally called Isabella Baumfree, rose and strode to the podium.

These two public moments intersect on several planes. Both Jordan and Truth were operating in traditionally white male–dominated arenas, which accepted uncritically patriarchal values as the norm for family and society. Both women had defeated the boundaries whereby the private sphere, or the home, was woman's place, whereas the public sphere, or society, was male's proper domain.

Both Jordan and Truth stood at the center of incongruous media moments in which the linguistic, visual, and tonal components of the camera's eye, in Jor-

Figure 13.1
Barbara Charline Jordan, Washington, D.C., in 1974

Courtesy of artist Lorena Garza.

dan's case, and the reporter's eyes and ears, in Truth's, invited analysis of sexism as a major problem connected with and as evil as racism in American society. They thus spoke the same language from different social locations. Each spoke from the authority of her own experience. When Truth spoke at Akron, no woman served in elective office in the federal government. Well over a century later, when Jordan spoke at the impeachment proceedings, a handful of women and several minority males held national elective office. Hence, inherent in the fabric of American social and political life in 1851, as well as in 1974, were the perogatives of race, sex, and class.

"Sexism like racism," declared James Cone (1991), "is freedom's opposite" (p. 274). In their remarks, the women argue for free will and for unfettered critical reasoning. Indeed, they construct what Cornel West (1994) calls a "prophetic framework of moral reasoning" (p. 48). In these pivotal moments, Jordan indirectly, and Truth directly, challenged the racist and sexist stereotypes that have historically thwarted black female creativity in this country. Therefore, this chapter argues that in analyzing the nature of their power as orators, two intriguing points emerge. First, Jordan's and Truth's particular uses of verbal strategies

Figure 13.2
Sojourner Truth, Akron, Ohio, in 1851

Courtesy of artist Lorena Garza.

position them within the tradition of black American female oratory. Second, given these women's positions within a complex sociopolitical environment, they operated as rhetors who successfully confronted gender and racial bias as they stood their ground and appropriated moral suasion for their particular aims.

Born into slavery at Ulster County, New York, Sojourner Truth bore five children and suffered cruel slaveholders who used her unusual physical strength and inflicted beatings to subdue her will. Escaping from slavery a year before New York officially emancipated its slaves in 1827, Truth traveled the country speaking for abolitionist and suffragist causes. Unable to read or write, she captivated her Northern audiences with her simplicity of expression, with her sincerity of purpose, and with her natural conversational style. Sojourner Truth's story is the stuff of legends, since she built quite a reputation for fearlessness coupled with a bit of folksiness. She is said to have successfully subdued a conductor who tried to evict her from a city trolley. Also, Truth's contemporaries relate the story in which she put a Rochester, New York, police officer in his place when she encountered him on a dark street. When the latter demanded that she give an accounting of herself, Truth paused, planted her cane firmly, drew up to her full six-foot height, and in her deep, resonant voice, replied, "I am that I am." The unnerved officer vanished, and Truth went on her way (Gates and McKay, 1997, p. 196).

While she advanced no systematic theory of rhetoric, Truth did use a series of artistic proofs to support her claims, most notably in her famous speech in 1851 at the Women's Rights Convention at Akron. Her oratorical moment was fraught with sexual, racial, classist, and political imagery. Situated at a time in American history in which her particular gender and race were maliciously excoriated, Sojourner Truth was an automatic object of suspicion, distrust, and disdain at the convention. A brief review of some of the virulent racial rhetoric of the day provides chilling context for her reception at Akron. The climate of racial distrust can be illustrated by the so-called white scholars who posted offerings of pseudoscience and bogus social theory to bolster their offensive claims against blacks. Harvard graduate Philip A. Bruce was the son of a plantation owner and slaveholder, the brother-in-law of Thomas Nelson Page, and the nephew of the Confederacy's secretary of war. His nineteenth-century publication *The Plantation Freedman* argued that blacks, " 'cut off from the spirit of White society,' had regressed to a primitive and thus criminal state. Bereft of the master's influence, Blacks were even closer to the 'African type' than the slaves had been" (Giddings, 1984, p. 27).

Bruce's stereotypical paradigms were especially demeaning to black women whom he described as "morally obtuse and openly licentious." Hence, "because they were women, their regression was seen as much worse than that of men" (p. 31). Toni Morrison has argued that the Africanist presence in the Americas "provides a way of contemplating chaos and civilization, desire, and fear, and a mechanism for testing the problems of freedom" (1992, p. 7). If we examine the impact of racism on those who perpetuate it on nonblacks, we discover that the obsession distorts the mind and replaces reason with a pretzel logic. So it was with Bruce and his cohorts.

Often those purporting to be sympathetic to black equality succumbed to received racist generalizations of the day. Indeed, one G. Vale, a newspaper publisher and mathematics professor, who once volunteered his services to Sojourner Truth on a legal matter, recorded his first impression of her—in condescension: "She has African features and no apparent mixture of blood; she is not exactly bad looking, but there is nothing prepossessing or very observant or intelligent in her looks" (Pauli, 1962, p. 122).

Vale's assessment begs the question of why he felt compelled to appraise Truth's appearance and intelligence in the first place. Therefore, a mixed bag of racist, sexist, and classist baggage accompanied Truth to the podium that day. Indeed, there were urgent whispers of protest to Frances Gage, convention chairperson, not to allow Truth to speak, lest "every newspaper in the land have our cause mixed with abolition and niggers" (Gates and McKay, 1997, p. 199). It appears that Gage herself may have had feet of clay and was unnerved by the clamors for Truth's silence (Giddings, 1984, p. 54). However, Truth did speak, and she was heard.

Sojourner Truth used several techniques, including turning the tables, reductio, ad absurdium, appeals to authority, as well as humor, to refute the claims that she had heard. But moreover, her rebuttal can be analyzed by what Steele and Redding (1962, pp. 83–91) call a values appeal. This paradigm uses patriotism, indicative when Truth calls for equality of opportunity for all people, a claim made at least indirectly by the Constitution.

Perhaps Truth's strongest values appeal is her inherent claim of the value of the individual and, in this case, praise for the ability of women to surmount the odds allayed against them by insensitive and unethical males. In addition, Truth appropriates a Puritan or pioneer morality as she stands alone on a racial island, separated as she was from her audience by color, economics, and gender.

Well, Children, where there is so much racket, there must be something out of kilter. ... The white man will be in a fix pretty soon. But what's all this about anyway? That man over there he says women need to be helped into carriages and lifted over ditches and to have the best everywhere. Nobody ever helps me into carriages, over mud puddles, or gets me any best places. And ain't I a woman? I have ploughed and I have planted. And I have gathered into barns. And no man could head me. And ain't I a woman? I have borne five children and seen them sold into slavery, and when I cried out in a mother's grief, none heard me but Jesus. And ain't I a woman? (McKissack and Mc-Kissack, 1994, p. 112)

Then, one by one, she addressed the male religious pedants: "You say Jesus was a man so that means God favors men over women. Where did your God come from? From God and a woman. Man had nothing to do with him" (p. 114). Next she attacks the myth of superior male intelligence, using humor and what passes for a simplistic reasoning. It is anything but: "Suppose a man's mind holds a quart, and woman's don't hold but a pint; if her pint is full, it's as good as a quart" (p. 114). Then Truth addresses her primary audience, the women: "If the first woman God ever made was strong enough to turn the world upside down all alone, these women ought to be able to put it back and get it right-side up again and now that they are asking to do it, the men better let 'em" (pp. 114–15).

The July 21, 1851, edition of *The Anti-Slavery Bugle* warmly praised Truth's delivery and described her audience's conversion, giving special attention to her "powerful form; whole-souled earnest gestures; strong ... tones" (Gates and McKay, 1997, p. 198). As Gates and McKay have pointed out, Frances Gage handed down a more elaborate and more dialectical Sojourner Truth than did the *Bugle* reporter, and hence her "reliability has been questioned" (p. 197). Further, in allowing Truth to speak, Gage may have been dabbling in seasonal niceties for her own substantive agenda. Frances Gage, like her political sisters Susan B. Anthony and Elizabeth Cady Stanton, was no particular friend to black rights. These women, as Paula Giddings (1984) holds, "viewed the strategy of expediency—despite its racist and classist implications, as ends justifying the means" (p. 125).

None of them was willing to speak with clarity and courage for black rights—men or women—if such a stance disturbed their own comfort. Indeed, white feminists and perhaps these women as well were present on one occasion when Truth was asked to show evidence of her gender. Truth suffered the indignity of having to bare her chest, and these women spoke not a word of protest (Russell, 1990, p. 7). As a black woman, Truth's clarity, vision, and courage as she challenged the prevailing stereotypes of her day represent a fine moment in black female public address.

No speech matters more to the oratorical history of black women in America than Barbara Jordan's impeachment statement in 1974. Before Jordan, there were important groundbreaking black female orators: Lucy Terry in the eighteenth century; Maria Stewart, Truth, Ida B. Wells-Barnett in the nineteenth century; and Mary McLeod Bethune, Fannie Lou Hamer, and Shirley Chisolm in the twentieth. It, therefore, was not a matter of Jordan's bringing black female oratory into the mainstream. It was already there. What Jordan did was to take on the major issue of the day—Watergate excesses—and to dissect it via a values paradigm and thereby render to her audience a transformative moment, in terms of sealing Nixon's political fate. Her statement *appeared* to transcend race, sex, and class, *even as it forced us to examine these verities* by the sheer imagery of the moment itself. Like Truth, Jordan could not escape the visual irony of a black female administering moral solace and ethical anchor to a nation and to a white male elite, sorely in need of both.

The substance of Jordan's statement was at once liberating *and* confining. Her cogent pronouncements liberated her audience *into* responsibility for the body politic with the aim of the ethical renewal of the nation. Jordan's speech situates her as a moral arbiter at the center of the national dilemma. She once taught a course in political ethics at Texas that included an essay called "The Conscience of Huckleberry Finn." The boy, bred in a racist Southern culture, is faced with the moral dilemma of either remanding Jim to the slave catchers or helping the latter to escape bondage. Huck's double-visioned self declares to his own mirrored reflection: "Alright, I'll go to hell, then." While technically aiding Jim's escape, Huck is nevertheless ignorant of Jim's humanity. He therefore does the right thing for the wrong reason, and because he accepts the ideology of the status quo, he is rendered morally helpless. Jordan had no such moral dilemma, as Paul Burka (1996) has pointed out, when she faced the cameras that July day to state her position on the impeachment question (p. 89). In fact, her credibility was already established in Texas before she ever sat before the cameras. She had distinguished herself as a debater at Phillis Wheatley High School at Houston, winning a tie with students from Harvard in a national contest; she had been the first black elected to Congress from the South since Reconstruction; and she was only one of a handful of freshmen legislators invited to sit on the

House Judiciary Committee. But she enjoyed no uncritical acceptance from the men in her political life. Indeed, when Jordan defeated black militant Graves for her congressional seat in 1970, the former called her an "Aunt Jemima." "It means," Jordan explained to a baffled white supporter, "my ass isn't black enough" (Burka, 1996, p. 110). But Barbara Jordan was always less concerned about the color of her derriere than she was about the color of her conscience—clear and colorless.

She opens with a tone of moral authority that the *Washington Post* pronounced "Churchillian" (Lind, 1996, p. 6). Jordan's debt to black southern preachers, notably to her own father, is evident in her appropriation of the triple structure, as when she declares that her "faith in the Constitution is whole, complete, total." As has been noted, Jordan was not the first black woman to rise to prominence on a public stage. But the image of the six-foot Jordan, intense, imposing, intellectual, was such as had never before been seen on that national forum. Despite her bulk, Jordan's voice was commanding, yet safe. Like Truth before her, Jordan's vibratory delivery offered a morally distinctive message.

Opening by reciting one of the most familiar phrases in American political language, "We the people," Jordan quickly acknowledges the exclusivity of her own people when the Constitution was written in September 1787. But she does not long tarry over this reality, thereby gaining common ground with her audience: "But through the process of amendment, interpretation, and court decision, I have finally been included in 'We the people' " (Bryant, 1977, p. 51). Jordan's assertion is not simplistic. The exclusivity with respect to gender, race, and class that influenced the Framers makes Jordan's presence in *this* chamber speaking on *this* issue—elitist male excesses and arrogance—prophetic as well as symbolic. She quickly moves to the key issue. By naming herself "inquisitor," she reimages and appropriates for her own purposes American political rhetoric. She, Barbara Jordan, has become an arbiter of the very instrument that had cast her as a mere footnote two centuries before. Jordan, whose race was legally invisible to the Framers, will now test the marvelous elasticity of the document largely created with whites males in mind. From the moment that she declares via triple structure that "my faith in the Constitution is whole. It is total. It is complete. I am not going to sit here and be an idle spectator to the diminution of the Constitution" (p. 51), Jordan commands her audience's attention. Using simple Bible tones, she cuts to the core of the ethical issue. And she validates her self-assignment as inquisitor by appealing to the authority of the *Federalist Papers*, No. 65.

The subjects of its jurisdiction are those offenses that proceed from the misconduct of public men. In other words, she takes her authority from a document that she is cognizant that her audience reveres. Closely reading the jurisdiction for her own actions and statements from the Constitution, she reminds us of the division of powers as set forth by the Framers: "We do not trust liberty to a particular branch." She enhances her own ethical appeal to her audience by her dismissal of partisan politics as the motivation for this process: "Common sense would be revolted if we engaged upon this process for petty reasons" (p. 53).

She then anticipates her opposition's claims that the proceedings may be premature, the evidence to support impeachment thin, and that there would be forthcoming clarification from the White House to clear up these issues. Jordan ties Nixon's inaction in the face of the Judiciary Committee's request for information to the concept of the rule of law: "The fact is that yesterday, the American people waited with great anxiety for eight hours, not knowing whether their President would obey an order of the Supreme Court of the United States" (p. 53).

By connecting Nixon's actions to specific impeachment criteria, Jordan alerts her audience to the seriousness of her imminent vote to impeach:

- James Madison: "If the President be connected in any suspicious manner with any person. . . ."
- Justice Story: "Impeachment is intended for the occasional, and extraordinary cases where a superior power is put into operation to protect their rights and rescue their liberties from violation." (marshalls the evidence, tagging it with "We know" to avoid the appearance of supposition)
- South Carolina Ratification Convention: "Those are impeachable who behave amiss or betray pubic trust." (delineates Nixon's gallery of documented falsehoods)
- Madison again: "A President is impeachable if he attempts to subvert the Constitution." (Nixon counseled aides to commit perjury) (p. 54)

After her careful juxtapositioning of Nixon's actions to the impeachment criteria, Jordan offers a proposition that she knows her audience will have to accept:

If the impeachment provision in the Constitution of the United States will not reach the offenses charged here, then perhaps that eighteenth-century Constitution should be abandoned to a twentieth-century shredder. Has the President committed offenses and planned and directed and acquiesced in a course of conduct which the Constitution will not tolerate? That is the question. We know the question. We should forthwith proceed to answer that question. It is reason and not passion which must guide our deliberations, guide our debate, and guide our decision. (p. 54)

Asserting finally the superiority of reason over passion in her argument assures Jordan's intent to proceed fairly with an aim toward the gathering of facts. Her use of triple structures as she hopes that reason will "guide our deliberations, guide our debate, and guide our decision" is a cogent appeal to the ethical dimension of argumentation. The key to Jordan's successful appeals lies in her use of a values-laden argument. In placing the Constitution as the centerpiece of her claims, she has situated the values of patriotism, the value of the individual as well as the individual's responsibility to uphold the laws of nation, and constructed, not unlike Sojourner Truth, a code of conduct predicated upon such founding principles as Puritan and pioneer morality. That she overwhelmingly makes her case is evident in the bipartisan reception that she received from both media and public responses to her statement.

CONCLUSION

In 1892, after more than a decade of courageous and often life-threatening crusades to research and to render coherently the truth about the psychosexual dimension of lynching in the southern United States, Ida B. Wells-Barnett sought to publish her findings in booklet form for wide distribution in the country but had no funds with which to do so. Two hundred and fifty black women honored her with a testimonial and a fund-raiser on October 5 at New York's Lyric Hall. The meeting was unprecedented in the history of black women in the country, and the phrase "Lyric Hall" became a psychic moniker for rallying the race, especially the women of the race, to the aid of one of its own. The conceptual aspect of an allegorical Lyric Hall, wherein a people seize the initiative to lend voice, talent, and resources for the specific aim of moral suasory, resonates in the oratorical skill of Truth and Jordan.

Sojourner Truth and Barbara Jordan challenge historical intellectual domination by decoding racial insincerity and moral frailty of their day.

At the center of each statement is a firmly held faith in the inherent justness of their claims and a belief that right will prevail, that fairness and decency will win the day. Although the women are miles apart in terms of time, place, and education, the essentialities of their individual messages are salient. Their statements marry imagery and idea in ways that their audiences immediately understood. As they appropriate a Puritan ethic that places the individual at the center of reason and morality, they invent a system of moral suasion that refocuses and redefines the role of race, sex, and class in American social and political debate. When Truth met Jordan, therefore, something in the machinery of the status quo defected, as the two collectively called for a needed "meeting at some Lyric Hall" (Giddings, 1984, p. 357).

REFERENCES

Burka, P. (1996, March). Major Barbara. *Texas Monthly*, pp. 88–111.

Cone, J. (1991). *Martin and Malcolm and America: A dream or a nightmare?* Maryknoll, NY: Orbis Books.

Gates, H. L., and McKay, N. Y. (Eds.). (1997). *The Norton anthology of African American literature*. New York: W. W. Norton.

Giddings, P. (1984). *When and where I enter: The impact of black women on race and sex in America*. New York: William Morrow.

Jordan, B. (1974, July 25). Address. Statement presented before the House Judiciary Committee, Washington, DC.

Lind, M. (1996, February). Jordan rules. *The New Republic.* p. 6.

McKissack, P. C., and McKissack, F. (1994). *Sojourner Truth: Ain't I a woman?* New York: Scholastic.

Morrison, T. (1992). *Playing in the dark: Whiteness and the literary imagination.* New York: Random House.

Pauli, H. (1962). *Her name was Sojourner Truth.* New York: Avon Books.

Russell, S. (1990). *Render me my song.* New York: St. Martin's Press.

Steele, E. D., and Redding, W. C. (1962). The American value system: Premises for persuasion. *Western Speech, 26,* 83–91.

West, C. (1994). *Race Matters.* New York: Vintage Books.

14

*Susan Stearns and
Meta G. Carstarphen*

Deconstructing Ellen:
Time, Sitcoms, and the
Meaning of Gayness

INTRODUCTION

On-screen, everything about the word scared her. Ellen Morgan, played by co-
medienne Ellen DeGeneres, was facing Susan, a successful television producer
played by actress Laura Dern, in a busy airport. "What is wrong?" she asked.
"Why do I have to be so ashamed? Why can't I just say the truth . . . be who I
am?"

The question addressed not only Susan but also the audience. We not only
saw "Ellen," the fictional character, but Ellen, the person, struggle to be true to
herself against social beliefs about homosexuality that she had internalized for
years. When Ellen finally did break through her fear, she turned to her new
friend, leaned over and said, "Susan, I'm gay." This announcement was mo-
mentous, for "Ellen" had inadvertently perched over a microphone when she
uttered those words and broadcast them to everyone via the airport loudspeaker.

It was impossible to overlook the symbolism of this "mistake." Ellen De-
Generes, who had publicly sidestepped questions about her own sexuality for
years, took a loud and very public step out of the closet. Everyone heard the
words the moment they left her mouth. For "Ellen" and Ellen DeGeneres, there
was no turning back. The actress had finally given power to her truth.

COMING OUT TO AN AUDIENCE

On April 30, 1997, television history was made when for the first time since
the development of the medium in the 1940s the main character on a popular

sitcom announced to the viewing audience that she was a lesbian. In a one-hour episode run during the crucial spring sweeps rating period, recently "out" comedian Ellen DeGeneres took the viewing audience through her character, "Ellen's" fear, pain, and joy of discovering and revealing her true identity.

The episode revolved around the relationship between Ellen Morgan and Susan, a television producer introduced to Ellen through her high school sweetheart, Richard (Steven Eckholdt), a TV news anchor. Susan, an "out" lesbian very comfortable with her sexuality, becomes the catalyst for Ellen's discovery that she, too, is gay, but only after several scenes in which Ellen puzzled over her lack of attraction to Richard while trying desperately to deny any desire for women.

When Ellen rushed to meet Susan at the airport and announced, during a touching and funny scene, that she indeed was a lesbian, the two embraced amidst the loud, drawn-out cheers and applause of the live studio audience. The remainder of the show chronicled Ellen's journey to full acceptance through discussions with her therapist and a nervous announcement to her friends, who were generally supportive and accepting of Ellen's new identity.

The public responded to "Ellen's" revelation, both in DeGeneres's real life and on the show, with a great deal of interest. Since 1994, when *Ellen* began on ABC, the gay and lesbian community, which knew for years that DeGeneres was a lesbian, followed the television show searching for the many clues she offered about her character's identity. Spurred on in part by activist organizations such as the Gay and Lesbian Alliance Against Defamation (GLAAD) and the Human Rights Campaign (HRC), gays and lesbians throughout the United States planned more than 1,500 parties and media events for the night "Ellen" finally came out on the show. GLAAD developed a "Come Out with Ellen" Web site, stating that if Ellen Morgan can come out to the world, "you can come out to your family, friends and co-workers" (GLAAD, 1997a). *Ellen* "clues lists" were circulated throughout the cyberspace community, and hundreds of news articles were published about DeGeneres, gays and lesbians, and the joys of coming out.

The night of the show's airing during "sweeps" week, *Ellen* was the number-one network television show. Forty-two million people watched the show, giving it a 35 percent share in the Nielsen ratings. This was more than twice the show's usual audience and roughly comparable to the average rating for *ER*, the number-one show on television. According to Bill Carter (1997a), television critic for the *New York Times*, because of the *Ellen* episode, ABC managed a "rare weekly victory in the prime-time ratings, beating NBC by almost a full rating point for the week" (p. C20). Carter also notes that DeGeneres was responsible for the number-four rated show during sweeps week; *PrimeTime Live* scored its highest rating of the year that week because of an interview with DeGeneres and her family.

Much of this overwhelming attention to Ellen, no doubt, was fomented by the news media's frenzy over all things DeGeneres. Renee Graham (1997) from the *Boston Globe* noted that DeGeneres's decision to come out inspired a great deal of interest within the public discourse.

DeGeneres's decision (which included her own coming out) has inspired newspaper polls and sound bites, debates about advertiser boycotts and lesbian cruise lines, and windy predictions running the gamut from grimly apocalyptic to gleefully euphoric. Self-appointed moral savior Jerry Fallwell has taken to calling the actress "Ellen DeGenerate," whereas one gay newspaper editor compared her to Jackie Robinson (Graham, 1997, p. C1).

MEDIA FRENZIES HEIGHTEN

Without a doubt, the publicity surrounding DeGeneres and her show had been enormous. A database search on Lexis/Nexis revealed the extent of the media attention given to the event. During the month of February 1997 when news leaked to the media that DeGeneres was considering coming out of the closet and bringing her character with her, coverage of DeGeneres and her show increased exponentially. During the month of March, there were more than 500 articles on *Ellen* in newspapers in the United States.

In April 1997, thousands more news articles were written about *Ellen*, 515 of which appeared in major newspaper, on April 30, the day the episode aired. Furthermore, thirty-one magazine articles mentioning DeGeneres were published in April, including the famous April 14 *Time* magazine article in which DeGeneres announced for the first time, "Yep, I'm gay." Eighty-seven Associated Press (AP) wire stories about DeGeneres also were distributed during April. Between May 1 and May 7, over 400 major newspapers ran stories mentioning DeGeneres. Throughout the month of May, there were forty-one magazine articles and thirty-five AP wire stories.

Television news was not to be left behind, however, DeGeneres appeared on numerous television news and interview shows, including *Conan O'Brien, Oprah, David Letterman*, the *Tonight Show, 20/20, PrimeTime Live, Entertainment Tonight*, and *E!* Clearly public interest in DeGeneres and the *Ellen* television show was running high in the weeks before and during the famous coming-out episode. Numerous news reports and analyses told us the event was historical in its significance—a "must see event." ABC promoted the show frequently and loudly, and television, magazine, and newspaper interviewers could not get enough information from and about DeGeneres. Not since the gays in the military controversy in 1992 at the beginning of President Clinton's first term in office had homosexuals and homosexual issues been so widely discussed and debated in the public discourse.

Gays and lesbians expressed a great deal of excitement over DeGeneres's coming out. Howard Rosenberg (1997), *Los Angeles Times* television critic, said in a September 24 article, "*Ellen* look[s] very much like a series of seminal importance, television's most significant comedy since CBS raised the curtain on racism and bigotry in *All in the Family* nearly 27 years ago. *Ellen* has an opportunity to diminish prejudice on a level not previously seen in TV" (p. F1).

DeGeneres told the press over and over again that she wanted to contribute to increasing society's acceptance level for gays and lesbians. After receiving the Emmy for best writing in a television comedy, DeGeneres told the Associated Press that such recognition is a "big nod" of approval from the industry and noted that she hopes her character will "help viewers see that there are gay people and we are OK, because growing up I didn't have that" (Lyons and Wallenfels, 1997).

Joan M. Garry, executive director of GLAAD, said "Ellen's acceptance speech not only touched each and every lesbian and gay man across the nation, it touched their families as well. Like every American parent, I want my three children to grow up in a world without hatred and bigotry, and Ellen's historic win last night is a great stride in the right direction for the television industry, and for our nation" (GLAAD, 1997b).

FROM ABSENCE TO MARGINAL PRESENCES

Clearly, a great deal of social significance was attributed to DeGeneres's coming-out process. For almost fifty years since the invention of television, lesbians and gays have suffered relative invisibility in their representation in the medium (Fejes and Petrich, 1993; Gross, 1995; Moritz, 1991). Media scholars theorize that this invisibility, or symbolic annihilation, is an indication of the traditional lack of cultural and political power lesbians and gays hold throughout society. Gross (1991) in particular sees symbolic annihilation as a way elites keep nonmainstream groups outside of society's power structure. "While the holders of real power—the ruling class—do not require or seek mediated visibility, those who are at the bottom of the various power hierarchies will be kept in their places in part through their relative invisibility" (p. 21).

The rare instances when lesbians and gays have been portrayed on television have generally shown homosexuals as deviant, sick, or abnormal (Gross, 1991; Moritz, 1991). Because viewers tend to believe that media portrayals are at least partially realistic (Gross, 1995; Katz and Liebes, 1987; Signorelli, 1989), and because many people have little known contact with lesbians and gays on a daily basis, such portrayals can form the basis for assumptions about members of these groups. Thus, researchers have found that people who watch more television have more negative attitudes toward lesbians and gays (Kerns and Fine, 1994).

In the late 1990s, however, television's approach to the lesbian and gay population appears to be shifting. As of January 1998, thirty gay, lesbian, or bisexual characters appear regularly on network television (GLAAD, 1997a). These characters tend to be portrayed in a positive manner, often more sensible and "together" than the heterosexual characters surrounding them, as with the lesbian couple on *Friends*.

Most significant, however, were the events that took place in April 1997. During that month, an actress on a well-loved sitcom announced to the world that both she and the character she played were lesbians. Ellen DeGeneres's revelation, which marked the first time in television history a lesbian actress played a lesbian lead character, precipitated a great deal of media and public attention. A measure of the mainstream audience's interest in DeGeneres's coming out can be seen in their response to both news reports about DeGeneres and the television show itself.

On April 14, 1997, *Time* magazine published the first interview with DeGeneres in which she announced to the public that she was a lesbian. According to *Time*'s circulation department in New York (D. Pearson, personal communication, March 16, 1998), the April 14 issue was met with a great deal of public interest. The single issue had a 54 percent return rate on the newsstands, meaning that of the 500,000 issues sent to newsstands, 228,000 were purchased by consumers. *Time* ranks these numbers as "very good" on a return rate scale from "bad to very good."

Two weeks after the *Time* interview, on April 30, 1997, *Ellen*'s coming-out episode was aired. The night of the show's airing, *Ellen* was the number-one network television show, garnering a 35 percent share in the Nielsen ratings. This translates to a viewership of approximately 42 million people.

Clearly, the reading and viewing public followed DeGeneres's coming out with a great deal of interest and anticipation. The implications of the event itself coupled with the public's interest in the event could have far-reaching implications for lesbians and gays. Fejes and Petrich (1993) note, for example, that the media play a primary role in the formation of gay and lesbian identity, both at the individual level and at the level of community. "Whether the dominant media discourse defines homosexuality as a perversion, sickness or crime or defines it as a normal expression of human sexuality has a significant impact on how individual gay males or lesbians view themselves and their relationships to society" (p. 397). Thus, positive portrayals of gays and lesbians, such as those shown on *Ellen*, could result in higher self-esteem and self-confidence for lesbians and gays.

Gross (1991) believes that more positive portrayals of homosexuals on television could have implications for society as a whole. He notes that television, which functions as a primary source of information about the world and about social value systems for many people in the United States, tends to "cultivate" mainstream, elite attitudes among heavy viewers. The transmission of mainstream attitudes is particularly effective when information is presented about a group most viewers know little about, such as gays and lesbians. "In the absence of adequate information in their immediate environment, most people, gay or straight, have little choice other than to accept the narrow and negative stereotypes they encounter as being representative of gay people" (p. 27). Thus, for heavy television viewers, ideas about what it means to be homosexual are transmitted and supported by television images of lesbian and gay characters. This serves to support the status quo by keeping homosexuality as a marginalized force within the society at large.

Gross theorized that the presence of healthy, nonstereotypic lesbians and gay men on television could begin to change the way society views homosexuality. "It [could] undermine the unquestioned normalcy of the status quo, and it [could] open up the possibility of making choices to people who might never otherwise have considered or understood that such choices could be made" (p. 30). Such a change might have implications for society as a whole. Not only would lesbians and gays find more positive images to foster their sense of identity as individuals and as a community, but also the mainstream audience could begin to view homosexuality as more mainstream itself, thus erasing boundaries that prevented lesbians and gays from gaining true political and social power.

CULTURAL FRAMEWORKS: IDEOLOGIES IN CONFLICT

It is too early to study the historical significance of Ellen DeGeneres's coming out, yet this chapter can be a starting point for researchers to consider long-term attitude shifts in this society about homosexuality. Specifically, this discourse/ideological analysis of two "firsts"—the April 14, 1997, *Time* magazine front cover that shows Ellen DeGeneres as she first comes out to the public and the April 30, 1997, *Ellen* sitcom episode in which DeGeneres's character first acknowledges that she is a lesbian—will look for ideological differences between the two texts that could point to a struggle over the meaning of gayness in modern American society. If such a struggle is revealed, mainstream attitudes and beliefs could be in the process of shifting toward a different view of homosexuality, which could have far-reaching implications for lesbians and gays and for society as a whole.

The differences between the way in which *Ellen*/DeGeneres and the *Time* magazine cover framed lesbianism are highly indicative of a struggle between the two over the meaning of the sign "I'm gay" in U.S. society. While *Ellen*/ DeGeneres sought to normalize gayness, to show the basic humanity of a lesbian, the *Time* magazine cover and inside article functioned to destabilize this attempt by accenting "I'm gay" as abnormal and marginal.

John Fiske (1992) notes that the meaning of any sign becomes part of an ideological social struggle. The sign can be spoken in different accents according to who is using it, and thus to accent a sign is to inflect its meaning with the social interests of a particular group against those of others.

When the word *nigger* is accented by contemporary black rap artists in their music videos, they are giving it their meanings of blackness, racial subordination, and prejudice against the historically dominant white ones. In doing so, they are exploiting the multiaccentuality of the sign "nigger" and are thus politically engaging in racial relations. The struggle over the sign "nigger" is not just a struggle over the meanings of a word but over who has the power to control those meanings. This is important, for the power to control the meaning of social experience is a crucial part of controlling the social relations, identities, and behaviors of those involved in that experience (Fiske, 1992, p. 299).

SIGNS, SYMBOLS, AND DIFFERENCE

A similar struggle was going on between *Ellen*/DeGeneres and *Time* magazine. The struggle was not only over control of gayness on television but over the power for lesbians and gays to control their own identity and to validate the meanings of their own social experiences. The *Time* magazine cover limited the meanings of the sign "I'm gay" to those that it connoted when spoken with the dominant accent, thereby taking it out of the realm of struggle. Ellen DeGeneres, on the other hand, was struggling to exploit what Fiske (1992) calls "multiaccentuality" or "heteroglossia"—the ability to speak difference from the dominant position in one's own accent and to engage in the struggle to make sense of social difference on one's own terms rather than submitting to those proposed and preferred by the dominant group.

The April 14, 1997, *Time* magazine cover is riddled with ambiguities. The cover is devoted to a large picture of a smiling DeGeneres crouching down on her heels with the words "Yep, I'm Gay" superimposed in large type over her right shoulder. Underneath the headline are two "teasers" for the story: "Ellen DeGeneres explains why she's coming out" and "The changing nature of sex on TV." Clearly, by devoting the cover to DeGeneres, *Time* is announcing to its readers that her "coming out" is a significant, newsworthy event.

But the text on the cover frames DeGeneres in the context of difference. The actress proudly and unambiguously asserts "Yep, I'm gay," leaving no question about her sexual preference. At the same time, she must also "explain" to the world why she is coming out. The word *explain* implies that the actress must decipher her actions to the public, that the process of coming out is not something people would naturally understand without justification. Implicit in this need for explanation is also an assumption that the readers of *Time* magazine are heterosexual and unfamiliar with the reasons why a person would choose to come out.

More ambiguities between homosexuality and heterosexuality can be found in the second teaser: "The changing nature of sex on TV." While the words imply shifts in social attitudes about sexuality—something that would be particularly appealing to marginalized sexual minorities like lesbians and gays— they also serve to limit DeGeneres's coming out to the context of the television world, thus assuring heterosexuals that the entire fabric of their belief system was not about to crumble because of DeGeneres's actions.

Visually, *Time*'s cover further continues to marginalize homosexuality. DeGeneres is shown in a crouching position, with her hands and her smiling face as the most visible parts of her body. The rest of her body is essentially hidden from the audience. The relative invisibility of DeGeneres's body is highly significant since she is essentially neutered. Her breasts, stomach, waist, thighs, and legs—all components of a woman's physical sexuality—are hidden in the shadows. In the photograph, these cloaked sexual body parts function as a metaphorical denial of DeGeneres's sexual identity. Homosexuality, then, becomes framed within the nature of ideas (the visibility of her head), rather than in the nature of the physical (the invisibility of the rest of her body).

CENSORSHIP RUMBLINGS

During the fall 1997 television season, after her (in)famous episode, DeGeneres continued her struggle to highlight gay issues on her television show. On October 9, ABC placed a "due to adult content, parental discretion is advised" warning at the beginning of an episode in which DeGeneres jokingly kissed a female co-star. The warning—not displayed on other programs that showed heterosexual adults kissing—sparked a controversy that almost led to DeGeneres's quitting the show.

"Where will it stop?" DeGeneres asked. "If you say, 'Don't watch a show that has gay people on it,' who's to say they won't one day say, 'Don't watch a show that has Black people on it, or Jews?' It's like if they had a Black show and put on a warning that said this show isn't suitable for viewers who don't like Black people. No other show on ABC, not *Spin City* or *Drew Carey* or *Dharma and Greg* would be forced to carry that kind of advisory for a scene like this. The only other ABC show that's ever had this label is *NYPD Blue*, and that has nudity and violence" (Bauder, 1997, p. D). She added that the parental warning undermined the goal of her show—to let gay children know there's nothing wrong with being gay—by telling children that they shouldn't watch the show.

In response to DeGeneres's anger, ABC, which admitted to worrying that the *Ellen* show might become "too gay," offered conflicting responses to her claims of censorship. Network executive Kevin Brockman said the warning was not meant to exclude viewers but was instead simply a way to educate concerned parents.

"The network has a responsibility to give viewers and parents as much information as possible so they can make educational decisions for young viewers," Brockman said. "The advisory on tonight's episode is simply meant to do just that provide additional information. It is not meant to exclude viewers" (Bauder, 1997, p. D6).

On the other hand, Patricia Matson, a corporate spokeswoman for ABC, claimed the message was placed before the show so that parents would have time to decide if their children should be allowed to watch the show. "We are ultimately the ones responsible for maintaining the standards for our audience," Matson said. "The promise we have made to our audience is to provide them with as much information as possible so they can decide what is appropriate for their children to watch" (Carter, 1997b).

Clearly, the parental warning, which appeared on all shows during the fall season, which was the first season that included direct references to Ellen's sexuality, was an attempt by ABC to dilute DeGeneres's homonormal agenda by limiting the sign "I'm gay" to the realm of ideas, rather than the physical. This toning down of the gay message was a way in which the television network attempted to limit lesbianism to a form that was comfortable for the dominant, mainstream audience.

Ellen Goodman (1997), columnist for the *Boston Globe*, noted that ABC's handling of *Ellen* points to the prevalence of homophobic attitudes throughout society. The resistance, she says, stems from an unwillingness to believe that lesbian and gay sexuality can be anything other than deviant:

No sooner does ABC agree to the notion of content labeling than they slap a parental discretionary advisory about adult content on the only show with an openly gay star. It's a bit like yelling, "Eek, hide the children. There's a lesbian in the room." The show is getting a warning label because of its sexual identity, not because of its sexual content. . . . In the latest Ellen flap, parents are being warned about homosexuality itself. That exposes a serious fault line in the coalition of Americans who have favored ratings, warnings, V-chips, any tool of defense against the overwhelming culture of sex and violence. There is a huge gap between those who do and those who don't believe in the possibility of wholesome homosexuality. The perceived moral danger in this sitcom isn't really its sexual content. It is rather that the show might actually succeed in portraying a gay woman as a fellow struggler, maybe even a happy one. (p. C1)

EXPANDING THE MEANING OF GAYNESS

In effect, then, the struggle over the warning message was over power—who had the right to define, or accent, gayness and who didn't. ABC, perceiving *Ellen*/DeGeneres from a heteronormal perspective, viewed her lesbianism as threatening and abnormal. The warning message therefore functioned as an attempt to both communicate this perspective to viewers and to put DeGeneres back in her place.

DeGeneres, perceiving ABC's heteronormal objective, fought back in two ways: first, by drawing a comparison between homophobia and racism and, second, by threatening to quit the show. Her response mirrors Gross's (1995) contention that lesbians and gays utilize several techniques in response to homophobic treatment in the media, including secession and resistance. DeGeneres practiced resistance in this case by voicing her anger to the media. When this didn't work, she threatened to secede from the mainstream press in order to gain greater control over her creativity and her message, which, according to Gross (1995), is "the ultimate expression of independence for a minority struggling to free itself from the dominant culture's hegemony" (p. 68).

The power struggle between DeGeneres and ABC gave rise to a political struggle that illustrated the deep ideological divisions separating U.S. society. On October 16, 1997, a week after the parental warning was placed on *Ellen*, Vice President Al Gore praised the *Ellen* television show. In a speech to the Hollywood Radio and Television Society, Gore singled out *Ellen* for her valuable contribution to society, along with other influential TV characters such as Archie Bunker and Oscar the Grouch. Speaking about the character played by De-Generes, Gore said, "[W]hen the character 'Ellen' came out, millions of American were forced to look at sexual orientation in a more open light" (HRC, 1997).

Gore's remarks sparked a controversy that illustrates significant differences between heteronormal and homonormal ideologies. Gay and lesbian organizations, as well as many liberal human rights organizations, were overjoyed by Gore's remarks, whereas many conservative groups were outraged that the vice president would label *Ellen* as socially beneficial. Elizabeth Birch, executive director of the Human Rights Campaign, said Gore showed courage and good character with his remarks. "Television is a mirror of society and, unfortunately, for a very long time, gay people were either invisible or highly distorted. By singling out a positive gay character on a groundbreaking show, the vice president has himself helped to lead Americans to view our community with greater openness" (HRC, 1997).

At the same time, Randy Tate of the Christian Coalition said Gore's remarks showed him to be out of step with the American public. "I'd use Ronald Reagan's one-liner: 'He's gone so far left, he's left America.' He's way out of the mainstream. This is nothing more than craven pandering to the Hollywood left" (Orin and Connor, 1997, p. A1). Former Vice President Dan Quayle said further, "I'm always surprised to hear politicians promoting the agenda of Hollywood elites. If there's anybody whose agenda needs promoting, it is the middle-class American family" (Marcus, 1997, p. A1). And Alan Keyes, conservative radio talk show host, called Gore's remarks "tragic and misguided." He said, "With this speech, Al Gore is making himself a champion of the most radical anti-family forces in America today. Clearly, he fails to understand or willfully ignores the grave threat of Hollywood's promotion of sexual licentiousness poses to the heart and moral character needed to sustain decent families" (PR Newswire, 1997).

The rhetoric of the responses to Gore's endorsement of *Ellen* mirrors closely the rhetoric surrounding DeGeneres in *Ellen*'s coming-out episode and on *Time*'s April 14, 1997, cover. In both cases, those speaking from a homonormal perspective sought to accent the sign "I'm gay" in order to promote a new openness and acceptance of homosexuals in American society. At the same time, those speaking from a heteronormal perspective sought to disenfranchise homosexuals by exploiting a mainstream accent on the sign "I'm gay," thus defining lesbians and gays as marginal and as threats to social stability.

CONCLUSION: GAYNESS REFLECTED OR REFRACTED?

In the most basic sense, then, the struggle evidenced by different accents on the sign "I'm gay" on the television show and in *Time* magazine, by both liberals and conservatives, represented a struggle between two ideologies: homonormality and heteronormality. As cultural studies theorists define ideology as a site in which negotiation of meaning occurs through struggle between various worldviews, the social construction of gayness in the *Ellen* phenomenon most likely will result not from homonormality nor heteronormality alone but from the friction between the two ideologies that were simultaneously viewed by the audiences for the television show, for the magazines, and for political news reports.

As we approach the next century, however, the television media appear to be more willing to present positive images of homosexuals. An indicator of this willingness is simply the fact that, for the first time in television history, a sitcom presented a main character who was a lesbian played by an actress who also was a lesbian. The implications of this shift could have far-reaching ramifications for lesbians and gays and for society as a whole. Not only could positive portrayals of gays and lesbians, such as those shown on *Ellen*, result in higher self-esteem and self-confidence for lesbians and gays (Fejes and Petrich, 1993), but they could also precipitate a transformation in mainstream attitudes about the deviance of homosexuality that could lead to different treatment of lesbians and gays in the future (Gross, 1991).

Some scholars have theorized that, whether fundamental ideologies will or will not shift because of *Ellen*, lesbians and gays will become an increasingly common sight in the media. According to Leonard (1998):

Essentially, I believe that television progresses to reflect society. However, this is done so with a cracked mirror. . . . It takes a bold move, such as "Ellen's" coming out episode, to test the public's tolerance. Nevertheless, once the initial controversy is accepted by the public, the sponsors, the network, then other programs will copy the topic. Ultimately, the topic will become naturalized as part of television culture. (p. 5)

What this naturalization means from a cultural perspective certainly is not clear. The challenge remaining, however, is to discover what new ideology will form at the site of the friction between heteronormality and homonormality. Can media scholars assume from the *Ellen* phenomenon that the public's view of homosexuality has begun to shift significantly? Or, on the other hand, could the television show and the news reports surrounding it simply be another form of marginalization and symbolic annihilation?

REFERENCES

Bauder, D. (1997, October 9). Will Ellen leave her show? *Chattanooga Times*, p. D6.

Carter, B. (1997a, May 7). Ellen by the numbers. *New York Times*, Late Edition (East Coast), p. C20.

Carter, B. (1997b, October 9). Star of *Ellen* threatens to quit over advisory. *New York Times*, p. E3.

Fejes, F., and Petrich, K. (1993). Invisibility, homophobia and heterosexism: Lesbian, gays and the media. *Critical Studies in Mass Communication, 10*, 395–422.

Fiske, J. (1992). British cultural studies and television. In *Channels of discourse, reassembled: Television and contemporary criticism* (2nd ed., pp. 284–326). Chapel Hill: University of North Carolina Press.

Gay and Lesbian Alliance Against Defamation. (1997a). Action alert [Online]. Available: http://www.glaad.org/glaad/press/970813.html [No date].

Gay and Lesbian Alliance Against Defamation. (1997b, September 15). Press release [Online]. Available: http://www.glaad.org/glaad/press/index97.html [No date].

Goodman, E. (1997, October 12). In the latest Ellen flap, parents are warned about homosexuality itself. *Boston Globe*, City Edition, p. C1.

Graham, R. (1997, April 30). What took the networks so Long? *Boston Globe*, City Edition, p. C1.

Gross, L. (1991). Out of the mainstream: Sexual minorities and the mass media. *Journal of Homosexuality, 21* (1–2), 19–46.

Gross, L. (1995). Out of the mainstream: Sexual minorities and the mass media. In G. Dines and J. M. Humez (Eds.), *Gender, race and class in media: A text-reader* (pp. 61–69). Thousand Oaks, CA: Sage Publications.

Hall, S. (1977). Culture, the media and the ideological effect. In J. Curran, M. Gurevitch, and J. Woollacott (Eds.) *Mass communication and society* (p. 34). London: Sage. As cited in Moritz, M. J. (1991), *American television and the creation of lesbian characters: An analysis of context, text and audience* (Doctoral dissertation, Northwestern University, 1991). *Dissertation Abstracts International*, DAI-A *52* (12), pp. 11, 13.

The Human Rights Campaign. (1997, October 17). Largest national gay political organization praises Vice President Gore's remarks about Ellen show [Online press release]. Available: http://www.hrc.org. [No date].

Katz, E., and Liebes, T. (1987). Decoding *Dallas*: Notes from a cross-cultural study. In H. Newcomb (Ed.), *Television: The critical view* (4th ed., pp. 419–32). New York: Oxford University Press.

Kerns, J. G., and Fine, M. A. (1994). The relations between gender and negative attitudes toward gay men and lesbians: Do gender role attitudes mediate this relation? *Sex Roles, 31* (5–6), 297–307.

Leonard, R. (1998, February). *Encountering the communication century: Ellen and the impact of gay and lesbian characters on television in the new century.* Paper/Roundtable Discussion, Western States Communication Association Conference, Denver, CO.

Lyons, S., and Wallenfels, J. (1997, September 15). Afterglow: The winners speak. Press release [Online]. Available: http://www.ultimatetv.com [No date].

Marcus, R. (1997, October 18). Gore bashed for Ellen comment: Conservatives call praise for gay TV character inappropriate. *Washington Post*.

Moritz, M. J. (1991). *American television and the creation of lesbian characters: An analysis of context, text and audience* (Doctoral dissertation, Northwestern University, 1991). *Dissertation Abstracts International*, DAI-A *52*(12).

Orin, D., and Connor, T. (1997, October 18). Gays make Gore their poster boy. *New York Post*, p. A1.

PR Newswire. (1997, October 17). Alan Keyes calls Al Gore's praise of homosexual themes an assault on the moral character of America.

Rosenberg, H. (1997, September 24). Power beyond the punch lines. *Los Angeles Times*, p. F1.

Russo, V. (1981). *The celluloid closet: Homosexuality in the movies*. New York: Harper & Row.

Schwichtenberg, C. (1987). The love boat: The packaging and selling of love, hetero-sexual romance, and family. In H. Newcomb (Ed.), *Television: The critical view* (4th ed., pp. 126–40). New York: Oxford University Press.

Signorelli, N. (1989). Television and conceptions about sex roles: Maintaining conven-tionality and the status quo. *Sex Roles, 21* (5–6), 341–59.

Smith, C. (1991). Sex and genre on prime time. *Journal of Homosexuality, 21* (1–2), 119–38.

Williams, S. (1997, September 10). Ellen jellin: Now that she's out, what's she about? *New York Daily News*, p. 69.

15

Kara Keeling

"We Got Next": The WNBA Advertising Campaign's Negotiations with "Femininity"

INTRODUCTION

A banner proclaiming "We Got Next" graced center court of each of the 1997 National Basketball Association (NBA) championship games, and a historic advertising campaign was launched during those games' commercial breaks. It was in the margins of the NBA's annual climax that the Women's National Basketball Association (WNBA) gathered enough momentum to propel it into a successful inaugural season. Never mind that the American Basketball League (ABL) had already signed most of women's basketball's best talent, completing its first season during the winter months amidst competition for fans from college and professional basketball. Never mind that the ABL's players were receiving far better pay than the majority of athletes in the WNBA. The WNBA had stars (especially after the marketing team had its say). The WNBA had supermodels, athlete/moms, corporate sponsors, and media deals guaranteeing them the best television coverage ever available to a women's professional basketball league. Sure, most of the 1996 U.S. Women's Olympic Basketball team wore ABL uniforms, but when the nets were rehung after the NBA championship game, it was the WNBA who hollered, "We got next!"

Background

Since the passage of Title IX of the Education Amendments of 1972, there has been a 2.1 million rise in high school participation in women's athletics from approximately 300,000 women who competed in 1971 (Lichtman, 1998,

p. 62). Title IX states, "No person in the United States shall, on the basis of sex, be excluded from participation in, be denied the benefits of, or be subjected to discrimination under any educational program or activity receiving Federal financial assistance" (quoted in Lichtman, p. 62). It was not until April 1997, however, when the Supreme Court upheld the 1993 ruling against Brown University by the First Circuit U.S. Court of Appeals in *Brown University v. Amy Cohen* that it seemed that universities would be forced into compliance with the law. That ruling, which requires "full and effective accommodation of women in collegiate athletics," means also that "schools must take the total population of university women into account when designing or cutting back on programs, rather than simply those women who have expressed an interest in sports participation" (Goldberg, 1993, p. 87). What exactly this will mean for the composition and priorities of athletic departments across the United States remains to be seen. But the striking coincidence of the Supreme Court's decision with the launching of the fifth and sixth attempts in the United States to found a professional women's basketball league indicates that, in any event, one of the effects of Title IX will have been the serious attempt to cultivate a sports fan market for women's athletics.

Over the past two decades, there have been four failed attempts to found a women's professional basketball league in the United States. In each case, a concerted effort was made to render the image of women's basketball less "mannish." As recently as 1991, the Liberty Basketball Association professional league for women modified the game of basketball in the name of making the games an appealing option for fans by using a lower basket, a shorter court, and a smaller ball in order to "speed up the game and allow women to dunk" (Ingram, 1991, p. 14). In addition to these fundamental changes, the Liberty Basketball Association also asked Danskin to design "uniform-colorful lycra unitards" for the women to play in. This league was short-lived, as were the three other attempts that preceded it (one of these attempts, the Women's Professional Basketball League, 1978–80, asked its athletes to go to charm school and to play on teams with names like the Fillies and the Does). More recently, the success of the 1996 Women's Basketball Olympic Team, composed of the first wave of Title IX babies, was quickly followed by the fifth attempt to create a professional league, the American Basketball League. Instead of attempting to alter women's basketball, this league, which completed its first season in March 1997, relies upon the talent and athletic ability of women athletes to make the game exciting. Jackie Joyner-Kersee and several other of the gold medal Olympians could be seen each weekend during their season on Black Entertainment Television.

Launching the WNBA

Although the American Basketball League has more than half of the best talent in women's basketball, including eight of the twelve members of the U.S.

Olympic team, the most recent league to tip off, the Women's National Basketball Association, started its inaugural season on June 21, 1997. This league, the WNBA, is supported by the NBA and has television contracts with NBC, ESPN, and Lifetime. Moreover, the league had secured ten corporate sponsors and spent $15 million on marketing by June 1997 (Lopez, 1997, p. 44). Accompanying these leagues are a host of attempts to cultivate a female sports fan market. Several women's athletic magazines, including a Sports Illustrated Quarterly, *SI Woman*, and dozens of new TV Sports programs are being developed.

As the 1997 NBA playoffs kicked into full gear, amid the barrage of beer, car, and insurance commercials, there were a series of advertisements for the WNBA. This advertising campaign, organized around the motto "We Got Next," stands as the most visible (and the most expensive) of the serious attempts to foster a market for professional women's basketball. It also stands as the first significant attempt to do so without altering the game itself or requiring its players to intentionally "feminize" themselves through colorful clothing or refined manners. Not particular to the game of basketball, the discursive convergence of "sport" with "masculinity" in the United States and the ways in which this convergence is also manifested in the images of "sport" have assigned to sports a particular importance in the continually contested production of commonsense understandings of embodied "masculinity" and "femininity" (Cahn, 1994; Cohen, 1993; Creedon, 1994; Messner, 1988). This chapter's concern is to demonstrate the ways in which by working to revalue an already existing collectivity, women's basketball players, the advertisements for the WNBA also worked to create another social formation, women's basketball fans, organized by and through the "socialized time" of the event. Through this demonstration, this chapter argues that the success of the WNBA depends upon the creation of a collectivity, defined here as women's basketball fans, glued together and made acceptable within a series of complex negotiations made with and at the site of femininity's socially acceptable limit.

THE "SPORTS/MEDIA COMPLEX" AND GENDER

Recently, research has been conducted that has been aimed at making visible the devices through which "the sports/media complex actively constructs audiences that are likely to see the men's Final Four as a dramatic, historic event that they simply 'must' watch, whereas fans are likely to see the women's Final Four as a nonevent or, at best, as just another game" (Messner, Duncan, and Wachs, 1996, p. 422). This work, like its predecessors, engages with organized sport as an important site of ideological contestation with prevailing social conceptions of "masculinity" and "femininity," including the ways in which these translate into unequal "power relations between men and women" (Messner, 1988, p. 199). Important to much of this scholarship is the understanding of the sports/media complex as primarily responsible for the continued devaluation of women's athletics (and, within the logic of their arguments, "femininity"). Such an understanding rests on the assumption that better and increased visibility, indeed, the construction of more "positive images" of women athletes, would constitute a significant challenge to male dominance over the determination of the "cultural meaning of organized sport," thereby challenging existing gender relations (Messner, 1988, p. 200). Within the framework of this scholarship, the recent efforts to establish a lucrative market for the WNBA without resorting to lycra unitards seem to pose just such a challenge to male dominance. However, it is here argued that this challenge is recuperated, not only through "the subtle (and not so subtle) differences in the quality of production and framing of the events, and in the gendered language of the commentators" (Messner, Duncan, and Wachs, 1996, p. 437), but, more importantly, through the very constitution of the televisual machine itself.

"SOCIALIZED TIME" AND FEMALE ATHLETICISM

For Richard Dienst, the attempt to articulate an understanding of television's complex relationship to global capitalism leads him, through a reading of Marx, to an understanding of television that hinges upon two important hypotheses. In Dienst's words, "[F]irst television works as a machine according to the basic Marxian account, serving as a transfer point between quantities of time already supposed as value, translating between the time of images and the time of viewing (always imperfectly) and thereby motivating further productions and circulations. Second, television appeared at a certain historical moment to incorporate everyday life and culture as 'free' time into the body of capital through the mediation of the image" (Dienst, 1994, p. 58). It is by putting these two hypotheses into collaboration with one another that Dienst is able to point out that in this historical moment "some share of what used to be called 'disposable time' is put at the disposal of television, so that non-work time becomes subject to the same kinds of antagonisms that cut across labor time" (p. 59). In order to preserve the WNBA's status as a televised spectacle, the image of women playing basketball must be pressed into "socialized time." That is, the image of women's basketball must be made to fit within that set of images that comprise and maintain hegemonic relations. Relying on this understanding of television's work within capitalism, work that is transformative of both time and space, Dienst argues that advertising and, by extension, television in its fundamental commercial function "socializes time by sending images of quantifiable duration, range, and according to its own cultural coordinates" (p. 61). In the case under consideration here, the demands placed upon the WNBA by the product itself, women's basketball, required that the advertising campaign valorize images of aggressive female athleticism while at the same time containing that female athleticism within a more familiar narrative.

The weight of the historical challenge to render female athleticism "acceptable" came to bear on the advertising campaign for the WNBA. As Susan Cahn's study of women in sports makes clear, with the popular reception in the early 1900s of the "athletic girl," finally "free from Victorian constraints," came an accompanying concern with the issue of "mannishness," already understood to be inherent to "sport" (Cahn, 1994, pp. 7–9). The early years of twentieth-century women's athletics were guided, at least in part, by the effort to resolve the issue of "mannishness" (p. 9). Driven by the need to sell the spectacle of women's basketball, the "We Got Next" campaign was an attempt to set the standards for the production of that spectacle as an image of value. This can also be understood in Dienst's more general terms: "By generating a realm of collective, shared time, and by setting the standards for the valorization of this time, television advances capitalism's temporal rule: everybody is free to spend time in their own way only because, on another level, that time is gathered elsewhere, no longer figured as individual" (Dienst, 1994, p. 62). It is this collective time (referred to here as "socialized time"), organized according to the demands of capitalism, that television, by its very nature, generates, maintains, and governs. Through the generation of socialized time television is also able to organize different collectivities, sometimes referred to as "markets."

What is at stake here in consolidating a collectivity around the spectacle of women's basketball? What negotiations are made on top of the image of women's basketball itself in order to do so? By interrogating the images of value that are these advertisements, the remainder of this chapter highlights the specific ways in which the televisual machine channels the "mannishness" in this image into the realm of already existing value. In so doing, it is also interested in marking the ways in which the mannishness customarily perceived in female athleticism threatens to spill out of those mechanisms meant to subvert it.

MARKETING "MANNISH" FEMALE ATHLETICISM

The WNBA logo is an exact replica of the NBA logo, except that the icon on the logo has breasts; it is a derivative of the established symbol for the NBA. The slogan adopted by the WNBA for its inaugural season, "We Got Next," allowed a way of making a direct reference to the fact that after the 1997 NBA playoffs the next teams on the court would be the women's teams. While in its common usage, the phrase "We Got Next" would mean that the team claiming to "have next" would play on that court against the team who just won, the understanding here was not that a WNBA team will play the 1997 winner of the NBA. Instead, the slogan made a claim only to a court and to an audience. However, the "street meaning" of "We Got Next" remained important because it implied a level of athletic achievement and, therefore, of entertainment that promised to strive to match that provided by the NBA. Moreover, it established a connection to Spike Lee's advertising campaign for the U.S. Women's Olympic team in which the members of the women's Olympic basketball team call "next" at a playground basketball court dominated by male athletes and then proceed to score point after point against them. Additionally, the street meaning of "We Got Next" established a connection to the standard practices of playground basketball and, therefore, to an already existing dimension of basketball culture. The promise of "excellence" carried by the slogan in this usage relied upon a comparison to the wildly successful NBA. This connection—the attempt to establish an equivalence between the two leagues—required that the WNBA engage directly with the same problems that brought about the downfall of the four leagues prior to it. That is, the advertisements for the WNBA, in using the NBA as a standard, were necessarily directly confronted with a socially and historically constructed image of "mannishness" in female athleticism, that consistent site of anxiety.

One of the major apparatuses used in the confrontation with mannishness visible in these advertisements is the creation of women's basketball stars. For these early advertisements for the WNBA, the images and names of Rebecca Lobo, Sheryl Swoopes, and Lisa Leslie carried with them a recognition of prior exceptional athletic achievement. Even if one didn't know who these women were before viewing the commercials, the commercials themselves established them as noteworthy through an insistence on the importance of name recognition and through the consistent framing of the athletes as if their celebrity were already well established. The additional cachet carried by Lisa Leslie's star text (apart from officially being the first women to dunk a basketball, Leslie is also an up-and-coming supermodel) was played upon in the advertisement I will refer to as the "runway advertisement."

"A WOMAN'S WORK IS NEVER DONE"

In the "runway advertisement," the three stars of the WNBA, in full face makeup, saunter down a hallway, presumably to a locker room to dress for a game, in runway formation. Relying upon its ability to present these women as women's basketball stars, the advertisement aligns women's basketball with the reigning bastion of women's femininity, runway modeling, but it does so only by erasing any representation of another commodity it is marketing—women's basketball.

In a different "We Got Next" commercial, the "woman's work" advertisement, fast-paced, quick shots of women playing basketball are accented by fast-paced rock music; a woman sings aggressively, urging the audience to shout. Intermittently, written messages appear in block letters on the screen featuring such action words as: "drive the lane," "pound," and "pass," before reminding us of the familiar adage that women's work never ends. Here, through the use of quick cuts, tilted framing, fast, energetic music, and fragmenting close-ups, women's basketball is presented as exciting, fast paced, and competitive, those same characteristics basketball fans demand from men's basketball. This particular advertisement, and in general those advertisements that presented images of women playing basketball, threatened to throw the supermodels-sauntering-in-to-play-a-game-of-basketball premise into crisis. Without lycra unitards, the image of mannishmess in female athleticism is channeled by the "woman's work" advertisement into the already existing realm of value, labeled "femininity," through the cliché of the never-ending nature of "woman's work." By attempting to expand the commonsense category of "woman's work" to include playing basketball, the commercial highlights the fact that, above all else, these are images of women playing basketball. At the same time, this deliberate attempt to channel the image of female athleticism into a narrative about "woman's work" marks a moment in which the mannishness in female athleticism is excessive to the mechanisms employed to direct it into the realm of the already acceptable. The use of the cliché here, instead of fully recuperating the mannish image, highlights the ways in which, in the words of Gilles Deleuze (1989, p. 18) in a related context, "something has become too strong in the image."

Presented out of the economic demand to cultivate a market of women's basketball fans, comprised, at least in part, by those fans accustomed to men's basketball, the televisual image of a fast-paced, competitive, women's basketball was ushered into television's "socialized time." In this way, mannish female athleticism is currently caught within the televisual machine, becoming " 'part of' the way in which value is constructed, distributed, and attached to bodies formed in the general circulation of labor, commodities, and money" (Dienst, 1994, p. 64). As recent research points out and as this chapter has sought to illustrate, the continued employment of devices such as "gender marking" and the construction of a "hierarchy of meaning" different from that of men's basketball (Messner, Duncan, and Jensen, 1993; Messner, Duncan, and Wachs, 1996) indicates that the spectacle of female athleticism remains a site of anxiety. As Susan Cahn's (1994) work makes clear, one important contemporary reason for this anxiety is the persistence of the association of "mannishness" with "lesbianism." One of the most significant goals of the "We Got Next" advertising campaign was to channel the image of value, female athleticism, into the hegemonic set of values that already undergirded perceptions of "femininity." This set of values does not include mannishness as a characteristic of female bodies primarily because of the lesbianism consequently perceived to be inherent in those bodies. Instead of challenging existing social relations, the "We Got Next" television advertising campaign strives to strengthen oppressive gender relations and homophobia.

CONCLUSION

To understand the "We Got Next" advertising campaign merely within the narrative of the continuing quest for more positive images of female athletes is to unfairly simplify the stakes involved in the televisual production of images. The "We Got Next" campaign did indeed mark the acceleration of the process of valuation of "mannish" female athleticism. However, an easy celebration of this acceleration in the process of the transduction of value conspires to obscure the ways in which the "socialized time" of the advertisements has been organized and valued in advance, obfuscating the homophobia and sexism that make possible such a celebration.

At the time this chapter was completed, the WNBA was wrapping up its second successful season. Many potentially productive areas of inquiry remain unexamined. An engagement with the televised WNBA games could open up, among other studies, rich analyses of the interplay between the image of a nonwhite female athlete and "femininity." In a related vein, an analysis of the much less expensive and much less extensive advertising campaign for the ABL would prove a productive historical complement to this chapter. Additionally, because the conclusions drawn in this chapter rely so heavily upon the TV advertisements for the WNBA and on the WNBA as televised spectacle, an analysis of a live WNBA game that is not experienced via television may provide an exciting site from which to discuss some of those images that television must render invisible.

NOTES

An earlier version of this chapter was presented at the 1997 Console-ing Passions Conference at Concordia University in Montréal, Québec.

This chapter has benefited greatly from extended conversations with Coach Rudy Keeling about basketball in general and the WNBA in particular. For those conversations and for much more, the author wishes to thank him. The author also wishes to thank Chandra Ford for her careful reading of this chapter and for her patient tolerance of frequent rants about women's basketball.

REFERENCES

Cahn, S. (1994). *Coming on strong: Gender and sexuality in twentieth-century women's sport*. New York: Macmillan.

Cohen, G. (Ed.). (1993). *Women in sport: Issues and controversies*. Newbury Park, CA: Sage Publications.

Cole, C., and Hribar, A. (1995). Celebrity feminism: *Nike Style*, post-Fordism, transcendence, and consumer power. *Sociology of Sport Journal, 12,* 347–69.

Creedon, P. (Ed.). (1994). *Women, media and sport: Challenging gender values*. Thousand Oaks, CA: Sage Publications.

Deleuze, G. (1989). *Cinema 2: The time image* (H. Tomlinson and R. Galeta, Trans.). Minneapolis: University of Minnesota Press.

Dienst, R. (1994). *Still life in real time: Theory after television*. Durham, NC: Duke University Press.

Goldberg, S. (1993, July). Title IX: School must follow regs. *ABA Journal*, p. 87.

Ingram, K. (1991, April). Not quite full-court press: Liberty Basketball Association plans. *Women's Sports and Fitness, 13* (3), 14.

Lichtman, B. (1998, March 1). Sexual discrimination and school sports: The Title IX compliance challenge. *USA Today*, p. 62.

Lopez, S. (1997, June 30). They got next. *Sports Illustrated*, p. 44.

Marks, R. (1997, July). Supermodels. *Sport, 88* (7), 46.

Messner, M. (1988). Sports and male domination: The female athlete as contested ideological terrain. *Sociology of Sport Journal, 5,* 197–211.

Messner, M., Duncan, M., and Jensen, K. (1993, March). Separating the men from the girls: The gendered language of televised sports. *Gender and Society, 7* (1), 121–37.

Messner, M., Duncan, M., and Wachs, F. (1996, November). The gender of audience building: Televised coverage of women's and men's NCAA basketball. *Sociological Inquiry, 66* (4), 422–39.

PART VI

VIDEO

16

Emile C. Netzhammer

Competing Rhetorical Strategies in the Gay and Lesbian Video Wars: *Marching for Freedom* and *Gay Rights, Special Rights*

INTRODUCTION

Beginning with Spring of Life Ministry's *The Gay Agenda* in 1992, anti-gay and -lesbian activism moved to a new frontier. Limited by the constraints of mainstream journalism and liberated by the decreasing costs and increased portability of self-produced media, both pro- and anti-gay and -lesbian organizations learned that producing their own programming for direct distribution on videotape provided some clear benefits (Deitcher, 1994, p. 29). The organization can control content from start to finish, not having to concern itself with the manner in which the press might edit quotes to construct a "balanced" message. The organization can reap some financial benefit from either sale of the tape or distribution of the tape to individuals sympathetic to the cause. Most important, the organization can include content that would otherwise never see the light of the television screen in people's homes—material that would be deemed inappropriate, inflammatory, or too biased for mainstream media.

Video activism certainly predates *The Gay Agenda*. Video surfaced in the abortion controversy in the early 1980s with the video release of *The Silent Scream* (1984), still widely circulated and available on the World Wide Web. Pro-gay and -lesbian and anti-gay and -lesbian video activism of the 1990s was different, however, in that a dialogue began through a series of videotapes released by various religious and gay rights organizations. Between 1993 and 1996, no fewer than ten videotapes directly addressed gay and lesbian civil rights. The video war was notable for more than just the number of tapes produced. To some extent, each video was a response to the salvo released in the opposition's latest production. *Hate, Lies and Videotape* (1993) was a direct response to *The Gay Agenda; It's Elementary* (1995), a response to *The Gay Agenda in Public Education* (1994). Other videos that supported the gay and lesbian rights movement included *Straight from the Heart* (1994), *Sacred Lies, Civil Truths* (1993), *To Support and Defend: The Role of Homosexuals in the Military* (1993), and *Always My Kid: A Family Guide to Understanding Homosexuality* (1994). Anti–gay rights organizations countered with *Gay March 93: What You Didn't See on Network TV* (1993), *Sexual Orientation or Sexual Deviation: You Decide* (1991), and *Civil Rights or Crisis in America* (1992). Some of these videotapes received airtime on cable access channels but most were circulated through direct distribution to individuals, religious groups, or community organizations, generally at a nominal cost. A number of the videos were shown to members of Congress and military leaders during the controversy over lesbians and gays in the military (Boxall, 1993; Pine, 1993). The tapes were then copied over and over again through a large underground network. Issues of copyright largely were ignored.

On April 25, 1993, the March on Washington for Lesbian, Gay and Bi Equal Rights brought hundreds of thousands of people to the Mall in Washington, D.C., filling the area between the U.S. Capitol and the Washington Monument. Depending on the video watched or the news story read, somewhere between 300,000 and a million people participated in the march, a controversy in and of itself ("Gays Demand," 1993; Harney, 1993; Zremski, 1993). Within three months of the March on Washington, a number of videotapes had been released. These tapes continued the rhetorical strategies employed in earlier tapes under the guise of presenting what happened in Washington on April 25. In fact, gay and lesbian leaders recognized that such events present a prime opportunity for the Right: "The argument went that Mid-America would be frightened off by our numbers and our rhetoric, and the inevitable press attention on the drag queens and the faeries" (Monette, 1994, p. 153). Preston (1992) noted that marches are "occasions when an enemy forces an identity onto the group" (p. 14). This was certainly true for the 1993 march. Imagery of the march, as well as the volumes of text that resulted, was co-opted for specific political purposes by the Right.

Two of the videos resulting from the March on Washington form the basis for this chapter: *Marching for Freedom* (1993) and *Gay Rights, Special Rights: Inside the Homosexual Agenda* (1993). Although the stated purposes of the videos are quite different—*Marching for Freedom* purports to be a keepsake for those who attended the march, whereas *Gay Rights, Special Rights* is intended as an exposé on the differences between gay civil rights and African American civil rights—the videos utilize many of the same "experts," the same visual imagery, and the same rhetorical strategies. *Marching for Freedom* in many ways anticipates the video offensive from the Right, creating a far different picture of the march, all the while employing the same rhetorical strategies.

This chapter analyzes the persuasive strategies employed in *Gay Rights, Spe-*

cial Rights (GRSR) and *Marching for Freedom (MFF)*. Specifically, it analyzes and compares the strategies and techniques used in the videos to determine their rhetorical impact. Ultimately, these videos, like all activist videos, are part of the larger context of social activism and must be seen in that light. However, a close analysis of these two examples reveals striking similarities in the rhetorical strategies used by pro- and anti-gay and -lesbian activists, even though their conclusions could not be further apart.

THE US/THEM RHETORICAL WARS

Even though *GRSR* and *MFF* are so different on the surface, a closer examination reveals a number of important similarities. The same three dichotomies quickly emerge in the rhetorical choices made in each video. Each participates in an overall us/them strategy of argumentation: similar/dissimilar, moderate/extremist, and good guy/villain. These strategies lead to a fourth dichotomy that pervades both videos from beginning to end—appeal to minority/majority status. In each video, the producers, as representative of gays and lesbians or representative of anti-lesbian and -gay religious conservative organizations, define themselves by their opposition to the subjects articulated in the other video. That is, in *MFF* gays and lesbians define themselves by defining the enemy, religious conservatives. In *GRSR*, the anti-gay and -lesbian rights video makers define themselves and their supporters by placing themselves in opposition to gay and lesbian rights supporters. In his study of the spotted owl controversy, Lange (1993) referred to this strategy as "a mirror effect in which each side castigates the other while proclaiming their own virtue" (p. 248).

One difference that emerges from the manner in which the videos are designed to function is that *Marching for Freedom* generally adopts an us/them strategy, whereas *Gay Rights, Special Rights* employs a them/us rhetorical strategy. That is, in *MFF*, the primary focus is on the "us" in the equation—gays and lesbians—with secondary emphasis placed on the "them." In *GRSR*, the emphasis is on the attack. The video focuses primarily on defining the other, with secondary emphasis on self-definition. In either case, however, each group is defined implicitly through its definition of the other us it attempts to inject its construction of homosexuality into the mainstream. Smith and Windes (1997) noted:

Contests between progay and antigay advocates can be understood as efforts to gain support for rival interpretive packages which frame same-sex orientation and behaviors as either sin, sickness, and crime or as benign difference and positive identity. When opportunity occurs to make variant sexuality a contested subject, coalitions of organizations, joined by movement clusters, sponsor rival interpretive packages in order to impose a dominant meaning on a public dispute. (p. 30)

By defining the opposition in ways that vilify or point out dissimilarities or extremism, each group then develops an identity for itself composed of positive and prosocial characteristics. They construct themselves as holding ideal and correct points of view, asserting that their arguments are unimpeachable. By interpreting "minority status," the activists move from a battle over public acceptance to one over judicial legitimacy.

THE VIDEOS: AN INTRODUCTION

Before analyzing the four dichotomies employed in each video, a brief description of the two videos demonstrates just how little these two videos appear to have in common. In purpose and in execution, *GRSR* and *MFF* seem so different as to be incomparable.

Produced by the National Gay and Lesbian Task Force (NGLTF) explicitly as a souvenir of the March on Washington, *MFF* documents the event with interviews and speeches but without the use of a narrator. The video is divided into segments that begin with extended musical interludes over video of specific activities of the march weekend: the parade, the parties, the rally, the commitment ceremony, AIDS demonstrations, and the Pentagon demonstration. Throughout these segments, interviews with marchers are used to articulate the variety of reasons people are in attendance. The video includes sound bites from speeches by gay and lesbian leaders, politicians, and Hollywood celebrities. With the exception of Torrie Osborne and Urvashi Vaid—at the time the current and immediate past directors of the NGLTF—no one appears more than once in the video. In addition to the speeches, *MFF* includes many of the musical and comedy performances on the stage at the rally. *MFF* is generally sedate. Images of tender embraces, children playing, and marchers walking arm in arm are plentiful. Images of the behaviors often defined as outrageous—drag, demonstrations that lead to arrests, leather and pierced bodies (but not sex)—are relegated to a five-minute segment titled "Expression of Self."

GRSR draws heavily on footage from the March on Washington, as well as President Bill Clinton's 1993 inauguration. It is overtly political. The video begins with a lengthy comparison of the African American civil rights movement and the gay and lesbian civil rights movement, focusing specifically on the reasons why "legally" gays and lesbians do not qualify for civil rights protection under the law. The video then articulates "four basic myths" of homosexuality, relying on its own stable of politicians, religious leaders, and experts to define what it is to be gay or lesbian. Osborne and others in attendance at the march also appear throughout the video, their words used to support the video's claims. The last half of the video delineates the impact that giving gays and lesbians civil rights protection would have on families, schools, businesses, and churches. Finally, in a segment reminiscent of *The Gay Agenda*, Cathy Kay, a registered nurse, lists the sexual activities that accompany the "behavior disorder that goes along with homosexuality." Throughout, scenes from the March on Washington are used as visual proof of the claims being made in the video.

The differences in intent and execution between the two videos do not hinder the video makers from adopting similar rhetorical strategies to get their messages across. Both videos make similar appeals to the viewer, setting themselves up as espousing the more acceptable and honest message.

Similar/Dissimilar

Although neither video is likely to command a widespread mainstream audience, both videotapes employ rhetorical devices to communicate to mainstream America that "we are just like you" and "they are not," "we are normal, and they are deviant." This is accomplished through visual appeals that reflect American values, speeches, and interviews in which individuals not only assert their "sameness" but also pointedly acknowledge the "differentness" of the opposition. Progay and -lesbian rhetoric often promotes an atmosphere of assimilation. The Right developed strategies to disabuse the public of the idea of gay and lesbian sameness and replace it instead with the notion of pathological difference (Smith and Windes, 1997, p. 31). *GRSR*'s and *MFF*'s use of imagery and words continues this rhetorical approach.

Both videos almost immediately wrap themselves in American cultural symbolism. *MFF* begins with images of American landmarks—from the mountains to the prairies—as individuals travel from all parts of the country to participate in the march. After the arrival segment, shots of D.C. monuments and buildings are plentiful. Speaking at the rally, Urvashi Vaid says, "The gay rights movement is an integral part of the American promise of freedom." *GRSR* has just as many monument shots and appeals to patriotism. Segments containing charts or lists of information generally place text over shots of the Supreme Court building or other Washington landmarks.

MFF implements a strategy that invokes the mainstream. Herrell (1993) argued that the appeal to sameness is a common development in lesbian and gay activism:

Presenting the gay community as composed of families, of churches and sports leagues, of clubs and professional associations, of everything about normative society except simply sexual behavior, has become the new strategy. The political agenda as frequently calls for the right to a conventional family life as for sexual freedom. In the era of AIDS, the personal script and collective myth for "coming out" (i.e., "coming out of the closet," telling others that one is gay) is based no longer on the sexual revolution of Stonewall but on a community of individuals and organizations involved in fundraising for research, taking care of people with AIDS, offering networks of support, and defending the rights of the infected; in short, not on acts of sex but on acts of love. (pp. 233–34)

MFF does exactly this. The message of sameness in *MFF* runs throughout the video. The images of marchers and subjects chosen for interviews demonstrate racial, professional, religious, and family diversity. In one of the first sound bites, a marcher says, "We're regular people, and that's what we need to show the rest of the country." The visual images that accompany the text of the video make a clear appeal to sameness. Many individuals are shown in their military or police uniforms or carrying children in familiar family portrait shots. Where the crowd shots alone don't communicate sufficiently, banners carried by the marchers and keys (superimposition of text by the video makers) provide more detail for the viewers. The images are not just of gays and lesbians but of gay and lesbian teachers, musicians, politicians, and athletes. While the video shows a tremendous range of diversity of individuals, in almost all cases gay men and lesbians are presented as ordinary.

This self-identification stands in stark contrast to the manner in which the opposition—primarily the Religious Right—is portrayed in *MFF*. The opposition is never portrayed visually. The producers made a decision not to include images of the counterdemonstrators present along the march route. However, the Right is always present in the rhetoric of the video—in the speeches and in the "on-the-street" interviews. One marcher observes:

I think this march is a response to the pressure the right wing has put on us. They don't have communists to go against, so now they're against gays. . . . Reverend Sheldon said—and I don't mean to call him reverend—Lou Sheldon said, "Look what the United States is coming to. They're organizing marches based on what they do in the bedroom." We're organizing marches because they won't get out of our bedroom.

In *MFF* the Right is out of the mainstream in that their values don't reflect mainstream values; their patriotism is not reflective of true American patriotism.

GRSR, of course, mirrors that view, using the same strategy to reach the opposite conclusion. The video uses images of gays and lesbians culled extensively from the march to construct difference. From the opening sequence to the title sequence four minutes later *GRSR* repeats the message that gays and lesbians are different because they falsely claim to be a minority and because they want "special rights." The video uses a racially diverse group of people to make this point, firmly reinforcing the sameness of anti-gay and -lesbian rights activists. Images of topless women follow lesbian marchers discussing political power. Images of marchers chanting, "We're here, we're gay, we're in the PTA" are followed by images of men performing in drag and children in the audience crying.

Marlin Maddoux, one of the expert commentators used throughout *GRSR*, argues:

One of the things that sex education does in the public schools is to tell the kids that there is no difference between homosexual lifestyles and heterosexual lifestyles. The aim of that is basically to break down any type of what they would call prejudice against the homosexual lifestyles. So, basically what Americans have to understand is that the agenda of the homosexuals is aimed at the children.

As he begins his last sentence, ominous music fades up, and slow-motion video is used to make these articulated differences menacing.

Religious Right sameness is articulated by indicating that anti-gay and -lesbian activists merely want what the rest of America wants. They want families to consist of a mother, father, and children. Christian Coalition head Ralph Reed and former Secretary of Education William Bennett say they are not antigay; they just want values to be taught in the home. Schools must focus on basic skills. These arguments are designed to resonate with the mainstream audience by suggesting that gays and lesbians undermine American values.

Moderation/Extremism

Almost a corollary to the issue of sameness and difference is an assumed posture that "our views are moderate; their views are extreme." Moderation and extremism are barometers of sameness and difference. Both videos articulate a position that is moderate and appropriate while attacking the other side for its militant views that are so far out of the mainstream as to be unacceptable. Smith and Windes (1997) observed, "In response to the charge that they are hate-filled bigots, many antigays strive to project an image of moderation and political centrism" (p. 34). Gay men and lesbians also strive to project an image of moderation in the face of charges that they are immoral and diseased sex fiends (Herrell, 1993, p. 233).

An early segment in *Gay Rights, Special Rights* has Larry Kramer in an agitated state recalling Martin Luther King's "I Have a Dream" speech. A portion of King's speech is followed by Kramer's speech, which begins, "To paraphrase . . ." The narrator then says, "Many failed to notice Mr. Kramer's substitution of the words 'sexual behavior' for 'skin color' as he misquoted the Reverend Dr. Martin Luther King on the steps of the U.S. Capitol." (Ironically, the quote shown in the video has Kramer saying "sexual desires.") Kramer is presented as the embodiment of gay extremism.

The images from the march in *GRSR* contain a lot of provocative imagery. Men in leather discuss uses for anything one might find in a hardware store. Shots of nudity, simulated sexual activity, drag, and emotional children are plentiful. Toward the end of the video, a concerned woman discusses public sex:

It averages between 100 and 150 men a day that walk down this bike path, one at a time, wearing different clothing according to their sexual perversion. They take the dirt paths off into the brush. They meet one another, and they do their sexual perversions right there in the open. They come out one at a time, walk into the park with the children. I've seen them talk to the children.

As absurd as some of the rhetoric may sound, it is very successful in projecting gay and lesbian extremism. These comments are juxtaposed with comments from cool politicians and religious leaders who are just stating the facts in quiet, authoritative terms that project moderation. William Bennett says, "No society can survive, obviously, unless it comes full forward in favor of hetero-sexuality, and no society in its right mind would do anything but that." Trent Lott and a host of African American religious leaders make the same calm appeals. Former Attorney General Edwin Meese says homosexuals have taken free speech to the extreme, a comment made over shots and sounds of marchers shouting antichurch slogans.

Marching for Freedom projects gay and lesbian moderation. A minister par-ticipating in the march says, "I think too often the church makes a negative witness, so I want to be here to make a positive witness on behalf of the church." Ministers at the rally speak of spiritualism; others speak of love and commit-ment. Imagery throughout the video has same-sex couples in quiet, tender em-braces. The mood is compassionate and supportive. Indeed, the theme of the march, "A Simple Matter of Justice," communicates that this is a perfectly rea-sonable position. Conversely, marchers talk of the Right as extremists, fighting against real family values and punishing decent people. One straight-identified marcher says, "I don't want anyone else to have to go through what we've gone through in Oregon—we're still going through." (She is referring to Proposition 9, an Oregon initiative sponsored by anti-gay and -lesbian activists.) Moderation is established by aligning gay and lesbian activists with a straight-identified woman. This happens on a number of occasions in *MFF*.

Vanderford's (1989) study of abortion rights rhetoric illustrated the impor-tance of a moderation/extremism tension in activist rhetoric:

Empowerment is also granted through legitimacy. Comparing themselves to their op-ponents, believers were able to define themselves as a moral force, combating corruption and injustice. The resultant self-righteousness encouraged action by empowering believ-ers, placing democracy, justice, and freedom on their side. (p. 177)

In both videos, projecting the opposition's extremism promotes the group's own legitimacy by making its views appear moderate.

Good Guy/Villain

Vanderford (1989) also noted that vilification is a strategy frequently em-ployed in the abortion rights controversy. It is a strategy of war that dehumanizes an opponent:

Vilification is a rhetorical strategy that discredits adversaries by characterizing them as ungenuine and malevolent advocates. Rather than differentiating opponents as good peo-ple with a difference of opinion, vilification delegitimizes them through characterizations of intentions, actions, purposes, and identities. (p. 166)

She noted that vilification is a strategy that ultimately can strip opponent activists of legitimacy in the debate. This strategy has become central to the controversy over lesbian and gay rights.

Both videos vilify the other side over and over again. Implicit in the repeated vilification of the opposition is the assumption that "we" are the good guys, the righteous, and perhaps the heroes. Lange (1993) noted, "As each group vilifies the other, so too does each side ennoble themselves. Both sides claim they have 'compromised'; both hold that 'science' favors their position; both imply 'morality' and 'the common good' as their guiding forces" (p. 249). Not only does the strategy ennoble, it situates the vilifier firmly with the moderate, similar positions discussed above. Sanger (1994) argued that "while the purpose is undoubtedly vilification, the participants in this video claim not to vilify at all but, rather, to simply have an honest disagreement with gay claims to special rights status" (p. 6). One's nobility increases when purporting to take the high road.

Throughout *MFF*, gay and lesbian marchers and speakers talk of protecting themselves from infractions by the Right. Usually, this vilification takes subtle forms, generally refraining from direct attacks on the Right. Actress Judith Light says the gay and lesbian civil rights movement is "a battle to replace divisiveness with acceptance, condemnation with compassion, rigidity with diversity and most of all hatred with love." A marcher says, "We're showing love for our families, not hating our children." In context, these comments are easily seen as an attempt to vilify the Right, particularly attacking them where they launch their greatest offensives, over the issue of children.

Gay Rights, Special Rights vilifies gays and lesbians in a number of ways. Images of marchers are almost always presented with ominous music and slow-motion effects that make the subject appear menacing. Gay men and lesbians are portrayed as a direct, insidious threat to the American way of life. In addition to the music, marchers' own words are turned against them in interviews. A member of a group of half-naked marchers notes, "We need to acknowledge in a legal and social way the reality of the range of different relationships people have in our society: men having relationships with men, women with women, men with women, triads, group marriages."

A major strategy used to vilify lesbians and gays is to portray them as predatory toward children. This argument is a long-held plank in the Religious Right arsenal (Smith and Windes, 1997, p. 31), and it is integrated throughout *GRSR*. "To allow sex with youth" is listed as one of the demands of the marchers, as is a demand for homosexual Scout leaders. Over the image of a young boy, the narrator reads text that appears on screen:

Michael Swift writes in gay community news, "We shall sodomize your sons, emblems of your feeble masculinity. We shall seduce them in your schools, in your dormitories, in your gymnasiums, in your locker rooms, in your sports arenas, in your seminaries, in your youth groups."

Nurse Cathy Kay notes that "all the groups—the sadomasochists, the pedophiles, the transsexuals"—were at the march. Implicitly, the fact that they are willing to take on this battle against the homosexual villain makes the Religious Right noble, heroic even.

In *Marching for Freedom*, gays and lesbians are exercising "moral leadership" and calling on Congress and others to follow suit. In *Gay Rights, Special Rights*, the Religious Right, typified by Lou Sheldon and Pat Buchanan, is the villain. Both videos adopt strategies to ennoble those who hold their views and vilify those who do not.

Minority/Majority

Similarity and difference place pro- and anti-gay and -lesbian rights groups at different points on a cultural spectrum. Moderation and extremism, as well as vilification and heroism, also mark the cultural positioning of these groups. The appeal to minority/majority status uses these strategies to move the debate to the jurisprudential realm. Oddly, since both sides make claims to mainstream status, their simultaneous claims to oppressed minority status is intriguing. Both progay and -lesbian groups and religious conservative groups articulate a clear connection to the African American civil rights movement for themselves and promote dissolution of any connection between their opponents and the history of civil rights in this country. This argument leads naturally to the claim that civil rights protection is warranted for us but not for them.

Gay Rights, Special Rights does not argue for the same civil rights protection for the Religious Right as it suggests African Americans need. Nonetheless, without calling for legal protection as a minority, the video clearly establishes the anti-gay and -lesbian rights activists as oppressed and less powerful than their opponents: "Antigays also cast themselves as warriors against an establishment dominated by 'elite secular humanists' who, according to antigay Frances Schaeffer, have 'become overwhelmingly dominant in about the last forty years' " (Smith and Windes, 1997, p. 38). After describing public sex activities in detail, an unidentified interviewee adds:

If it was a heterosexual problem, it would be taken care of and it wouldn't be permitted. However, because these are homosexuals and so many rights and privileges and ordinances—city ordinances—have been provided that protect them, all of the agencies are fearful to take any action against them.

The more direct strategy employed in *GRSR* is a string of experts who argue that gays and lesbians are not a legal minority and, therefore, are not entitled to legal protection.

GRSR particularly spends the first third of the tape employing strategies that attempt to sever any connections between African American civil rights protection (deserved) and gay and lesbian civil rights protection (undeserved). An important corollary to this argument is the assumption—articulated as fact in the video—that minority status is given only to members of groups discriminated against for being who they are. Lesbians and gays are not a minority because they are discriminated against for what they do (Schacter, 1994, p. 294). That is why the narrator's switch from "sexual desires" in Larry Kramer's speech to "sexual behaviors" is critical to the argument advanced in *GRSR*. The introduction includes a parade of experts who discuss the consequences of minority protection for gays and lesbians. Trent Lott, for example, says such protection "threatens to undermine and belittle the entire civil rights efforts of the 1960s."

Beyond the dire consequences predicted in the video, however, *GRSR* develops a detailed argument as to why gays and lesbians do not constitute a minority. The video draws on language of Supreme Court cases, focusing particularly on the need for "immutable characteristics." Since homosexuality is constructed as something that is done, rather than who someone is, it is not an immutable characteristic.

Having concluded that gays are not a minority, the video exposes the "myths" that are "the foundation on which the gay political platform has been built." African Americans, Hispanics, and Asians lead this analysis, which strengthens the connection between the Right and minority groups and serves to confound and obliterate the connection between gays and lesbians and "true" minorities.

Deitcher (1994) was dubious that this ultimately would be a successful rhetorical strategy:

Gay Rights, Special Rights: Inside the Homosexual Agenda exploits the anti-gay bigotry that is as prominent within communities of color as it is among white Americans. It is a matter of historical record that the Christian right includes a great many people who consistently have opposed the goals and tactics of the civil rights movement. *Gay Rights, Special Rights* recasts this racist assembly as champions of the epochal struggle to overcome white supremacy in America, and as guardians of its legacy. (p. 33)

But as Sanger (1994) argued, the makers of *GRSR* promote themselves as champions of civil rights, "as standing for equality and against discrimination toward true minorities" (p. 10). The strategy is seductive when taken in context.

MFF clearly mirrors the assertions in *GRSR*. Here gay men and lesbians are minorities in need of protection from the conservative oppressors. The March on Washington is constructed primarily as a civil rights demonstration. Testimony from marchers throughout the video employs civil rights discourse. A racially diverse group of young men say, "We're not allowed to go home until we have our rights. That's what everyone said." An older woman notes, "I wasn't here to see Martin Luther King give his speech in Washington in 1963, but I wanted to be here because this is history and this will be our decade." She is followed immediately by a very young woman who adds, "We're all here to send a message to the federal government that we have to update the civil rights codes to include gays, lesbians, and bisexuals."

Torrie Osborne, who figures prominently in both videos, puts gay and lesbian civil rights in a historical context:

In the '60s, the civil rights movement fought the lie that you had to be white, the women's movement of the '70s revolutionized the very concept of power, and let us remember today that it was lesbian leadership that created that vision. And in 1969 those brave drag queens and working class dykes at Stonewall laid siege to the last lie and catapulted us to this moment in history, into this movement that proclaims our right to love and to desire whom we choose. By 1980 our movement was growing, we had begun to come out, and we had begun to fight for our rights, and then we began to die.

The images and speeches of Benjamin Chavez (then head of the National Association for the Advancement of Colored People), Patricia Ireland (National Organization for Women president), and Sharon Pratt Kelly and David Dinkins (mayors of D.C. and New York City) also connect the movement to the history of civil rights movements in this country.

CONCLUSION

Images of the 1963 Civil Rights March on Washington figure prominently—both literally and figuratively—into *Marching for Freedom* and *Gay Rights, Special Rights*. A portion of Martin Luther King's "I Have a Dream" speech is included in both videos, resulting in a connection between the African American civil rights movement and both the pro– and anti–gay and –lesbian rights movements. Ultimately, the constant references to African American civil rights struggles in *MFF* contextualize gay and lesbian civil rights into a forty-year history of fighting for social justice. *GRSR* does the same thing, arguing, however, that, in historical context, gays and lesbians are strange bedfellows with African Americans.

While the rhetorical strategies used in *GRSR* urge the viewer to renounce a connection between gay and lesbian civil rights and African American civil rights, they promote a strong connection between the viewer and antigay and -lesbian activists. Reflecting the opposite view, *MFF* urges viewers to see gays and lesbians as they see themselves. To accomplish these goals, both videos project an image of moderation and sameness with the viewer. They promote themselves as the nobler fighters in a battle with the evil other. An interesting by-product of the rhetorical strategies employed in both videos is that in their attempts to project moderation and sameness the videos reconceive the civil rights battles that predate the gay and lesbian civil rights movement as moderate themselves. The civil rights battles of the 1960s become benign movements that all moderate, right-thinking people supported. Depending on the video, gay and lesbian civil rights are either a simple, logical next step in this history or the product of extremists who have no claim to the past civil rights movements.

Marching for Freedom and *Gay Rights, Special Rights* could not be more different in the positions they urge the viewer to adopt. However, they take the same path to get to their respective conclusions and reach their goals. They rely on the same persuasive strategies, they use the same visual imagery, and they adopt the same rhetoric. They both provide a reading of the March on Washington that is designed to construct the viewer's interpretation of that event and generalize past it to all gays and lesbians. In that regard, the videos stand as participants in a dialogue over gay and lesbian rights. The march provided the catalyst, but ultimately it was just a convenient tool that allowed the pro- and anti-gay and -lesbian activists to construct messages that they could disseminate far more widely through the medium of television. The videotapes become the lasting interpretation of the march. Both *Gay Rights, Special Rights* and *Marching for Freedom* employ similar us/them strategies that attempt to create an affinity between the viewer and the activist. Building on this perceived affinity, each video then attempts to win the viewer over to its position.

In the end, both *MFF* and *GRSR* are about whether gays and lesbians deserve civil rights protection. The rhetoric is designed to wage the debate in the social and jurisprudential arenas. The 1993 March on Washington becomes the battlefield onto which these issues are imposed. The march provided many opportunities for footage that supported both positions. Both videos ended with appeals to the viewer to bring this issue home, to local political leaders and to Congress. They expressed the need for grassroots activism.

Gay Rights, Special Rights and *Marching for Freedom* stand as interpretations of an event. The event is long over, but the videotapes continue to circulate and give the March on Washington decidedly different meanings. They are shown often, and the rhetorical strategies they employ are used frequently in social activism, making the video battles an important part of the ongoing battle over gay and lesbian civil rights.

REFERENCES

Boxall, B. (1993, April 21). Video presents case for gays in the military. *Los Angeles Times*, p. B3.

Deitcher, D. (1994). The gay agenda: Attempts by conservative groups to repress gay and lesbian art. *Art in America, 82,* 27–35.

Gays demand march recount. (1993, April 27). *Sacramento Bee*, p. A12.

Harney, J. (1993, April 26). Crowd counters' totals differ, organizers say police 700,000 off. *USA Today*, p. A10.

Herréll, R. K. (1993). The symbolic strategies of Chicago's Gay and Lesbian Pride Day Parade. In G. Herdt (Ed.), *Gay culture in America: Essays from the field* (pp. 225–52). Boston: Beacon.

Lange, J. I. (1993, September). The logic of competing information campaigns: Conflict over old growth and the spotted owl. *Communication Monographs, 60,* 239–257.

Monette, P. (1994). *Last watch of the night*. New York: Harcourt Brace.

Pine, A. (1993, January 28). Issue explodes into an all-out lobbying war. *Los Angeles Times*, p. A1.

Preston, J. (1992). What happened? *Out/look, 4*, (3), 8–14.

Sanger, K. (1994, November). *The Religious Right and the illusion of moderation: "Gay Rights, Special Rights: Inside the Homosexual Agenda."* Paper presented at the annual conference of the Speech Communication Association, New Orleans, LA.

Schacter, J. S. (1994). The gay civil rights debate in the states: Decoding the discourse of equivalents. *Harvard Civil Rights–Civil Liberties Law Review, 29* (2), 283–317.

Smith, R. R., and Windes, R. R. (1997). The progay and antigay issue culture: Interpretation, influence and dissent. *Quarterly Journal of Speech, 83*, 28–48.

Vanderford, M. L. (1989). Vilification and social movements: A case study of pro-life and pro-choice rhetoric. *Quarterly Journal of Speech, 75*, 166–182.

Zremski, J. (1993, April 26). Gays buoyed by Washington march; organizers, park police disagree over crowd estimate. *Buffalo News*, p. 1.

VIDEOGRAPHY

Always my kid: A family guide to understanding homosexuality. (1994). Houston: Steve Baker.

Civil rights or crisis in America. (1992). Lancaster, CA: Springs of Life Ministries.

The gay agenda. (1992). Lancaster, CA: Springs of Life Ministries.

The gay agenda in public education. (1994). Lancaster, CA: Springs of Life Ministries.

Gay march 93: What you didn't see on network TV. (1993). Falls Church, VA: Christian Action Network.

Gay rights, special rights: Inside the homosexual agenda. (1993). Anaheim, CA: Traditional Values Coalition.

Hate, lies and videotape. (1993). Washington, DC: National Gay and Lesbian Task Force.

It's elementary. (1995). San Francisco: Women's Educational Media.

Marching for freedom. (1993). Washington, DC: National Gay and Lesbian Task Force.

Sacred lies, civil truths. (1993). New York: Gay and Lesbian Emergency Media Campaign.

Sexual orientation or sexual deviation: You decide. (1991). Lancaster, CA: Springs of Life Ministries.

The silent scream. (1984). Cleveland, OH: American Portrait Films.

Straight from the heart. (1994). San Francisco: Woman Vision Productions.

To support and defend: The role of homosexuals in the military. (1993). Los Angeles: Parade Pictures.

17

Julie L. Andsager

Contradictions in the Country: Rituals of Sexual Subordination and Strength in Music Video

INTRODUCTION

In 1997, country music celebrated its "Year of the Woman," thanks to the unprecedented commercial and critical success of new female artists LeAnn Rimes and Shania Twain, as well as entrenched country stars Trisha Yearwood and Reba McEntire. This chapter examines how women (and girls) in country music used their considerable influence to portray sexuality and gender roles in videos. Because love and romance are the primary themes of today's country songs, sexual rhetoric is salient in its video.

Popular country music videos by five prominent female artists were critically examined for this chapter. The artists represented the broad range of women's portrayals in video, although the songs the videos supported focused on either heartbreak or love:

- Deana Carter's 1996 debut album sold more than 3 million copies, while her first single won the 1997 single of the year ("Deana Carter," 1998). Carter's trademarks were her bare feet and her authenticity as the daughter of a well-known country guitar player. Carter was a slim, blonde woman in her early thirties.

- Terri Clark's image was unique as a tall, dark-haired woman in jeans, boots, and a cowboy hat. Clark released her debut album in 1995 and won two top new female artist awards ("Terri Clark Biography," 1998). She was one of few women to play guitar in her videos.

- Faith Hill, a blonde in her twenties who first appeared on the country charts in 1993, enjoyed both critical and commercial success in the 1990s ("Faith Hill," 1998). Her girl-next-door image matured in 1997 when she became involved in literacy projects, married a top male singer, and became a mother.

- The first single from Mindy McCready became a top-selling hit in 1996; after her debut, McCready successfully changed her image to tone down her makeup and clothing. Her songs tended to focus on women's independence and friendship ("Mindy McCready," 1998). McCready was in her early twenties, very slim, and blonde.

- In 1991, Trisha Yearwood released her debut album, then went on to win numerous country music awards and sell more than 7.5 million records ("Trisha Yearwood," 1998). The most widely known of these women, Yearwood appeared on television situation comedies and commercials and performed at the 1996 presidential inauguration. In her early thirties, Yearwood was tall with brown hair and projected a friendly image.

Image has never been more important to country artists, as country music, like rock music before it via MTV (Music Television), used music video to establish artists' images and sell their music. New country artists could "go cut an album, produce a couple of videos—and they've got national exposure" (Pinkston, 1997, p. B1). Country music videos were aired on two networks: CMT (Country Music Television), an all-video format seen in 38 million TV homes nationwide, reaching into 56 percent of all cable TV households; and TNN (The Nashville Network), which played about two hours of videos each day and reached 68 million U.S. households ("When the Dust Settles," 1997). Both country channels debuted in early 1983, dramatically changing the face of country music marketing because videos made "instant stars" out of musicians, as opposed to the years it took to build an image in the pre-video era (Bufwack and Oermann, 1993).

But what images were country music's women suggesting in the late 1990s? To be sure, the days of female country artists as token "girl soingers" were long over, and their images had undergone drastic changes over the last six decades and more. In more than six decades, female artists have spanned the range from the calico-clad girl next door to the cowboy's sweetheart in buckskin and boots; from the carefully coifed, sequined show queen to the relaxed styles of a California country-rocker (Bufwack and Oermann, 1993). These images evolved over the years as country music itself moved from hillbilly and Appalachian music into a genre that reached a broader market than ever, as country music became the top radio format in the United States during the 1990s.

Modern women and girls tended to elude any such classification. One of the top-selling female artists of the 1990s, Shania Twain—who used music video to promote herself more effectively than any other country singer, male or female—offered an often-contradictory mirage of images. She was a "no-nonsense sex symbol—a take-charge woman line-dancing down the middle of the road, splitting the difference between feminine compliance and feminist effrontery" and promoted "the flirtatious co-existence of glamor [*sic*] and self-empowerment [as] country's Cosmo-girl, a fantasy that works for both men and women" (Johnson, 1998). Although Twain may have exuded both strength and submission from video to video and occasionally within individual videos, other female artists tended to embody one quality or the other but seldom both. Twain's chameleonlike video image was not representative of country video. To facilitate analysis and discussion in this chapter, then, videos by women with well-defined images were examined. Specifically, five videos by top-selling artists were analyzed; each video was in high rotation during the end of January 1997, as TNN's *Music City Tonight* variety program celebrated the "Year of the Woman."

COUNTRY MUSIC

Despite its popularity, scholars seldom study country music; indeed, no published work has yet examined country music video in and of itself. One reason for this void is suggested by Buckley (1978), who contended that much of the public perceives country music as "an artistic and intellectual wasteland . . . a persuasive medium for the transmission of rural conservatism" (p. 293). Indeed, major studies of the genre tend to be histories of country music that focus on its roots in the rural South and the men who expanded its horizons to the nation via the Grand Ole Opry (see, for example, Rogers, 1983; Tichi, 1994). These volumes reified the belief that "[c]ountry music really participates in a long-term American tradition in which genius [is] considered to be male" (Tichi, 1994, p. 201). However, women have long been influential in country music's development as songwriters, artists, musicians, and producers (Bufwack and Oermann, 1993). Still, the long-held belief that male artists sell more product than female artists—from the 1940s to the early 1960s, country music shows assumed they needed only one "girl singer" (Jensen, 1993)—has not quite faded in Nashville.

But women were integral to country music because love is the foundation of a large portion of country songs. Certainly, the portrayal of women in country music has often focused on their sexuality and desire for love, perhaps because country is steeped in the values of love, family, and the work ethic—with all that those values encompass, good and bad. An analysis of the lyrics of forty top country songs during the mid-1980s found that the woman in country music "appears to make maximum use out of her only resources—emotional support and her sexuality" (Saucier, 1993, p. 255) because her status was derived from her ability to get and keep a man. Saucier concluded that the roles of lover, wife, and mother were the most appropriate for women in country lyrics, but men did not fare much better—their roles were most often defined as lover and provider. For the audience, songs and their lyrics cannot easily be separated from the artists who perform them, though, and artist gender seems to matter in how the audience perceives various topics. When analyzing the success of country songs in the late 1970s, Jaret (1993) found that male artists were more likely to stay on the charts with songs with honky-tonking and sexual themes. Female artists' songs about their rambling men and other sad love stories were more likely to sell than those on other topics. Thus, whether it has been industry-

or audience-created, country music has long seen a disparity between the sexes in terms of their portrayal in songs and the topics they should sing about.

The gender disparity may have in part resulted from country's place as an intensely personal medium. Country music historians Bufwack and Oermann (1993) argued that women's role in the genre has traditionally reflected the lives of the majority of American women, however: "It describes poverty, hardship, economic exploitation, sexual subjugation, and limited opportunities. Sometimes it is self-defeating and reactionary, painful and despairing. But it also contains outspoken protest and joyful rebellion, shouts of exaltation and bugle calls of freedom" (p. x). Thus, arguably more so than other genres, country music is rife with the contradictory feelings inherent in relationships and sexuality.

In the 1990s, as the themes of country music have evolved beyond the old drinking and cheating songs into more enlightened portrayals of male-female relationships, some of the gender role disparity has crept into country music video. While the love songs of the 1990s were "helping to, if not erase, then at least recast many of country's male-female stereotypes into more enlightened models" (Altman, 1997, p. 256), a viewing of the fare on CMT suggested that the visual imagery present in videos was not keeping pace with country's comparatively progressive lyrics. Moreover, the traditional male dominance in the country genre was glaringly apparent on CMT: A study conducted in 1997 found that, in a random sample of twenty-four hours of videos, more than 94 percent of CMT video directors were male, and male artists' videos were played almost three times as often as female artists' (Andsager and Roe, 1999). Because a fairly small number of female artists garnered any significant airplay on CMT, it is important to consider the images they presented regarding love and sexuality, the most common topics for country songs in the late 1990s.

MUSIC VIDEO

Gender in popular music videos has been extensively discussed and analyzed. Aufderheide (1986) suggested that music videos are natural subjects for study of gender and gender roles because the short, imagery-based video's "lack of a clear subject carries into its constant play with the outward trappings of sex roles" (p. 69). The three-minute medium often operated on easily identifiable signs to convey a story quickly and vividly. However, in Kaplan's (1987) comprehensive analysis of MTV, she argued that rock music video was not monolithic but rather "constructs several different kinds of general address and modes of representing sexuality" (p. 89) and offered the viewer a means of negotiating among gender portrayals.

Gender role negotiation in music video has been categorized in slightly varying ways. A study of MTV and BET (Black Entertainment Television) videos suggested three general themes in portraying girls and women ("Women in Music Videos," 1996). These were:

- "Conventional woman," in which the emphasis was on physical appearance and the woman's role was merely to satisfy a man's desire;

- "Independent woman," where women were strong, were self-reliant, and demanded equality, even in sexual relationships; and

- "Internal paradox," in which male or female characters were portrayed in conflicting gender roles in a single video.

The juxtaposition of these three categories allowed female viewers to "construct the particular gender identity she finds most satisfactory from the paradoxical images presented" ("Women in Music Videos," 1996, p. 8). It was apparent from these studies that female artists and characters tended to follow some fairly well-defined conventions in their roles in music video, leaning toward either the victims of sexism or the leaders of independence.

Early studies of gender in music videos also focused primarily on sexism in MTV. In the mid-1980s, researchers found that slightly more than half of the MTV videos they examined portrayed women in a condescending manner (Vincent, Davis, and Boruszkowski, 1987); less than two years later, a replication indicated that condescending treatment had declined sharply, occurring in about 40 percent of the videos analyzed (Vincent, 1989). What was most salient about these studies was the finding that male artists' videos were much more likely than female artists' to portray women in a condescending way in both studies. In the latter study, female artists were twice as likely as they had been in the first study to portray women as fully equal, suggesting an improvement in the way they were able to negotiate gender in the medium. At the same time, female characters' clothing in the videos became more seductive (Vincent, 1989; Vincent, Davis, and Boruszkowski, 1987), and not surprisingly, female characters and artists wore less clothing in videos than males (Seidman, 1992). The increase in allure of clothing worn suggested a backlash to the growing level of independence female artists began to portray in their own videos.

Just as country music itself has been the subject of little research, content analyses have seldom examined country music videos. Tapper, Thorson, and Black (1994) included country videos from The Nashville Network in their comparison of music videos across genres; they found that, not surprisingly, all of the country music videos in their sample were performed by white artists, 79 percent of whom were male. More recently, a study replicating Vincent's (1989; Vincent, Davis, and Boruszkowski, 1987) MTV studies found that female artists' videos on CMT were four times more likely than male artists' to portray women as fully equal, whereas the male artists' videos were three times more likely to use condescending images (Andsager and Roe, 1999). Female characters in country videos also wore more alluring clothing than males and were most frequently cast in the role of the male artists' love interests. Unlike their counterparts in rock music who often played sexual predators or strippers, though, the country female characters were pictured in conventional roles such as bride, pregnant wife, or girlfriend.

The disparity between gender role portrayals in male and female artists' videos—both in country and rock—was largely due to the control that established female artists often exerted over their images. "Female musicians are actively participating in making the music video form work in their interest, to assert their authority as producers of culture and to air their views on female genderhood" (Lewis, 1995, p. 500). This assertion may have been true for women who gained a foothold in the music industry, but for new country artists, the fact that country music video is dominated by male directors (as mentioned above) may have impeded certain visions of female gender, emphasizing those more consistent with male notions of gender and sexuality.

RITUALS OF SUBORDINATION

Signs of sexuality are often transmitted more subtly in music video than the rough categorizations of gender roles can capture, however. And as artists and directors become (presumably, at least) more sensitive to the images that gender roles create in video, nonverbal cues such as body language should become increasingly important as signals to convey messages about gender and sexuality. Indeed, nonverbal signs may "act in such a way not only to embody hierarchical relations but perhaps more importantly, to uphold and to justify them" (LaFrance and Henley, 1994, p. 290). Thus, although female country artists may have appeared to be "fully equal" according to the conventional means of content analysis discussed above, a close examination of their nonverbal signs suggested disparities among them in strength and sexual rhetoric.

Goffman (1976) noted the prevalence of nonverbal cues that characterize gender relations in cultural products such as advertisements. He defined certain gender displays—particularly expressions of "femininity"—as rituals of subordination that can "affirm a contrary picture" of men and women "who happen to be in the same social situation" (p. 8). Gender displays can be so culturally ingrained within individuals, then, that they can undermine a conscious effort to portray women as fully equal. It is important to emphasize that these signs are not biological or instinctual but rather socially constructed. Therefore, the viewer's interpretation of them is "due primarily to those institutionalized arrangements in social life which allow strangers to glimpse the lives of persons they pass" (p. 23). This supports the notion that certain displays, symbols, and gender roles are often employed in music video to convey messages in an immediate way—similar to the function of print advertisements, upon which Goffman's work was based.

Nonverbal gender displays can incorporate a wide range of behaviors. Among the most common are facial expression or gaze; posture, gestures, or orientation to others; touching; and people's use of space (LaFrance and Henley, 1994). Because female artists in music videos were often pictured alone (or somewhat distant to other characters), the focus here was on displays that are subordinating in and of themselves, not necessarily in relation to other individuals. In Goffman's (1976) discussion, a number of nonverbal gender displays that he contended are more likely to be performed by females comprise the ritual of subordination. Licensed withdrawal involved averting the gaze from a situation, suggesting an element of trust in that other people in the area are presumed unthreatening. Withdrawal rendered women "dependent on the protectiveness and goodwill of others who are (or might come to be) present" (Goffman, 1976, p. 57). Canting referred to lowering parts of the body—usually the head, or bending the knees or waist—leaving the impression of submissiveness or ingratiation. It appeared to reduce the body size, indicating a subordinated posture. Similarly, reclining was the ultimate canting, as this position both inhibits physical defense and provides "a conventionalized expression of sexual availability" (p. 41). These signs may indicate subordination to others who were either present in the scene or whose presence was implied, as by a camera's gaze. Conversely, holding the body and head in an erect posture reflected unashamedness, superiority, or disdain.

Other subordination behaviors may have more directly implied sexual subordination. Ritualistic touching may involve caressing or cradling an object (Goffman, 1976); a touching more common in music videos was self-touching, which Goffman argued conveys "a sense of one's body [as] being a delicate and precious thing" (p. 31)—thus highlighting the body, something particularly salient in many videos about love. When a man is present, hand-holding and other "tie-signs" may occur. Although hand-holding was considered nonsubordinating, it can signal submissiveness if one partner appears to pull the other along. A shoulder hold, on the other hand, was indicative of sexual proprietorship in what was portrayed as a romantic relationship. Finally, clowning was a ritual of subordination that can assume many forms. For Goffman, all of these are demeaning. However, in male-female relationships such as those often enacted in music video, an important form of clowning to note was the "mock assault," which involved one partner chasing the other, playfully threatening. The mock assault was considered to suggest fun, but "underneath this show a man may be engaged in a deeper one, the suggestion of what he could do if he got serious about it" (p. 52).

VIDEO ANALYSIS

Nonverbal displays such as these appeared in country music video quite regularly. To examine how behaviors inherent in the ritual of subordination were evinced, discussion will now turn to five videos that were at the top of CMT's rotation schedule in spring 1997. The videos portrayed romance and heartbreak; however, the contradictory displays of strong and subordinate women render the imagery vastly different among the videos with the same themes.

In *We Danced Anyway* (1996), Deana Carter reminisced about a romantic getaway from the past. The video was set in Puerto Rico on a beach and in a city. It opened to a waist-down shot of Carter—barefooted, as she was throughout the video, while her lover was shod—kicking water along the beach in a short, sleeveless black dress, then showed her playfully running away from her lover. Later, he caught her around the waist and threatened to throw her into the water as she kicked in protest. The lover held Carter by the hand or waist in nearly every scene in which they both appeared. The lyrics suggested that the video images recounted her memories of the vacation, but despite the togetherness these imply, Carter danced alone for the camera. In turn, she wore a long, gauzy gown, lifting its skirt up as in a curtsy; she leaned flirtatiously into the camera in a low-cut sundress; she turned cartwheels in shorts and a white t-shirt. She threw her bare arms into the air, then behind her head as if to caress her hair. Finally, she rolled on the beach in the wet v-neck t-shirt and shorts, ending in a supine position.

The video was interspersed with shots of older men (apparently to add "color") who stared, then smiled into the camera, suggesting that they were watching Carter and admiring her actions—almost as if they were complicit with the viewer. Thus, in nearly every scene Carter assumed some form of canting behavior. The imagery suggested that perhaps she was trying to appease her lover, whose perspective the viewer seemed to be taking.

Whether the subordination present in this video was the product of director or artist was unclear. The imagery projected in this video seemed to coincide with the way Carter's publicity framed her songwriting and personality. She was described as "delicate yet strong, wistful yet direct, the wisdom of a grown woman tempered by the wonderment of a still innocent young girl" ("Deana Carter," 1998). These contradictions were not apparent in the *We Danced Anyway* video, however, in which Carter embodied Goffman's (1976) rituals of subordination.

If love subordinated Carter, heartbreak rendered Faith Hill seemingly powerless in *It Matters to Me* (1996). In the song, Hill's lover had hurt her by withdrawing after an argument. The setting for the video was the stage of a darkened auditorium. No other characters appeared. Throughout the video, the barefooted Hill wore a sleeveless black gown with a plunging neckline. As she sang of her desperation, she alternately stared into space for the camera's gaze and then directly into the lens for close-up shots. She frequently caressed her neck, shoulders, and chest, occasionally grabbing handfuls of hair as if ready to tear it out. Hill paced in small circles, clutching and twisting the skirt of the gown. In the most disturbing scenes, she lay prone, stroking her face and arching her back as she appeared to moan; flashbulbs inexplicably punctuated the scene. The overall impression was one of a woman going mad, helpless with the loss of her man.

Similar images were presented in another heartbreak video, *Maybe He'll Notice Her Now*, by Mindy McCready. A heavily made-up McCready spent most of the video sitting or lying on a bed in obviously posed positions, wearing a series of sleeveless gowns, seldom looking into the camera.

McCready has since decried these images and others presented in her early videos, however, as false and unnatural. For her second album, McCready said she demanded "No retouch, no make-up, no airbrush. I wanted the girls who see it to say, 'Oh, I look like that. Mindy looks just like we do' " ("Mindy McCready," 1998). This statement indicated that female artists' images—and music videos—were contrived to present a hegemonic view of beauty and sexuality. Combined with the subordinated sexual rhetoric presented in videos such as those discussed above, these images reinforced the traditional notions of submissiveness as feminine and sexy.

But another group of women in country music counteract such imagery. For example, a broken heart had no such devastating effect on Trisha Yearwood in *Everybody Knows* (1996). In this upbeat song, Yearwood complained that everyone except herself knew how to end the heartache over her lost love, but she needed no sympathy. Although the lyrics themselves suggested that she is depressed, the video's signs suggested otherwise. The scenes in the video took place in a colorful hotel room and a small studio. Throughout, Yearwood sang forcefully and directly into the camera, often in close-ups, seldom smiling. Indeed, her face dominated the frame. The intimate setting and close camera shots suggested that she was commiserating with the viewer. She wore loose-fitting casual suits and long-sleeved blouses, dancing occasionally in the studio scenes. Yearwood did not interact with the other characters—her mother talking on the telephone, the hotel maid (played by Yearwood's grandmother), or the handful of men offering her solace in the form of martinis, religion, and chocolate—though she acknowledged them with her dismissive facial expressions. At the end of the video, she closed with a defiant "Yeah!" and shut the hotel room door, pushing the viewer out of her space.

More difficult to find in country video was a strong portrayal of a woman in love. In Terri Clark's *Emotional Girl* (1996), she warned her potential love interest that she was unpredictable and emotional. The stereotypical lyrics stood in marked contrast to the video imagery accompanying them. Clark was a tall woman who wore a cowboy hat, jeans, and boots throughout the video, which took place at an outdoor café and in a soundstage. In the café scenes, Clark was having lunch with her agent and apparently trying to flirt with him—applying lipstick, leaning close to him—but he was oblivious, too busy planning her career. Meanwhile, two construction workers attempted to catch Clark's attention. She finally abandoned the agent to join the construction workers on their girder, seemingly becoming one of the guys. This imagery was rife with gender role contradiction, as Clark's attempts at traditional feminine sexual rhetoric failed to catch the attention of the man she wanted but eventually set her free from her role as the "star" whose time and movement he controlled (when the construction workers lured her away with their admiration).

Interspersed with this story were scenes of Clark playing guitar in a sound-stage as she assumed a traditional male mode of handling the guitar and moving aggressively about the set. Like Yearwood, she nearly filled the frame of these scenes. Clark made eye contact with the camera and smiled frequently, appearing to challenge the viewer to ignore the warning in her lyrics.

CONCLUSION

These videos were fairly representative of the two general images of female artists in country music. One group, represented by Carter and Hill—and formerly by McCready—suggested an ingratiating woman who often served as an object for the camera to view; as a subordinate, she appeared desperate if her lover abandoned her. As she reclined on the beach, floor, or a bed, she seemed sexually available. Moreover, the bare feet popular in such videos symbolized the woman's limited range, both physically and professionally. These nonverbal displays indicated that women tend to depend on men for protection and love. Their submissiveness endangered them, suggesting that they could easily be victimized by heartbreak or even physical threats. Much as the woman in country music lyrics of the past was characterized as dependent on her sexuality, modern country music video depicted some women in the same way, despite the genre's more progressive lyrics.

But a number of strong female country artists contradicted the imagery offered by their counterparts. Yearwood and Clark, among others, projected independence and self-reliance as they gazed directly into the camera. Few, if any, rituals of subordination appeared in their videos. Their directness and aggressive postures suggested that women can control their sexuality and, perhaps more important, challenged the traditional country theme that women must rely on men and romance for fulfillment. Further, this stronger woman interacted with male characters (if any) on a more nearly equal basis, and she was fully clothed. Although strong female artists have always been a presence—for example, Loretta Lynn and Kitty Wells—in the genre, women such as Yearwood and Clark resisted the nonverbal gender signals that permeated many other videos, sending a clear message that they were not to be trifled with.

What constituted the difference among these variations in gender display? Although the strong group of artists may have been slightly older as a whole, there was not more than a dozen years' range in the ages of the women discussed above. The women categorized as submissive in these videos all tended to be blond, slight, and very fit, whereas their counterparts appeared taller, with larger frames—which may have been an artifact of the closer, more direct camera angles used in their videos—and more average body types. The first group was clothed in traditionally feminine, alluring styles; the second group was more fully clothed.

It would not be accurate, however, to contend that these variations constituted substantive differences in the artists themselves or the songs they selected.

Rather, the sexually subordinated images that some of the artists developed—or that were created for them by publicists, agents, and directors—seemed to be products of conventional gender roles and traditional gender themes in country music. These images apparently sold products and built fan bases, as the women who employed such sexual rhetoric tended to be more commercially successful, as indicated by the phenomenal success of Carter's first album and Twain's *The Woman in Me*, which surpassed Patsy Cline's work as the top-selling country album by a female artist.

As the genre continues to evolve, though, female artists may become more likely to assume the new and progressive roles that were beginning to emerge in a segment of country music videos. Certainly, Yearwood and others who presented images of independence and sexual strength—such as Mary Chapin Carpenter and Patty Loveless—have garnered the lion's share of critical success, suggesting that there is room for both types of women in country music. The presence of two contradictory images of women in country video, however, upheld the old notion that women's sexuality and role in love must either be subordinate to men's or independent and possibly superior—but apparently not both. In reinforcing rituals of subordination through female artists' video imagery, then, some commercially successful country music ironically maintained stereotypical, submissive gender roles at a time when the industry proclaimed its gratitude for female artists' contributions to its expanding economic horizons.

REFERENCES

Altman, B. (1997). Women in music: Country just ain't what it used to be. In S. Biagi and M. Kern-Foxworth (Eds.), *Facing difference: Race, gender, and mass media* (pp. 255–58). Thousand Oaks, CA: Pine Forge Press.

Andsager, J. L., and Roe, K. (1999). Country music video in country's Year of the Woman. *Journal of Communication, 49* (1), 69–82.

Aufderheide, P. (1986). Music videos: The look of the sound. *Journal of Communication, 36*, 57–78.

Buckley, J. (1978). Country music and American values. *Popular Music and Society, 6*, 293–301.

Bufwack, M. A., and Oermann, R. K. (1993). *Finding her voice: The saga of women in country music*. New York: Crown Publishers.

Carter, D. (1996). *We danced anyway*. Studio Productions (Producer), and Pistole, R. (Director). Nashville, TN: Capitol Nashville.

Clark, T. (1996). *Emotional girl*. Bateman, B. (Producer), and Merriman, M. (Director). Nashville, TN: Mercury Nashville.

Deana Carter. (1998). Country.com: Country music, racing, outdoors, TNN, CMT [Online]. Available: http://www.country.com/music/artist-alpha-f.html [1998, March 10].

Faith Hill. (1998). Country.com: Country music, racing, outdoors, TNN, CMT [Online]. Available: http://www.country.com/music/artist-alpha-f.html [1998, March 10].

Goffman, E. (1976). *Gender advertisements*. New York: Harper & Row.

Hill, F. (1996). *It matters to me*. Thorpe/Phillips (Producer), and St. Nicholas, R. (Director). Nashville, TN: WEA/Warner Brothers.

Jaret, C. (1993). Characteristics of successful and unsuccessful country music songs. In G. H. Lewis (Ed.), *All that glitters: Country music in America* (pp. 174–185). Bowling Green, OH: Bowling Green State University Popular Press.

Jensen, J. (1993). Patsy Cline, musical negotiation, and the Nashville sound. In G. H. Lewis (Ed.), *All that glitters: Country music in America* (pp. 38–50). Bowling Green, OH: Bowling Green State University Popular Press.

Johnson, B. D. (1998). Shania revealed: The queen of country wants to step out of the packaging and prove herself on the stage. *Macleans* [Online]. Available: http://www.macleans.ca/newsroom03298/cov1032398.html [1998, April 4].

Kaplan, E. A. (1987). *Rocking around the clock: Music Television, postmodernism, and consumer culture*. New York: Routledge.

LaFrance, M., and Henley, N. M. (1994). On oppressing hypotheses: Or differences in nonverbal sensitivity revisited. In L. Radtke and H. J. Stam (Eds.), *Power/gender: Social relations in theory and practice* (pp. 287–311). London: Sage Publications.

Lewis, L. A. (1995). Form and female authorship in music video. In G. Dines and J. M. Humez (Eds.), *Gender, race and class in media: A text-reader* (pp. 499–507). Thousand Oaks, CA: Sage Publications.

McCready, M. (1996). *Maybe he'll notice her now*. Fanjoy, T. (Producer), and Hershleder, J. (Director). Nashville, TN: BNA Records.

Mindy McCready. (1998). Country.com: Country music, racing, outdoors, TNN, CMT [Online]. Available: http://www.country.com/music/artist-alpha-f.html [No date].

Pinkston, W. (1997, March 2). Won't touch that dial: Westinghouse to change little at CMT, TNN. *The Tennessean*, pp. E1–E2.

Rogers, J. N. (1983). *The country music message: All about lovin' and livin'*. Englewood Cliffs, NJ: Prentice-Hall.

Saucier, K. A. (1993). Images of men and women in country music. In G. H. Lewis (Ed.), *All that glitters: Country music in America* (pp. 241–258). Bowling Green, OH: Bowling Green State University Popular Press.

Seidman, S. A. (1992). An investigation of sex-role stereotyping in music videos. *Journal of Broadcasting & Electronic Media, 36*, 209–16.

Tapper, J., Thorson, E., and Black, D. (1994). Variations in music videos as a function of their musical genre. *Journal of Broadcasting & Electronic Media, 38*, 103–13.

Terri Clark biography. (1998). Mercury Nashville Artists [Online]. Available: http://www.mercurynashville.com/mercurynashville/artists/clark_terri/biography.html [1998, March 10].

Tichi, C. (1994). *High lonesome: The American culture of country music*. Chapel Hill: University of North Carolina Press.

Trisha Yearwood. (1998). Country.com: Country music, racing, outdoors, TNN, CMT [Online]. Available: http://www.country.com/music/artist-alpha-f.html [No date].

Vincent, R. C. (1989). Clio's consciousness raised? Portrayal of women in rock videos, re-examined. *Journalism Quarterly, 66*, 155–60.

Vincent, R. C., Davis, D. K., and Boruszkowski, L. A. (1987). Sexism on MTV: The portrayal of women in rock videos. *Journalism Quarterly, 64*, 750–55, 941.

When the dust settles. (1997, March 2). *The Tennessean*, p. E1.

Women in music videos: Conflicting, contradictory messages and models. (1996, Summer). *Media Report to Women, 24*, 8.

Yearwood, T. (1996). *Everybody knows*. Beresford, R. (Producer), and Wenner, G. (Director). Nashville, TN: MCA Records.

18

Joseph W. Slade

Inventing a Sexual Discourse: A Rhetorical Analysis of Adult Video Box Covers

INTRODUCTION

Sufficient numbers of Americans subscribe to Woody Allen's dictum that "sex is not dirty [pause] unless it's done right" to give credence to corollaries: (1) that sex can be appreciated as performance and (2) that only properly "dirty" representations of sex can reliably arouse. Accordingly, producers of pornography have flooded the market with kinky and athletic video fantasies that gays, lesbians, and heterosexuals can share with partners or enjoy by themselves. Even so, the adult video industry is still very much in transition: Enhanced private and social orgasms aside, precisely what Americans want from pornography is no more clear than what, exactly, they do in bed. Trying to discover what turns audiences on requires not only experimentation with video scenarios but also the invention of a discourse to describe and promote performances. When fantasies can be mass-produced, then marketing must discover (create?) niches of desire; commerce has overcome traditional American sexual reticence by fashioning for the adult video box cover a hybrid discourse suitable to the public venue of rental stores. *Adult Video News*, the industry bible, boasts that "while backwards in almost every other way of doing business, porno producers have gotten the box cover art down to a science"; in terms of that packaging, the adult video is "among the best-marketed product in the world" (Ross, 1993, p. 6).

Speaking about pornography in America leads to categories never envisioned by Michel Foucault. Despite attempts by various groups to demonize sexual materials to fit ideological, gendered, or religious dichotomies of good and evil, the contention that pornography is monolithic is a fiction. The term *pornography* embraces many genres and many media representations, all of them with their own dynamic, all of them in continuous dispute. As Walter Kendrick has pointed out, "[P]ornography is not a thing but an argument" (Kendrick, 1987 p. 178). The inability to agree stems from ancient inarticulateness about sexuality. Discomfort with sexual candor and differences in gender, class, religion, age, ethnicity, region, and community, not to mention psychological idiosyncrasies, have worked against formation of a standardized discourse.

What common meanings exist have often derived from pornographic genres, each of which creates its own lexical and semiotic universe. Mistrustful of a medical rendition of human sexuality that academics have shown to be just as socially constructed as other versions, Americans still draw on pornographic sources for their sexual folklore. The appropriation of vulgar language and images is a process understood since Farmer and Henley published *Slang and Its Analogues* (1890/1904), the classic study of obscenity in the English language, but modern information economies accelerate the movement of words and ideas from margins to mainstream. A recently syndicated editorial cartoon depicted a young woman who asks her grandmother to name "the biggest change you've witnessed in your lifetime." The grandmother's reply: "How even nine-year-old girls now use the word 'sucks' " (Horsey, 1998). *Boogie Nights* (1997), a mainstream film much praised for its patronizing of the adult industry, punctuated its script with terms such as "cum shot" and "blow job." Talk-show hosts routinely invite porn stars to titillate audiences with the vernacular of their trade; the *New Yorker* regularly publishes articles about print and videographic pornography (de St. Jorre, 1994; Faludi, 1995) and in the process domesticates wild images from hard-core industries; and signs for Hooters restaurants are almost as familiar as golden arches. "Deep Throat" may mean one thing in Washington, another in the hinterlands, but tracing the term is easy, especially when it is kept vibrant by repetition on video box covers.

Adult Box Covers as Ghettoed Genre

Adult video boxes (at 9 inches by 5 3/4 inches) seem to have been pumped with steroids. Distributors originally made them larger than standard sleeves to prevent store staff from inadvertently racking adult with mainstream family fare. Retailers now complain that adult tapes take up an extra 40 percent of shelf space (Ross, 1993, p. 5), but expanded surfaces have one distinct advantage: They can display more messages on all sides.

Linguistic convention holds that geography shapes discourse, so that novel systems of representation are most likely to arise in physically bounded sectors, whether the subculture be a tribe in the Carpathians or a gang on the South Side of Chicago. Though some adult videos are sold by mail, most are displayed in a retail outlet's "adult" ghetto. Boxes thus speak to a semiclosed community. Adult sections are not all-male preserves: Aware that women rent about 40

Figure 18.1
Video Box Cover

Courtesy of Steve Hirsch, Vivid Video. Used by permission.

percent of all adult tapes (Williams, 1989, p. 231), outlet owners try to ensure comfortable browsing. Many outlets shelve gay tapes separately; the authentic lesbian video, though developing (Conway, 1997, p. 91), has not generated enough examples to be clustered apart. Shelving schematics, in short, are themselves texts of the sort Foucault found so fascinating. That Americans rent millions of tapes, and that women and minorities are now shooting hard-core scenarios (Royalle, 1993; Suggs, 1997), suggests that the need for sexual fantasies cuts across gender and ethnicity, though just how is not clear.

Thus distributors target "imagined communities" whose tastes in sexual performance they try to guess. Research on *actual*—rather than experimental or theorized—audiences for pornography is just beginning, pioneered by Gross (1996, pp. 161–176). Gross points out that "the public" condemns pornography and believes that the government should regulate it at the same time that millions of Americans consume it. He examines the messages of a porn film as they mutate—the conceived text, the production text, the produced text, the transmitted text, the received text, the perceived text, the social/public text—on their way to an audience that Gross believes is average and normal. The power of pornography rests on a shared secret: Almost no one will admit to finding it arousing. Humans lie about pornography as often as they lie about sex itself; what they say they find erotic is not what they rent. Aware of the audience's capacity for self-deception, distributors understand that consumers must be able to tell the video from its cover.

CHANGES IN THE MARKET

Straight, gay, or lesbian hard core depicts masturbation, genital contact, or penetration—sexual performance. Also lumped in this category are videotapes devoted to particular objects of desire. These foreground obsessions range from large breasts and penises to bondage, footwear, rubber, leather, and so on; these may or may not lead in the videos to actual climax but nonetheless locate and fix sexual cues. Around 7,500 new straight, gay, lesbian, and amateur titles appear each year. Eight percent of these come from German, Scandinavian, Italian, French, Hungarian, or Asian companies. According to *Adult Video News*, Americans spent about $4.2 billion on adult video tapes in 1996 (Schlosser, 1997, p. 45; Slade, 1997, pp. 2–3) or roughly 11 percent of the amount they spent at fast-food burger franchises such as McDonald's (Lubow, 1998, p. 40); the average American household now watches six porn videos per year (Andersen, 1998). As in most industries, a handful of big companies dominates; given the control of distribution by VCA, Vivid, Evil/Elegant Angel, Sin City, Western Visuals, and a few others, Americans outside major cities do not encounter more than a fraction of the industry's annual output.

ELEMENTS OF BOX DISCOURSE:

John Fiske defines *discourse* as "a language or system of representation that has developed socially in order to make and circulate a coherent set of meanings about an important topic area" (Fiske, 1994, p. 94). Where box covers are concerned, codes drawn from oral, print, and graphic media constitute an ensemble of representations. Components are commercial, legal, and promotional inscriptions; titles; name brand stars and directors; photographs; vernacular language; and fetishes.

Commercial, Legal, and Promotional Inscriptions

Three inscriptions are conventional. The first is the UPC label, so ubiquitous as to be invisible, a reminder that the videotape is a commodity marketed like any other; the UPC tracks inventory, sales, and rentals for distributor and retailer. The second is the Section 2257 notice, a statement of compliance with the federal requirement that records the ages of all performers be kept by the producer. Although designed to harass makers of pornographic videotapes, this law has had the unintended consequence of bringing accounting and management techniques to an industry notoriously careless with them. Ironically, the sign of official disapproval almost certainly enhances appeal. The third is the sticker announcing an award (e.g., Best Video of 1997 or Best Oral Scene of 1996) bestowed by *Adult Video News* or another trade journal. Because mainstream media seldom review adult films, award notices take the place of blurbs reproduced on legitimate video sleeves. Like other messages on the box cover, the inscriptions contradict without canceling each other, marginalizing a quasi-outlaw industry (the Section 2257 notice) that seeks recognition (the award stickers) through standard commodification (the UPC label).

Titles

Upscale distributors prefer suggestive titles (*Night Tales, Sailor in the Wild, Dark Angel*) on the assumption that their audiences lean toward Calvin Klein eroticism. Lowball distributors choose flat-footed titles (*Tit City, Shaved She-Males, Snatch Shots*), on the assumption that *their* targeted viewers respond to raw vulgarity. In between are parodies of mainstream artifacts, a traditional function of pornography visible in titles such as *Blazing Bedrooms, Sex Trek II: The Search for Sperm, Honey, I Blew Everybody,* and *The Last Condom;* the archness, however adolescent, is a reminder that sexual humor laughs at both social convention and sex itself. Some are amusingly alliterative (*Dick of Death*), many are double entendre (*Powertool, Club Head, Deck His Balls with Holly*), a few trade on imagined proclivities of nationalities or regions (*Hungarian Anal Rhapsody, San Francisco Lesbians, Eurosluts*), and rare examples are disarming (*Topless Brain Surgeons*). Having signed a charismatic performer, the producer determined to get marquee value will work the star's name into the title: *A Portrait of Christy* [Canyon]; *The Legend of Joey Steffano;* or *Deep Inside Racquel Darrian.* In a special category are purloined tapes of celebrities not normally associated with the sex industry (*Pam and Tommy Lee: Hardcore and Uncensored*), as well as spins on notorious media events (*John Wayne Bobbitt Uncut*).

Titles may hint at acts not in the videotape, a practice more common in the past, when reference to a "piece of tail" or allusions to "rears," say, did not guarantee anal intercourse. Promising and then delivering that particular behavior helped establish the popularity of series such as *Caught from Behind* and *Rump Humpers.* As the foregoing suggests, titles can cue particular fetishes: long-running series bear titles such as *Girls from Hootersville* and *The Girls of the Double-D.* The titles of *Where the Boys Aren't* and *Strap-on Sally* appeal to males interested in watching ersatz lesbian encounters between heterosexual stars. Similar titles seem self-fulfilling: It was doubtless inevitable that *Every Woman Wants a Penis*, a scenario laden with strap-on sex toys, would spawn *Every Woman Wants Two Penises*, in which the females sport harnesses with double dildos.

Names Above the Title: Stars and Directors

Appearances on afternoon talk shows, cable specials, or striptease circuits have made celebrities of performers who also maintain fan clubs with mail, telephone, and e-mail addresses. Because Dyanna Lauren, Jenna Jameson, Sunset Thomas, Sean Michaels, and Tom Byron in the straight market and Dallas Taylor, Tim Lowe, Marco Rossi, and Ryan Idol in the gay have large followings, their contracts guarantee their names above the title. Even so, boxes customarily list *all* the video's performers prominently at least once; today's spear-carrier may be tomorrow's diva. Performers often choose punning, parodistic, or fanciful stage names, as in Dave Hardman, Randy Spears, Woody Long, Paul Coxxx, Dru Berrymore, Anna Malle, Caressa Savage, Wendy Whoppers, Jen Teal, Sid Deuce, and Vince Voyeur. Actors refer to themselves as "performance artists," and some (e.g., Annie Sprinkle) support their "serious" endeavors by working in porn (Burana, 1998). The reputations of major directors such as John Leslie (the *Voyeur* series), Andrew Blake (*House of Dreams*), John Stagliano (the *Buttman* series), John Travis (*Powertool*), and Jim Steel (*The Roommate*) also draw fans.

Still Photographs as Collages

The box front or display side is usually given over to full-length depiction of the star. Photographers can key-light flesh until it glows and airbrush jaded veterans into innocent ingenues. Nudity is rare (the front of the box might be visible from family sectors of the store), though skimpy costumes reveal curving biceps, breasts, crotches, and buttocks. Male and female performers seem genuinely to enjoy posing for "cover art" and readily adopt the hipshot, quarter-turned, pin-up pose beloved of Hollywood fan magazines and sports posters. In a culture that worships performance on screen, it is hardly surprising that pornography takes on glamour for clerks trying to avoid employment at McDonald's, and it is here, on the cover, that the glamour seems most cool. Front covers inscript desire through conventional standards of beauty and sexiness; the social construction of those standards is most obvious when the cover features a transvestite, a transsexual, or merely a performer who owes her bust to surgery.

The visuals on the normally obscured reverse are different. Here up to twelve small photos augment text. Static photos tour the nude star's flesh, push fetishes such as lingerie or high heels, or set intercourse in an office. Action frames not only indicate video content but also sequence encounters in genre patterns. Frames may depict female stars masturbating, making love to another woman, next coupling with a male, then joining an orgy, and finally devolving into monogamy. The formula first destabilizes, then restabilizes desire: The performer surrenders to sexual chaos in order to be ravished by her own sexuality before the world rocks back into place. Gay formulas are similar, though the lexicons of positions and the protocols for orgasm differ.

Competition and postmodern impatience with logical sequence have led to the abandonment of scripted plots that were always precarious to begin with. Though hardly as silent as early stag films, contemporary videos have replaced language with the wordless pageant of bodies, giving prominence to unscripted performance rather than story lines. As a consequence, box photos have become more explicit. Pictures foreground genitals, or freeze shooting sperm to resemble explosions in action films; spectacle provides rhetorical meaning for both (Browne, 1998). In cycling homosexual and/or heterosexual intercourse to orgasm, photo sequences mimic the Laban system of dance notation (a system of pictographic symbols for performance positions) by representing bodies in various postures of congress. Some texts enumerate acts ("Six Cum Shots! Four Anals! Two Double Penetrations!") so that photos can confirm a coherent pictorial narrative. Among interesting semiotic issues raised by such trains of images is that of faces photographed during (real or dramatized) orgasm. Whether expressions are socially constructed or not, faces almost always register orgasmic pleasures as intensities indistinguishable from pain, a factor that helps explain the confusion surrounding sexual representations.

Because photos are sometimes so small that it is not always evident who is coupling with whom, gender slides toward instability even on "straight" boxes. Constant "lesbian" scenes aside, other activities—anal intercourse in particular— bend gender practice, a reminder of Gore Vidal's remark that "there are no homosexual people and no heterosexual people, only hetero or homo acts" (Katz, 1995, p. x). Photos and videos typically represent women as masculinized, just as the pornographic genres of the billion-dollar women's romance industry feminize men; Vance (1984, p. 11) insists that hard-core genres urge sexual autonomy on females even as it subordinates them. Moreover, even casual observers can see that waving about large numbers of heterosexual penises will lead inevitably to homoerotic or pan-sexual novelties. Gender disputations have to an extent always animated hard-core role-playing and experimentation (Slade, 1997, p. 1), which is why the study of pornographic fantasy has spurred Queer Theory and Performance Theory. Both suggest that behavior is a game of impersonation conducted through rituals of signs. Some theorists (Butler, 1990, 1993) believe that gender is performance, that performance calls gender into being; the semiotic analyses of "performed gender" by Butler (1997) and Chisholm (1995) could easily be applied to boxes. In short, covers not only inscript desire but also negotiate gender.

Old and New Vernaculars

At one end of their range, adult covers emulate Hollywood sleeves by identifying the product as comedy, romance, adventure, or drama and by placing the emphasis on plot rather than sex. Although the latter is clearly the key ingredient, the cover employs euphemisms, so that "delicious fantasy" can allude to cunnilingus or daydream. The more developed the plot, the more reticent will be the language on the cover. The diction for *Le Parfum de Matilde* (1995), a costume drama, is typical.

The very distinguished Sir Remy lives alone in an aging castle, with only his servants and his memories of his departed wife Matilde. Her scent—if not her essence—seems to fill every room. She was a magnificient bitch, known for her wild orgies thrown for the benefit of her perversions and for the amusement of her husband. She was truly an unequalled wonder. Until now. Until Eva. Join Europe's reknowned director Marc Dorcel in his essential masterpiece, *Le Parfum de Matilde* [*sic*]—with Draghixa playing the enchantingly beautiful Eva. As she is joined by a cast of European superstars. Named AVN's Best European Production of 1995. For good reason. And brought to you by Vivid. For obvious reason.

Covers may assert that plot is unimportant even where it is developed, thus finessing a central issue for video pornography: that of the narrative's destruction by the intrusion of sexual scenes that disrupt normal fictional sequence. The box copy of *Boiling Point* (1996) does not fictionalize the performers and actually undercuts the narrative itself:

Dyanna [Lauren] is engaged to Mark [Davis], per her father's wishes. Along comes Colt [Steele], a drifter on his way to Dyanna's heart. Will she follow through with the marriage? Or will she follow Colt to Mexico? (After the incredible bachelorette party, the double dp's, and the wild bar scene, you won't care. You'll be too busy rewinding the tape to watch the whole thing all over again.) Get The Point. *Boiling Point*. Only from [director] Toni English and Wave Film.

The implication is that the plot is hackneyed anyway, that a larger complicity—a shared voyeurism—binds viewer and producer, and that what counts is performance.

A Language of Excess

At the other end of the range is what Bataille (1985, pp. 25–28) calls a language of excess and transgression. Most vulgar is the amateur video box. Shot by husbands, wives, and neighbors and distributed erratically, amateur videos enshrine a warts-and-all eroticism. Covers promise an unrehearsed "real" intercourse between partners who are turned on by each other, as opposed to professionals who couple without passion. Amateur tapes extend the tradition of the stag film, which was shot ineptly, then laced with illiterate intertitles as indices of authenticity (Slade, 1984, p. 150). On amateur covers, vulgar terms for intercourse provide the gerunds of choice, and grammar faults and tortured syntax compete with ancient metaphors: "polish his knob," "munch her carpet," "hide the salami." Copywriters cull such expressions from the storehouse of oral obscenity. Hoffmann (1965, 1973) has demonstrated that folklore helped shape the early American stag film by providing numerous narratives, motifs, characters, and language for the genre; Legman (1990, p. 417) maintains that *all* folklore is erotic.

Oral traditions have always shaped written, visual, and electronic pornography. Writing on the rhetoric of Tijuana Bibles, or dirty comic books, Kripke speaks of this indigenous American pornographic genre as "a rich repository of the vernacular of the 1930s and 1940s" (Kripke, 1997, p. 11). Kripke classifies coarse humor in eight-page comics in six categories: (1) alliteration, as in "ram that rotten round rod up that rusty rump"; (2) puns, as in " *'Tom Cat's Revenge by Claud Balls'* "; (3) traditional jokes, as in the perennial favorite, "She was pure as the driven snow, but she drifted" (see also Barreca, 1991); (4) limericks, doggerel, ersatz regional speech dialects; (5) demeaning racial and cultural stereotypes; (6) occupational jargon—as in a radio repairman's complaint that his partner's "socket is too tight"—and underworld and sports lingo—as in a character's getting his "bat up again to play another inning"—used as wordplay.

Sport motifs abound on boxes, as does the jargon of brokerage houses *(Wanda Whips Wall Street)*, corporations *(Corporate Assets)*, and auto shops *(Garage Girls)*, not to mention prisons, barracks, and factories. Other elements in Kripke's list are evident in the vernacular on the box for *Semen for Seven*, volume 17 of the series Creme de la Face, written by the director and performer Rodney Moore, self-styled "King of Cream." "WHERE ELSE CAN YOU FIND SEVEN MONSTER FACIALS ON ONE TAPE?" asks a row of capitals on the reverse, where explicit photos show semen on the faces of five women. The text is vulgar in the extreme, beginning with: "Kali is at the yacht show wishing she could be a captain's slut. 'I'm your captain,' says Rodney, who promises to show her his 'vessel.' " Coarsely comic metaphors for various kinds of intercourse proliferate in the passage. Most crudely represent ejaculation (as in a "Rodney Blast"), or "cum shots," though raucous references to race, body fat, and axillary and pubic hair also abound. Kipnis (1992) has noted that such offensiveness, especially as a weapon of class consciousness, is deliberately disturbing because it is aimed at what the author of the text thinks of as erotic pretense. Moore's crude references to body parts and fluids are designed to subvert bourgeois standards of taste, to restore authenticity to desire. In such a context, "dirty jokes function as a sign for both sexual difference and class difference" (p. 380).

The Vocabulary of Performance

One can dismiss the passage as demeaning to women and the overweight, but its near-demented rush of repellent metaphors and fetishes (semen, body hair, corpulence) structures gonzo fantasy while distancing aspects not to everyone's taste. Interpreting the text as macho boasting—though it is certainly that—

misses the mocking, corrosive nature of obsession (perhaps experienced to the full only by adolescent males unwillingly awash in their own sperm) that provides the subversive and antisocial meaning of many pornographic messages. It is not so much a language of entitlement and empowerment as it is of uncertain order. Patton notes that cum shots "enhance the illusion of control over ejaculation" (Patton, 1991, p. 381). "Clearly," says Patton, "few heterosexual men engage in this practice in real life. The men in porn are paid to *control* their orgasm, their sexuality, not for their partner in the film but for the viewer" (p. 379). Patton maintains that performance overshadows realism. Richard Dyer (1985) deplores the prevalence of the cum shot in gay films because it represents the "ideology of the visible" and reinforces a narrative that "is never organized around the desire to be [penetrated], but around the desire to ejaculate" (p. 228).

Rodney's discourse transforms ejaculations into measures of successful performance, a notion that helps explain the current video fascination with female ejaculation (e.g., *How to Female Ejaculate*). According to Bataille (1986), because Western civilization itself is an artificial construct, it locates eroticism in those acts that distance themselves from reproduction. Impulses toward pornographic representation are thus not a "natural" response to sexuality but are nevertheless quintessentially human attempts to preserve and violate taboos. Where women might see in Rodney's monologue a symbolic reversal of breastfeeding, an infantilization of women fed on "drool," males may see a rebellion against the destiny imposed on them by gonads. Iconographic orgasms—in videos and on their boxes—punctuate scenarios, bring them to closure, and establish the dominance of pleasure over reproduction, thus enabling hard-core videos to present themselves as installments in an epic of triumph over biology.

Even copywriters aiming at a wider audience need a vocabulary to describe pornographic spectacle. So do reviewers of adult videos in search of colorful but precise idiom. The term *facial* (in Rodney's box copy above), of course, is a neologism invented to designate ejaculation onto the face of a partner, and "cum shot" itself is only a few decades older. Authors of video guides append glossaries of their neologisms (Riley, 1994, pp. 625–628). Reviewers and box editors use *anal* as a verb, as in "to anal," following a period of experimentation with "to back door" or "to rear-end." Those expressions, in turn, were attempts to avoid *sodomize* and its vulgar translations, all of which are associated with homosexuality, or equally vulgar terms for heterosexual anal penetration, which, while clear enough, connoted an aggression not intended. "To anal" is genderless and need only be contextualized to refer to gay or heterosexual acts.

Ingenuity helped translate into language a form of anal intercourse in which a woman is seated aside a reclining man, facing his legs so that a low camera angle can "read" simultaneously his penis, her crotch, her rear, and her face as she moves up and down. The official Kinsey Institute for Sex, Reproduction, and Gender notation for that position is rendered as "♀ sup ♂ rec ventral/dorsal seated An HT" for "female on top seated with her back facing the head of a reclining male in anal heterosexual intercourse." Simplifying matters, box writers called the position "a reverse cowgirl anal," which is both precise and self-parodic, and the term became standard within five years. Adopted with similar speed is the abbreviation "DP," or "double penetration," in which a woman serves as the filling in a "sandwich," between a penis in her vagina and another in her anus. Although representations of double penetrations are ancient (scenes can be found on Hellenic vases), the term "DP" has become common only in the last decade, as the act has become the triple lutz of a porn actress's skate toward stardom. While double penetrations may symbolize the alleged insatiability of the female, and invoke taboos against homosexuality and scatology, the act has less to do with sexual enjoyment than with achieving an apogee of performance and is treated as such in box cover copy.

The Role of Fetishes

Critics of pornography mistakenly assume that desire is monolithic, diffuse, and unfocused and that all forms of erotica similarly affect all those who come in contact with them. According to the classic ethnography of porn stores, consumers are far more discriminating:

The man who could not have an orgasm without looking at big breasts ignored everything else in the store. Another, who fantasized about blond pubic hair, showed no interest in big breasts unless they happened to be on a woman who also had blond pubic hair. The man who liked pictures of transvestites thought that the customer who bought pictures of young men was sick, and the men who liked bondage had no common interest with the men who wanted the soft-core magazines. Often it seemed that the men who liked to read written stories had little interest in the picture magazines. Each man had a narrow range of fantasy and showed interest only in the precise kind of pornography that sustained this fantasy; as far as he was concerned, the rest was trash. There were no connoisseurs of pornography as a whole, no little old men in raincoats who got equal thrills from bondage, incest, and interracial rape. Even within the extreme monotony of pornography, there was a marked specialization of fetishes and fantasies that kept the users separate and isolated in their antisocial pleasures. (Weatherford, 1986, p. 45)

Marxist, anthropological, Freudian, or Lacanian perspectives on fetish make for divergent definitions—as commodity, as venerated object, as paraphernalia as cultural force (Slade, forthcoming)—but the "official" definition of fetishism is "recurrent, intense sexually arousing fantasies, sexual urges or behaviors involving the use of nonliving objects (e.g., female undergarments)" (American Psychiatric Association, 1994, p. 526). Sexologists more broadly use fetish to designate a surrogate for more logical or "normal" genital fixations, where the surrogate can be another erogenous zone, like breasts or buttocks, or some artificial substitute, like clothing, that entices and excites. Most people respond to sexual triggers: One woman prefers small buttocks on men, whereas another is keen on wedge-shaped chests, body hair, or small nipples. Ordinarily, however, we call a person a fetishist when he responds sexually only to a specific object embedded in a specific script; because the fetish encapsulates his psychological history, he looks not for originality but for singularity. Carefully scripted scenarios of sado-masochism, for example, appeal only to statistical minorities. Given the idiosyncratic character of sexuality, it is silly to maintain that stimulus and response are universal. Two of the most common myths, that all men are turned on by images of brutalized women, or that all women are stimulated by rape fantasies, are naive and possibly dangerous. Whether or not one can argue with tastes, on the other hand, some tastes clearly are shared. *Adult Video News* alerts outlet managers to cassettes featuring bondage, female domination, infantilism, foot worship, latex and rubber garments, and other classic, psychologically genuine fetishes (Masters, 1993, p. 60) but also to merely popular preferences (men who resemble John Travolta, say) driven by shifting hierarchies of fashion rather than compulsive obsession. Because they are irreducible, save to psychological interpretation, true fetishes are their own meaning. Defined loosely, fetishes are mere tastes—at least partially constructed—and they offer the box designer a palette of sexual colors. Using such preferences in videos is less about signification—since symbol is there made specific—than it is a matter of packaging, a task that falls to box cover designers. The more familiar the fetishes, the more easily they can be read, and a skilled designer will weave corsets, stockings, high heels, blond hair, long legs, large breasts, and big penises into a textual version of fusion cuisine. Whatever else one might say about mildly fetishistic tastes, they add variety, spice, and depth to pornography. More to the point, they are guaranteed to attract some customers in a highly competitive market. As Stoller (1985) has remarked, "[A] fetish is a story masquerading as an object" (155), which means that the box cover need only establish a fetish's presence in order to set a narrative in train.

CONCLUSION

When a director opts for loosely linked vignettes or compilations of fetishes, the lack of a traditional narrative places a special burden on the box cover copywriter (or, in cheaper productions, the distributor, who has to write copy himself). Some dodge the responsibility by appealing instead to the ultimate effect of pornography, as in this text for the cover of *Beach Fucking Brazillians*, an import carrying the warning "Entire Video Is Spoken in Portugese! No English!": "Hey Everybody it's volume 3 of this Brazillian line, and if you're like me you still don't know what the hell is going on. But the sex is great, and we have not seen any of these girls before. Now isn't that why we buy sex tapes to begin with? There is a bunch of people in this volume and they're doing it on the beach. That's how I got the clever title. So sit back and watch the Brazil [*sic*] sex thing. Good Beating [as in masturbating], Al Borda [the distributor]."

Borda's lower-class language and the grubby stills on his cover assert the primacy of the physical over the social and the cerebral. When Borda denies any meaning beyond the performative, when he implies that all he hopes to do is stimulate masturbation, he is giving voice to the pornographer's fantasy of getting beyond language, beyond even representation, to a quotidian, nonsymbolic reality. Viewers may share that essentialist fantasy as they share in the more conventional fantasies of performance advanced by video and box, which are not so different from reveries of success, heroism, or hitting the lottery.

Because box covers are texts announcing and anticipating other texts, offering in a sense representations of representations, they demand a level of logic and coherence often missing from the videos themselves. Through inscriptions, language, and graphics, covers make plausible the universe to be found on the cassettes they contain. That universe is one of perpetual randiness, similar in reductiveness to the power struggles envisioned by antiporn critics. In the porn world, however, no one has any power, only the kinetic impulse provided by fantasy. In this world, no one wears underwear, strangers couple at first introduction, the absence of condoms never leads to disease or pregnancy, women never chafe and men never suffer from impotence, and people can reach orgasm in any position. Viewers understand this world, of course, just as they understand that ballets are about bodies in motion and love conquering all, not about fallen arches, overweight thighs, or sensible costumes and shoes. While deconstruction might focus on what is not on the box, pornographic videos—and their covers— have little to do with self-esteem, wealth, secular happiness, or other trophies of middle-class life but a lot to do with biological imperatives and socially constructed ideals of beauty and performance. Box covers anticipate this world for a public increasingly willing to be entertained and stimulated by it. Pornographic videos are recordings of performance, whether their rhythms are those of musical comedy (Williams, 1989) or the operations of a star system (Dyer, 1979). Box covers are the program notes.

REFERENCES

American Psychiatric Association. (1994). *Diagnostic and statistical manual of mental disorders* (Rev., 4th ed.). Washington, DC: Author.

Andersen, K. (1998, March 30). Blunt Trauma. *New Yorker*, pp. 13–14.

Barreca, R. (1991). *They used to call me Snow White . . . but I drifted: Women's strategic use of humor*. New York: Viking.

Bataille, G. (1985). *Visions of excess: Selected writings 1927–1939* (A. Stoekel, Ed., and A. Stoekel, C. R. Lovitt, and D. M. Leslie, Jr., Trans.). Minneapolis: University of Minnesota Press.

Bataille, G. (1986). *Erotism: Death and sensuality* (M. Dalwood, Trans.). San Francisco: City Lights.

Browne, N. (1998, April 20). The "big bang": The spectacular explosion in contemporary Hollywood film [Online]. Available: www.cinema.ucla.edu/strobe/bigbang/default/num [1998, April–present].

Burana, L. (1998, May 5). Can stripping support the arts? *Village Voice*, pp. 138–140.

Butler, J. (1990). *Gender trouble: Feminism and the subversion of identity*. New York: Routledge.

Butler, J. (1993). *Bodies that matter: On the discursive limits of sex.* New York: Routledge.

Butler, J. (1997). *Excitable speech: A politics of the performative.* New York: Routledge.

Chisholm, D. (1995). The "cunning lingua" of desire: Bodies—language and perverse performativity. In E. Grosz and E. Probyn (Eds.), *Sexy bodies: The strange carnalities of feminism* (pp. 19–41). New York: Routledge.

Conway, M. (1997, July). Spectatorship in lesbian porn: The woman's woman's film. *Wide Angle, 19* (3), 91–113.

de St. Jorre, J. (1994, August 1). The unmasking of "O." *New Yorker*, pp. 42–50.

Dyer, R. (1979). *Stars.* London: British Film Institute.

Dyer, R. (1985, March). Male gay porn. *Jump Cut, 30*, 227–229.

Faludi, S. (1995, October 30). The money shot. *New Yorker*, p. 64.

Farmer, J. S., and Henley, W. E. (1904). *Slang and its analogues.* 7 Vols: London: Privately Printed. (Original work published 1890–1904)

Fiske, J. (1994). *Television culture.* New York: Routledge.

Gross, L. (1996). Marginal texts, marginal audiences. In J. Hay, L. Grossberg, and E. Wartella (Eds.), *The audience and its landscape* (pp. 161–76). Boulder, CO: Westview.

Hoffmann, F. (1965). Prolegomena to a study of traditional elements in the erotic film. *Journal of American Folklore, 78*, 143–148.

Hoffmann, F. (1973). *Analytical survey of Anglo-American traditional erotica.* Bowling Green, OH: Popular Press.

Horsey. (1998, April 12). [Editorial Cartoon]. *Seattle Post-Intelligencer Syndicate.*

Katz, J. (1995). *The invention of heterosexuality.* New York: Dutton.

Kendrick, W. (1987). *The secret museum: Pornography in modern culture.* New York: Viking.

Kipnis, L. (1992). (Female) desire and (female) disgust: Reading Hustler. In L. Grossberg, C. Nelson, and P. Treichler (Eds.), *Cultural studies* (pp. 373–91). New York: Routledge.

Kripke, M. (1997). The lingo of the Tijuana Bibles. In B. Adelman (Ed.), *Tijuana Bibles: Art and wit in America's forbidden funnies 1930s–1950s* (p. 11). New York: Simon and Schuster.

Legman, G. (1990, October–December). Erotic folksongs and ballads: An international bibliography. *Journal of American Folkore, 103*, 417–501.

Lubow, A. (1998, April 19). Steal this burger. *New York Times Magazine*, pp. 38–43.

Masters, S. (1993, November). Alternative sexuality and the video retailer. *Adult Video News, 8* (12), 60, 62.

Patton, C. (1991). Speaking out: Teaching in. In D. Fuss (Ed.), *Inside/out: Lesbian theories, gay theories* (pp. 373–86). New York: Routledge.

Riley, P. (1994). *The x-rated videotape guide 4.* Amherst, NY: Prometheus Books.

Ross, G. (1993, February). The next ten years: How to improve the adult video business. *Adult Video News Tenth Anniversary Supplement*, pp. 4–5, 6, 8, 10.

Royalle, C. (1993, Winter). Porn in the USA. *Social Text, 11* (4), 23–32.

Schlosser, E. (1997, February 10). The business of pornography. *U.S. News & World Report*, pp. 44–48.

Slade, J. W. (1984, Summer). Violence in the hard-core pornographic film: A historical survey. *Journal of Communication, 34* (3), 148–63.

Slade, J. W. (1997, July). Pornography in the nineties. *Wide Angle, 19* (3), 1–12.

Slade, J. W. (forthcoming). *Pornography: A reference guide*. Westport, CT: Greenwood.
Stoller, R. (1985). *Observing the erotic imagination*. New Haven, CT: Yale University Press.
Suggs, D. (1997, October 21). Hard corps: A new generation of people of color penetrates porn's mainstream. *Village Voice*, pp. 39–40.
Vance, C. S. (1984). Pleasure and danger: Towards a politics of sexuality. In C. S. Vance (Ed.), *Pleasure and danger: Exploring female sexuality* (pp. 1–27). Boston: Routledge and Kegan Paul.
Weatherford, J. M. (1986). *Porn row*. New York: Arbor House.
Williams, L. (1989). *Hard core: Power, pleasure, and the frenzy of the visible*. Berkeley: University of California Press.

VIDEOGRAPHY

Beach fucking Brazillians. (1997). Los Angeles: Bordavision.
Blazing bedrooms. (1987). Rhodes, P. (Director). Los Angeles: LA Video.
Boiling point. (1996). English, T. (Director). Van Nuys, CA: Wave Video.
Boogie nights. (1997). Ahlberg, M. (Director). Los Angeles: New Line Cinema/Home Video.
Buttman's big butt backdoor babes. (1995). Stagliano, J. (Director). Arieta, CA: Evil Angel Video.
Buttman's big tit adventure 1–3. (1991–95). Stagliano, J. (Director). Arieta, CA: Evil Angel Video.
Buttman's European vacation 1–3. (1992–95). Stagliano, J. (Director). Arieta, CA: Evil Angel Video.
Caught from behind (20 vols.). (1982–97). Freeman, H. (Director). Chatsworth, CA: Hollywood Video.
Club head. (1990). Rhodes, P., and Lincoln, F. (Directors). Canoga Park, CA: Caballero Home Video.
Corporate assets. (1985). Paine, T. (Director). Los Angeles: Essex.
Dark angel. (1997). Blake, A. (Director). Los Angeles: Studio A.
Deck his balls with holly. (1992). Rainer, J. (Director). New York: Starmaker Video.
Deep inside Racquel Darrian. (1994). Emerson, W. (Director). Chatsworth, CA: VCA.
Dick of death. (1985). Mitchell, S. (Director). Los Angeles: Visual Entertainment Productions VCR.
Dripping with desire. (1994). Edwards, E. (Director). Panorama City, CA: Dreamland.
Eurosluts #2. (1994). Marino, F. (Director). New York: Coast to Coast Video.
Every woman wants a penis. (1995). No dir. credited. Los Angeles: S. S. Productions.
Every woman wants two penises. (1997). No dir. credited. Northridge, CA: Midnight Productions.
Foreskin fantasies. (1984). No dir. credited. West Hollywood, CA: Adam and Co.
Garage girls. (1981). Neeallum, R. (Director). North Providence, RI: Cal Vista.
Girls from Hootersville (9 vols.) (1993–95). Hollander, B. (Director). Los Angeles: Silver Foxx.
The girls of the double-D (14 vols.). (1986–90). Various dirs. Canoga Park, CA: CDI Home Video.
Honey, I blew everybody. (1992). De Mille, C. B. (Director). Northridge, CA: Midnight Video.

House of dreams. (1990). Blake, A. (Director). Canoga Park, CA: Caballero Home Video.
How to female ejaculate. (1996). Fatale, F. (Director). San Francisco: Fatale Video.
Hungarian anal rhapsody. (1992). James, B. (Director). Los Angeles: Odyssey Group.
John Wayne Bobbitt uncut. (1994). Los Angeles: Leisure Time.
The last condom. (1988). Spinelli, A. (Director). Chatsworth, CA: Plum Productions.
The legend of Joey Steffano. (1994). Steel, J. (Director). Van Nuys, CA: VividMan.
Night tales. (1997). Enright, J. (Director). Chatsworth, CA: VCA.
Nurse tails. (1994). Leslie, J. (Director). Chatsworth, CA: VCA.
Pam and Tommy Lee: Hardcore and uncensored. (1998). Los Angeles: ieg.
Le parfum de Matilde. (1995). Dorcel, M. (Director). Van Nuys, CA: Vivid.
A portrait of Christy. (1990). Thomas, P. (Director). Van Nuys, CA: Vivid Video.
Powertool. (1987). Travis, J. (Director). Tarzana, CA: Catalina.
The roommate. (1994). Steel, J. (Director). Van Nuys, CA: VividMan.
Rump humpers (18 vols.). (1991–94). No dir. credited. Woodland Hills, CA: Glitz Video.
Sailor in the wild. (1983). Higgins, W. (Director). Tarzana, CA: Catalina Video.
San Francisco lesbians #6. (1994). No dir. credited. Tennent, NJ: Pleasure Productions.
Semen for seven (1997). Moore, R. (Director). Los Angeles: Odyssey Group.
Sex Trek II: The search for sperm. (1991). Fox, S. (Director). Chatsworth, CA: Moonlight
     Entertainment.
Shaved she-males. (1994). Dior, K. (Director). Tennent, NJ: Pleasure Productions.
Snatch shots. (1991). Pontello, C. (Director). Chatsworth, CA: A.F.V. Releasing.
Strap-on Sally (8 vols.). (1993–1996). Gunn, J. (Director). Tennent, NJ: Pleasure Pro-
     ductions.
Tit city. (1993). Marino, F. (Director). Woodland Hills, CA: Sin City Video.
Topless brain surgeons. (1997). Centerbury, S. (Director). Woodland Hills, CA: Legend
     Video.
The voyeur (10 vols.). (1994–98). Leslie, J. (Director). Arieta, CA: Evil Angel.
Wanda whips Wall Street. (1982). Christian, J. (Director). Los Angeles: Vid-X-Pix.
Where the boys aren't (5 vols.). (1989–92). Blue, J. (Director). Van Nuys, CA: Vivid
     Video.
Working stiffs. (1990). Johnson, T. (Director). Los Angeles: Altomar/Adam and Co.

PART VII

FILM

19

Anthony Enns

Sexual Imagery and the Space of Love

INTRODUCTION

From the Hays Production Code of the 1930s to pornography on the World Wide Web, sexual imagery has always been a contested marked boundary of representation, of what may be represented and what may not. But sexual imagery has also marked the boundary line for the relation between signs and things, the very limit of representation itself. In classic Hollywood cinema, love scenes typically reached their climax when the lovers kissed, and this was usually followed by a fade or dissolve to the next scene. The act of making love had no place in these narratives, or rather it occupied an invisible space that was only suggested by the kiss and the dissolve. Contemporary films obviously have much more freedom in their use of sexual imagery—even television programs, such as *NYPD Blue*, are able to generate enormous publicity by showing underrepresented parts of the male anatomy—but it is equally as obvious that this freedom hasn't made them any more successful at representing love. So what is the relationship between sexual imagery and love, or rather what is the relationship between visual representations of the space of the body and the space of love?

When I took sex education in junior high, I was taught that sexual intercourse was an event that occurred between two people who were *in love*. But what did I know of love? It is certainly possible to teach sex (illustrations seem particularly helpful), but is it possible to teach love? My sex education instructor encouraged my class to postpone sexual activity until we were "ready," presumably meaning until we were "in love," but the curriculum didn't include lessons on how to know what love was. Is it even possible to imagine what those lessons might have been, beyond simply, "You'll understand when you're older"? Love is clearly a type of knowledge that cannot be taught, but ironically this inability to teach love is also the guarantee of love's existence. It is precisely because love cannot be taught, because it remains a mystery, that we are able to talk about it and to feel some degree of confidence that we know what it is we are talking about.

There is a group of writers/motivational speakers in the self-help industry who claim to teach knowledge of love, but most of them do so by outlining a system of rules for courtship and marriage, a code of conduct that is supposed to show people how to love each other the "right" way. These texts often assume that desire cannot be trusted, that there is a "bad" or "unhealthy" love that readers should avoid. These books differ radically from the courtly love manuals of the Middle Ages, such as Andreas Capellanus's *The Art of Courtly Love*, whose purpose was to outline strategies of seduction; even the distinction between healthy and unhealthy love seems to be a uniquely modern phenomenon. But what is most interesting about these works is that they show how the attempt to teach love actually negates it: It is precisely at the moment when one attempts to systematize love, to remove it from the realm of experience and resolve its mystery into clarity, that knowledge of love is brought under suspicion.

So what is the guarantee of love's existence in the absence of any concrete evidence? When my sex education instructor defined sexual intercourse as an event that occurred between two people who were in love, he was suggesting that love was a place lovers could occupy, a place they could be "in," and he was also configuring the act of sex as the visible guarantee of that invisible place. However, when he encouraged us to postpone sexual activity, he was reversing this configuration: Love became the guarantee of sex. Narratives often struggle with this dilemma of cause and effect: Is sexual intercourse the manifestation of love, or is love the revelation of sex? Does knowledge of love open up the possibility for sexual relations, or does sexual experience impart knowledge of love? This is not the sort of dilemma for which there is any solution, but it does reveal that narratives create a space for love just as they create a space for the body, that the relationship between these spaces is constantly being negotiated, and that the representation of this spatial relation is culturally determined. This chapter will briefly explore historical trends in the representation of the space of love, with particular emphasis on recent works of film that mark a contemporary shift in representation toward a conflation of the space of love and the surface of the body.

THE BODY OF GOD

In order to understand how the Middle Ages understood the space of love, it will be helpful to return to the problem faced by twentieth-century sex education classes: If love cannot be taught, how can it be known? Augustine struggled with a similar question in his treatise *On Christian Doctrine* (1958), where he asked how it was possible to know something one didn't understand (Augustine was referring specifically to knowledge of the Trinity). To speak about this, Augustine developed the following distinction between things and signs: "All doctrine concerns either things or signs, but things are learned by signs. Strictly speaking, I have here called a 'thing' that which is not used to signify something else. . . . There are other signs whose whole use is in signifying, like words" (p. 8). All signs are things, but not all things are signs, and this distinction between things and signs made it possible for Augustine to speak about things that could not be spoken—namely, God.

In order to understand Augustine's logic, it is important to note that he did not speak about God directly: "[N]othing worthy may be spoken of Him . . . he is called *Deus*. Although He is not recognized in the noise of these two syllables, all those who know the Latin language, when this sound reaches their ears, are moved to think of a certain most excellent immortal nature" (p. 11). In other words, Augustine believed that God was not "recognized," or signified, in the sound of the word *"Deus,"* but rather this sign suggested that there was some thing that could not be signified; the distinction between signs and things, therefore, allowed Augustine to speak about an *absence* in signification.

After establishing the relationship between signs and things, Augustine made a further distinction between two types of things: those to be "enjoyed," the category that applied to God, and those to be "used," the category that applied to worldly things:

[I]t is to be understood that the plenitude and the end of the Law and of all the sacred Scriptures is the love of a Being which is to be enjoyed and of a being that can share that enjoyment with us. . . . [T]he whole temporal dispensation was made by divine Providence for our salvation. We should use it, not with an abiding but with a *transitory* love and delight like that in a road or in vehicles or in other instruments, or, if it may be expressed more accurately, *so that we love those things by which we are carried along for the sake of that toward which we are carried.* (p. 30, emphasis added)

Augustine envisioned a relationship not only between signs and things but also between love and the movement of bodies in space: What held them together was the presence of God or rather the space of God's body (as delineated by the points of the Trinity). Love, for Augustine, was love of God, and this was a thing for which there was no sign, a thing that could not be signified. The things of the world, which could be signified, were not to be enjoyed for themselves, but rather they were to be used, like "vehicles," to bring him closer to God, and the love of these worldly things was a secondary or "transitory" love.

In this way, Augustine believed that love between people on earth brought them closer to God in heaven. Their love was not contained within their own bodies, but rather it resided in God's body; love was the movement of their bodies in space toward God. Just as signs pointed toward things, so did the things of this world point toward heaven, and just as Augustine's distinction between signs and things allowed him to speak about an absence in signification, allowed him to speak, in other words, about something he did not know, so did his distinction between God's body and worldly bodies allow him to speak about love.

THE LAW OF ALLIANCE

In *The History of Sexuality* (1990), Michel Foucault analyzes the transformation of this classical Christian notion of love and the body into the modern discourse on sexuality. Foucault traced this transformation through the invention of pornography in the sixteenth century, obscenity and censorship laws in the seventeenth century, and finally, in the nineteenth century, psychoanalysis and its categorization of perversions. According to Foucault, the traditional Christian notion of "flesh" was based on the "law of alliance," the pre-Christian model of kinship and marriage:

[T]his is one of the most significant aspects of this entire history of the deployment of sexuality: it had its beginnings in the technology of the "flesh" in classical Christianity, basing itself on the alliance system and the rules that governed the latter; but today it fills a reverse function in that it tends to prop up the deployment of alliance ... with psychoanalysis, sexuality gave body and life to the rules of alliance by saturating them with desire. (p. 113)

Augustine's notion of love, therefore, sheds light on the birth of sexuality; it shows how sexuality was introduced to pre-Christian models of social relations or alliance, such as marriage, and how alliance was originally the guarantee of knowledge of love. Today, however, the positions of sexuality and alliance have reversed: Alliance is no longer the foundation of sexuality, but rather sexuality has become the foundation of alliance. The guarantee of knowledge of love, therefore, has shifted from alliance to sexuality. Foucault attributed this reversal to psychoanalysis and its infusion of desire into familial relations. Regardless of whether alliance or sexuality form the guarantee of knowledge of love, however, such knowledge still remains predicated on an absence or lack in signification; psychoanalysis merely replaced the body of God with the notion of the Other.

INTIMACY AND ALIENATION

In order to illustrate the contemporary use of absences in the representation of the space of love, this chapter will analyze a series of films made between 1988 and 1994 that contain both love narratives and sexual imagery and that address the difficulty of representing the space of love through such imagery. Before examining these films, however, it will be helpful to consider the theory

Walter Benjamin outlined in his essay "The Work of Art in the Age of Mechanical Reproduction." Benjamin was critical of film technology because it denied the viewer the ability to contemplate the image: The moving picture controlled where the viewer's perception was allowed to go and how long it was allowed to remain there. He also believed that contemplation was the experience of the object's authenticity, its presence in time and space, which the film image obliterated. "That which withers in the age of mechanical reproduction," he wrote, "is the aura of the work of art" (1969, p. 221). The "aura" is what made the work unique, and Benjamin added that the move toward reproductions of works of art was motivated by the "desire of contemporary masses to bring things 'closer' spatially and humanly, which is just as ardent as their bent toward overcoming the uniqueness of every reality" (p. 223).

This paradoxical movement in mass culture that Benjamin observed in 1935— a simultaneous movement toward increased intimacy and increased alienation— was a crucial insight into the cultural negotiation of the space of love and its relationship to the space of the body. Ever since the Middle Ages, cultural shifts in the representation of the space of love have tended toward decreased spatial distance and increased temporal distance. These shifts in representation have clearly indicated a desire to be spatially closer to love, to have a more intimate experience of love, but they have also created an increased temporal distance between the space of love and the movement of bodies. For example, when love was mediated through God's body, intimacy was only possible in heaven, but love between people on earth was experienced directly as the movement of their bodies toward God: The spatial distance between people's bodies and the body of God was therefore infinite, but the experience of their movement toward God, the experience of their own bodies, was immediate. Cinematic representations of the space of love functioned in the opposite way: The film image appeared to offer a more intimate relation between viewers and the space of love, but it simultaneously alienated viewers from the experience of their own bodies.

THE CUT

Several films from the late 1980s addressed both the cinematic representation of the space of love and the spectator's dual involvement toward increased intimacy and alienation. One of these films was Giuseppe Tornatore's *Cinema Paradiso* (1988), which illustrated film's ability to represent the space of love as an absence, the desire of the viewer to use film as a means of achieving intimacy, and the inability of film to deliver this intimacy. At the beginning of the film's narrative, a town priest demands that all love scenes be cut from the films shown at the town's only cinema, a practice that the townspeople abhor. There are several scenes that show the cinema's audience watching in rapt attention as lovers on the screen stare longingly at each other and begin to embrace only to be interrupted by an abrupt cut in the film, which then skips to the next scene as the audience begins to yell and hiss. The priest's act of censoring is motivated within the narrative by his desire to impose Christian morality on the townspeople; it appears, therefore, that the use of absences in representing the space of love is rooted in a form of sexual repression. However, on closer examination it appears that the opposite is true: As Foucault (1990) points out, sexuality "has been expanding at an increasing rate since the seventeenth century" (p. 107). The priest's act of censoring actually serves to fuel the discourse of sexuality, or in this case the desire of the townspeople, and it is this discourse of sexuality, not its silencing, that serves as a foundation for the space of love.

The priest's act of censoring is also an exaggeration of a film technique that is already being employed: the strategy of obscuring and concealing the movement of bodies in order to present the space of love as an absence or a lack in signification. The actions of lovers on screen do not represent the space of love; rather, they suggest an absence within the text that is able to guarantee love's existence. The obvious cut between scenes announces the fact that there is a gap in the text, that there is an invisible space that is clearly part of the text but that is missing from the text itself; in other words, this absence is felt by the audience as a very real presence because the cut is so readily apparent.

As the film's protagonist grows up, he himself becomes a filmmaker, and the first thing he films is a woman who later becomes his one true love. When he is older, he returns to the town and is sad to see that the cinema has closed. (He is sad, also, to learn that prior to its closing the cinema had exclusively shown pornographic films, possibly the cause of the cinema's failure.) In his mother's house he finds the old footage of his true love, and by watching the footage he attempts to recapture his intimacy with her. The film thus acknowledges its own presence outside of time and space, its constant distance from the viewer, and the difficulties inherent in creating a space for love within the cinematic image. The protagonist's surrogate father, the blind projectionist, gives him a reel of spliced love scenes that the priest had censored decades before, and the film concludes with a series of these scenes. They serve as a reminder to the protagonist, as well as to the viewer, that there are spaces in the cut, spaces that cannot be represented on film, and that these are the spaces where love resides.

Another of these films was Steven Soderbergh's *Sex, Lies and Videotape* (1989), which seemed to criticize the impulse to construct a cinematic space of love while at the same time it attempted to construct such a space itself. One of the main characters in the film is a mysterious drifter who can only have an orgasm while watching videos of women discussing sex, discussions that usually focus on the women's acts of masturbation. One woman discusses masturbating on an airplane without anyone noticing. Another woman actually masturbates while the videocamera records her. There is a strange interplay of intimacy and alienation at work in these videos; the videographer seems incapable of sexual relations with another body, as do the women, but they are all able to relate to the narratives/representations of bodies mediated through video. The videographer needs to watch the women on video in order to have an orgasm, but the women themselves cannot be anonymous; he must be present during the recording of the interviews. The video thus serves as a reminder of the experience of his own body in their presence, but it is the removal of the videos from the events they record, their temporal distance from the women in time and space, that makes them arousing.

This use of videotape is also interesting in light of Benjamin's theories. It could be argued that videotape is a natural extension of Benjamin's critique of film: Videotape is even more spatially close to the viewer than film, and yet the experience of video is less unique than the experience of film. There is also an element to cinema that is ritualistic: Films are artifacts that reside in specially designated buildings, and audiences must undergo a kind of journey to view them. Videotape is entirely lacking this ritualistic quality.

Soderbergh's film, on the other hand, culminates in the videographer's interview of his friend's wife. The husband learns about this video and breaks into the videographer's apartment to watch the tape. His fear is that the video contains images of his wife having sex, but when he watches it, all he sees are his wife and his friend talking. Their conversation eventually leads to silence and then static. The husband is unable to find any evidence of adultery, yet he knows that his wife and his friend are in love. The space of their love can only be represented by silence and static—visual and audible absences—and it is precisely this lack, this absence of evidence, that makes the existence of their love clear.

In his shooting diary for the film, Soderbergh described an earlier version of this scene in which the video interview ended with the wife and the videographer "dry humping" on the sofa. His decision to cut this scene reveals the power of the cut in constructing film narratives. An attempt to convey the love between these characters through the movement of their bodies would have been an attempt to create a seamless film, a film without cuts, a film in which nothing was unrepresentable, where everything was also a sign.

EROTIC ART

Cinematic love narratives are uniquely suited to this model of representing the space of love, but a modern crisis in the representation of the space of love can be seen in several films from the early 1990s in which traditional genre categories, such as romance, erotica, and pornography, were blurred. These films attempted to dissolve the gap between the space of love and the space of the body, to create images in which nothing was lacking, where there was no absence in signification.

One of these films was Pedro Almodovar's *Atame!* (1989), which was released in the United States in 1990 as *Tie Me Up! Tie Me Down! Atame!* was an attempt to create a pornographic film that also told a love story. This attempt can be seen as part of Almodovar's larger project of representing the human body as a very real and physical entity; in this film, however, Almodovar took this project to its natural conclusion by showing his characters having sexual intercourse. The plot of *Atame!* focuses on a mental patient who kidnaps a porn actress and ties her up in a hotel room, confident that he can win her love if only they spent some quality time together. The woman rejects the man at first and asks him to buy drugs for her, but when he returns, having been beaten brutally by drug dealers, the woman takes pity on him. As she cleans his wounds, the man says she reminds him of his mother. The woman is visibly moved by the remark: She sighs, closes her eyes, and touches his face, and finally they kiss. These are all standard tropes of the traditional love scene, but rather than cutting away after the lovers kiss, the camera stays on the couple as they begin to have intercourse. The camera remains in a static shot until the end of the love scene, when the camera cuts to a shot of the lovers in a multifaceted ceiling mirror; the image of their lovemaking is multiplied into several smaller images, thus heightening the spectacle of the sex act.

This love/sex scene is a fascinating narrative move because it creates a shift in viewer-character identification. At first, the viewer is asked to identify with the male protagonist, and the woman is presented as the object of his desire. When they begin to have intercourse, however, the viewer no longer sees the woman from the protagonist's perspective. The use of the static camera and the mirror shot force the viewer to witness the scene from an omniscient point of view, a perspective that is more common to works of pornography. The distinction between pornography and the traditional love narrative lies in this absence of viewer identification: In pornography, the distance between the viewer and the image is necessary, but in a traditional love narrative the opposite is true. Almodovar succeeds in melding the two genres by using this technique of shifting perspective.

A similar practice was used in *Erotique* (Borden et al., 1994), a collection of four short films by women directors that addressed various issues concerning gender, sexuality, and cinema. Clara Law's contribution to the project, a short film titled *Wonton Soup*, was an attempt to combine erotica with the love narrative. The story concerns a young Chinese couple who are reunited in Hong Kong. The boy is attempting to regain the girl's affections and asks his uncle for advice. The uncle shows him ancient Chinese erotic texts and tells him which sexual positions to use and which foods will increase his libido. The uncle's teachings represent a completely non-Western kind of sexuality: the *ars erotica*, or the "erotic art."

According to Foucault (1990), this erotic art is based solely on pleasure and the body itself: [T]his knowledge must be deflected back into the sexual practice itself, in order to shape it as though from within and amplify its effects. In this way, there is formed a knowledge that must remain secret. . . . Consequently, the relationship to the master who holds the secrets is of paramount importance; only he, working alone, can transmit this art in an esoteric manner and as the culmination of an initiation in which he guides the disciple's progress with unfailing skill and severity. (p. 57)

By teaching his nephew the erotic art, the uncle becomes a master revealing his "masterful secret" to his disciple. The film thus offers a radically different model of sex education than the kind I received in junior high, which was not based on the experience of the body but rather on a scientific approach to the body, on the translation of pleasure and bodily sensations into language or discourse. Western civilization has no *ars erotica*, but rather it practices what Foucault refers to as a *scientia sexualis*, "a form of knowledge-power strictly opposed to the art of initiations and the masterful secret" (p. 58).

Even within this non-Western model of sex education, however, absence remains central to the representation of the space of love. The boy does his best to follow his uncle's advice, but even with his knowledge of the erotic art he fails. The young couple have sex in a wide variety of positions and locations throughout the city, thus attempting to construct a space for love through the movement of their own bodies and the location of their bodies in space, but something is always missing. At the end of the film, the girl begins to weep, and it is clear that their relationship is over. This ending is highly untraditional for a love narrative, and in many ways the film more closely resembles a work of pornography. But Law's film is far more complicated than a work of pornography. While it does manages to create images of bodies as objects of desire for the viewer, it also asks the viewer to identify with these bodies, and the means by which this identification succeeds is through the plot move at the end of the film. By showing the inability of sexual imagery to represent the space of love, the narrative engages the viewer as both voyeur and participant. The viewer is able to desire the young couple, to have distance from them, and yet simultaneously to identify with them, to be intimately involved in their story and to empathize with them. Law succeeds in melding the two genres by telling a story in which the lovers have fallen out of love.

A more complex fusion of perspectives can be seen in Peter Greenaway's *The Cook, The Thief, His Wife & Her Lover* (1989). A man and a woman exchange glances across a crowded restaurant. They meet secretly in the women's lavatory for fear they will be discovered by the woman's husband. The woman, Georgina, tells her husband a joke when he comes to fetch her: "You know what they say about men who hang around women's lavatories? They are asking to have their illusions shattered." So are the viewers of Greenaway's films, which attempt to shatter every illusion about the body. Just as Almodovar shows his actors copulating, Greenaway presents the body as a real, physical entity, and the pleasuring of the body becomes synonymous with the creation of a space for love. There is nothing beyond the surface of the body, and there is no space through which the body moves; the body is its own universe.

The woman's husband, Albert, is the villain in the narrative, and his villainy seems to lie in his insatiable appetite, his inability to experience pleasure, and his unusual sexual practices: He is unable to have intercourse with his wife, but instead he reaches orgasm by inserting objects into her vagina, such as toothbrushes and spoons. When Albert begins to suspect that his wife is having an affair, the lovers move their meetings to a kitchen pantry, where they make love surrounded by the kitchen staff. Georgina's lover, Michael, says her eyes are beautiful, but she replies, "And you have a wonderful prick." Even their pillow talk seems to deny that anything exists beyond the surface of their flesh. The space of their love is created exclusively by the movement of their bodies in space, and the guarantee of their love does not lie in any absence in signification but rather in the fact that their lovemaking is *witnessed*. This is revealed in a conversation between Georgina and the cook, Richard, that occurs near the end of the film:

GEORGINA: What did you see? How can I know that he loved me if there were no witnesses?

RICHARD: If you love him that does not seem to be a very necessary question.

GEORGINA: Yes it is. . . . How could I know that it was real unless somebody else was watching?

RICHARD: I saw him kissing you on the mouth, on the neck, behind your hair. I saw him undressing you. I saw him kissing your breast. I saw him put his hand between your legs. . . . I saw you kiss him on the mouth. I saw you lie under him on the floor of the pantry. I saw him take you from behind. I saw you take his penis in your mouth. I saw you.

GEORGINA: Do lovers always behave like that?

RICHARD: My parents behaved like that. . . . Lovers in the cinema sometimes behave like that. . . . In my fantasy, lovers always behave like that.

The behavior of lovers, the movement of lovers' bodies, becomes the space of love, and its guarantee, the guarantee that one can possess knowledge of love, is that the behavior is *seen*. Richard's perspective is the perspective of the viewer, and thus the viewer's desire for the character becomes the means by which the character's love is guaranteed. Greenaway succeeds in melding the two genres by positioning desire for the body as a form of viewer identification: The viewer's detached relationship to the bodies on screen becomes the means by which the lovers in the narrative are shown to be in love.

CONCLUSION

Atame! and *The Cook, The Thief, His Wife & Her Lover* were two of the first films to receive an NC-17 rating by the Motion Picture Association of America (MPAA). This experimental rating was applied to three films in 1990, the year it was introduced; the first was Philip Kaufman's *Henry and June* (1990). The NC-17 rating was originally designed for films that contained explicit sexual material but that could not be classified as pornography. The fact that this rating was instituted at the turn of the decade therefore reveals that there was a popular assumption that explicit sexual material could be employed to represent love and that films that incorporated this new kind of sexual imagery needed to be clearly differentiated from the other, "obscene" kind.

Many directors had been calling for a revised rating system prior to 1990, including David Lynch, who suggested the RR rating, but despite this interest within the film industry, the NC-17 rating turned out to be very unpopular. It not only limited film distribution, but it was also criticized for the way it was employed by the MPAA. Peter Travers (1990), for example, suggested that the MPAA had a moral agenda behind its usage of the NC-17 rating, arguing that *Henry and June* was equally as explicit as Dennis Hopper's *The Hot Spot* (1990) but that the latter was merely rated R because the lesbian characters in the film were punished at the end (p. 95). Therefore, rather than hailing a new kind of sexual imagery, the NC-17 rating merely became a new kind of censorship.

Despite its lack of popularity, however, this rating and the films that were involved in its implementation signal a fundamental change in the way our culture represented the space of love. Regardless of the various methods individual directors employed to negotiate the space of love and the movement of bodies, this new model of representing love marked a radical shift away from the representation of love as an absence in signification and toward the conflation of the space of love and the surface of the body. The danger of this new model, however, was precisely the danger that Benjamin (1969) described in connection to new technologies of mechanical reproduction: It was a model in which viewers were closer, spatially, to other bodies but even farther from the uniqueness of their own reality, their own bodies, their own pleasure. While it appeared to grant viewers more knowledge of intimacy, it actually increased their alienation. While it seemed to be liberating because it detached sexuality from the law of alliance, it actually remained part of the broader discourse of sexuality, what Foucault (1990) calls the *scientia sexualis*. Like students watching a sex education film, the viewers of these films were taught that sex was an event that occurred between people who were in love and that knowledge of love, the guarantee of love's existence, was made possible because they were there to watch.

REFERENCES

Almodovar, P. (Writer and Director), and Almodovar, A. (Producer). (1989). *Atame!* [Motion Picture]. Miramax, El Deseo.

Augustine, St. (1958). *On Christian doctrine* (D. W. Robertson, Jr., Trans.). New York: Liberal Arts Press.

Benjamin, W. (1969). *Illuminations* (H. Zohn, Trans.). New York: Schocken Books.

Borden, L., Treut, M., Law, C., and Magalhaes, A. (Writers and Directors), Wood, C., and Herman, V. (Producers). (1994). *Erotique: An erotic journey as seen through the eyes of women* [Motion Picture]. Beyond Films Ltd.

Capellanus, A. (1969). *The art of courtly love* (J. J. Parry, Trans.). New York: W. W. Norton.

Foucault, M. (1990). *The history of sexuality* (Vol 1). New York: Vintage Books.

Greenaway, P. (Writer and Director), and Kasander, K. (Producer). (1989). *The cook, the thief, his wife & her lover* [Motion Picture]. Miramax, Allarts and Elesevier-Vendex, Allarts Cook-Erato Films-Films Inc.

Hopper, D. (Director), and Lewis, P. (Producer). (1990). *The hot spot* [Motion Picture]. Orion Pictures.

Kaufman, P. (Co-writer and Director), and Kaufman, P. (Producer). (1990). *Henry and June* [Motion Picture]. Walrus and Associates Ltd.

Soderbergh, S. (Writer and Director), Newmyer, R., and Hardy, J. (Producers). (1989). *Sex, lies and videotape* [Motion Picture]. Outlaw Productions.

Tornatore, G. (Writer and Director), and Cristaldi, F. (Producer). (1988). *Cinema paradiso* [Motion Picture]. Cristaldifilm, Films Ariane.

Travers, P. (1990, November 1). An X by any other name. *Rolling Stone*, p. 95.

PART VIII

CYBERSPACE

20

Kimber Charles Pearce

Third Wave Feminism and Cybersexuality: The Cultural Backlash of the New Girl Ordcr

INTRODUCTION

With a greater emphasis on networking than organization, "Third Wave feminism," or Generation X's "New Girl Order," has secured a foothold in cyberspace in the form of "zines" and World Wide Web sites with names like Bitch, Brillo, Bust, gURL, Hues *(Hear Us Emerging Sisters)*, and Maxi. Twenty-something "Third Wavers," who have experienced less of what their mothers defined as oppression, have turned to the Internet to further a new version of cultural feminism that answers what thcy havc perceived as the shortcomings of the "Second Wave" of feminism, which began during the 1960s. Central to the project of Third Wave feminism, as it has manifested itself on the World Wide Web, has been the representation of a thoroughly emancipated, all-encompassing, sexual chic—a "fishnet feminism," as detractors have labeled the image.

Third Wave feminism's guiding concept that "the personal is cultural" has embraced a cultural feminism that rose to prominence during the early 1970s as a commitment to women's emancipation through individual lifestyle choices and sexual freedom. The "Grrls" network—a loose coalition of Third Wave Web sites—has been devoted to contesting male stereotypes of female social and sexual roles. But more significantly, Generation X feminists have challenged what they have identified as the sexual orthodoxies of their Second Wave feminist mothers' narrow and humorless attitudes toward women's and men's sexuality.

The generational conflict over Second and Third Wave feminists' perspective on sexuality has pitted representational politics against structural politics within the women's movement. According to M. C. McGee (1998), the rift between representational and structural politics has fragmented all of American liberalism, from which the women's liberation movement emerged. With the rise of new communication technologies, McGee has argued that the "relationship between surface and depth [in American liberalism] has exactly reversed itself" (p. 175), so that the primary goal for Left coalitions, including feminists of all stripes, is no longer to break down structural barriers to equality, as it was during the 1960s. Sexual discrimination has assumed new forms, many of which have appeared as mutations and expansions of demeaning representations of women in media culture, not only in print and on radio and television but most strikingly on the newest technological medium, the Internet. With ongoing changes in the modes of delivery of sexist messages, the struggle for contemporary feminists has been to propagate fresh social, political, and economic affinities within a system that is always being influenced in consequential ways by mass media representations.

Images of Third Wave sexuality on the World Wide Web have answered the challenge of representational politics in America. Third Wave representations have been made possible by the grammars of the Internet, which have accommodated experimentation with ambiguous and multiple sexual personalities. The Internet presence of the New Girl Order, in particular, has opened up possibilities for young women to test the boundaries of their own sexuality as members of a generation raised in the context of a mass-mediated conversation about transgendered, bisexual, gay, and other sexual orientations. This chapter analyzes Third Wave representations of sexuality on the World Wide Web—an "affinity" driven medium of mass communication that has posed both opportunities and obstacles for the sexual politics of technocultural feminism.

THIRD WAVE FEMINISM AND SEXUALITY

By using the Internet to propagate innovative representations of female sexuality. Third Wave feminists have eschewed their Second Wave mothers' commitment to structural politics on behalf of gender equality. As a concern that has virtually displaced the idea of "gender" as a locus of feminist ideology, the construct of "sexuality" has become vital to the technocultural feminism that has been practiced in the Third Wave movement. "Sexuality," Jackson and Scott (1996) have argued, "involves our sexual feelings and relationships, the ways in which we are or are not defined as sexual by others, as well as the ways in which we define ourselves" (p. 2).

In contrast to Third Wavers' concern with sexuality, Second Wave feminists' focus on "gender" has emphasized "the social shaping of femininity and masculinity, to challenge the idea that relations between women and men were ordained by nature [biological determinism]" (p. 2). Zavarzadeh (1994) has summarized the advantages that "postgender" feminists, including the cyber-oriented

Third Wavers, have found in stressing "sexuality" over "gender": " '[S]exuality'—as a postgender notion that marks the 'excessive play of desire'—is considered to open up more room for the aleatory workings of the subject and its freedom" (pp. 292–93). Third Wavers have viewed their emphasis on sexuality as a path to deliverance from the Second Wave preoccupation with opposing biological determinism. These denizens of cyberspace have found their alternate focus on sexuality more conducive to the online discussions and role-playing they believe will lead them to a better understanding of feminist "community."

SEXUAL AFFINITIES AND THE THIRD WAVE NETWORK

The Internet has provided an expedient communication medium for the growing Third Wave feminist network. As M. E. Price (1995) has written, "Societies reveal themselves and can be differentiated through the distinctive webs of social intercourse that are the consequence of particular domestications, adaptations, or responses to innovations in modes of communicating" (p. 64). Third Wave feminists' use of the Internet as an instrument of sexual representation has been a compelling case in point. In a landmark essay on postmodern feminism—"A Manifesto for Cyborgs"—D. Haraway (1985) has described an ongoing leftist political impetus that fits the Internet activities of Third Wave feminists:

The recent history for much of the U.S. left and U.S. feminism has been a response to crisis by endless splitting and searches for a new essential identity. But there has also been a growing recognition of another response through coalition—affinity, not identity. (p. 73)

"Affinity groups," or coalitions linked together by common interest, have thrived on the World Wide Web. The "Grrls" network of Third Wave feminists has arisen as an affinity coalition, linked not by organizational identity but instead by a loosely shared stake in confronting cultural paradigms of sexuality and related issues.

As an affinity-driven medium through which search engines access Web sites and subject matter of particular interest to the user, the World Wide Web has been well suited to the representational politics of Third Wave networking and coalition building. Individual women have searched and posted information, tested ideas, and self-disclosed in a cyberspace community that has not demanded a physical presence nor any commitment to an actual organizational identity. In fact, Third Wavers have resisted physical organization as an ineffective means for realizing cultural change and have placed their faith in what they see as the vast potential of telecommunications to effect change in American society. As one Third Wave associate of a self-described "amorphous group of activists and media intervention superstars"—the Barbie Liberation Organization—has declared of "embodied" organizations: "[A]dvocacy groups don't seem to work . . . you end up in this victim status" (Eubanks, 1997).

A significant amount of Third Wave networking has occurred on "college nodes" of the Internet, at educational institutions where women can access the World Wide Web as part of their tuition and fees. A group of women in the Interactive Telecommunications Program at New York University, for instance, have published the Third Wave Web site gURL, a play on the online acronym for "Uniform Resource Locator." gURL and similar "webzines" have targeted a technologically savvy audience of high school–and college-aged women by combining feminist politics and popular culture. Reminiscent of the shock media tactics of radical "politico" groups of the 1960s, such as those of the Women's International Terrorist Conspiracy of Hell (WITCH), the webzines have employed sexually explicit language and provocative graphics to inject shock and humor into feminist critiques of the body, relationship issues, and sexual representations promulgated in media culture. Influenced by the thought of feminist and queer scholars, who have been largely responsible for putting the construct of "sexuality" on the academic agenda, the mostly college-affiliated designers of "Grrls" Web sites have used entertainment values as a pretext to indoctrinate young women into the ways of the Third Wave movement and to attack what they have seen as the sexual essentialism of Second Wave feminism. On their Web sites, Third Wavers have resisted sexual essentialism and have operated within the male-driven political economy of the World Wide Web to further a commitment to polyvocalism and multisexualism. M. J. Herrup (1995) has offered a testimonial that has revealed how Third Wavers have used the simulated environment of the Internet to evade the essentialism of conventional identity politics:

In cyberspace, a realm in which the body is not physically present, where confirmable identity markers such as anatomy and skin color are no longer visible, the fluidity of identity is thrown into high relief. . . . [I]t was in cyberspace that I discovered an on-line sexuality that questioned my "predilections" and asked me to rethink my identity. (pp. 240–41).

LIBERTARIANISM AND THIRD WAVE FEMINISM

Third Wave affiliates of a self-described "digital elite," or "digerati," have aimed to forge a coalition of disparate feminist lifestyle affinities by exploring issues of sexuality through the interactive medium of the Internet. Politically, their conversations, self-analyses, and consciousness-raising activities in cyberspace have reflected an aggressive, individualistic style of feminist libertarianism. L. S. Brown (1993) has written of the libertarian position, "Supporters of the individualist approach believe . . . that the human individual is capable of exercising free will and that this capacity to make choices defines what it is to be human" (p. 11). With respect to sexuality, Third Wave feminists have espoused a rhetoric of sexual libertarianism on the World Wide Web that has sought to accommodate all individual desires, even masochistic urges that would have been considered contrary to the feminist agenda of a generation ago. D. Minkowitz (1995) has posed a suggestive question that Third Wavers ask of feminist sexuality: "How can women give it up enough to let someone see us writhe, claw, moan, and beg, the bitches in heat we've fought forever not to become?" (p. 79).

As Minkowitz's query has insinuated, Third Wavers have been skeptical of the collectivist position toward sexuality that Second Wave feminists popularized during the 1960s. According to H. Hartmann (1981), the structural politics of Second Wavers, which has been greatly influenced by Marxism, has tended to "subsume the feminist struggle into the 'larger' struggle against capital" (p. 2). S. Smith (1991) has described the Second Wave orientation toward the individual as an "experiential politics," which has sought to expose patriarchal hegemony and uncover "the truth about the self's experience, the sources of oppression and strength, the essential differences [from men] in body, psyche, and modes of knowing and being in the world" (p. 188).

Collectively and at an individual level, Second Wave politics has embraced an essential, oppositional identity and has endorsed women's sexual freedom as part of a movement toward "social change." However, unlike the Third Wave vision of an unconstrained female sexuality, the terms of the Second Wave endorsement of a sexually liberated identity were conceived within the context of Marxian historical materialism, in which the history of male repression and commodification of the female body were seen as part of the division of labor in a class struggle. As C. A. MacKinnon (1996) has explained: "[T]he organized expropriation of the sexuality of some for the use of others defines the sex, woman" (p. 182).

The Second Wave movement, in contrast to the Third Wave network on the Internet, has promoted physical organization, embodied revolution, and a high suspicion of male sexuality. E. Willis (1992) has identified an insoluble contradiction in the "sexuality" plank of the Second Wave platform, a dilemma to which Third Wavers have strenuously objected:

The idea that in the interest of equality women's sexual freedom must be expanded and men's restricted has a surface common-sense logic. Yet in practice it is full of contradictions. For one thing, the same social changes that allow greater freedom for women inevitably mean greater freedom for men. (p. 26)

The Second Wave double-bind concerning sexuality has stated that women should have the right to express their sexual needs freely but that sexual freedom should in no way be defined by men. Willis (1992) has noted the damaging effect of the incongruity of Second Wave notions of feminist sexuality: "The ironic consequence has been the development of feminist sexual orthodoxies that curtail women's freedom by setting up the movement as yet another source of guilt-provoking rules about what women should do and feel" (p. 27). Third Wave feminist R. Walker (1995) has confirmed the deleterious consequences of Second Wave sexual orthodoxies and has written of her personal dilemma with those norms: "Curiosity about pornography, attraction to a stable domestic partnership . . . interest in the world of S/M . . . for me and my sense of how to make a feminist revolution, they represented contradictions that I had no idea how to reconcile" (p. xxx).

Third Wave Web sites have addressed the contradictions of Second Wave conceptions of sexual freedom, including the lack of clarity on issues such as traditional women's demands for marriage and monogamy; the tendency of the sexual revolution to provide opportunities for men to have sex with women without love, respect, or responsibility; and the arguments of separatist lesbians that sexual contact with males is inherently oppressive. Whereas, historically, Second Wavers have failed to "organize" the various positions on feminist sexuality into a coherent structural politics, Third Wavers have abandoned the project. As an alternative, they have used the Internet to build representational "affinities" among women with different views of sexuality in an attempt to alter feminist discourse and the concept of feminist community.

THE MOVEMENT AND THE MEDIUM

In Third Wavers' efforts to establish feminist affinities in cyberspace and to transform Second Wave sexual norms, they have encountered a medium that is impersonal yet efficient at reducing social distance through electronic information exchange. Third Wavers have been sensitive to the social paradoxes of the Internet and have embraced what media analyst J. Meyrowitz (1985) has termed the "situational geography" of the medium—the social condition created by the relationship between the physical and informational setting (media environment).

"Situational geographies" have arisen from interactions between electronic media and users and have undermined traditional relationships between physical settings and embodied social situations. Given this tension between media contexts and human interactions, the rhetorical challenge for Third Wavers in making their online movement alluring has been to persuade World Wide Web "surfers" that communication in cyberspace can match or prevail over the pleasures of face-to-face interactions. The idea of an "online sexuality" has been vital to Third Wave affinity building, as has rebellion against Second Wavers' efforts to promote physical organization and identity politics as axioms of feminism.

CYBERSEX AND THIRD WAVE FEMINISM

In representing an online sexuality, Third Wavers have blurred the boundaries between the physical and nonphysical. They have promulgated on the World Wide Web what A. Balsamo (1995) has labeled a "thick perception" of the human body as "a social, cultural and historical production" (p. 217). From this perspective, the body has been explored as a symbolic construction rather than a biologically determined object. The "online body" of Third Wave Web sites has merged the "organic/natural" and the "technological/cultural" to the point where the Internet user and medium have been conjoined in a cybersexual union. An Internet author, who has written a "rant" (editorial) for the Third Wave webzine Brillo under the pseudonym "Weeber" (1997), has made the "cybersex" connection explicit:

Machines are easy. . . . Everyday, we are creating more and more intimate relationships with them. . . . [W]e girls need to invent our own technological improvements over those overrated things called human relationships. Why not begin this process of breeding with machinery now, while the pesky risk of pregnancy is (as of yet) impossible.

Such representations of a "wired" intimacy between the Web "surfer" and her computer have signaled a Third Wave acknowledgment of the Internet's situational geography. The paradoxical condition of being alone for hours in front of a computer, while at the same time connected to millions of other users, has been represented as pleasurable in a masturbatory sense—empowering as a communicative mode of self-gratification. One Third Waver has described the sensation: "[T]here is that sexy sort of appeal of the Internet. You're all alone in your house, nobody's supposed to be watching you, and you can do anything you want" (Eubanks, 1997).

Both as an analogue to the situational geography of cyberspace and as the topic of online discussion, female masturbation has been a polysemous theme on Third Wave Web sites. Traditionally, the act has not been openly discussed in mainstream media settings, nor in face-to-face interactions among women. As the editors of *MouthOrgan* have guest-written for the webzine Maxi: "We've never understood why there's so much shame and guilt associated with masturbation. . . . [W]omen have historically been conditioned to not admit they touch themselves, and to be ashamed if they do it and enjoy it" ("Guest-written," 1998). As a trope for "surfing" the Internet, female masturbation has provided Third Wavers a multipurpose metaphor for virtual self-discovery and liberation from physical dependency on others to fulfill desires. The double entendre Third Wavers have made of masturbation has been extended to the pedagogical content of their webzines, which has prescribed sexual fantasizing and role-playing in cyberspace as forms of feminist self-help.

CYBERTHERAPY IN THE THIRD WAVE MOVEMENT

Departure from the physical world into cyberspace has brought Third Wavers an empowering (but illusory) sense of "connected" anonymity, which has allowed them to experiment with multiple online personalities and self-disclose information about themselves that they would not otherwise reveal in the most intimate, embodied social situations. Links on Third Wave Web sites to electronic bulletin boards and interactive "chatrooms" have encouraged Web "surfers" to post their frustrations about actual (and online) relationships and to engage in sexual fantasies to gain virtual experience in activities about which they are curious. For example, one could be a lesbian for a day. For Third Wavers, the World Wide Web has provided an emotional refuge in which to test that identity without incurring the social obligations and repercussions that pursuit of an actual encounter might bring. One webzine has even encouraged women to become the producers of their own pornography as a way of foiling the male-dominated industry that thrives on the Internet (Sawyer, 1996).

Zines directed to younger, high school–aged women, such as gURL, have offered online consciousness-raising sessions by posting testimonials concerning body image and self-esteem, with personal narratives that can be retrieved by clicking the mouse-pointer on graphical icons represented by body parts: big nipples, small nipples, lips, hips, and legs. By mixing and matching iconographic hairstyles, garments, and accessories, young Third Wavers have constructed and reconstructed stereotypical representations of teenage males with interchangeable images of the "rasta guy," the "jock," the "skate punk," and other choices.

The online activities of Third Wave feminists have provided for catharsis of female sexual angst as they have exposed and repudiated both Second Wave and chauvinistic conceptions of sexuality. By using the Internet to achieve a fluid sense of self-definition against rival views of female sexuality, Third Wavers have resisted the ways that they have been defined as sexual by others and have expanded control of their own identity. E. R. Mason (1997) has conveyed the idea: "The potential for social transformation [is] through interaction, through communication and recognition. This could occur not simply because I am another user, but because my identity is expanded through its recreation on the 'Net." The recognition of a spectrum of sexual identities has been critical to the Third Wave brand of technocultural feminism in the form of a tolerance for all things homosexual, heterosexual, and every orientation in between. As a "wired" version of "personal politics," the movement has held that online enactments of multiple, fluctuating sexual identities will lead to increased self-awareness and solidarity in the larger network. The threat that older Second Wavers have perceived is that the Third Wave acceptance of stereotypically heterosexual practices associated with male dominance will bring late twentieth-century feminism full circle back to where it was in the 1960s.

CONCLUSION

Even Third Wavers have differed about the future of their feminist movement on the Internet. There has been much debate about whether the positioning of the "Grrls network" on the World Wide Web, and in a few other domains in the public sphere, will place the movement too far out on the cultural fringe to be effective at inducing social and sexual transformations. The editor of the webzine Brillo (1997) has addressed the downside of activism in cyberspace: "While Internet denizens may be talking about sharing ideas and eradicating boundaries, what we get in practice, for the most part, are caricatures, misrepresentations and dis-realities. About 1% of the world is on-line" ("In Bed with the Devil," 1997). Indeed, to a significant degree, the situational geography of the Internet has threatened to remove Third Wave activists from the face-to-face deliberations in political life that their feminist mothers have performed in embodied feminist organizations. On the other side of the argument, some have seen the proliferation of Third Wave Web sites as evidence that the movement is thriving and effective. They have refused to accept the "live by the 'Net, die by the 'Net" maxim: "There are leaders out there for us, a lot of them are online. Once we're connected, our strength will grow" ("Things Are Changing," 1998).

Perhaps the online destiny of Generation X's Third Wave feminism may be best understood in light of the nature of the Internet itself. As a representational medium, the World Wide Web has provided a virtual domain in which young women have composed their own sexual identities with a sense of liberation from the material world. Nevertheless, as K. Robins (1995) has warned, "The institutions developing and promoting the new technologies exist solidly in this world. . . . Because it is a materially straitened and socially divided world, we should remember how much we remain in need of politics" (p. 137).

To endure as a feminist presence into the twenty-first century, Third Wavers will have to relocate their virtual culture in the real world and bridge their representational politics with the kind of structural initiatives their mothers began in the 1960s. To be sure, the Internet has become more and more of a medium of structural change in society. But there have been limits to the Third Wave fetishization of technology as a site of affiliation around the construct of "sexuality." At best, the cyber-oriented Third Wave movement has provided women a voice in the ongoing evolution of Internet technology and has served as a conceptual testing ground upon which "sexuality" has been the key to a recognition of the bonds and fissures among women. At worst, the movement has diverted the attention and energies of a generation of young women from participation in embodied public forums. While the future of Third Wave feminism is yet to be determined, much of it will depend on how the leaders of the movement navigate between the demands of civic life and the virtual world of emerging technologies.

REFERENCES

Balsamo, A. (1995). Forms of technological embodiment: Reading the body in contemporary culture: In M. Featherstone and R. Burrows (Eds.), *Cyberspace, cyberbodies, cyberpunk: Cultures of technological embodiment* (pp. 215–37). Thousand Oaks, CA: Sage Publications.

Brown, L. S. (1993). *The politics of individualism: Liberalism, liberal feminism and anarchism.* Montreal, Canada: Black Rose Books.

Eubanks, V. (1997). Hacking Barbie with the Barbie liberation organization. *Brillo* [Online], *1*. Available: http://www.virago-net.com/brillo/No1 [No date].

Guest-written by *MouthOrgan's* Editors. (1998). *Maxi* [Online]. Available: http: //www.maximag.com [No date].

Haraway, D. (1985). A manifesto for cyborgs: Science, technology, and social feminism in the 1980s. *Socialist Review, 80*, 65–107.

Hartmann, H. (1981). The unhappy marriage of Marxism and feminism: Towards a more progressive union. In L. Sargent (Ed.), *Woman and revolution: A discussion of the unhappy marriage of Marxism and feminism* (pp. 1–41). Boston: South End Press.

Herrup, M. J. (1995). Virtual identity. In R. Walker (Ed.), *To be real: Telling the truth and changing that face of feminism* (pp. 239–251). New York: Anchor Books.

In bed with the devil. (1997). *Brillo* [Online], *2*. Available: http://www.viragonet. com/brillo/No2/rant.htm [No date].

Jackson, S., and Scott, S. (1996). Sexual skirmishes and feminist factions: Twenty-five years of debate on women and sexuality. In S. Jackson and S. Scott (Eds.), *Feminism and sexuality: A reader* (pp. 1–31). New York: Columbia University Press.

MacKinnon, C. A. (1996). Feminism, Marxism, method and the state. In S. Jackson and S. Scott (Eds.), *Feminism and sexuality: A reader* (pp. 182–190). New York: Columbia University Press.

Mason, E. R. (1997). Resisting erase-ism on the 'Net by E. R. *Brillo* [Online], *3*. Available: http://www.viragonet.com/brillo/erasism.htm [1998].

McGee, M. C. (1998). Fragments of winter: Racial discontents in America, 1992. In C. Corbin (Ed.), *Rhetoric in postmodern America: Conversations with Michael Calvin McGee* (pp. 159–188). New York: Guilford Press.

Meyrowitz, J. (1985). *No sense of place: The impact of electronic media on social behavior*. New York: Oxford University Press.

Minkowitz, D. (1995). Giving it up: Orgasm, fear, and femaleness. In R. Walker (Ed.), *To be real: Telling the truth and changing that face of feminism* (pp. 77–85). New York: Anchor Books.

Price, M. E. (1995). Free expression and digital dreams: The open and closed terrain of speech. *Critical Inquiry 22*, 64–89.

Robins, K. (1995). Cyberspace and the world we live in. In M. Featherstone and R. Burrows (Eds.), *Cyberspace, cyberbodies, cyberpunk: Cultures of technological embodiment* (pp. 135–55). Thousand Oaks, CA: Sage Publications.

Sawyer, S. (1996). Reinventing porn. *The Nerve* [Online]. Available: http://www. journalism.berkeley.edu/magazines/nerve/porn.html [1998].

Smith, S. (1991). The autobiographical manifesto: Identities, temporalities, politics. *Prose Studies, 14*, 186–212.

Things are changing. (1998). *Riotgrrl* [Online]. Available:http://www.riotgrrl.com/ archive [No date].

Walker, R. (1995). Being real: An introduction. In R. Walker (Ed.), *To be real: Telling the truth and changing that face of feminism* (pp. xxvix–xl). New York: Anchor Books.

Weeber. (1997). Multiple orgasms through multi-tasking. *Brillo* [Online], *2*. Available: http://www.virago-net.com/brillo/No2 [No date].

Willis, E. (1992). *No more nice girls: Countercultural essays*. Middletown, CT: Wesleyan University Press.

Zavarzadeh, M. (1994). Ideology, poststructuralism, and class politics: Rethinking ideology critique for a transformative feminist politics. In A. Kibbey, K. Short, and A. Farmanfarmaian (Eds.), *Sexual artifice: Persons, images, politics* (pp. 292–324). New York: New York University Press.

21

Paul Martin Lester

Girls Can Be Doctors and Boys Can Be Nurses: Surfing for Solutions to Gender Stereotyping

When my daughter, Allison, was 7-years-old, I casually asked her what she wanted to be when she grew up.

"A nurse," she answered immediately.

Her quick reply was not totally unexpected. She had been visiting many nurses and doctors for most of her young life. Suffering from ear infections for several years, she recently had recovered from an operation in which tubes were placed in her ears to stop her infections. (Now, as an active 10-year-old I can happily report that she's the first one in the pool as her ears have totally healed.)

But when she answered that she wanted to be a nurse so rapidly, a tiny alarm bell went off in my head.

"You can certainly be a nurse," I answered, and added hopefully, "but you can also be a doctor."

She immediately laughed as if that idea was the funniest joke she had ever heard.

"Girls can't be doctors," she asserted.

The alarm bell was now sounding like a buzzer at the end of a basketball game.

"Oh yes they can," I replied a little too forcefully. "And boys can be nurses."

Again, she erupted into a fit of laughter.

I definitely was getting a headache from this ringing in my head.

—Lester, "Faint"

THE PROBLEM WITH STEREOTYPING

The problem as a parent educating a child on how stereotypes control thought and action is that what she sees and learns in her own life are reflected and reinforced by what she sees and learns from media messages. Trying to neutralize the stereotypes presented by the media is a daunting task. At best, there are only tiny victories to show for the effort. She might be persuaded to put down her Barbie dolls or concede that maybe being a doctor is a possibility, but given the constant stream of negative views, it is a hard mind-set to overcome. And given such popular television sitcom characters as Ally McBeal, characterized as "a ditsy 28-year-old Ivy League Boston litigator who never seems in need of the body-concealing clothing that Northeastern weather often requires," it is little wonder that *Time* magazine devotes a cover to the issue of whether feminism is dead (Bellafante, 1998).

Stereotypes are difficult to analyze because there is always some truth in them. If men are often characterized in commercials as insensitive, beer-drinking, sex-crazed, muscle-bound louts, that's because many men fit that description. If women are portrayed on magazine covers as fashion-frenzied, sexually alluring airheads with few career goals other than to smile for the camera, there are many who wouldn't disagree with that characterization. And since the media are composed of members from society, stereotyping is often a part of the message.

Willard Enteman (1996) writes of the meaning of *stereotyping*:

While the origin of the word "stereotype" has been almost entirely lost in the dim recesses of linguistic history, it is most closely associated with journalism as a trade. The older print people among us will remember that the original stereotype was called a *flong*, which was a printing plate that facilitated reproduction of the same material. Thus, a stereotype imposes a rigid mold on the subject and encourages repeated mechanical usage.

. . . The purposes of the stereotype are the same as in the print history: They are grounded in laziness. In standard economics, efficiency is another term for laziness. The person who substitutes a stereotype for careful analysis simply does not want to work harder than necessary to achieve a superficially acceptable result.

For visual communicators, whether photographers, videographers, filmmakers, cartoonists, or graphic artists, stereotypes are useful devices because they are easily understood and make a clear, if unfair and at times hurtful, point. As Everette Dennis has written, "For cartoonists, such depiction is part of their job description, but for communicators charged with an accurate representation of news and information, even entertainment fare, they can be damaging and dangerous." (Lester, 1996).

Because of the biases of media personnel that are based on ethnicity, economics, education, and experience, certain cultural groups receive too much and others too little attention because of preconceived stereotypical views. But responsibility for the images created must be shared between image makers and image consumers. Boycotting a product, turning a page, changing a channel, or walking out of a movie theater because of an offensive message does not absolve anyone's blame. The offending generalization still exists.

Another difficulty with negating the effects of media stereotypes is a result of how the brain processes visual information (Lester, 1995). Nerve cells in the visual cortex at the back of the brain combine to reproduce four visual cues for a person—color, depth, form, and movement. When these cues are linked in our minds with pictures in our memory, images remain with us for years. Consequently, pictures are highly emotional objects. Aristotle was the first to recognize the power of emotional messages to persuade others. His logos, ethos, and pathos combination of logical argument, credibility, and emotion worked to convince persons in ancient Greece and works today for political spin doctors and motion picture trailer producers. Because pictures affect a viewer emotionally more than words alone do, pictorial stereotypes often become misinformed perceptions that have the weight of established facts. These pictures can remain in a person's mind throughout a lifetime.

WHAT ARE PICTORIAL STEREOTYPES?

The list is endless and always injurious: African Americans play sports. Latinos join gangs. Native Americans drink alcohol. Wheelchair-using individuals are helpless. Gay men are effeminate. Lesbians wear their hair short. Older adults never have sex. Anglos are racist. Homeless people are drug addicts. These and other stereotypes are perpetuated by visual messages presented in print, television, motion pictures, and computers—the media (Lester, 1997).

The media typically portray members of diverse cultural groups within specific content categories—usually crime, entertainment, and sports—and almost never within general interest, business, education, health, and religious content categories. When we only see pictures of criminals, entertainers, and sports heroes, we forget that the vast majority of people—regardless of their particular cultural heritage—have the same hopes and fears as you or me.

Although it is important to study the messages themselves, it is equally vital to study the underlying motives behind stereotypical portrayals. And more likely than not, the motive behind stereotypical coverage in the media is economic. David Shaw wrote a three-part series for the *Los Angeles Times* on the crumbling wall that traditionally separated the advertising and editorial departments of newspapers and other media institutions (Shaw, 1998). The unfortunate trend is becoming undeniable: Marketing concerns at many media organizations are more important than community concerns.

The stereotypes we see in society and in the media are a result of what is expected and what sells. Consequently, the list of stereotypical portrayals of women is endless—any cover of a women's magazine will do. A stereotype is reinforced when the image seen in life or in the media doesn't surprise. Think of women in a typical beer commercial or models in a Victoria's Secret catalog: What images come to mind? When your preconceived idea matches the reality of the media presentation, you've got yourself a stereotype—and a powerful one at that. It is one that is extremely difficult to overcome.

The Mattel toy company, for example, raises stereotypes to new, unexplored levels with its Barbie line of dolls, outfits, and accessories. Recently the toy manufacturer introduced Cool Shoppin' Barbie with an unlimited credit limit MasterCard that sings "credit approved" when run through a tiny toy scanner (Hua, 1998). The blond, blue-eyed, man-and-material-crazed, and unrealistically thin icon of male stereotypical desire now has her little smiling head filled with dreams of unlimited use of plastic. Despite a record 1.35 million people filing for bankruptcy last year largely because of credit card abuse, the doll is an obvious attempt by marketing wizards at MasterCard to enforce brand loyalty early in a child's development. Stereotypes persist by those who don't see the larger societal effects of a product or message.

Fortunately, it appears that letters to Mattel, in newspapers, and on the Internet have convinced those responsible to curtail future editions of the happy shopper. And that's an important aspect to consider. Stereotypes get their life from apathy. If no one complains, there's no one to blame and commercial interests continue their business as usual.

Looking pretty—whether in commercials, on magazine covers, or as anorexic plastic parts—is rewarded in our society as an end in itself. Smiling with healthy hair and thin features is enough to warrant lucrative contract deals and boys by the bushel. Far too often women are exploited as scantily dressed, objectified hood ornaments without active roles, purpose, or much to do.

THE WORLD WIDE WEB: A SOURCE FOR POSITIVE PORTRAYALS

But there's a place that is a haven for realistic and supportive images that defy the commercially inspired stereotypes. This place is called the World Wide Web. The Web is not a place for grazing passively. It is a medium where users learn to take an active role in the media messages they seek. The sure way to combat negative stereotypes is to change society—an almost impossible task. Until that day, however, individuals learning to be users of the media with critical opinions and discriminate tastes instead of passive readers and viewers is a more realistic goal. The Web can help teach that form of critical analysis.

Here is a small sample of sites on the Web that don't offer stereotypical views of girls and women:

With its images of jogging girls, microscopes, and electric hand tools, the "Just for Girls" site,

• www.girlscouts.org/girls/

sponsored by the Girl Scouts of America, is an apropos place to start one's journey looking for positive portrayals of girls and women on the Web. Among its many features is a "Women's History Month" link that includes information about women scientists, sports heroes, and even wartime photojournalists. In the "Computers and Cyberspace" feature of the "Links for Girls!" section, you can learn about computer-related professions and such notables as Grace Hopper, the creator of the computer language Pascal.

Billed as the first Web site to create content specifically for women, "Women.com Networks"

• www.women.com

was established in 1992. With pleasing graphics and a simple, easy-to-navigate design structure, Women.com Networks includes links to such special sections as "Women's Wire," "MoneyMode," "Beatrice's Web Guide," "Prevention's Healthy Ideas," "Stork Site," and "Crayola Family Play." This successful commercial site that accepts advertising targets "affluent, decision-making women who seek the highest quality news, information and entertainment online."

Maxi is an aesthetically pleasing "webzine"

• www.maximag.com/

with a mission statement that stresses the creators' serious approach to issues affecting women:

Maxi is a place to talk about those experiences, where we can read intelligent thoughts on the issues and objects that have meaning in our lives, whether it's lipstick or politics or sex. We believe in looking at the positive as well as the negative. Women need a friendly environment in which to empower and inspire ourselves; in response to that need, we've created *Maxi*. (*Maxi*, 1998)

A search engine for women is called "Femina," Latin for *woman*. Its site

• www.femina.com/

contains alphabetized links from "Arts and Humanities" to "Society and Culture." Part of the joy of the Web is to discover sites within sites. within sites.

A graphic-intensive and yet content-rich Web site, "BreakupGirl.com"

• www.breakupgirl.com

offers, as the name suggests, solace, community, and hints for recovering from a love affair gone wrong with intelligence and humor. The postcard section offering e-mail cards a user can send to an insignificant other is alone worth a trip to this site.

When "*stereotype*" was entered in the search window, four sites were found: *InterMountain WOMAN,*

• www.marsweb.com/imwoman/

"a magazine that claims to present, 'no diet, no romance, no stereotype' "; *Packaging Horizons,*

• www.packaginghorizonsmag.com

"a quarterly publication dedicated to changing the stereotype and raising the awareness and visibility of women and minorities in the packaging industry"; "Women's Issues,"

• womensissues.miningco.com/

a site devoted to "the lives, events and cultural stereotypes that shape women's lives"; and "Smash!"

• www.dandyweb.com/smash/

a chatroom and listserv link "smashing stereotypes" with links

• www.dandyweb.com/smash/womenlink.html

to information about general body images, eating disorders, and positive portrayals.

The introduction message for the "Smash!" Web site is worth noting:

SMASH! The Stereotypes is the organization that finally says, Be Who You Are!!!!! Forget about the expectations of society and culture and dare to follow your own mind, heart and dreams. Maybe you are a different size or shape than the world says you ought to be. Maybe you are in a profession that has long been considered for men only. Maybe you have a hobby that used to be only for "the guys." Or maybe you just look at the world in a wholly unique way and are tired of being told that you should conform to the standard image of being a woman—whether it is the image purveyed by patriarchy, or the one purveyed by a particular set of feminist theorists or another. You just want to be who you are, but doing that is a SMASH! to the stereotypes. So what? Welcome to YOUR place!!!!! (Smash, 1998)

Perhaps a bit strident in its rhetoric, the "Smash!" message nonetheless conveys a proactive spirit concerning negative stereotypes of women. This attitude is reflected within Web sites with nontraditional spellings of the word *girl.*

One example of this new in-your-face attitude manifesting on the Web is the "Cybergrrl"

• www.cybergrrl.com

Web site. With links to books "by women about women," doing business in foreign countries, sexual information, and educational opportunities, the site is another in a quickly growing collection of Web resources for women that offers timely and useful services for any Web surfer.

In a reference to the Web address acronym for the uniform resource locator (URL), *gURL*

• www.gurl.com/hq/

is a highly graphic Web magazine with the usual array of hypertext links including "shoutouts," in which members are asked to "shoutout to us and other gURLs about life, liberty and the pursuit of gURLness."

Finally, there is The Body Shop. From a small store on the south coast of England opened in 1976, Anita Roddick's The Body Shop has grown to an international corporation with 1,491 stores in forty-six countries. The company is known for its innovative environmentally safe products and business philosophy that balances earnings with ethics. With a hemp-colored background, The Body Shop's Web site

• www.the-body-shop.com/

contains company and product information and a link to *Full Voice,*

• www.the-body-shop.com/fullvoice.html

where you will meet Ruby, a digitally altered alternative to the usual visual messages of women in fashion.

As described on the *Phoenix New Times* Web site:

When the Body Shop's most recent ad campaign featured Ruby posters and postcards of "Ruby" (she was originally nameless, but consumers adopted the name Ruby after "Rubenesque") it started showing up around the country in magazines as part of the company's "international campaign on self-esteem and body image." *(Phoenix New Times,* 1998)

Full Voice is an online magazine produced by The Body Shop staff that advocates a nonstereotypical philosophy within such sections as "Ideal ... Real," "What is beautiful?" and "Self Esteem." The Web site is a model for merging corporate and cultural sensibilities.

Figure 22.1
Body Shop Ad

Courtesy of The Body Shop International Plc. Used by permission.

HOPE FOR THE FUTURE?

Quick: Name five important or influential women—real or from fiction—in all of history. If you find that assignment difficult, you should ask yourself why women have been denied throughout recorded time a place of equal value among men. When sixty-seven students (forty-two were women) from a southern California university class concentrating on the mass media were given that task, here are their top answers:

Men (Top 5 Answers)	Women (Top 5 Answers)
1. Mother Theresa	1. Hillary Clinton
2. Harriet Tubman	2. Princess Diana
3. Rosa Parks	3. Their Mother
4. Joan of Arc	4. Rosa Parks
5. Princess Diana	5. Mother Theresa

It is gratifying to note that the top choices are similar and are not celebrities in the traditional Hollywood definition. Perhaps the answers indicate the best way to overcome stereotypes in the media and throughout society—education. Nevertheless, there is much work to be done when "five times more boys than girls use computers at home" and "parents purchase twice as many technology toys and products for their sons as they do for their daughters" ("Growing Up Cyber," 1998, p. 10). Once again, we see stereotypes in the media because society stereotypes.

At least as indicated by surfing the Web, there is a new sensitivity to stereotyping, especially with regard to women. Does such a trend have a positive payoff for concerned parents?

Three years after I asked my daughter about her future career plans that started this piece, I asked her the same question. But this time the alarm bells didn't go off.

"A teacher, Dada, like you," she replied confidently.

"It's a good gig, Allison," I admitted. "But you know," I added, "you can also be Dean of the School or President of the University."

She smiled, looked me in the eye, and asked, "Do you think I'm nuts?"

I'm so glad I had a daughter. I know boys. I was once a boy. I can't learn from boys. Seeing a girl grow from the ground up is a challenge and a joy that constantly teaches me how we should all strive to do better.

REFERENCES

Bellafante, G. (1998, June 29). Feminism: It's all about me! *Time*, p. 58.

Body Shop. (1998). [Online]. Available: http://www.the-body-shop.com [1999].

BreakupGirl.com. (1998). [Online]. Available: http://www.breakupgirl.com [1999].

Cybergrrl. (1998). [Online]. Available: http://www.cybergrrl.com [1999].

Enteman, W. (1996). Stereotyping, prejudice, and discrimination. In P. M. Lester (Ed.), *Images that injure pictorial stereotypes in the media* (pp. 9–14). Westport, CT: Praeger.

Femina. (1998). [Online]. Available: http://www.femina.com/ [1999].

Full Voice. (1998). [Online]. Available: http://www.the-body-shop.com/fullvoice.html [1999].

Growing up cyber. (1998, April). *LA Weekly*, p. 10.

gURL. (1998). [Online]. Available: http://www.gurl.com/hq [1999].

Hua, V. (1998, April 2). Parents give credit card Barbie a low rating. *Los Angeles Times* p. D1.

InterMountain WOMAN. (1998). [Online]. Available: http://www.marsweb.com/imwoman/ [1999].

Just for Girls. (1998). [Online]. Available: http://www.girlscouts.org/girls/ [1999].

Lester, P. M. (1995). *Visual communication images with messages.* Belmont, CA: Wadsworth.

Lester, P. M. (Ed.), (1996). *Images that injure pictorial stereotypes in the media.* Westport, CT: Praeger.

Lester, P. M. (1997). Images and stereotypes. In E. D. Cohen and D. Elliot (Eds.),
Journalism ethics (p. 69). Santa Barbara, CA: ABC-CLIO.

Lester, P. M. (1998). Faint. In *The spiral web: On the nature of coincidence* [Online].
Available: http://commfaculty.fullerton.edu/lester/writings/spiralweb.html [1999].

Maxi. (1998). [Online]. Available: http://www.maximag.com/ [1999].

Packaging Horizons. (1998). [Online]. Available: http://www.packaginghorizonsmag.
com [1999].

Phoenix New Times. (1998). [Online]. Available: http://www.phoenixnewtimes.com/
extra/ruby.html [1999].

Shaw, D. (1998, March 29–March 31). Breaching the wall. *Los Angeles Times*, p. A1.

Smash! (1998). [Online]. Available: http://www.dandyweb.com/smash/ [1999].

Smashing Stereotypes. (1998). [Online]. Available: http://www.dandyweb.com/smash/
womenlink.html [1999].

Women.com Networks. (1998). [Online]. Available: http://www.women.com/ [1999].

Women's Issues. (1998). [Online]. Available: http://womenissues.miningco.com/ [1999].

Index

About the Editors
and Contributors

JULIE L. ANDSAGER is an Assistant Professor in the Edward R. Murrow School of Communication at Washington State University. Her research focuses on public opinion toward free expression and on media framing of gender issues.

JACQUELINE BACON received her Ph.D. in English from the University of Texas at Austin in 1997. She is currently an independent scholar, who specializes in the rhetoric of marginalized nineteenth-century Americans, particularly women and African Americans. Her articles have appeared in *College English, Nineteenth-Century Prose*, and *Rhetoric Society Quarterly*.

CECELIA BALDWIN is an Associate Professor at the School of Journalism and Mass Communication, San Jose State University. She has taught at Cornell and the Newhouse School of Public Communication at Syracuse University.

DIANA YORK BLAINE, an Assistant Professor of American Literature at the University of North Texas, researches images of dead women in literature. She serves as book review editor for *Studies in the Novel* and is on the board of the International Programme for Pynchon Studies.

MARK CALLISTER is an Associate Professor in the Communication Department at Western Illinois University, where he teaches courses in persuasive campaigns, persuasion, research methods, and advanced organizational communication. His primary research interests include the impact of incongruent visual and verbal messages in advertising on information processing.

META G. CARSTARPHEN is Associate Professor of Journalism at the University of North Texas. A former magazine editor, she received the "Best Feature" awards twice from the American Business Press as a result of her contributions to in-depth reports on the emerging digital watch industry and on discrimination in the jewelry industry, respectively. She continues an active writing career as a contributing writer for the *Dallas Morning News, Our Texas* magazine, *Black Issues in Higher Education*, and others.

ELIZABETH DIETZ is currently working on her A.B.D. at the University of Iowa. Her thesis, "Partiality: Love, Memory and Fragments in Early Modern England," explores the way in which subjectivity in the English Renaissance (especially 1590 to 1660) is constructed through acts of amorous looking.

PHYLLIS PEARSON ELMORE holds a Ph.D. in English from Texas Woman's University and teaches rhetoric and literature at North Lake College. Her sabbatical research on black American female oratory as this relates to political activism was presented at the International Society for the History of Rhetoric at the Amsterdam Meeting in July 1999.

ANTHONY ENNS is a Teaching Fellow in the Department of English at the University of Iowa. His work has appeared in *Popular Culture Review, The Pannus Index*, and *Postmodern Culture*. His essay "The Space of Love: Toward a New Sexual Imagery," presented at the 22nd Annual Meeting of the Semiotic Society of America, provided the basis for his contribution to this volume.

LINDA K. FULLER, Professor of Communications at Worcester State College, has produced over 200 professional publications and conference reports and is the author/(co-)editor of eighteen books, including *Beyond the Stars: Studies in American Popular Film, Community TV in the US, Media-Mediated Relationships, Women & AIDS*, and *Dictionary of Quotations in Communications*.

JACQUELINE C. HITCHON holds a joint appointment in the Department of Agricultural Journalism and the Department of Family and Consumer Communication. She has published in *Communication Theory, Communication Research, Journalism and Mass Communication Quarterly, Political Communication*, and other scholarly publications.

KARA KEELING is currently completing her Ph.D. in English at the University of Pittsburgh. Her primary research and teaching interests include film, media studies, African American studies, and Queer Theory.

JACQUELINE J. LAMBIASE is an Assistant Professor of Journalism, at the University of North Texas. Much of her research focuses on gender in cyberspace, as well as on women's voices and representations in mass media. She is a recent contributor to Bosah Ebo's *Cyberghetto or Cybertopia? Race, Class and Gender on the Internet* (Praeger, 1998).

PAUL MARTIN LESTER is a Professor of Communications at California State University at Fullerton. He is the author or editor of seven books including *Images that Injure: Pictorial Stereotypes in the Media, Visual Communication*

Images with Messages, and *Photojournalism: An Ethical Approach*. In addition, Lester has published numerous articles in major communications journals and has lectured throughout the United States, Canada, South Africa, and the Netherlands.

KEVIN R. MALY is a program director at Equality Colorado, a civil rights organization that works on behalf of gay, lesbian, bisexual, and transgendered people and other marginalized populations. He is also a faculty member in the School for Professional Studies at Regis University in Denver.

KATHY BRITTAIN McKEE is an Associate Professor of Journalism in the Department of Communication at Berry College. Her teaching areas include media law and ethics, media writing and editing, and public relations. Recent research has focused on visual images in magazines, films, and music videos.

DEBRA MERSKIN is an Associate Professor in the School of Journalism and Communication at the University of Oregon. Her research interests include the representation of women and minorities in the media and media dependency theory. Recent publications have appeared in *Journalism and Mass Communication Quarterly, Journalism Educator*, and *Journal of Communication Inquiry*.

SUSAN E. MORGAN is Assistant Professor of Communication at the University of Kentucky, where she teaches health communication, persuasion, and intercultural and interpersonal communication. Her primary research focus is persuasive message design for health campaigns targeting multicultural audiences.

GENE MURRAY teaches mass communication at Grambling State University. He served as professional freedom and responsibility chair for the Minorities and Communication Division of the Association for Education in Journalism and Mass Communication. Murray is a cofounder and coadviser of the Lincoln Collegiate Chapter of the Society of Professional Journalists.

EMILE C. NETZHAMMER is Dean of Arts and Humanities and Professor of Communication at Buffalo State College. His research and teaching interests include the mediated representations of underrepresented and marginalized groups.

CAROL J. PARDUN is an Assistant Professor of Advertising and Public Relations at the University of North Carolina at Chapel Hill. She has published articles in *Communication Reports, Youth and Society*, and *Journal of Broadcasting & Electronic Media*. She collaborates with Kathy Brittain McKee for research on religious images in popular media as well as product placements in film.

KIMBER CHARLES PEARCE is an Assistant Professor of English and Director of the Communication Certificate Program at Saint Anselm College. His research and teaching concentrations are in rhetorical theory and criticism. He is the author of several essays on rhetoric, feminism, and political discourse.

ALLESSANDRIA POLIZZI received her bachelor's and master's degrees in English from California State University at Fresno. She has published articles on H.D.'s feminist aesthetic and on women poets of World War I. She is currently writing her dissertation on work drives and identity construction in early twentieth-century American literature.

SHIELA REAVES holds a joint appointment in the School of Journalism and Mass Communication and the Division of Continuing Studies. Her research interests focus on ethics and the impact of digital manipulation and the growth of the Native American press. She has published in *Journalism and Mass Communication Quarterly, Newspaper Research Journal, Visual Communication Quarterly*, and *Journal of Mass Media Ethics*.

TOM REICHERT is an Assistant Professor and member of the Advertising faculty in the Department of Journalism at the University of North Texas. His primary research interests include message and advertising effects and the impact of sexually oriented appeals on message processing and persuasion.

JOSEPH W. SLADE is Director of Graduate Studies at the School of Telecommunications at Ohio University. He is the author of *Thomas Pynchon* (1974; 1990), coeditor of *Beyond the Two Cultures: Essays on Science, Technology, and Literature* (1990), and author as well of some fifty articles on film, literature, culture, and electronic media. His *Pornography: A Reference Guide* will appear soon from Greenwood Press.

SUSAN STEARNS holds a bachelor's degree in English from the University of Maryland and a master's degree in journalism from the University of North Texas. Stearns plans to pursue a Ph.D. in the near future, with an emphasis on media analysis.

SUSAN C. ZAVOINA is an Associate Professor and Coordinator of the photojournalism sequence within the Department of Journalism. Zavoina teaches advanced photojournalism classes, including digital imaging and multimedia. She was chosen as a Research Fellow for the Poynter Institute for Media Studies to complete a study comparing and contrasting photo editing for newspapers publishing online and in print. Zavoina has also received a grant from the Freedom Forum Foundation to complete a vision documentation of the affect of litter on parts of the Texas coastline.

ISBN 0-313-30788-1

EAN

9 780313 307881

90000>

HARDCOVER BAR CODE